A GUIDE TO THE
HUMAN RESOURCE BODY OF KNOWLEDGE™
(HRBoK™)

A GUIDE TO THE
HUMAN RESOURCE
BODY OF KNOWLEDGE™
(HRBoK™)

SANDRA M. REED, SPHR

WILEY

Library of Congress Cataloging-in-Publication Data

Names: Reed, Sandra M., author.
Title: A guide to the human resource body of knowledge / Sandra Reed.
Description: Hoboken, New Jersey : John Wiley & Sons, Inc., [2017] | Includes
    bibliographical references. |
Identifiers: LCCN 2017007870 (print) | LCCN 2017013310 (ebook) | ISBN
    9781119374893 (pdf) | ISBN 9781119374916 (ePub) | ISBN 9781119374886
    (cloth) | ISBN 9781119374930 (oBook)
Subjects: LCSH: Personnel management.
Classification: LCC HF5549 (ebook) | LCC HF5549 .R447 2017 (print) | DDC
    658.3–dc23
LC record available at https://lccn.loc.gov/2017007870

Printed in the United States of America

10 9 8 7 6 5 4 3 2 1

As always, I must dedicate this work to C^3, who continue to be the inspiration for every single decision I make. To Christopher, thank you for believing in me and celebrating the big moments in my life, even when I stubbornly cling to my wallflower status. To my Rowdy friends, thank you for force-feeding me balance (and alternative housing in rainstorms) when I need it the most. Each of you has given me a particular type of love, support, and encouragement, allowing me to live a life of passion. My wish for each of you is an abundance of the same.

Contents

Acknowledgments

The industry of human resources (HR) has many voices, several of which are represented in this work. The construction and deconstruction of the ideas contained here are intended to be a reflection of the work of passionate and dedicated HR practitioners around the globe. While sure to inspire conversation and debate, the primary purpose of this volume is to serve those practitioners—guiding new careers, providing insights on the application of HR principles, accompanying the preparation efforts of certification seekers, and offering perspectives on the past, present, and future of our field.

Critical to these aims are the subject matter experts who juggled tight deadlines, travel commitments, teaching and work schedules, the holidays, sickness, and my incessant e-mails and questions in review of the content for accuracy and clarity. While any errors to the content are certainly my own, I offer my sincere thanks to the following reviewers for their thoughtful guidance and expertise:

Pantelis Markou, PhD
Vice President of Human Resources,
    Adjunct Professor of Business
    Psychology
Mikimoto America Co. Ltd.

Karla J. Kretzschmer, SPHR
Owner
Karla K Enterprises, LLC

Joan E. Moore, JD, SPHR
President
The Arbor Consulting Group, Inc.

Tracy Jimenez, JD
Consultant
The Arbor Consulting Group, Inc.

Cameron Evans, JD
President
Evans Law Group, PC

Dr. Rita Fields, SHRM-SCP
Associate Professor of Management,
    Madonna University
Workforce Strategist, Copper Phoenix
    Consulting, LLC

Roger Herod, SPHR
Global Mobility Consultant

Lee S. Webster, SPHR, GPHR
Director, Employee Relations
University of Texas Medical Branch at
    Galveston

I often joke about geeking out over those who have had a significant impact on my career or helped shape my thinking. In this way, having Dave Ulrich write the Foreword to this book was a career highlight. My first read of his book *The HR Value Proposition* many years ago helped root within me the goal of educating HR professionals on how to be the most valuable players within any organization. My abundant thanks for his patience and flexibility with the schedule, and generosity in sharing his profound insights with us in this text. Additionally, many thanks to Andy Fleming of Way to Grow, Inc. for a delightful conversation where he shared with me his thoughts regarding twenty-first-century employee development. His work is well worth a deep dive beyond the scope of this publication. The professionalism and thoroughness of the case study provided by Jack and Patti Phillips from the ROI Institute is an excellent example of why their group has set the standard for measuring business outcomes. Katrina P. Merlini's phenomenal case study on the important concept of organizational justice is also well worth the time it takes to digest, and I am indebted to her for her professional courtesy and contribution to my lifelong learning objectives in the area of industrial-organizational (I-O) psychology.

Navigating the ins and outs of the publishing process would have been impossible without the direction, guidance, and project management skills of Jeanenne Ray at John Wiley & Sons. I always picture her in my mind at her desk pressing buttons, flipping toggles, and pulling levers, working her magic to keep our project on track. Additionally, the optimism and hard work of Chris Webb were instrumental in getting this manuscript from concept to launch—many thanks to Jeanenne, Chris, and their team at Wiley.

Finally, I must acknowledge the dedication of the leaders at the HR Certification Institute®. Their vision for our industry is unflinchingly represented by the precision and excellence of their core staff; their commitment to the principles of the profession of HR is a testament to why HRCI® has and will continue to lead the certification efforts of HR practitioners across the world. It was a pleasure working with Amy Dufrane, CEO, Kerry Morgan, Rebecca Hastings, Inga Fong, and the many others I came into contact with through the course of this manuscript development. Thank you for the opportunity to serve the HR community through this work.

Acknowledgments from the First Edition

The process of building out the *Human Resource Body of Knowledge*™ (HRBoK™) is evolutionary, requiring the time and attention of many practitioners. I would be remiss if I failed to acknowledge the professionalism and expertise of those that worked on the inaugural edition of this guide.

HR Certification Institute® (HRCI®) recognizes and thanks the many individuals who assisted with the creation of the first edition of the HRBoK Guide.

The following individuals comprised the HRBoK Working Group:

Chair:	John D. Varlaro, PhD, MBA, SPHR, GPHR
Vice Chair:	Linda J. Haft, MS HRM, SPHR, CCP

Subgroup Leaders:

Business Management and Strategy:	Javiel Lopez, SPHR, MS
Workforce Planning and Employment:	Lynda D. Glover, MA, SPHR
Human Resource Development:	Lori L. Rolek, SPHR
Compensation and Benefits:	Alisa Guralnick, SPHR
Employee and Labor Relations:	Karla M. Knowlton, MAOM, PHR, GPHR
Risk Management:	Nancy L. Hill-Davis, MHSA, MJ, SPHR, CHHR

Working Group Members:
Amy Gulati, GPHR, SPHR, PHRca, CPDM
Armando A. Villasana, MBA, PHR
Diana Kroushl, SPHR
Doris M. Sims, SPHR
Gary W. Sexton, SPHR, CLRS
Kathusca Johnson, PHR

Lee S. Webster, JD, MBA, SPHR, GPHR
Lin Little, SPHR
Lori S. Goldsmith, SPHR, GPHR
Pantelis Markou, PhD
Q VanBenschoten, MBA, SPHR, CFE
Rafael M. Uzeda de Oliveira, CHRL, PHR, GPHR
Roland C. Howell, SPHR, GPHR
Ron Drafta, CIH, CSP, SPHR
Sharon L. Beaudry, JD, SPHR
Shiva Dubey, MBA, CCP, GRP, PHR
Stephen I. Otterstrom, SPHR
Sue S. Stalcup, SPHR, LPC-MHSP
Victoria Clavijo, SPHR

Project Consultant Team:

PSI Services

Rory E. McCorkle, PhD, MBA, SPHR, CAE, NPDP
Beth Kalinowski, MBA, SPHR
Siddiq Kassam, MS
Alexandra Kassidis
Melissa McElroy

HRCI HRBoK Team:

Amy Dufrane, EdD, SPHR, CAE, CEO
Linda K. Anguish, SPHR, GPHR
Rebecca R. Hastings, SPHR, PHRca
Inga Y. Fong, SPHR, GPHR
Naomi M. Cossack, SPHR, PHRca

About the Author

Sandra M. Reed, SPHR, is a leading expert in the certification of human resource professionals, and has had 20 years of practical HR experience. She is the author of the fourth edition of the *PHR/SPHR: Professional in Human Resources Certification Study Guide* and *PHR/SPHR Exam For Dummies*. Sandra is a sought-after, engaging facilitator of human resource and management principles, with a strong focus on strategic business management and employee development. She is currently the owner of epocHResources, a management and consulting group based in California. She holds a bachelor of arts in applied psychology with an emphasis on industrial-organizational (I-O) psychology from Florida Tech University and an adult vocational teaching credential from California State University, San Bernardino. She has been SPHR certified since 2007.

Foreword

HR Rising to the Opportunity

Dave Ulrich

Rensis Likert Professor of Business at the University of Michigan and Partner, the RBL Group

The professionals who commit to helping organizations and people succeed through human resource (HR) practices have impact because they recognize and respond to the unprecedented opportunities available in today's business world. This exceptional volume holds the Human Resource Body of Knowledge (HRBoK™), offering both conceptual frameworks and practical tools to enable HR professionals. Let me set the context for the opportunities implicit in this work with three simple tenets.

First, it is a great time to be in HR. HR is not about HR, but about helping organizations and individuals in organizations be more successful. Organizational success includes investor confidence (evidenced by market value), customer commitment (evidenced by customer share), and community reputation (evidenced in social responsibility). Individual success includes measures of productivity (evidenced by output/input indicators), as well as personal well-being (evidenced by sentiment indicators).

Four forces make HR more central to organization and individual success: the context of business: social, technological, economic, political, environmental, and demographic changes (STEPED); the increased pace of change: volatility, uncertainty, complexity, ambiguity (VUCA); the demise of employee well-being (individuation, isolation, indifference, intensity); and the requirement to be outside-in (attend to customers, investors, and communities). Collectively, these four forces shift HR to center stage of organizational and individual success. Competitors can access and match financial resources, strategic insights, and technological platforms. HR issues around talent, leadership, and capability become differentiators that are more difficult to copy, but critical to success.

Because HR is not about HR, HR analytics are less about an HR scorecard, and more about how HR practices and HR professionals impact business results. For example, increasingly HR insights are less about innovations on how to hire, train, or pay people, and more about how the hiring, training, or compensation choices impact and deliver value to stakeholders outside (e.g., customers, investors) and inside (employees) the organization. These business-based analytics provide leaders with information to make more informed choices about HR practices, and HR professional standards become clearer.

It is a great time to be in HR because HR matters more than ever in the value creation process.

Second, we know what it takes to be successful. As the HR profession evolves, it becomes more evident how to be a successful HR professional, both in terms of managing a career and in terms of developing competencies that matter.

HR Career Mosaic

When diagnosing choices that make up an HR career, there has been an evolution from a career stages (stage 1, 2, 3) logic to a career mosaic based on two questions:

1. Where do you work? There are four choices where HR professionals can work (generalist, specialist, geography commitment, or outside HR).
2. What level or type of work do you do? There are three levels, each with increasing scope for HR work (individual contributor, manager, or leader).

These two questions shape an HR mosaic so that HR professionals may create a personal career path that works for them (see Figure F.1).

Within this mosaic, HR professionals may embark on a number of career paths as evidenced in the options in Figure F.1. Three examples of HR career paths are:

Functional specialist (1, 2, 3, 4) These HR professionals take increasingly senior jobs within a functional expertise (e.g., compensation, training, organization development, labor relations). With each career move (1, 2, 3, 4), they expand their scope within their chosen functional expertise.

Specialist to generalist (A, B, C, D, E) These HR professionals move from specialist to generalist world and back again (with a stint in geography). As they move back and forth, they gain awareness of the types of HR work.

Broad-based experience (a, b, c, d, e) These HR professionals have careers that offer broad exposure and experience, including work outside the HR function (e.g.,

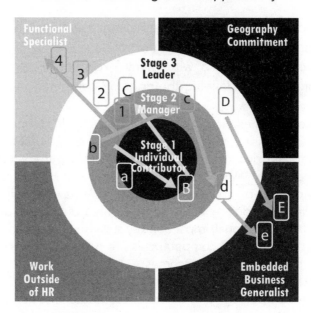

Figure F.1   HR Career Mosaic

in operations, marketing, or consulting). They are likely to be seen as business experts who happen to work in HR.

Obviously, within this mosaic a host of other career paths exist. The HR career mosaic reflects choices HR professionals make about how to manage their careers.

HR Certification and Competencies

HR certification ensures that HR professionals know the body of knowledge (theory and research) that underlies HR. Certification validates base knowledge and ensures that HR professionals are legitimate. This volume offers exceptional insights into the certification requirements in six areas of HR functional expertise:

1. Business management and strategy
2. Workforce planning and employment
3. Human resource development
4. Compensation and benefits
5. Employee and labor relations
6. Risk management

Becoming certified in these areas enables HR professionals to deliver insights that will have impact.

In addition, HR professionals need to be competent. There are an increasing number of HR competency models created by HR associations and by organizations working to upgrade their HR professionals. Having researched and published on HR competencies for 30 years (primarily with Professor Wayne Brockbank from the University of Michigan, but also with many exceptional colleagues), we have identified four principles of defining the right HR competencies.[1]

1. HR competence definition is *not* the goal; defining HR competencies that create positive outcomes *is* the goal. Most competency models ask the question "What are the competencies of HR professionals?" This is the wrong question. The question should be: "What are the competencies of HR professionals that have greatest impact on business performance?" We have shown that different HR competencies have differential impact on three outcomes: personal effectiveness of the HR professional, impact on key stakeholders, and business results. HR is not about HR, and HR competencies are not about the competencies, but about how they deliver key outcomes.
2. HR competencies are determined less by self-report and more by how those competencies are perceived by others. HR competencies should be assessed not only by the HR professional but by those who observe the HR professional. People generally judge themselves by their intent; others judge them by their behavior, so it is important to evaluate both intent and behavior.
3. Global HR competencies exist, but they also may vary by geography, industry, size of organization, level in the organization, role in the organization, gender, time in role, and so forth. We empirically show that 50 to 60 percent of HR competences are essential to all circumstances, and then 40 to 50 percent vary by setting.
4. Key HR competencies change over time. Having done seven rounds of major studies over 30 years with a total of more than 100,000 respondents, we can say with some certainty that every four to five years, 30 to 40 percent of HR competencies evolve. For example, in recent rounds of our research, we have seen a rise in the importance of HR technology and HR analytics.

In our most recent research, we identified nine competencies for being an effective HR professional, as shown in Figure F.2.[2]

Table F.1 summarizes the key questions and our findings from this recent research.

In brief, we know what it takes to be successful in HR. Regardless of career path, HR professionals require a combination of certification and competence. Certification gives one a license to act; competence ensures the right actions.

Third, HR professionals can rise to their opportunities. Through hundreds of HR interventions, we have learned how to be a better HR professional and how to build better HR professionals. In both cases, there are four steps to upgrading HR professionals.

First, create a theory or standard of what it means to be effective. The six domains of certification in this volume and the example of HR competencies cited earlier suggest a standard of what it means to be or build effective HR. The "be, know, and do" of these expectations may become a standard for effective HR.

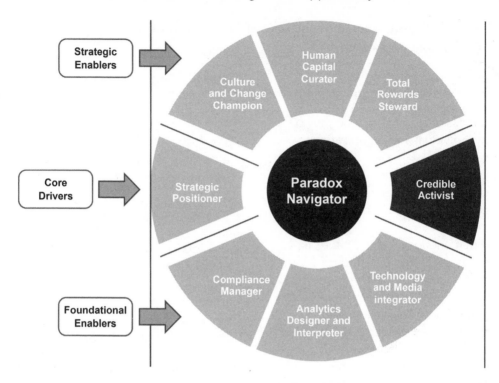

Figure F.2   2016 HR Competency Model—Round 7

Second, assess HR professionals against the standards and behaviors. Some of this assessment may come from personal profiling, and some may come from 360-degree assessments. These assessments highlight strengths that can be built on and weaknesses that can be overcome. People are more likely to change when they have clarity about what to improve.

Third, improve HR professionals through a host of development experiences. We have organized these development experiences into three categories. First, work experiences come when HR professionals take on new and demanding assignments, work on special projects, and/or receive coaching. Most learning comes from personal experience with trial and error. Second, training and development experiences come from learning in more structured education settings. Training is more effective when it emphasizes learning solutions, adapts to different learning styles, is focused on specific business challenges and personal behaviors, and is measured by accountable impact. Third, people learn from life experience. Some of life experience can be structured, such as using corporate philanthropy as a leadership development opportunity (e.g., IBM service corps offers aspiring leaders a way to learn by participating in IBM's community service). But many life experiences create incredible forums for learning, such as raising children, participating in community organizations, traveling to new countries, reading and exploring new

Table F.1   Key Questions and Overall Findings from HR Competency Research

Key Question	Overall Finding
1. What are the competencies of HR professionals, and how do they differ by individual and organizational context?	• Nine overall competency domains • Three core drivers; three strategic enablers; three foundational enablers
2. What competencies do HR professionals require to be personally effective (i.e., to be invited "to the table")?	Be a credible activist who builds relationships of trust and takes advocacy positions.
3. When engaged "at the table" (in business discussions) and HR professionals represent themselves, what competencies are required to add value to key stakeholders?	• If inside (employee, line), be a credible activist. • If outside (customer, investor), be a strategic positioner.
4. When engaged "at the table" (in business discussions) and HR professionals represent the HR department's practices and policies, what competencies are required to add value to key stakeholders?	For the most part, the competencies of individual HR professionals that have an impact on stakeholder outcomes are the same as the collective competencies of HR professionals, with a few exceptions (culture, change, and analytics) where the collective competencies have business impact.
5. What competences do HR professionals require to drive business results?	Navigate paradox (manage tension and divergent-convergent cycle), followed by strategic positioner and technology and media integrator.
6. What is the relative importance of the competencies of HR professionals versus the activities of the HR department in driving business results?	• Recognize the importance of the HR department (about four times the impact of the individual on business results). • Build capabilities (information/external sensing, speed, culture, collaboration, efficiency, customer responsiveness).

ideas, representing one's organization to public audiences, and simply being an active observer of one's world.

Each HR professional should have an individual development program that lays out a road map to becoming a better HR professional. Each HR department should be investing in HR professional development either through HR career management (see previous discussion), through HR academies for HR professionals, or through other HR development opportunities.

Fourth, evaluate HR improvement. Wanting to change indicates a desire, but without measures to track change, desires often languish. To rise to their opportunities, HR professionals should track not only their personal improvements, but the impact of these improvements on desired outcomes. Personal change can be monitored through sequential 360-degree assessments that track how others perceive change. Organization change can be tracked through the impact of HR on desired outcomes. For example, we have created the leadership capital index that offers investors a way to measure how HR impacts investor value.

These four steps essentially propose HR for HR. Often HR encourages leaders and others to define, assess, improve, and evaluate in order to grow. When HR professionals apply the same logic to themselves, they can make real progress.

Conclusion

What is the hope for the ideas in this book? To help HR practitioners, academics, and thought leaders deliver more value from a shared set of best practices and benchmarks. Whether you are a student of HR, an international HR professional, a seasoned practitioner, or a professional influencer, it is indeed a great time to be in HR. We know what it takes to be successful, and because of this, HR professionals can be valued business partners by rising to the opportunities.

Notes

1. Dave Ulrich, Wayne Brockbank, Mike Ulrich, and Dave Kryscynski, "Toward a Synthesis of HR Competency Models: The Common HR 'Food Groups' or Domains," *People and Strategy* 4 (Fall 2015): 56–65.
2. Dave Ulrich, David Kryscynski, Mike Ulrich, and Wayne Brockbank, *Victory through Organization: Why the War for Talent Is Failing Your Organization and What You Can Do about It* (New York: McGraw-Hill, 2017).

1

The Human Resource Body of Knowledge

HRBoK^{TM}

The way organizations of today utilize the human resource (HR) department tells the story of HR. Some companies continue to view HR as personnel departments and compliance officers, managing the transactions of payroll, processing new hire paperwork, and terminating nonperformers. The second type of company uses human resources to its strategic advantage. Organizations of the second type recognize and support the valued contributions of a high-functioning HR department, delivering outcomes through people management, group management, and ultimately the management and understanding of the organization as a whole (see Figure 1.1).

The Building Blocks

The inconsistencies in the ways companies use their HR competencies mirror nearly perfectly the evolution of the profession. As the business landscape has changed, the HR industry has changed as well, and some businesses and industries have been better at keeping the two aligned than others.

The early twentieth century was characterized by enormous growth in industrialization and the country's labor pool. Large factories in the northern states expanded beyond textiles and into the middle states, creating a boom of work and many lifetime jobs. This industrialization required more workers, and the European immigrant population from countries such as Italy and Hungary grew as a result. Railroads expanded, decreasing the cost of transportation. Workers

1

Human Resource Management

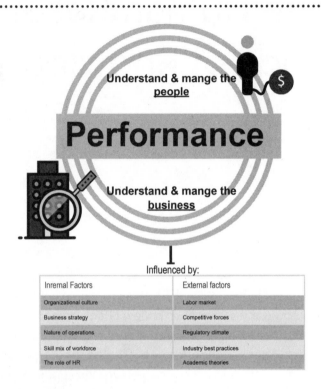

Figure 1.1   Human Resource Management

continued to organize for better working conditions. Human resources had a new job, and it was the *industrial relations* manager—relations with labor unions and interactions between humans and processes, and between humans and machines.

Industrial Relations

The relationship between an employer and its employees

The relationship between the management of an industrial enterprise and its employees, as guided by specific laws and regulations

---

Automating manufacturing processes fostered the development of mass production, bringing a whole new perspective to the workplace. For the first time, U.S. businesses had to think about managing full-scale operations and the people it took to perform them. How should large companies be structured? How should the work be organized? How should people be managed? Personnel became a *staff unit*, an independent department whose job was to advise all *line management* functions.

It wasn't just businesses that were seeking answers. The government took a keen interest in the way these taxpaying giants were behaving, and began influencing how businesses would be run through laws. HR added new responsibilities to its job description: policy maker and *compliance* officer.

Staff Units

People who support line management

Work groups that support the major business of an organization with activities such as accounting, customer service, maintenance, and personnel

Line Management

People who create revenue for organizations

Work groups that conduct the major business of an organization, such as manufacturing or sales

Compliance

Obedience, conforming

Following established laws, guidelines, or rules

As companies evolved and thought leaders of the day discovered that businesses could significantly influence individual employee behavior to achieve strategic goals, the transactional nature of HR work was not enough. Everything was in motion, with a mix of moving targets made up of the competitive and the resource management needs of the business (financial, physical, and knowledge). HR began to address the interpersonal skills of the workforce, applying principles of communication, leadership, and team-building skills. The human relations role of HR came to be. As the market deepened into international waters and competition increased, it became essential to employers that they find, develop, and retain key talent, adding the development and management of a *human capital strategy* to HR's increasingly important role.

Human Capital Strategy

Employment tactics, plan for managing employees

Methods and tools for recruiting, managing, and keeping important employees

The academic and scientific communities were experiencing momentum similar to that of other industries. As technological and economic progress was made in the workplace, psychology and the social sciences were creating a bank of empirical evidence on how best to manage organizational, individual, and group performance through systematic interventions. This work formed the basis for industry best practices around *organizational development*. Enter HR as the behavioral scientist.

Organizational Development

Planned process to improve an organization

Planned process that uses the principles of behavioral science to improve the way an organization functions

---

Finally, the globalization of the workforce and business structures created a need for HR practices across geographic borders. Decreased trade barriers, the search for new markets, the rapid development of technology, and the rise of e-commerce platforms have all contributed to the internationalization of business. HR was tasked with international human resource management (IHRM) strategies—adapting home country practices to global conditions.

It was and continues to be clear that the evolved HR role of industrial relations, compliance, human relations, strategy, organizational development, and IHRM has formed a powerful discipline from which organizations could push their competitive performance.

The HR Profession

In the late 1960s, a study by Cornell University found that a profession is defined by five main characteristics.[1] They were:

1. A profession must be full-time.
2. A profession must have a national professional association.
3. A profession must have a certification program.
4. A profession must have a code of ethics.
5. Schools and curricula must be aimed specifically at teaching the basic ideas of the profession, and there must be a defined common body of knowledge.

Based on this, the American Society of Personnel Administration (ASPA) began to design a formal human resource profession, seeking to frame the context from which the practice would be performed. These activities included organizing the existing academic principles into a formal program to teach human resources. It gave influence to the formal association of the ASPA, which morphed eventually into what is now the Society for Human Resource Management (SHRM). A code of ethics was adopted, serving to guide the highest standards of professional behaviors. In 1973, the ASPA Accreditation Institute (AAI) was formed to meet the professional certification requirements. The first certification exams were given in 1976. The AAI as we know it today is called the Human Resource Certification Institute® (HRCI®).

All of these efforts served to create the six domains of human resource management (HRM). The foundation of *human resources* is built upon the human resource body of knowledge—the HRBoK™.

HR

Human Resources

Function within an organization that focuses on implementing organizational strategy, as well as recruiting, managing performance, and providing direction for the people who work in the organization

---

The Six Domains

This book is organized according to the six domains of human resources that are rooted in HR's origins, but have evolved to reflect current conditions. These domains are reviewed in more detail next.

Business Management and Strategy

The domain of business management and strategy (BMS) is the area where HR experts look at the organization as a whole while establishing goals and outcomes for its parts. It is the foundation for all other HR activities, providing macro-level direction through strategy development and operational direction through business management.

The goal of this domain is to develop and support the company's mission, vision, and values. HR is expected to shape policies and HR programs around the company identity and employer brand while supporting the behaviors that achieve strategic goals and objectives.

All of the aforementioned outcomes are served when HR professionals are adept at managing change on a local and global scale, and being accepted as organizational leaders (see Figure 1.2).

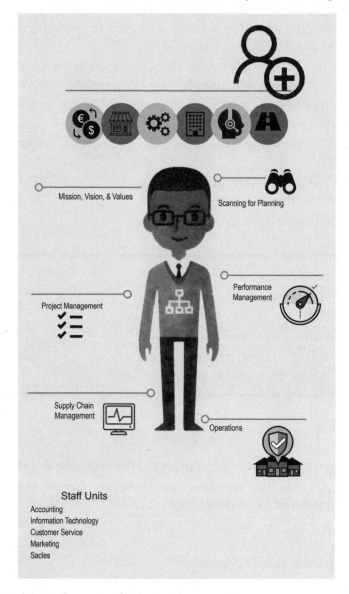

Figure 1.2   The Influence of Contemporary HR

Workforce Planning and Employment

If BMS is strategically focused, the domain of workforce planning and employment (WPE) is operationally focused. This is where HR practitioners are experts in recruitment, selection, and employee separation. These two practices are the bookends of the life cycle of the employee; the other domains address all areas in between (see Figure 1.3).

Key to all the activities of HR in this domain is alignment:

- *Aligning jobs to company goals and activities.* Using the principles of job design, HR supports productivity outcomes through work flow analysis.

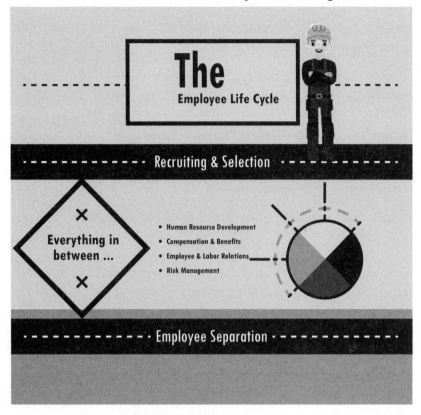

Figure 1.3   The Employee Life Cycle

- *Aligning jobs to people and people to organizations.* This is known as fit. HR uses both job and company data to predict the success of new hires and separate those with poor fit.
- *Aligning resources to strategy.* By systematically reviewing company business plans and strategies, HR determines the human capital requirements to achieve business goals. This includes both staffing up and downsizing.

Human Resource Development

In the domain of human resource development (HRD), HR supports organizational strategies through managing performance. It begins with conducting needs assessments to identify gaps between current performance and the desired state. This is followed by building programs that address the gaps. These programs may be people oriented, such as performance management systems and leadership development, or process oriented, such as through quality initiatives.

Additionally, the management of individuals requires expertise in motivating adults to do the work, developing tools beyond the paycheck. Understanding how employees learn and paying attention to what employees need form the basis for employee training and development activities.

Compensation and Benefits

While compensation and benefits (CAB) are not the sole motivating factors for workers, poor management of the programs results in highly dissatisfied workers. CAB programs are heavily influenced by the concepts of equity and loyalty:

- Perceptions of justice are very closely linked to CAB programs.
- Compensation and benefits programs increase employee loyalty.

Both of these concepts are linked with the *psychological contract*: the mutual expectation of an exchange of fair behaviors, implied and codified over time through experience. Employers expect employees to do their best work, remain loyal, and stay until work is completed. Employees expect fair pay, promotions, and job security.

Psychological Contract

Beliefs that influence the employee-employer relationship

An unwritten agreement of the mutual beliefs, perceptions, and informal obligations between an employer and an employee, which influence how they interact

The reception other HR programs receive in terms of employee engagement and responsiveness must pass first through the psychological veil of CAB programs. Additionally, employers need their CAB programs to remain competitive while dealing with increasing labor and health care costs. Employers pay a cost above and beyond employee base wages, and this burden must be factored into the design of all CAB programs to deliver a return on investment (ROI) and retain the company's value (see Figure 1.4).

Employee and Labor Relations

Key to understanding and practicing human resources is knowing that each domain is connected and dependent upon the functioning of each department. When one domain of HR is dysfunctional, performance in the other domains is, to varying

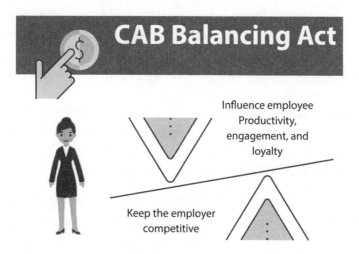

Figure 1.4   CAB Balancing Act

degrees, impaired as well. Perhaps in no other area is this as true as in employee and labor relations (ELR). The management of the relationship between the employer and the employee forms the energy of the company culture, the pulse of employee performance. The artful practice of communication is the conduit through which information flows, and determines both the speed of transfer and the obstacles encountered along the way.

It is in this domain that discipline and terminations are processed and management under the watchful eye of an employee union is done. Both of these conditions may be fraught with emotion and conflict, requiring the true advocacy role of human resources to be practiced, serving the needs of both the employer and the employee.

Risk Management

Risk management (RM) is the domain of HR that manages employee health, safety, and security, along with protecting the employer from loss and liability. Identifying personnel as human assets, while impersonal, does give clarity to the need for protection. HR is tasked with protecting all assets of the organization, from the human to the physical and, in the twenty-first century, the information assets for all *stakeholders*. Employers have a duty of care regarding their workers, and an obligation to protect the company from risk. Both are underscored by compliance with safety, security, and governance laws.

Education and prevention are at the heart of all RM programs. When employees understand the hazards associated with their work and are taught how to protect themselves from said hazards, then injuries, accidents, and near misses decrease. When financial and purchasing accountability processes are developed, controls are introduced to protect assets.

HR helps the companies they serve conduct risk assessments, working with internal and external experts to identify threats and build behavioral and environmental controls to reduce exposure. Response plans must be built and tested for if (when) the controls fail, and refined as conditions change.

Stakeholder

An interest holder in an organization

A person, group, or organization that has a direct or indirect interest in the organization (for example, owners, investors, employees, suppliers, unions, or the community)

The Age of Organizational Behavior

Gary Vaynerchuk tweeted[2] that a company environment is about the people, not about whether there is a foosball table in the break room; this is a great example of the bridge between human relations and organizational behavior (OB). By definition, OB is both theory based and practically applied, using analytical techniques of people, group, and organizational factors. Kinicki and Fugate in their phenomenal book *Organizational Behavior*[3] defined OB's focus as managing people within and between individual, group, and organizational levels.

Human relations formed in response to evidence that organizational behavior influences individual behavior. How people are treated, and how they *think* (perceive) they are being treated makes a difference in how they perform. For this reason, companies began investing and experimenting with the human side of production as opposed to focusing only on outputs. The quality of leadership, the way communication flowed, and the way coworkers interact formed best practices to engage and retain a talented workforce.

Capital is an interesting word meaning "wealth in the form of assets" (www .businessdictionary.com). This definition and that of human capital are rooted in possibility: If a company has financial assets, it can direct those resources to solve problems. Similarly, if a company has a wealth of knowledge workers, it can deploy them to solve problems, take advantage of opportunities, and, ultimately, successfully compete in its market. A current or future employee with the right knowledge, skills, and abilities represents a company's ultimate ability to both sustain its existence and thrive by taking advantage of opportunities and reducing threats through the power of its people. The individual talents of the employees influence the overall competencies of a group, collectively accumulating to drive organizational performance.[4]

In this way, organizational behavior and human relations must drive the management of the human resources of public, private, and nonprofit businesses. This translates into the design of HR programs, policies, and processes that influences not only the behaviors of the people, but the behavior of the organization as well.

Structuring Human Resource Departments

In every sense, all managers are HR managers. They are responsible for making hiring decisions, providing performance feedback, making recommendations for training and promotions, and taking corrective action when necessary. As a company grows, these responsibilities may get lost or diluted under the increased burden of operations. Additionally, asking managers to keep track of the labor compliance factors—which become increasingly onerous as employers add staff—is unrealistic and risky. As the company grows, so does the need for a structured human resource department.

A quick Google search of the phrase "human resource job titles" resulted in these first five:

1. Category Manager, HR
2. Chief Happiness Officer
3. Chief Human Resources Officer
4. Chief People Officer
5. Client Facing Human Resources Specialist

There is some speculation that "human resource" is out of date in a job title, failing to reflect the complex roles and responsibilities of this discipline. This is evidenced by the five job titles listed, but also by a growing trend by large companies such as UPS, Adobe, and Airbnb to include "employee experience" in the titles and job responsibilities of their HR talent.

Regardless of what they are called, most companies staff their human resource departments based on the total number of employees. Typically, a company will hire someone to focus solely on human resource tasks when it reaches 80 employees. While the first hire could be administrative, operational, or strategic, most midsize companies find they need an operationally oriented hire to provide midlevel support. Priority tasks include managing payroll, recruitment, selection, and training. These roles are reviewed next.

Department of Labor, Bureau of Labor Statistics, RIASEC

There are three resources in this section that are used to illustrate the talent structure of an HR department. They are:

1. *U.S. Department of Labor (DOL) O*NET.* The DOL undertook a formal job analysis of nearly every job in the United States, collecting information from employers on job content, context, tasks, duties, responsibilities, work environment, and much more. This section calls upon the DOL's findings to provide examples of how companies are utilizing their HR talent.
2. *U.S. Bureau of Labor Statistics (BLS) Occupational Handbook Outlook.* The BLS compiled and continues to provide regular updates to the outlook of jobs in the United States, including projected growth.
3. *Holland's RIASEC (realistic, investigative, artistic, social, enterprising, and conventional) model of vocational choice.* This model of personality demonstrates the interests of individuals who gravitate toward work in the HR field. The DOL used the RIASEC to identify work interests. Holland believed six personality factors influence career choice. They are:

    1. **Realistic (doers)** Realistic occupations frequently involve work activities that include practical, hands-on problems and solutions. They often deal with plants, animals, and real-world materials like wood, tools, and machinery. Many of the occupations require working outside, and do not involve a lot of paperwork or working closely with others.

    2. **Investigative (thinkers)** Investigative occupations frequently involve working with ideas, and require an extensive amount of thinking. These occupations can involve searching for facts and figuring out problems mentally.

    3. **Artistic (creators)** Artistic occupations frequently involve working with forms, designs, and patterns. They often require self-expression, and the work can be done without following a clear set of rules.

    4. **Social (helpers)** Social occupations frequently involve working with, communicating with, and teaching people. These occupations often involve helping or providing services to others.

    5. **Enterprising (persuasive)** Enterprising occupations frequently involve starting up and carrying out projects. These occupations can involve leading people and making many decisions. Sometimes they require risk taking and often deal with business.

    6. **Conventional (organizers)** Conventional occupations frequently involve following set procedures and routines. These occupations can include working with data and details more than with ideas. Usually there is a clear line of authority to follow.

Table 1.1   The RIASEC Model and Those Who Choose HR

	Doers: Realistic	Thinkers: Investigative	Creators: Artistic	Helpers: Social	Persuaders: Enterprising	Organizers: Conventional
Human resource manager				X	X	X
Human resource specialist				X	X	X
Training and development manager				X	X	X
Compensation, benefits, and job analysis specialists					X	X
Payroll and timekeeping clerks					X	X

Source: U.S. Department of Labor, O*NET.

The RIASEC model and corresponding theory of vocational choice, when applied to the sample HR jobs listed in Table 1.1, reveal a trend in the types of folks attracted to the work of HR. This data should be used by organizers of a human resource department to ensure they get the right blend of talent into the department, and consider any service gaps based on the current personality mix of the department and needs of the company.

Human Resource Manager: Enterprising, Social, Conventional

Characterized by the RIASEC as "persuasive helpers who like to organize," human resource managers plan, direct, and coordinate the administrative functions of an organization. They oversee the recruiting, interviewing, and hiring of new staff; consult with top executives on strategic planning; and serve as a link between an organization's management and its employees.

Work Styles

1. **Integrity** Job requires being honest and ethical.
2. **Stress tolerance** Job requires accepting criticism and dealing calmly and effectively with high-stress situations.

3. **Leadership** Job requires a willingness to lead, take charge, and offer opinions and direction.
4. **Dependability** Job requires being reliable, responsible, and dependable, and fulfilling obligations.
5. **Initiative** Job requires a willingness to take on responsibilities and challenges.

Job Outlook

Employment of human resource managers is projected to grow 9 percent from 2014 to 2024, faster than the average for all occupations. As new companies form and organizations expand their operations, they will need human resource managers to oversee and administer their programs, and to ensure firms adhere to changing and complex employment laws. Strong competition can be expected for most positions.

Human Resource Specialist: Enterprising, Conventional, Social

Human resource specialists recruit, screen, interview, and place workers. They often handle other types of human resource work, such as those related to employee relations, compensation and benefits, and training.

Tasks

Human resource specialists perform tasks such as:

- Prepare or maintain employment records related to events, such as hiring, termination, leaves, transfers or promotions, using human resources management system software.
- Interpret and explain human resources policies, procedures, laws, standards, or regulations.
- Hire employees and process hiring-related paperwork.
- Inform job applicants of details such as duties and responsibilities, compensation, benefits, schedules, working conditions, or promotion opportunities.
- Address employee relations issues, such as harassment allegations, work complaints, or other employee concerns.

Job Outlook

Employment of human resource specialists is projected to grow 5 percent from 2014 to 2024, about as fast as the average for all occupations. Human resource specialists will be needed to handle increasingly complex employment laws and health care coverage options. Most growth is projected to be in the employment services industry.

Compensation, Benefits, and Job Analysis Specialists: Conventional, Enterprising

Compensation, benefits, and job analysis specialists conduct an organization's compensation and benefits programs. They also evaluate position descriptions to determine details such as a person's classification and salary.

Work Styles

1. **Integrity** Job requires being honest and ethical.
2. **Analytical thinking** Job requires analyzing information and using logic to address work-related issues and problems.
3. **Attention to detail** Job requires being careful about detail and thorough in completing work tasks.
4. **Dependability** Job requires being reliable, responsible, and dependable, and fulfilling obligations.
5. **Adaptability/flexibility** Job requires being open to change (positive or negative) and to considerable variety in the workplace.

Job Outlook

Employment of compensation, benefits, and job analysis specialists is projected to grow 4 percent from 2014 to 2024, more slowly than the average for all occupations. Outsourcing compensation and benefits plans to consulting firms will limit employment growth in most industries. Job prospects should be best for those with previous human resources work experience.

Training and Development Managers: Conventional, Enterprising, Social

Training and development managers plan, direct, and coordinate programs to enhance the knowledge and skills of an organization's employees. They also oversee a staff of training and development specialists.

Tasks

Training and development managers perform tasks such as:

- Prepare training budget for department or organization.
- Evaluate instructor performance and the effectiveness of training programs, providing recommendations for improvement.
- Analyze training needs to develop new training programs or modify and improve existing programs.
- Conduct or arrange for ongoing technical training and personal development classes for staff members.
- Plan, develop, and provide training and staff development programs, using knowledge of the effectiveness of methods such as classroom training, demonstrations, on-the-job training, meetings, conferences, and workshops.

Job Outlook

Employment of training and development managers is projected to grow 7 percent from 2014 to 2024, about as fast as the average for all occupations. Job prospects should be very good, particularly in industries with a lot of regulation, like finance and insurance.

Payroll and Timekeeping Clerks: Conventional, Enterprising

Payroll and timekeeping clerks compile and record employee time and payroll data. They may compute employees' time worked, production, and commissions, and may compute and post wages and deductions, or prepare paychecks.

Tasks

Payroll and timekeeping clerks perform tasks such as:

- Process and issue employee paychecks and statements of earnings and deductions.
- Compute wages and deductions, and enter data into computers.
- Review time sheets, work charts, wage computation, and other information to detect and reconcile payroll discrepancies.
- Compile employee time, production, and payroll data from time sheets and other records.
- Process paperwork for new employees and enter employee information into the payroll system.

From HR to Employee Experience

As alluded to in the Introduction, HR has a bit of an identity crisis, and it's no wonder with the rapid growth and elevation of business needs of the past several decades. The fracturing of the industry through manufactured or generic job titles has not served HR's overall credibility well. Companies that don't know how to use HR will not use HR. They will rely instead on the status quo: performance management systems that nearly everybody agrees are unsatisfactory, hope as a workforce strategy, and boxing HR into compliance and transactional exchanges between people. Of course, not all companies do this; many are tapping into the strategic competencies of their HR leaders to drive the change from "HR" to "employee experience." The point is that HR leaders take control and participate in the adaptations of the HR profession where appropriate, lending their voices and best practices to mold the discipline, and committing to their own professional development through the activities described in the next section.

The Development of HR Competencies

Competencies are defined as the knowledge, skills, and abilities (KSAs) necessary to do a job well. Senior leaders must be able to develop strategy and lead change. Generalists must have a working grasp on labor law. All HR staff must understand the fundamental activities of an HR department.

Competencies

The abilities needed to do well in a specific job

The skills, behaviors, and knowledge that are needed to succeed in a specific job

Human Resource Manager

While no two companies have HR management needs that are exactly alike, there are fundamentals to the KSAs and work activities of a functional human resource department. The following uses information from the DOL to identify the required competencies of an HR manager that apply across industrial, geographic, and other divides.

Knowledge

Personnel and human resources Knowledge of principles and procedures for personnel recruitment, selection, training, compensation and benefits, labor relations and negotiation, and personnel information systems.

Clerical Knowledge of administrative and clerical procedures and systems such as word processing, managing files and records, stenography and transcription, designing forms, and other office procedures and terminology.

Administration and management Knowledge of business and management principles involved in strategic planning, resource allocation, human resources modeling, leadership technique, production methods, and coordination of people and resources.

Customer and personal service Knowledge of principles and processes for providing customer and personal services. This includes customer needs assessment, meeting quality standards for services, and evaluation of customer satisfaction.

Skills

Active listening Giving full attention to what other people are saying, taking time to understand the points being made, asking questions as appropriate, and not interrupting at inappropriate times.

Speaking Talking to others to convey information effectively.

Reading comprehension Understanding written sentences and paragraphs in work-related documents.

Critical thinking Using logic and reasoning to identify the strengths and weaknesses of alternative solutions, conclusions, or approaches to problems.

Abilities

Oral comprehension The ability to listen to and understand information and ideas presented through spoken words and sentences.

Oral expression The ability to communicate information and ideas in speaking so others will understand.

Written comprehension The ability to read and understand information and ideas presented in writing.

Work Activities

Communicating with supervisors, peers, or subordinates Providing information to supervisors, coworkers, and subordinates by telephone, in written form, by e-mail, or in person.

Getting information Observing, receiving, and otherwise obtaining information from all relevant sources.

Interacting with computers Using computers and computer systems (including hardware and software) to program, write software, set up functions, enter data, or process information.

Staffing organizational units Recruiting, interviewing, selecting, hiring, and promoting employees in an organization.

Consider the KSAs and work activities in the context of hiring for this role. What job related preemployment tests might you use to predict success on the job? What interview questions might you write to determine fit? What instrument would you use to measure oral expression and written comprehension?

As the title search results suggest, organizations are grappling with how to best utilize current and developing competencies of the HR industry. The purpose of the HRBoK is to provide the blueprint from which the business and HR leaders of today may build out their HR culture: the cultivation of living things. Adopting the HRBoK throughout organizations and academia ensures consistency in the profession, weaving integrated patterns of knowledge and practice to affect organizational performance. HR must be an adaptive, learning industry, one with a never-ending capacity for professional development and growth while still performing from best practice benchmarks.

Degrees

Most colleges and universities have robust human resource management programs from which formal degrees are available. It is worth using curriculum as a filter through which to understand what the academic community believes to be important elements to the practice of HR.

For example, human resource undergrads at DePaul University will be educated in areas such as training and career development, compensation and benefits, and recruitment and selection. Other required courses include labor economics, leadership and global human resource management, and organizational development.

As you can see by the core requirements, the curriculum invests heavily in the ability of human resources to be proficient in the six domains of the HRBoK while incorporating global influences within and outside of the United States. This includes viewing the competitive marketplace through the lens of a *global organization*. When this concept is applied to HR, it reflects the need for human resource professionals to develop competencies in management of one labor market and all its diverse components.

Global Organization

An organization that views the world as one market

An organization that views the whole world as one market, and does not divide it into separate markets by country

---

Other universities run HR certificate programs, which develop student proficiencies in human resource and leadership through classes, workshops, and on-site training. Continuing an HR education is a best practice that serves the student, the employer, and the employees who are dependent upon the HR practitioner to take their role seriously. See Figure 1.5 for a view of the cascading transmission of HR and business knowledge and competencies from the sciences to the workplace.

Professional Certification: Seven and Strong

Achieving professional human resource *certification* is a mark of excellence and commitment. Certification programs are different from certificate programs such as the ones offered at many universities. Certification programs:

- Require specific experience and education.
- Require recertification, making sure your skills stay up to date.
- Allow you to put the letters after your name.

The credentials demonstrate *mastery* over the three e's: education, experience, and an exam covering a body of knowledge and practical competencies to designate a person as a dedicated, credible practitioner. When hiring in the human resource field, any one of HRCI's seven *credentials* serves as a reference of talent within the scope of the HR discipline.

While you can't teach talent, you can certainly influence the exponential effect that professional certification will have on a career. Talent without direction literally has no place to go. Professional certification is an integral piece in a *career management* system that can address many of the moving parts of knowledge and competency that will serve an individual's desire for a career path paved with excellence, confidence, job satisfaction, and pay increases. If we can't create a logical, systematic career path for ourselves, how will HR be able to do it for employees?

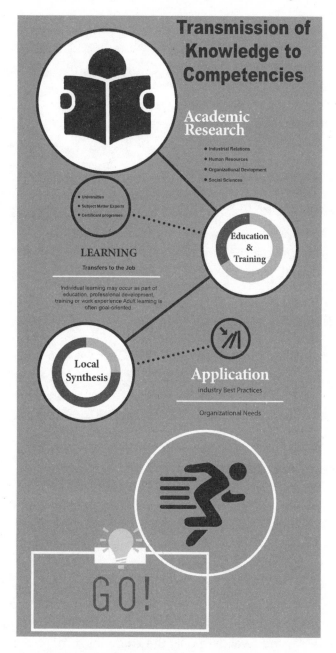

Figure 1.5   Transmission of Knowledge to Competencies

Certification

A procedure to grant an official designation

Confirmation of specific achievements or characteristics given by an authority, usually by issuing a certificate or diploma after a test

(continued)

(*continued*)

Mastery

Ability, expertise

Great ability and knowledge of some subject or activity

Credentials

Certified documents, diplomas

Proof of a person's earned authority, status, or rights, usually in writing (for example, a university diploma, a digital certification badge, or other proof of passing a professional exam)

Career Management

Planning and controlling the professional development of an employee

Preparing, implementing, and monitoring the career path of employees, with a focus on the goals and needs of the organization

The Importance of Accreditation

Accreditation through the National Commission for Certifying Agencies (NCCA) for professional or personnel certification programs provides validation from an impartial third party that the program has met recognized national and international credentialing industry standards for development, implementation, and maintenance of certification programs. The NCCA describes accreditation as the number one reason to choose one professional certification over another. It's important to note that there are only a few accrediting bodies (such as NCCA and ANSI) that evaluate a whole certification program; others validate only the exam instrument itself.

> HRCI certifications are also the only accredited HR certification program in the market, and have been in place for over 40 years.
> —from HRCI.org;
> Used with permission by Human Resource Certification Institute, Inc.

The NCCA standards were developed to highlight the essential elements of a high-quality program, focusing on the processes and products of certification organizations. In order to be applicable to all professions and industries, the

NCCA standards do not evaluate exam content. The NCCA determined that program content validity is demonstrated with a comprehensive job analysis conducted and analyzed by experts, with data gathered from experts and practitioners.

> HRCI's certification exam items and exam forms are developed and peer reviewed by subject matter experts with diverse HR experience developed in numerous industries, company sizes and levels of expertise. Each exam is built based on an exam blueprint (Exam Content Outline) which is developed through a structured, research-based practice analysis study. All exams are competency-based and all but the aPHR are practice-based and require demonstrated professional-level HR experience.
> —from HRCI.org;
> Used with permission by Human Resource Certification Institute, Inc.

The Exams

Headquartered in the United States, HRCI has been credentialing human resource professionals for decades.

As an independent nonprofit organization, the company follows an accredited practice to certify human resources professionals over seven exams. These exams deliver upon HRCI's vision that "People and organizations perform better because of us."

The bank of seven certification exams is reviewed next.[5]

aPHR

The newest of HRCI's seven professional-level exams, the aPHR exam is appropriate for an entry-level HR practitioner with a high school diploma or global equivalent. It is also an excellent choice for someone who has been in human resources, but does not meet the exempt level requirement to test for one of the other exams. The aPHR exam content is sorted into six functional areas:

1. HR Operations
2. Recruitment and Selection
3. Compensation and Benefits
4. Human Resource Development and Retention
5. Employee Relations
6. Health, Safety, and Security

The tasks that may be expected of an aPHR candidate are represented in Table 1.2. Hiring a successfully credentialed aPHR candidate means that employers may rely on the new hire to perform many of the administrative duties of HR, from coordinating orientation, on-boarding, and training to maintaining data for employee record keeping throughout all functions of HR. Operationally, aPHR

Table 1.2　Typical aPHR Tasks

Administrative	Operational	Strategic
Access, collect, and provide information and data to support HR-related decisions (for example, recruiting, employee relations, training, safety, budgeting, needs analysis, off-boarding, termination)	Comply with all applicable laws and regulations	Communicate the organization's core values, vision, mission, culture, and ethical behaviors
Maintain employee data in human resource information system (HRIS) or system of record	Coordinate and communicate with external providers of HR services (for example, recruiters, COBRA administrators, employee recognition services)	
Maintain, file, and process HR forms (for example, notices, announcements, new hire forms, salary forms, performance, termination paperwork)	Provide internal customer service by answering or referring HR-related questions from employees as the first level of support	
Prepare HR-related documents (for example, reports, presentations, organizational charts)	Communicate information about HR policies and procedures	
Post job listings (for example, company website, social media, job boards)	Identify risk in the workplace	
Manage applicant databases (for example, enter data, access records, update records)	Minimize risk by conducting audits (for example, I-9, workers' compensation, employee records)	
Coordinate interview logistics	Document and update essential job functions with the support of managers	
Arrange for tests and assessments of applicants	Screen applicants for managers to interview	
Coordinate the employment offer (for example, start date, salary, benefits)	Answer questions from job applicants	
Administer postoffer employment activities (for example, execute employment agreements, complete I-9/e-Verify process, coordinate relocation, immigration)	Interview job candidates	
	Communicate compensation and benefits programs and systems	
	Coordinate activities to support employee benefits programs (for example, wellness, retirement planning)	
	Resolve routine employee compensation and benefits issues	

Administrative	Operational	Strategic
Coordinate payroll-related information (for example, new hires, adjustments, paid time off, terminations)	Conduct orientation and on-boarding for new hires, rehires, and transfers	
Process claims from employees (for example, workers' compensation, short-term or long-term disability benefits)	Conduct employee training programs (for example, safety regulations, emergency preparedness, presentation skills, time management skills)	
Coordinate training sessions (for example, logistics, materials, tracking, registration, evaluation)	Monitor completion of performance reviews and development plans	
Coordinate the logistics for employee relations programs (for example, recognition, special events, diversity programs)		

Note: Used with permission by Human Resource Certification Institute, Inc.

candidates are well versed in processes that provide employee support by being knowledgeable about compensation and benefits, policies, procedures, and essential job functions.

The aPHR exam is 2 hours and 15 minutes in length, and comprises 100 multiple-choice questions and 25 pretest questions.

Professional in Human Resources, California® (PHRca®)

This is currently the only exam that is state specific, focusing on Compensation/ Wage and Hour, Employment and Employee Relations, Benefits and Leaves of Absence, and Health, Safety, and Workers' Compensation. To be eligible, individuals must have one of the following:

- At least one year of experience in a professional-level HR position + a master's degree or higher,
- At least two years of experience in a professional-level HR position + a bachelor's degree, or
- At least four years of experience in a professional-level HR position + a high school diploma.

This exam has 100 scored and 25 pretest questions, and is administered over a 2-hour, 15-minute time frame.

Professional in Human Resources® (PHR®) and Senior Professional in Human Resources® (SPHR®)

The PHR and the SPHR exams share core content. They are designed to measure a candidate's knowledge and competencies in the six functional areas described in this book:

1. Business Management and Strategy
2. Workforce Planning and Employment
3. Human Resource Development
4. Compensation and Benefits
5. Employee and Labor Relations
6. Risk Management

The Professional in Human Resources exam supports HR professionals with generalist or operational titles. These professionals generally focus on the HR operation as opposed to the operation of the organization as a whole. The PHR is both knowledge and competency based, requiring successful candidates to have one of the following:

- At least one year of experience in a professional-level HR position + a master's degree or higher,
- At least two years of experience in a professional-level HR position + a bachelor's degree, or
- At least four years of experience in a professional-level HR position + a high school diploma.

In addition to these PHR knowledge and competency requirements, a Senior Professional in Human Resources adds the dimension of executive-level strategic planning to his or her value set. An SPHR has a breadth and depth of knowledge in the functions of human resources and the functions of business. Eligible candidates will have one of the following:

- At least four years of experience in a professional-level HR position + a master's degree or higher,
- At least five years of experience in a professional-level HR position + a bachelor's degree, or
- At least seven years of experience in a professional-level HR position + a high school diploma.

Both the PHR and SPHR exams are 3 hours long, and are 150 questions with 25 pretest questions in length.

Global Professional in Human Resources® (GPHR®)

As much of this book's content reflects, there is a growing need for aligned global professionals with *cross-border* human resource experience. Competent professionals are eligible to sit for the 3-hour GPHR exam, consisting of 140 + 25 pretest questions, if they have one of the following:

- At least two years of experience in a global professional-level HR position + a master's degree or higher,
- At least three years of experience in a professional-level HR position (at least two in global HR) + a bachelor's degree, or
- At least four years of experience in a professional-level HR position (at least two in global HR) + a high school diploma.

Professional in Human Resources, International® (PHRi®) and Senior Professional in Human Resources, International® (SPHRi®)

A recent addition to the bank of seven exams are the PHR and SPHR international. As their titles suggest, these exams are appropriate for HR leaders practicing in a country outside the United States. PHRi-eligible candidates have work experience in a single international setting using technical and operational principles, and are tested with 145 + 25 pretest questions in a 3-hour, 15-minute period. Certificate seekers are eligible if they have one of the following:

- At least one year of experience in a professional-level HR position + a master's degree or global equivalent,
- At least two years of experience in a professional-level HR position + a bachelor's degree or global equivalent, or
- At least four years of experience in a professional-level HR position + a high school diploma or global equivalent.

SPHRi candidate careers have been more oriented toward senior-level HR competencies across multiple HR domains within a single international setting. To be eligible for the exam, SPHRi candidates must have one of the following:

- At least one year of experience in a professional-level HR position + a master's degree or global equivalent,
- At least two years of experience in a professional-level HR position + a bachelor's degree or global equivalent, or
- At least four years of experience in a professional-level HR position + a high school diploma or global equivalent.

The SPHRi exam is administered over 2 and a half hours, with 105 + 25 pretest multiple-choice questions.

Cross-Border

Country to country

Taking place across the geographic boundaries of two or more countries (for example, cross-border trade)

How the Exams Are Scored

The *Angoff method* is a way to establish exam scoring standards. It is used by test developers to determine a passing score. Subject matter experts (SMEs) evaluate the content of each exam question and predict how many minimally qualified test takers would get the correct answer. An average of the judges' scores is used to establish the cutoff for a passing grade.

Each exam taker seeking to pass one of the seven exams will take a test that includes pretest questions. These are questions that are being evaluated for validity and level of difficulty before they are rotated into the scored bank of tests used to determine an individual score. In this way, the integrity of the process and the quality of the exam item are measured.

All of HRCI's exams are pass-or-fail based on a range of scores from 100 to 700. Successful candidates will achieve a minimum *scaled score* of 500. The raw score is the actual number of items answered correctly on the test. The scaled score represents the difficulty level of the random exam the test taker received, and is shown only to those who do not pass.

It is recommended that you do *not* leave a question unanswered. Scoring is based on the number of correct answers, so leaving an item blank eliminates the possibility of that item counting in your scaled score.

Angoff Method

An exam scoring process

A way to set the standard score for passing a test

Scaled Score

An adjusted score

A conversion of a raw score to a common scale that can be used for comparison

How to Prepare for Exams

The most important step toward a successful exam experience is to ensure you select the proper exam. The practice of human resources requires lifelong learning through a mix of professional development activities. Starting with the PHR before the SPHR, for example, gives you the opportunity to develop benchmark knowledge and learn the operational job content of those you will eventually be managing. Measuring yourself against the content of the PHRi before the SPHRi ensures that you have a quality platform from which to base all other professional development activities. Certification is a journey, not an event.

Very few individuals sit for these exams with little or no preparation. The degree to which you prepare is based on your unique work experience and education and should include a mix of activities to ensure you are looking at the content from multiple perspectives.

Consider Exam Content Weights

The exam content outline for each of the exams shows the percentage of content for each functional area. This serves as a guide for test takers to know where to concentrate their study efforts.

Practice Exams

Certification seekers must conduct their own type of *gap analysis* to identify where they are compared to where they want to be. HRCI offers practice exams for most of the test banks. The practice exam results show your individual score in each functional area, allowing you to concentrate your study effort in the area where it is most needed.

Gap Analysis

A technique used to compare the current state with the future desired state

An analysis process that helps organizations or people compare their actual performance with their potential performance

Study Groups versus Self-Study Methods

There is no single way to study for these exams that is best. Knowing your individual *learning style* and personality will help you choose whether to go it alone or join a group to help prepare for your chosen exam.

Study groups have the advantage of learning from each other, holding one another accountable to stay on track. It is helpful to have others encourage you when you need it, and clarify content when necessary. Study groups can be self-formed, but many are led by experts who can guide you through exam content.

Successful self-studiers are those who have a high degree of self-discipline and are committed to the process. Staying organized and on track and reaching out to alternative resources when content is new or complex characterize those for whom self-studying is best.

Techniques for both groups should include reading content from exam prep resources, watching videos from credible sources, creating presentations focused on critical content, and *always* seeking to find ways to relate exam content to the job.

Both approaches should utilize an 8-, 12-, or 14-week study plan to work through the exam content outline.

Learning Style

The way a person learns

The way people process new information and learn most effectively (for example, some people learn best visually, through lectures, or by reading. Others learn best by action or doing)

The Importance of Recertification

Newly certified HR professionals need to recertify every three years. This is achieved by engaging in professional development activities designed to increase the depth of existing knowledge, or to learn something new related to the domains of HR. Successful exam takers may recertify credentials in one of two ways: retake the exam or earn credits. Many choose to earn the 60 recertification credits over the three-year active window rather than sit for the rather difficult exam again.

Approved recertification activities fall into any of the following categories:

Continuing education Part of the HRCI code of ethics is that HR professionals commit to professional development. This is achieved through formal and continuing education activities such as classes, workshops, seminars, and webinars.

Instruction Teaching an HR class or a topic on which you're an expert is another way to earn recertification credits. Instruction can be paid or voluntary.

On-the-job training (OJT) Training that occurs on the job is valuable, as these exams are experienced based. These types of credits need to be for tasks or responsibilities that are new to your role.

Research/publications With the abundance of online publishing, blogs, and e-newsletters, plenty of opportunities are out there for you to write on an HR topic that may be trending or of interest to other professionals.

Leadership Leading teams or projects or groups through interventions is another way to log recertification hours. Keeping track of any documentation that demonstrates the nature of the leadership, the relation to exam content, and the amount of time spent is important for your recertification application.

Professional membership Log any professional memberships you have in local, industrial, national, or global associations for additional credits.

While many pre-approved programs are available, you may submit work or educational activities for consideration with your recertification activities.

An easy way to track recertification credits is to regularly log into your HRCI account, and submit credit activities as you achieve them. When the time comes to recertify, you simply review for accuracy and submit, rather than scroll back through e-mails and calendars for dates, locations, content, and credits.

Once successfully certified, don't forget to claim your digital badge! Proof of your certification, this digital seal can be used on social media, e-mails, personal websites, and resumes. The badges securely link to HRCI to verify your active credential, protecting the integrity of the reference.

HRBoK™

The practice of HR is influenced by academia, politics, the economy, technology, and globalization. It draws upon research from the disciplines of psychology, anthropology, the social sciences, and business management. If that isn't enough, HR professionals must be intimate with the details and nuances of the industries in which they practice, such as finance, health care, manufacturing, and construction. HR professionals must be lifelong learners, as the practice of HR adapts as research emerges and business conditions change. Those who do not seek to advance their knowledge run the risk of becoming irrelevant in a very short period of time or of damaging their relationships with employers and employees through errors and omissions.

The HRBoK™ is the helix of human resources, a learning DNA shaped by past practices and evolving needs. Organic in nature, it reflects the need for an organization's human resources to serve in a consulting role more often than a policing role. It underscores the value of fostering a performance culture across all company departments through thoughtful, systematic programs with clear targets and regular measurements. The HRBoK positions practitioners to globally represent the discipline of HR with up-to-date and relevant best practices while functioning

Figure 1.6   Human Resource DNA

under the highest professional standards in service to the stakeholders who are counting on them. In short, the HRBoK is the cornerstone for a community in practice (see Figure 1.6).

Notes

1. HR Certification Institute, "A Brief History." Retrieved from https://www.hrci.org/about-hrci/overview/history.
2. Gary Vaynerchuk, "Work Required," September 14, 2016, Twitter.com/dailyvee.
3. A. Kinicki and M. Fugate, *Organizational Behavior* (New York: McGraw-Hill, 2011).
4. Ibid.
5. Exam eligibility and accreditation details found on pages 23–31 are used with permission by Human Resource Certification Institute, Inc.

2 | Business Management and Strategy

Introduction

Where do businesses come from? The fact is that there have been some forms of enterprise for thousands of years. From small businesses built upon individual skills and barter systems to import/export services for cross-country and across-oceans transport all the way through the formalized state-run corporations and academic institutions, the early businesses had the same fundamental needs as the companies of today: *human capital strategies* and competitive *supply chain management (SCM)*.

The *functional HR* practices in business management and strategy (BMS) embrace HR as a *business partner*. With a strong emphasis on managing the people and processes required to keep businesses up and running, a *dedicated HR* professional must be capable of:

- Applying general business principles
- Leading change efforts
- Acting as a strategic partner for all functions of HR
- Applying business strategies to operational activities
- Achieving international human resource management goals
- Integrating industry best practices and academic theories
- Orienting HR activities toward the bottom line

The *human resources (HR)* function focuses on implementing business strategies that combine the needs of the business with the needs of the people doing the work. This chapter serves as a resource for HR in an advisory role for all business functions. HR professionals must be able to create relationships with *HR partners*, and develop and administer programs that operate from a set of blueprints designed by master builders—architects, experts, and skilled individuals—with the shared objective to do well, and competitively, the business of work.

HR

Human resources

Function within an organization that focuses on implementing organizational strategy, as well as recruiting, managing performance, and providing direction for the people who work in the organization

HR Partner

An ally in providing HR services

A manager or department that has a relationship with HR in order to provide services to the organization

HR Business Partner

Strategic role for human resources

A role in which the human resources function works closely with an organization to develop strategies and achieve business results

Dedicated HR

Person committed to human resources in an organization

A human resources position that works only on HR responsibilities within an organization

Functional HR

Dedicated tasks of the human resources position in an organization

The human resources role within an organization that focuses on strategy, recruitment, management, and the direction of the people in the organization

Human Capital Strategies

Employment tactics plan for managing employees

Methods and tools for recruiting, managing, and keeping important employees

Supply Chain Management (SCM)
The steps taken from initial planning through customer support
Process of planning, implementing, and controlling operations, which begins with acquiring raw materials and continues to customer delivery and support

General Business Principles

HR professionals wear many hats and need to possess a variety of skills in order to serve business outcomes. Often acting as internal consultants, their continuing value to the organizations that employ them comes from understanding all aspects of the business, not just the practices of the HR department. Knowing company financials, building programs to serve organizational goals, evaluating the efficacy of strategies both before and after implementation, and helping companies prepare the workforce for future needs are all activities that contribute to HR professionals as trusted organizational leaders.

Business Entities, Functions, and Structures

The interrelatedness of all business functions is often demonstrated through the management of human resources. HR policies, procedures, and rules must be broad enough to apply to all employees yet specific enough to meet unique company and regulatory needs. Additionally, improving employee engagement and productivity and designing work that is free from safety hazards are other influences that HR helps to manage through organizational design decisions. This entails HR pros understanding the big picture environment of business entities, department functions, and organizational structures. These design features help dictate the plans, policies, programs, and procedures necessary to achieve HR outcomes linked to business strategy.

Business Entities

There are several different types of business structures that are defined by the Internal Revenue Service (IRS):

Sole proprietorship A business that is owned by a single person. Income is generally reported under personal income tax forms and includes liability for self-employment taxes.

Partnerships A partnership exists when two or more individuals legally join together to form a business. Each person is actively involved in the business by contributing money and labor, and both expect to share in the benefits of profitability and the risk of loss. In a partnership, the business entity does not pay income tax. Instead, gains or losses are "passed through" to each partner's personal income tax returns. In this structure, partners are not considered employees, and self-employment taxes apply.

Corporations A corporation is a business in which stock is sold to shareholders in order to fund operations. The profits of the corporation are taxed to the corporation when earned, and then taxed again to the shareholders when distributed to them as earnings (called a double tax). Shareholders do not deduct corporate losses from their personal taxes.

S corporations S corporations are entities that elect to pass profits and losses, income, and deductions through to the shareholders. These are then reported on the shareholders' personal income taxes as opposed to a corporate tax return. This allows S corporations to avoid the double tax described for regular (C) corporations.

Limited liability companies (LLCs) An LLC is a state-by-state-granted business structure that is a hybrid of a corporation and a partnership, with most states allowing for a single member. If there are two or more partners, it may be classified as a partnership for tax filing purposes. LLCs are not taxed as a corporation; profits and losses are passed through to the members. Self-employment taxes generally apply.

In addition to the IRS definitions, there are other ways a business can be organized, either initially or as part of an overall business strategy. They include:

Franchising *Franchising* is a business structure in which a company sells licensing rights to another group or individual, allowing the franchisee to conduct for-profit business under the franchisor's brand and supply chain practices. Fast-food restaurant chains are a common example.

Joint ventures (JVs) A *joint venture (JV)* is a type of time-based partnership between two businesses, often with shared goals or *aligned* to maximize resources. For example, in 2011 Microsoft joined with General Electric to form Caradigm, a company focused on streamlining health care analytics. Similarly, a *strategic alliance* may be formed by two or more companies to pursue similar objectives.

Equity partnerships When an individual or group decides to *invest* funds for *start-ups*, they may do so using an *equity partnership* structure. Simple Sugars, a skin care company, appeared on the television show *Shark Tank*, and agreed to a 33 percent equity partnership with Mark Cuban in exchange for a $100,000 investment in this *turnkey operation*. Investments may also be used to pay for *up-front costs* associated with getting a business off the ground.

Subsidiaries A *subsidiary* is a company with 50 percent or more *ownership interest* by a parent company. Odwalla Inc. is a subsidiary of the Coca-Cola Company, two major beverage brands successfully leveraging market position.

Foreign subsidiaries Similar to a subsidiary, a *foreign subsidiary* is 50 percent or more owned by a parent company headquartered in another country, such as Revlon Beauty Products of Spain, a foreign subsidiary of Revlon, Inc., headquartered in the United States. These may be formed using a *foreign direct invest (FDI)* strategy to obtain control. *Greenfield* and *brownfield operations* are two types of FDIs, in which an investor decides what type of operations to invest in and makes decisions such as to whether to buy, *lease,* or build new facilities.

In each of these examples, ownership is a major theme. Ownership determines who is the employer of record, data for financial reporting, and tax obligations, among other things. In each method described, the business operates to some degree (fully or partially) independent of the owner. Franchisees may use a company brand, recipes, and operational setups, but they own their business with independent profit-and-loss statements (P&Ls). Joint venture organizations may share resources, but often act as independent groups with different funding, strategies, and goals. A passive equity partnership may have a percentage owner who stays out of the day-to-day operations, but any partner with more than 20 percent equity may have to provide personal guarantees for business *loans.* Subsidiaries in many cases have their own brand identity, but will be captured in the parent company's financials. Knowing how this works is important for human resource pros, as different regulations and business strategies will need to be planned for, addressed, and managed.

Franchising

A business model that involves licensing

Selling a license for the use of a trademark, product, or service in order to do business a certain way and receiving ongoing payment for the license

Joint Venture (JV)

Partnership between two or more organizations

When two or more organizations work together and share risks and rewards

Align

Line up, make parallel

To place in a line or arrange in a similar way

(continued)

(continued)

Alliance

Agreement, cooperation

A partnership between organizations that helps both sides

Strategic Alliance

An agreement to cooperate between two organizations

An arrangement between two organizations to pursue common goals and share resources. Unlike a joint venture, the organizations do not form a new legal entity.

Investment

A commitment of money for expected return

Money and capital that is spent in order to make more money (for example, stocks, bonds, real estate)

Start-Up

A new business venture

A company or business that recently began operating and is in an early phase of development

Equity Partnership

Business arrangement with financial investors

An agreement for a person or an organization to own part of a company by providing start-up funds to the new business

Turnkey Operation

A business that is ready to operate

A business that includes everything needed to start operating in a certain location

Up-Front Costs

Paid or due in advance

Paid in advance, or invested as beginning capital

Subsidiary

A company that is controlled by another company

A company whose voting stock is more than 50 percent owned by another company. The company with the majority interest is called the "parent company"

Ownership Interest

Equity in a company

Owning part of a company or business

Foreign Subsidiary

A legal term defining ownership of a foreign company

A company that is more than 50 percent owned or controlled by a parent organization in another country

Foreign Direct Investment (FDI)

Ownership of a business or property by a foreign entity

An overseas investment in structures, equipment, or property controlled by a foreign corporation

Greenfield Operation

New business facility built in a new location

Start-up of a new business plant or operation, usually in a new location

Brownfield Operation

Previously used land

Reuse of land previously used for industry or manufacturing

Lease

A contract to use a property

An agreement for a person or organization to rent a property (lessee) from its owner (lessor) for a specific period of time and amount of money

(continued)

(continued)

Loan

Lending of money or goods

Money or goods that a person or organization lends temporarily, usually charging interest

Business Functions

As Figure 2.1 shows, there are many functions that are relevant to all business types, regardless of the number of employees. HR professionals must have an understanding of the workings of each department in order to plan for and contribute to the overall management of internal and external resources, including time, money, technology, and, of course, the talent. HR needs to know the business model(s) the company is pursuing to achieve revenue (how it makes money) and profit margins on products and services. Becoming experts in how work flows between departments and ultimately to the customer contributes to the design of HR strategies, programs, policies, procedures, and processes. Creating risk management plans, hiring qualified talent, building training programs, designing pay systems, and complying with country-specific regulations are just a few examples of how a working knowledge of business makes for a stronger (and more valuable) HR professional.

Finance and Accounting   Managing a company's finances is similar to managing human resources: it requires strategic planning for the management and direction of the financial resources toward business goals.

On an operational level, reports such as the balance sheet, cash flow statement, and income statement help human resources understand what is driving decisions about spending, growth, and expense management. For example, when a company experiences growth of 20 percent or more, cash starts to get tight. This is often because cash for *overhead* costs associated with increased sales, services, or equipment *purchases* goes out at a rate greater than cash is coming in. Additionally, finance will help employers calculate the *internal rate of return* on financial and other investments, and calculate overall net income expectations for the period being evaluated. While growth plans and targets are necessary, they may also impact HR's ability to pay for necessary talent or get approval for new programs or services. Three financial reports help HR understand the big picture and contribute to planning for budget surpluses and shortfalls:

1. *Balance sheet*
    The balance sheet is a basic financial statement that shows three things: assets, liabilities, and equity. Assets are what show as positive on the balance

Figure 2.1   Business Functions

sheet. They include equipment, facilities, patents, and the balance due on accounts (monies owed by customers)—anything that is owned by the business that may be converted to cash. Liabilities are those items for which a company owes money. They may include *outstanding loans* and accounts payable obligations. Equity refers to ownership, as described in an earlier section. A balance sheet at its most basic shows *assets = liabilities + equity*. The remaining balance is an indicator of organizational financial health.

2. *Income statement*

An income statement is a snapshot of a company at any given time. It shows, in its most basic form, *sales – expenses = net income*. Income statements are often used by employers to review how they are doing compared to the previous year.

3. *Statement of cash flows*

The cash flow statement is focused on tangible money in the bank. *Cash* is a term that is used by businesses to measure how much money they have available at any given time. Negative cash flow occurs when revenue is coming more slowly than the rate at which money is going out. Positive cash flow is the opposite. Note that neither negative nor positive cash flow is an indication of profit or loss; it simply reflects the amount of money an employer has available to operate. Companies may expand or contract spending based on this single indicator.

The accounting function refers to the operational tasks associated with crunching the numbers every day, week, month, quarter, and year to determine a company's *financial viability*. Similar to a human resource department, accounting personnel may be generalists or specialists.

There are different accounting methods that may be used. Cost accounting relates the costs (fixed and variable inputs) of producing goods or services with sales revenue to aid in decisions about labor levels, equipment purchases, and product pricing. Financial accounting is focused more on company assets and liabilities. The *accrual* method of accounting captures transactions as they occur (both sales and expenses) rather than when money is paid or received such as in cash basis accounting.

The general accepted accounting principles (GAAP) govern the tasks and reporting requirements associated with finance and accounting. As of 2017, the Securities and Exchange Commission (SEC) is still considering the formal adoption of the International Financial Reporting Standards (IFRS) for U.S. companies operating in multiple countries. Some U.S. companies with foreign subsidiaries have begun to integrate their GAAP practices with IFRS where allowed by law.

The finance and accounting functions of business are an excellent example of when *co-sourcing* is a good management strategy. A combination of accounting and finance staff, coupled with reliance on *third parties* such as CPA firms, is a practical example of managing the complex tasks of these critical functions.

Budgeting Budgeting is both an independent annual practice and also a function of the strategic planning process. Intervention strategies that come out of the planning process will require additional financial resources, and for that, a budget must be developed. A good question to ask during planning sessions comes from management guru Peter Drucker, who declares that the essence of strategy is deciding what *not* to work on (Drucker 2001). This allows for planning for a shift of resources or adding as an action item the securing of a separate source of financing as needed.

The human resources function has its own budget, which should include all labor for the organization. This is driven from workforce planning sessions and annual operating expenses related to the activities of the HR department. An HR budget should include anticipated salary increases and planned hiring. This is part of providing data for human capital projections.

A practical view of what is reflected in an HR budget may be taken by considering what money is spent on within the HR department on a daily basis. Examples include downsizing efforts, anticipated training costs, outplacement services, or HR software updates that may be necessary to achieve an organization's plan. Recognition program awards should be included, along with years of service awards or attendance incentives. Consider safety awards, attorney fees, performance incentives, and recruiting costs. With the rising cost of health insurance and other benefits, it is also necessary to forecast and budget for insurance increases.

The two main budget methods are:

Incremental Incremental budgets are built up from the previous years. Depending on goals and objectives, personnel needs, capital expenditures such as adding equipment, and one-time costs are all items that may be added on top of a department's or company's normal overhead. These are sometimes called static budgets, in that targets are established and then outcomes are measured against those targets.

Zero-based A *zero-based budget* starts from scratch each year. This allows department heads and executives to scrub expenses and justify the budget based on *return on investment (ROI)*, necessity, value, and alignment with strategic objectives.

Overhead

Business operating expenses

Direct costs associated with operating a business, such as rent, salaries, benefits, equipment, technology, and so on

(continued)

(continued)

Purchase

Buy

Acquire something through payment or barter

Internal Rate of Return

A way of measuring profits

A calculation of the average return each year during the life of an investment

Outstanding Loan

An unpaid debt

Money that a person or organization has borrowed but not yet paid back

Financial Viability

Ability to survive financially

The ability of an organization to achieve financial goals, growth, and stability, while also paying expenses and debt

Accrual

A method of accounting

An accounting method that recognizes a company's financial performance by recording income and expenses at the time a transaction occurs, rather than when a payment is received or an invoice is paid

Co-Sourcing

Using both internal and external resources to perform a service

A business practice in which the employees of a company work with an outside organization to perform a service

Third Party

A term describing those who are not directly involved in a transaction

A person or group in addition to those who are directly involved, such as a company that supplies outsourced services to an organization

Zero-Based Budgeting

An approach to financial planning and decision making

A budgeting process that requires that every budget item is approved instead of only budget changes being approved. No reference is made to previous budget expenditures.

Return on Investment (ROI)

A financial calculation to evaluate an investment

Performance measure used to evaluate the financial outcome of an investment

Research and Development (R&D)   The research and development (R&D) department is tasked with innovation. The need to design new products or refine current products exists for all companies, and often arises in response to the findings of market research or new technology. In some companies, R&D is its own department. In others, it is folded into a marketing department.

Marketing and Sales   Marketing and sales are separate yet closely related functions that exist to create and fulfill demand for company products and services. The sales function involves persuading customers to buy a company product or engage in a service. Marketing activities provide businesses with insights to help them engage with their stakeholders and promote the company brand, all while supporting the development and execution of business strategies.

Source: DILBERT © 2004 Scott Adams. Used by permission of ANDREWS MCMEEL SYNDICATION. All rights reserved.

Operations   The operations function is all about producing the goods and services that are designed by R&D and sold through sales and marketing. Many companies use the term *production* to categorize activities related to operations. This refers to manufacturing processes that make products. For other companies, the term supply chain management (SCM) is more appropriate, which is in and of itself a major management system. According to Investopedia, SCM includes managing "every business that comes into contact with a particular product, including companies that assemble and deliver component parts to a manufacturer." In this way, operations is an end-to-end chain linking raw material sourcing with delivery to the consumer, and all parts in between. Similarly, the *value chain* is built upon identifying what a customer is willing to pay for: quality and service. Customers are not willing to pay for inferior raw materials, production downtime, or the costs to fix defects.

Considering core competencies is another way to understand the operations function of business. This term can refer to a company's core product or the service offering for which the company is best known. Through this filter, a car wash company's core competency is washing cars, and everything else is ancillary. The term also refers to a particular excellence in any given area that allows the company to beat out its competitors. In the car wash example, the company may compete based on its environment (live operators, complimentary vacuums, a gift shop) for differentiation from its quarter-operated, carport-style counterparts. In essence, a core competency is identified by reviewing where a company invests its time and labor resources—it is a tangible declaration of "This is how we win." See the feature for an example of a strategic core competency at Wal-Mart.

Value Chain

Model of how businesses create value

Model of how businesses receive raw materials, add value to the raw materials, and sell finished products to customers

---

MICHAEL PORTER, WAL-MART, AND CORE COMPETENCIES

According to the *Harvard Business Review*, a core competency of Wal-Mart is buying power (Schrage 2013). This refers to one of Michael Porter's five forces that affect a company's competitiveness in the marketplace. Buying power is the ability to leverage size and quantity of supplier orders to reduce the wholesale price of a product. The purchasing power of Wal-Mart allows the company to fulfill its mission of "Saving people money so they can live better." Because of its high buying power, Wal-Mart can purchase or manufacture a product at a lower cost than its competitors, making this a primary competitive strategy for the company.

Information Technology (IT) Information technology (IT) is a network of systems connecting hardware, software, databases, and company information into a cohesive, user-friendly, secure package. IT needs of companies often are based on size and capacity needs. A small mom-and-pop shop may be able to get by with a single computer connected to the Internet to use for basic word processing, accounting, and inventory needs. Smaller businesses often out-source any task beyond the basics through retainers or pay-as-you-go services. Larger companies may need a more robust system of interconnected units beyond simple data retrieval and storage, requiring the hiring and management of technical staff.

Knowing the needs of and for a department is often a function of how companies are structured. This will dictate the way work is distributed and is a source for opportunities to develop organizational capabilities.

Organizational Structures

Organizational structure is much more than a chart of authority; decisions about structure are used to streamline processes, support efficiencies, simplify decisions, and establish reporting hierarchies. An organization is a single entity—a being, if you will—made up of many moving, interdependent parts. The right structure will support the unrestrained flow of information so that organizational system compo-nents and stakeholders are well served. This structure is visually represented by an *organizational chart (org chart)*.

Organizational Charts (Org Charts) According to Kinicki and Fugate in *Organiza-tional Behavior* (McGraw-Hill, 2011), there are four main dimensions of an organiza-tional structure that are graphically represented through an org chart:

1. **Hierarchy of authority** In this dimension, there are linear connections that illustrate *chain of command*. This assigns who is responsible for which employ-ees, often in terms of performance management and direction of effort.

2. **Division of labor** While the hierarchy of authority references people manage-ment, the division of labor often shows who is responsible for which processes.

3. **Span of control** *Span of control* is how many people report to a single supervisor. A wide span of control indicates several employees, whereas a narrow span of control indicates few.

4. **Line and staff positions** Line managers are generally made up of people within the organization who are responsible for revenue generation. Think production staff and the salespeople who sell the company's products. On an org chart, these are often depicted with solid lines connecting them in the hierarchy. Staff units are support functions and include accounting, IT, and human resources. These roles are often depicted with dotted lines on an org chart. One important distinction between line and staff managers is that staff managers have the authority to advise and direct the efforts of all line managers, not just direct reports. In this capacity, HR serves as an adviser for all managers and employees.

Organizational Structure

The grouping of employees and processes

The way that employees and processes are grouped into departments or functions in an organization, along with a description of reporting relationships

Organizational Chart (Org Chart)

Diagram showing reporting relationships

A graphic representation of how authority and responsibility are distributed within a company; it includes all work processes of the company.

Chain of Command

Order of authority

The sequence of power in an organization, from the top to the next levels of authority

Span of Control

The number of employees a manager supervises

The number of employees who report to one manager in an organization. The more people that a manager supervises, the wider the span of control.

What is depicted on the org chart is determined by how the functions of the business are sorted and ordered. There are many different ways to design this, and they include both traditional and nontraditional formats.

Traditional Structures   Traditional structures are those that are more commonplace, characterized by clear boundaries and relationships:

Functional In probably the most common structure, an organization divides departments based on *functional areas*. Think production, accounting, and IT as some examples, with employees reporting to a manager, who reports to an executive. *Functional structures* may be divided using a *front-back* format, a design that divides work based on customers and production.

Divisional In the divisional structure, organizations sort authority and tasks by company divisions or brands. Consider a financial institution's division of commercial products such as lending being separate from the investment side of the business services, an example of a divisional *product structure*. A corporation that divides the structure based on physical regions is an example of a *geographic structure*.

Matrix A *matrix structure* looks more like a jungle gym than a ladder, because it *integrates* the functional structure with divisional components. Employees often report to two managers—a functional manager in charge of a department and a brand manager in charge of a product line.

Hybrid A *hybrid structure* is useful for companies that have unique customer or operational needs. This type of organizational structure is a blend of any of the other structures.

Functional Area

Group of people performing similar tasks

A department in which people have similar specialties or skills (for example, the accounting or IT department in an organization)

Functional Structure

Group of people performing similar tasks

A department or division where people have similar specialties or skills (for example, the accounting or IT department in an organization)

Front-Back Format

An organizational design that separates customer service and production

An organization that has two parts: one part that focuses on the customers and the market (the front), and one part that develops products and services (the back)

Product Structure

A way of organizing a company

A method of organizing a company in which the departments are grouped by product

Geographic Structure

Organizational model based on location

An organizational model in which divisions, functions, or departments are organized by location in a specific country or region

(continued)

(continued)

Matrix Structure

A system of reporting where employees have both vertical and horizontal relationships

A system of managing staff where employees have more than one reporting relationship (for example, they could report to a direct supervisor as well as a team leader)

Integrate

Combine, mix together

To combine or bring together different parts

Hybrid Structure

A vertical and horizontal organizational model

An organizational model that combines different operational, functional, product, and geographic structures

Less Traditional Structures

Flat line/horizontal Generally organized around a need for collaboration, a flat line structure seeks to reduce boundaries and coordinate the efforts of all employees toward a desired outcome. Cross-functional teams may be a popular strategy in this kind of environment.

Hollow In this design, organizations seek to limit what functions are completed in-house, and focus instead on core competencies. Many (or all) other functions are outsourced. Companies who excel at design or marketing may take on hollow structures in which production and accounting are outsourced.

Modular Modular structures are characterized by strategic business units (SBUs) that focus on individual pieces of a whole product. Components are separated into smaller *work units*, and companies may choose to outsource functions to save labor costs or improve quality. Modules focus on very specific quality standards and creating depth in supplier relationships to reduce the risks of defects or an inability to meet demand surges.

Virtual The lack of a physical structure is what characterizes a virtual organizational structure. Generally temporary in nature, this structure brings together partners to a project, each of whom brings a level of expertise and core competencies to form a well-rounded business entity. This effort is focused on capitalizing on market opportunities. In some cases, competitors, suppliers, and customers compose a *virtual team* involved in product or service delivery, with shared rewards. The work is usually conducted online and via videoconferencing. One example is the mobile phone industry. Service providers such as AT&T and Verizon have captured vast market shares of cell phone service. For this reason, most phone manufacturers must work together to design and manufacture components for compatible phones.

Work Unit

Smallest work group in a company

A business function that produces one product or focuses on a single area

Virtual Team

People who work together in different locations or time zones

A group of people who work in different times, locations, or organizations, who communicate using technology

---

HR as a Strategic Partner

There is a significant need for HR to take the lead in linking business strategy with day-to-day operations. While one must account for the many variables that exist from one business to another, there are a few central practices that guide a human resource practitioner toward serving as a valued strategic partner. These are reviewed in more detail next.

Mission, Vision, and Values

HR contributes in a very real way to building a *company culture*. The process of building organizational mission, vision, and values (MVV) serves as a platform for many company programs, including workforce strategies, operational practices, and international actions. MVVs serve as a guide for behavior, providing a cornerstone for behavioral expectations. In the chapter Workforce Planning and Employment, the MVVs are cited as a basis for building an employer brand—the perception that internal and external individuals have of the business.

A *mission statement* describes the purpose of an organization, and remains constant throughout the life cycle of the company. A good mission statement is simple in form, focused on the primary reason that a company exists. Google's mission statement is "to organize the world's information and make it universally accessible and useful." There are some cases where business decisions compete with the mission. When Google decided to modify its offerings in China to comply with government regulations amounting to censorship, the company felt it was a more ethical option than leaving the world's largest population without Internet access. This strategy had to be revisited yet again in light of the 2010 cyber-attacks that appeared to stem from the Chinese government. In these cases, the company's vision and values can clarify direction.

A *vision statement* is forward-thinking, describing what the future looks like for a company that is evolutionary in nature. While still a macro view, a vision statement provides further clarification of the company's long-term orientation. The American Red Cross has a vision statement combined with what the organization calls a strategic intent: "Be recognized by the people and organizations we serve, as well as others in our field, as the provider of choice for blood, plasma and tissue services. This will be accomplished by commitment to quality, safety and use of the best medical, scientific, manufacturing and business practices."

As will be discussed in a later section regarding business ethics, *values* serve as a guideline for how a company does business. Ben & Jerry's, the ice cream maker, has a grouping of values statements that orient the consumer (and employees, and the public, and suppliers) to what is most important to the company. These statements include ingredient sourcing and purchasing practices, manufacturing practices, and "giving back" practices. HR often serves in an *advocacy* role to help employers direct their resources to programs with shared rewards. HR professionals reinforce these organizational values by communicating them to the workforce, modeling them in their own professional behavior, and coaching managers and executives on how to behave in accordance with agreed-upon values. Internally, values guide decisions about employee performance, as illustrated in Figure 2.2.

The organizational climate is the experience that stakeholders have when engaged with the business. The climate is served by how well (or how poorly) the MVV is integrated into operational activities. From the mission, business strategies and *cascading goals* are built that are aligned with the mission. If a company chooses strategies that are out of alignment with a mission, vision, or value, an identity crisis may occur, compromising the quality of decision making that affects service, productivity, quality, and ultimately company survival.

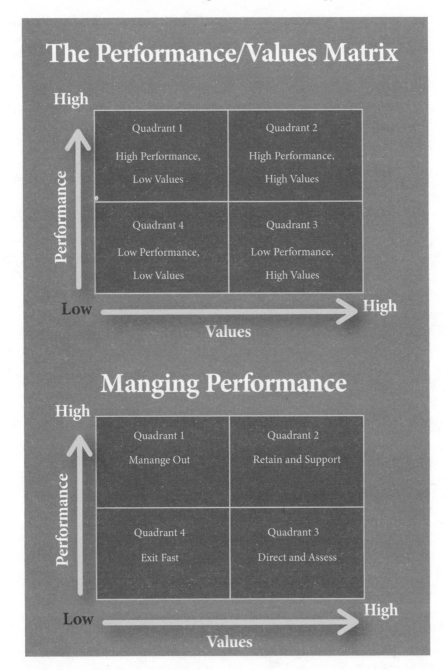

Figure 2.2   The Performance/Values and Managing Performance Matrices

Company Culture

The beliefs and behaviors of an organization

The values, language, rules, procedures, expectations, and processes that affect how employees of an organization think, act, and view the world

Mission Statement

A description of the purpose of an organization

A short description of the main purpose of an organization, which does not change (unlike strategy and business practices, which can change frequently)

Vision Statement

Declaration of what an organization wants to become

A written statement that clarifies what the organization wants to be in the future

Values

Beliefs of a person or social group

The lasting beliefs of members of a culture about what is good or desirable and what is not

Advocacy

Support, encouragement

Supporting an idea or cause, influencing outcomes

Cascading Goals

Goals that flow from the top to the bottom of an organization

Goals that an organization sets at a high level, which flow down as goals for departments, and then become goals for specific people

Strategic Planning and Analyses

> If you know the enemy and know yourself, you need not fear the result of a hundred battles. If you know yourself but not the enemy, for every victory gained you will also suffer a defeat. If you know neither the enemy nor yourself, you will succumb in every battle.
>
> —Sun Tzu, from *The Art of War*

Strategy has been defined as a careful plan of action. Avoiding a business strategy of "ready, fire, aim" is accomplished through strategic planning and structured actions led by courageous, competent HR leaders. In order to be valued as business leaders, HR professionals must seek to understand the *internal forces* and *external forces* affecting every business function.

The planning stage of the strategic support role of HR involves helping a company define its mission, vision, and values, and setting objectives on how outcomes will be achieved.

In *strategic planning*, the participants seek to analyze the conditions affecting competitiveness, develop solutions and plans of action, implement said plans, and evaluate the effectiveness of interventions. This includes anticipating growth or decline that will require an organizational response. There are five accepted steps to the strategic planning process:

1. **Analyze data** Data collection is the primary activity of this stage. Information is gathered by scanning the internal and external environments and through the use of forecasting techniques. Both are covered in more detail in an upcoming section.

2. **Develop objectives and goals** From the MVV and findings of environmental scanning, cascading goals are developed, often using the acronym *S.M.A.R.T. goal setting*:

   Specific The goal reflects the MVV but is specific enough to direct the behavior of line and staff managers in action planning.

   Measurable The goal has clearly identified milestones, often with a description of start and stop conditions.

   Action-oriented Goals describe the action steps that must be taken to fill the gap between current and desired state, with responsibilities assigned to departments or individuals.

   Realistic The goals are capable of being achieved, whether a *stretch objective* or the gathering of low-hanging fruit.

   Time-based The time frame is established and agreed upon.

3. **Implement solutions** At the center of organizational development are planned interventions staged in order to change conditions—either behavioral or

structural. These interventions may be time based, such as updating roles and responsibilities for all jobs on an annual basis, or may be single events such as making structural changes to improve work processes. Ultimately, solutions should map directly back to the problem being solved or strategy to be executed.

4. **Evaluate efficacy and monitor progress** Some strategies and plans work better than others, and HR must take steps to know which are which. Part of the strategic planning process must identify the methods that will be used to measure the effectiveness of programs. It is in this stage that evaluation and real-time refinement of plans and strategies take place. Performance standards that are set in order to meet a new customer need, for example, must be measured and addressed if they are falling short. Employee recognition for goal achievement may be necessary, particularly if new behaviors are being tested. Establishing controls may take the place of employee self-monitoring, or engineering controls may be designed to eliminate behavioral choice. These are all examples of evaluation efforts HR may lead to measure the success or failure of business initiatives.

The strategic planning process requires a good deal of organizational skills, which is often how HR is utilized in the process. This is about much more than simply keeping track of progress on a Gantt chart or spreadsheet. HR brings expertise in matters such as job design, organizational restructuring, data regarding the internal skill set of the workforce, *process-flow analysis*, and the development of standard operating procedures to aid in the achievement of goals.

As a management function, organizing the work to incorporate tangible business needs with the more mercurial needs of the people is top priority. In management planning, supervisors are called upon to understand the day-to-day nature of what needs to get done. This involves a heavy dose of resource management, in which leaders make decisions about the best way to organize and resource the necessary tools.

Leadership activities are often directed at meeting the needs of employees and projects. This involves coordinating resources into a smoothly running engine, not a smoke-spewing, belching machine requiring constant mechanical interventions. Organizational leaders—both HR and supervisors—must have the ability to take the strategic inputs gathered during the planning and organizing process, and put them into action through others in order to achieve company objectives. Leading requires individuals to make quality decisions that balance the demands of all stakeholders. External needs such as regulatory compliance, employee needs such as fairness, and business needs such as profitability—these are examples of the competing demands for management attention that the leading effort must embrace.

Strategy

Plan of action

A plan of action that starts with examining the current state of an organization and then deciding how to achieve the best state for the organization's future

Internal Forces

Drivers of change inside an organization

Key people and influences inside an organization that shape its future (the opposite of external forces, such as the economy and competitors)

External Forces

Events an organization cannot control

Things that occur outside of an organization that might affect its financial health, employees, products, services, or customers (for example, political, economic, or environmental challenges)

Strategic Planning

Process of defining the organization's future direction

The process of defining a company's direction for the future in four stages: analysis, development, implementation, and evaluation

S.M.A.R.T. Goal Setting

Process used to help achieve business success

Applying specific, measurable, action-oriented, realistic, and time-based goals to help a company achieve business success

Stretch Objectives

Goals that require maximum effort

Setting personal or business targets that require extra effort to achieve

(continued)

(continued)

Process-Flow Analysis

Method of assessing critical business functions

A diagram used to assess business processes; sometimes called "process mapping"

Forecasting

Part of both generalist and senior-level HR tasks includes forecasting, planning, and predicting the impact that any HR program may have on the workforce. *Forecasting* is the practice of using information to make educated guesses about future conditions to be used to make decisions.

Data gathering through research methods is a primary function of forecasting activities. In primary research, HR personnel make direct contact with the research subjects, often through surveys and focus groups. For example, a company that publishes wage data information would survey target markets about company pay and benefits practices. In secondary research, HR draws from previous research conducted by experts, such as when purchasing a wage survey from the authors.

Analyzing the research is the second step in forecasting conditions. HR applies *quantification* techniques when they interpret data that can be numerically or statistically measured.

A popular way to interpret numerical data is through measures of central tendency. These approaches attempt to find commonalities or patterns through sets of data and establish *norms*, data that may be relied upon to represent typical or frequent conditions. The most common measures of central tendency are:

Mean The *mean* is an average of a group of numbers achieved by finding the sum of a series of numbers and then dividing the sum by the number of values. The average of the series 2, 4, and 6 is found by adding $2 + 4 + 6 = 12$ and dividing it by 3, which results in an average of 4.

Median The *median* works by ordering numbers by smallest to largest and identifying the value where half the numbers are higher and half are lower. If there is an odd number of values, the one in the middle is the median. If there is an even number of values, the average of the middle two is the median.

Mode Perhaps the easiest to identify, the *mode* is the value that occurs most frequently in a series of numbers.

Financial statement analysis provides HR with data used to identify trends, such as when labor costs surge. If these surges happen every year right around June and production has a 30-day learning curve, HR may plan to begin hiring efforts in April or May on the basis of financial analysis.

Pie charts and graphs are often used to visually present quantitative research findings.

In qualitative research, nonnumerical or less tangible measures are gathered and analyzed. Stay interviews and opinion surveys may be conducted to find out what employees value from their employer, or their levels of job satisfaction. Anonymous surveys seeking feedback about a supervisor may be undertaken to make recommendations for management training programs. File studies may be conducted to pull archival separation data, or to research average personnel ratings in a critical area.

Regardless of the type or nature of the research, all data collection instruments should be valid and reliable. This increases the quality of the data collected, and the legal defensibility should the use of the data be called into question.

Forecasting

A planning tool that helps with future decisions

Analyzing the probability of future outcomes to help lessen uncertainty

Quantification

Counting and measuring

Giving a number to a measurement of something

Norms

Standards, averages

A standard model or pattern that is considered typical

Mean

A way to calculate the average of a series of numbers

An average determined by adding up a group of numbers, and then dividing that total by the number of numbers. For example, to calculate the mean of 10, 20, 30, 40, 50: first, add the numbers (10 + 20 + 30 + 40 + 50 = 150), then count the numbers (5), and then divide the total by the number of numbers (150/5 = 30).

(continued)

(*continued*)

Median

The middle value in a series of numbers

The middle number in a series. For example, in the series 13, 13, 13, 13, 14, 14, 16, 18, 21, the median is 14, with four numbers to the left and four numbers to the right.

Mode

The value that occurs most often in a series of numbers

In the following series of numbers, 8 is the mode: 6, 5, 8, 3, 7, 8, 9, 8, 4.

Environmental Scanning

"In a vacuum" is a phrase that refers to the fact that organisms do not function without other influences; all environments have shaping forces that drive company behaviors—no business exists independently or in a vacuum. So it is with organizations, and the leaders within. Consider Jack Canfield's leadership assertion that:

> Leaders cannot work in a vacuum. They may take on larger, seemingly more important roles . . . but this does not exclude them from asking for and using feedback. In fact, a leader arguably needs feedback more so than anyone else. It's what helps a leader respond appropriately to events in pursuit of successful outcomes. (Western n.d.)

Using the same quote, substitute the word *companies* for the word *leaders*:

> Companies cannot work in a vacuum. They may take on larger, seemingly more important roles . . . but this does not exclude them from asking for and using feedback. In fact, a company arguably needs feedback more so than anyone else. It's what helps a company respond appropriately to events in pursuit of successful outcomes.

This demonstrates that a business is an entity in which forces may be identified, molded, measured, and used to positively affect business outcomes. All businesses exist for a reason. These reasons may be profit-centered or mission-centered, but you can be sure there is an internal and external environment in which the participants feed off one another with only one of three results: grow, maintain, or decline. *Environmental scanning* is the practice of identifying the internal and external factors that drive company strategies, business goals, and daily decisions.

One example is that of retail giant Macy's. The company announced that it is eliminating more than 10,000 jobs by closing 60+ brick-and-mortar stores beginning in 2017 in order to focus more on online sales. The struggling retailer is the first of many that are feeling the pinch from online retailers like the U.S.-based Amazon and China's Alibaba. These external forces are requiring businesses to react.

HR helps to identify external sources to gather information related to an organization's ability to take advantage of opportunities or to reduce threats to survivability. A gap analysis is then used to compare the actual state to the desired state from which plans of actions may be mapped.

Organizational attention deficit disorder (ADD) may occur when everyone is working on one's own project, or the company has too many projects going on at once, choking off resources and spreading teams thin. There must be an environment defined by boundaries in which companies may plan, react, perform, and measure. Both internal assessments and external analysis aid in identifying these environmental business boundaries.

Environmental Scanning

Gathering internal and external information for strategic purposes

Acquiring and using information about the internal and external business environments that influence an organization's strategy (for example, determining how to respond to a talent shortage)

BACK TO THE FUTURE

My 6-year-old self had a wicked set of roller skates—hot pink leather, bright purple stoppers, and fluorescent, glow-in-the-dark laces. Without knowing anything else about me, can you guess about how long ago this was? No need to get specific—if you answered "more than 40 years," you are correct! Roller skates were all the rage in the 1970s, and skate manufacturers were enjoying the financial fruits of their product's popularity. In fact, my roller skates were cool right up until I got an Atari for Christmas. Video games had arrived in my house. Now, the roller skate manufacturers had a problem. They had successfully navigated the business stages of infancy and growth, but were going to jump to decline if they didn't fully embrace the maturity stage of their life cycle. A strategic plan had to be centered on the threat of lost consumers to technology. Executives must have understood the need to direct financial resources toward

(continued)

(*continued*)

research and development, and the generation of new products that would meet the mercurial tastes of their 6-year-old consumers. This meant potentially dropping back into the infancy stage of manufacturing a new product, with all the relevant tasks such as building work instructions, designing marketing campaigns, and training staff in the new processes or techniques.

In 1981, a new competitor entered the rink—a company called Rollerblade. The founder was focused on redesigning the market by improving on the existing single-line blade technology. By 1988, Rollerblade sales were up to $10 million. The industry as a whole hit half a billion dollars in sales in the 1990s. The roller skate manufacturers that were fluid enough to respond to the new design made up a large percentage of those industry sales. By capitalizing on the existing skill sets of their workers and manufacturing facilities, the transition wasn't as cumbersome as it could have been. And what happened to the roller-skating companies that did not have the foresight to strategically plan to address both the threat and opportunity in the industry? They pole-positioned themselves onto an asteroid and took a trip straight to the Death Star.

SWOT Audits (Internal and External) Analyzing the internal strengths and weaknesses and the external opportunities and threats is the purpose of a *SWOT audit*. SWOT audits are most often used to assess the company as a whole, but may also be useful as a tool for department analysis as well.

In a company SWOT audit, HR works with the executive team to analyze a bird's-eye view of the company's strengths and weaknesses. For example, some companies may have a highly skilled workforce or a high-quality product. Weaknesses may include untrained labor or outdated equipment. Externally, data must be gathered about opportunities that technology, consumer, or customer behavior is creating, and about threats to a company's viability, such as a lagging economy.

The availability and skill sets of local talent are also factors that should be reviewed during a *SWOT analysis*. This helps forecast and plan for the human capital needs to successfully achieve business goals. One example is Reno, Nevada, where Fremont, California–based visionary car company Tesla chose to build its battery manufacturing plant. Many industry insiders were a bit surprised by this move because the area was not known for its abundance of manufacturing workers. In order to meet demand, Tesla began hiring large groups of out-of-state workers to staff the plant. This strategy resulted in 350 union construction workers walking off the job to protest the hiring of these nonlocal workers willing to work for less, especially because Tesla had received a billion dollars in tax breaks in exchange for agreeing to hire local workers.

In a department-specific SWOT audit, HR facilitates the identification of department-by-department strengths and weaknesses. The management teams of many organizations can provide valuable information about what their needs and goals are. HR can act as a facilitator of the brainstorming sessions with managers to first

Table 2.1   Factors of a SWOT Analysis

Internal Factors	Strengths and Weaknesses	Opportunities and Threats	External Conditions
	• Employee skill sets • Software functionality • Marketing capability • Brand recognition • Leadership effectiveness • Process management and quality • Cash flow • Innovativeness	• Factors of competition • Regulatory constraints • Depth in supplier relationships • Industry changes • Technological advances • Economic factors	

Current capabilities: both the good and the bad   ← *A strategic plan will address the gaps.* →   Current and future needs based on opportunities and minimizing or eliminating threats

explain the process and why being honest and thoughtful about team strengths and weaknesses is so important. HR may also help management identify strategies the department heads would be willing to consider in order to maximize strengths and minimize weaknesses. This information will be highly useful when building out the strategic plan, and represents the thoughts, goals, and needs of the management team who will be charged with implementing the final strategies. See Table 2.1 for a look at sample SWOT information.

One other important note: Some managers may get caught up in the form of a SWOT analysis at the expense of content. While a strength could very well be phrased as an opportunity, the important thing to consider at this stage is capturing the data, and identifying individual behaviors or department interventions that will drive action after the plan is established.

SWOT Audit or Analysis

Strategic planning method

A strategic planning technique used to assess the internal and external environment in which a company operates, its strengths and weaknesses (internal), and opportunities and threats (external)

PEST Analysis (External)   A *PEST analysis* may be used to complete the external threat and opportunity portion of the SWOT analysis.

PEST (or STEP) is similar to SWOT in that it is used as a filter through which to assess factors affecting organizational competitiveness.

Political   The political climate can be both a help and a hindrance to the company strategies. Consider, for example, fair trade agreements. An American company may be considering opening a production facility in India. An analysis of fair trade agreements will identify the need for decent wages and safe working conditions for all locations outside of the home country. *Political unrest* in some countries may result in decisions to not compete there, or to offer danger premiums for expats on assignment.

The availability of tax incentives or stipends at both a local level and a national level is also important to consider. With the suburban saturation of large, big box retailers, there are more urban governments in New York, Chicago, and Washington, D.C., that are seeking to shrink their high unemployment numbers and increase their sales/property tax funds by courting companies such as Wal-Mart and Home Depot. A 2014 report by Americans for Tax Fairness found that Wal-Mart saved more than $70 million in direct "economic development subsidies by state and local governments." These were achieved through a combination of tax abatements, sales tax rebates, infrastructure development, and site improvements. Regardless of how an individual feels about these types of subsidies, they are a viable consideration for companies seeking cities from which to base or grow their operations.

It's interesting to note that state and local politics has a significant impact on a company's ability to compete. For example, in order for some cities to approve big box stores, they may require payment of a living wage to employees that could exceed the federal minimum wage by several dollars. See the "Corporate Welfare" feature for an example of the bubbling mess of results that can happen when governments and fairness aren't properly mixed with business.

CORPORATE WELFARE

Manchester, Connecticut, is a bucolic town characterized by local library sleepovers for kids and autumn activities such as scarecrow-making contests. In 2016, Bob's Discount Furniture planned to build a brand-new 103,000-square-foot corporate office in town, adding about 125 jobs to its existing workforce. In anticipation of the sales and property tax revenue, the state promised a $7 million low-interest loan, a $1.7 million grant to train employees, and up to $11 million in tax credits. Other companies receiving grants such as these are obligated to pay a living wage as part of the deal, but Bob's was exempted from the living wage requirement. The controversy exploded when it was discovered that the company was controlled by Bain Capital, a multibillion-dollar investment firm boasting as one of its founders 2012 presidential candidate Mitt Romney. Small businesses claimed that Bob's was receiving a form of "corporate welfare" out of line with all principles of fairness. Local workers protested the loss of a higher wage. And HR students can use Bob's as an example of when the political and regulatory environment may cultivate a pro-business climate that—right or wrong—drives organizational decision making.

Economic Economic factors affecting organizational competitiveness are built upon the health of the local, state, and federal economy. A town's low wages or high poverty levels may benefit from a business with a cost leadership strategy as opposed to a higher-priced brand competing on product differentiation. *Lagging economic indicators* and *leading economic indicators* are key barometers to use when analyzing the local, national, or global economy. In this way, HR must stay plugged into business and industry news that both track historical trends and forecast economic changes.

Social Social and political pressures often join forces to shape a company's decisions about how and where to compete. In a new political era, for example, companies that used to outsource may face social pressures to remain in the United States, as is the case with Carrier of Indiana.

Another example of social and/or political forces is emerging in the area of work/life balance. What was once a more social trend is beginning to stir in bellies of lawmakers, making it prudent for HR to pay attention and advise executives on how to engage. Some examples: As of January 2017, French companies with more than 50 workers must guarantee a "right to disconnect from [work-related] e-mails outside office hours" to improve work/life balance. The employment ministry of Germany bars its managers from contacting staff during off-hours, except during emergencies. In 2014, the automaker Daimler began allowing employees to use an automated setting that deletes any work-related e-mails received while on vacation. These companies—whether compelled by law or driven by social pressure—are responding to social needs accordingly through their HR teams.

Demographics is a large part of the social impact a company's strategies may have. Offering domestic partnership benefits in the absence of laws requiring them sends a message about diversity, and influences the ability of a company to source talent based on values. Designing HR programs that allow for job sharing and worker training may help retain an older workforce. Some cultures have a more *parochial* view, resistant to American business methods. Adopting global ethics policies about where and when to do business internationally helps form the competitive identity of a company.

Technological Technology as a driver for change has not slowed a bit in the past decade or so. From desktop to laptop to mobile to cloud, the rate of obsolescence in technological tools is rapid. Organizations must balance the need to use technology to compete with the cost of adopting technology, and the resulting training needs of both the workforce and consumer. Security and privacy concerns continue to declare their presence, especially through the "Internet of things" practices (connecting everyday objects to the Internet). Coffee makers connected to a mobile app are great until a hacker uses the connection as a conduit to other, more sensitive data. The electronic storage of confidential employee, customer, and financial data must be accounted for when technology is used as a path to achieve any strategic goal.

HR plays a vital role in monitoring the legal and regulatory, social, economic, and technical environment for trends and changes. This role may involve creating professional presentations and developing a clear and concise communication style to update managers and executives on emerging trends or recommended changes. This includes using the language of business, the language of HR, and the language of money. Belonging to HR associations, attending local trade meetings, and pursuing continuing education all help HR become (and remain) a trusted business adviser.

PEST Analysis

Method of gathering external data for organizational analysis

Political, economic, sociopolitical, and technological (PEST) data that is gathered and reviewed by organizations for planning purposes

Political Unrest

Disturbance or turmoil about government issues

Unrest, agitation, or turmoil about a government's actions or beliefs

Lagging Economic Indicators

Signs that confirm change in the economy

Signs that confirm the economy has already changed (for example, the unemployment rate)

Leading Economic Indicators

Signs that predict the future of the economy

Signs that show ahead of time that the economy will change (for example, a predicted rise or fall in interest rates)

Demographics

Data, information about people

Statistics about groups of people that give information such as age, gender, income, and ethnic background

Parochialism
Narrow interest or view
A view of the world that does not consider other ways of living and working

Employee Capability/Skills Assessments (Internal)

Assessing the internal environment is the bookend to the SWOT and the PEST analysis activities. An important role HR can play is helping the executive team understand the general skill set, experience base, and overall capabilities of the employees. Strategies will be developed that address the gap between where the employees are and where the company needs them to be. As an example, assume the executives at a manufacturing company declare their intent to start marketing and selling products online through websites such as Amazon.com. HR can lead the internal assessment by asking questions such as:

- What knowledge or skills do current employees have to take on this new method of selling?
- What new knowledge or skills will be required to successfully roll out this strategy?
- Should the task belong to the sales team or to the customer services team?
- Will the employees be paid a commission?
- What kind of training will be required?
- Can current employees absorb the job tasks, or will new hires be required?
- Is this a function that perhaps could be outsourced?
- How will success or failure be measured?

HR may use the data collected from the internal assessment to pivot to the more external questions around the practices of a company's competitors.

Business Metrics

Metrics are a fundamental aspect to HR being a contributing strategic partner, particularly because labor and its fruits have a direct impact on profitability and business sustainability. Data collected through metric collection provide tangible information from which to make business decisions and set strategies. This means that HR must identify what information is to be collected, and set up systems that will capture and report the data. Additionally, metrics in and of themselves are just a bunch of numbers. HR must help analyze and interpret the data using internal and external benchmarks to measure the achievement of an organization's strategic goals.

Metrics can be created for nearly any business process. Most will focus on current state, desired state, and baselines. Several data analysis methods exist and are explored over the course of this book. The most common business metrics are reviewed next.

Cost-Benefit Analysis (CBA)

A *cost-benefit analysis (CBA)* compares all costs (tangible and intangible) of a program in order to calculate the value of the project. The analysis also includes a review of the lost opportunity cost should a company decide not to proceed with a project. In a CBA, it is recognized that there are future values based on interest and inflation; in this case, the current value should be factored in. Because some values are presented in units of time or volume as opposed to just monetary values, scoring a CBA may be easiest by using averages, percentages, or ratios.

HR uses CBAs for several activities through all stages of the life cycle of a business. In start-ups, fees or equity structures associated with funding the burden on building up are analyzed. Scenarios for growth are evaluated as companies flourish and the cost of adding staff is compared to realistic measures of capacity and output. Short-range (6–12 months) and long-term (3–5 years) planning horizons are important in the growth stage of the life cycle. Companies entering the maturity stage evaluate the CBA of employee training programs to create depth in knowledge, and plans are built to survive worst-case scenarios. A declining organization may need to evaluate the retention value of employee benefits when compared with premium and administration costs, or the benefits of outsourcing noncore services as a way to phase out production.

Key Performance Indicators (KPIs)

As with all measurement, *key performance indicators (KPIs)* are expressed as quantifiable outcomes that may be used to measure progress toward performance goals. Financial KPIs may be set as part of a master or operating budget expressed as targets for real-time decision making. KPIs for marketing may include customer-acquisition costs or new contact rates. Accounting departments may establish KPIs for time-bound activities, such as at month end or accounts receivable over 30, 60, or 90 days.

Balanced Scorecards

Balanced scorecards attempt to balance data collection and analytics between financial and nonfinancial measures of success. Cited as a framework to capture metrics, the scorecard reflects financial measures such as profit, internal business practice measures such as shipping times or productivity, customer measures such as loyalty or satisfaction, and learning activities such as how people are hired and knowledge management goals.

The balanced scorecard can be a highly complex system to track and manage. HR should assist companies in building a measurement tool that first and foremost is aligned with strategic outcomes while still considering the time it will take to complete, data accuracy, and ease of use.

Digital Dashboards

Dashboards provide at-a-glance views and status of real-time company performance. Often made up of visual graphics such as charts, funnels, or thermometers, dashboards show a snapshot of a particular condition, with links to additional details for drill-down capabilities as needed.

While the initial investment costs to build a program that extracts data from multiple sources may be high, the returns in terms of future daily resource consumption are often worth it.

Cost-Benefit Analysis (CBA)

A process of measuring business decisions

A financial review of various options to determine if the benefits are greater than the costs

KPI

Key performance indicator

A measure an organization uses to see its progress and show what it needs to improve

Balanced Scorecard

An analysis technique

A method or tool that organizations use to measure the success of their strategies by looking at both financial and nonfinancial areas

---

Technology at Work

HR as a practice has benefited as much as any department in terms of the types of technology available to do the work of the people. Smaller companies may be able to use systems that are narrower in scope, such as a human resource information system (HRIS) or talent management system (TMS) that support recruiting, record keeping, performance management, and other modules. Larger companies may prefer a larger, networked program that links information between departments, such as an *enterprise resource planning (ERP)* system.

Cloud computing has significantly grown in use in the past decade. Different from on-premises software that requires a local server and physical updates, cloud computing uses the Internet to manage data. New hire paperwork can be processed through electronic forms and automated work flow, eliminating paper files and HR time to walk an employee through the packet. *Employee self-service* technology for benefits allows individuals to access their files, making simple changes such as updating their personal information, enrolling in benefits, submitting expense reimbursements, requesting time off, and more. Timekeeping can be achieved via mobile apps that allow employees to work with location services to clock in to remote sites. These are just a few examples of how cloud computing can serve many of the back-office and administrative functions of HR.

Technology has also delivered the company *intranet*, a private *network* with access granted to employees only. CEOs may post videos with messages for employees across all geographic sectors. HR may post a people directory with department and employee contact information. Standard operating procedures, reference guides, and the employee handbook may be digitally stored for employee access. Forms may also be retrieved from a company intranet, making this a highly practical tool with direct results on HR efficiencies.

Special considerations must be accounted for in the use of technology at work. The *user interface* manages how people interact with the computers. It has impact on the external tools used for processing such as *ergonomics*, and internal factors such as usability and graphics. If the technology is difficult or cumbersome to use, HR can very quickly erode any time gains by having to train or aid employees in the use of the systems. Managing the employee experience with technology is ever-evolving and has led to ensuring that new technology investments provide functionality and an intuitive user experience that does not require any special training.

HR has the responsibility to lead and oversee any technological transitions, working hand in hand with internal IT staff (in some cases hiring them) or researching how to best outsource the task, either just for installation or to include ongoing support.

Workforce Analytics

Workforce analytics are used to predict employee behavior, talent needs, events, and risks while directing the efforts of human resource departments, plans, and programs. Analytics gather data to conduct *trend analysis* to predict and respond to outcomes. For example, churn models can be built to identify root causes of employee turnover such as length of commute, time to pay raise, and attendance. This data are then cross-referenced with information related to historical attrition trends to predict employees who are likely to separate. Another example is employee benefits offerings. Some large companies are using benefits platforms such as Castlight Health to help their employees make more informed decisions about their health care and wellness choices. This leads to healthier workers and reduced health care costs. Castlight uses data from employee searches on its site to tailor recommendations to the workers.

Workforce analytics tracking mechanisms are often built into employee engagement software programs and internal portals, raising questions about employee privacy and employer liability concerns. Decisions about what information to collect, when to collect it, and how to use the information must be considered using a combination of IT, executive, and risk management resources. HR serves in an advisory role representing the ethical and privacy concerns of employees, and implements tools such as disclosure notices to protect their companies from risks.

The rapid development of data collection on both a macro scale and a micro scale has been a boon—and a beast—for HR practitioners. Touted in some cases as the solution to the perceived passé practices of employee surveys, focus groups, and the humble suggestion box, HR analytics can help companies improve employee physical and mental health, receive real-time feedback on employee morale, manage performance, and ease the burden of HR administrative tasks.

Care must be taken, however, to not turn analytics into an overused machine that deconstructs the talent of people into a numbers report. Analytics can help tell a story filled with insights to inform decision making, leading to greater organizational effectiveness. HR must advocate for practices that leverage data to create solutions that are personal in application—the human in human resource, the person in personnel. This means taking technology and making it user friendly, and humanizing the mass amounts of data that workforce analytics is able to provide.

Global Integration

In some cases, multinational businesses will build production and manufacturing services in another country, but perform other tasks on a global basis. To do so, shared technology, global communication systems and a global IT infrastructure must be built. A network-based framework includes a robust internal team but also access to global resources that have capacity to deal with local or regional conditions. A global communications system is not just about the hardware connections—it's also about building connections with the people, seeking to engage with consistent messaging, providing tools and resources to a remote staff, and delivering messages from top management that improve alignment with the employer mission, vision, and values.

ERP

Enterprise resource planning

Computer software that combines information from all areas of an organization (such as finance, human resources, operations, and materials), and also manages contact with people outside the organization (such as customers, suppliers, and stakeholders)

Cloud Computing

A type of computing that uses groups of servers and resources, made available on the Internet

Using a network of remote servers hosted on the Internet to access, manage, and process data, rather than using a local server

Employee Self-Service

A method allowing employees to access and update data

A trend in human resources management that allows employees to handle many job-related tasks (such as updates to their personnel data) using technology

Intranet

A private computer network with limited access

A restricted computer network that allows only authorized people to access the site (for example, a company intranet that allows only its employees access to its data)

Network

People or things that are connected

A group of people who connect with one another; a computer system that allows people to access shared resources and data

User Interface

Software that allows people and machines to share information

Software that allows a human and a computer to share information

Ergonomic

Safe and comfortable equipment

Designed to be comfortable and avoid injuries (for example, an ergonomic chair or keyboard)

Workforce Analytics

Metrics used in HR strategic planning

Metrics used to determine the effectiveness of HR functions, such as turnover rates, organizational culture, and succession planning

Trend Analysis

A review of historical data to predict future outcomes

Gathering information from the past to identify patterns that will help predict future outcomes

---

Standing on the Shoulders of Giants: Strategies' Leading Experts

In order to be of any use, the data collected from internal and external assessments must be applied toward something. In this way, the competitive landscape is the target. The company must be able to address how to best position itself (and corresponding strengths and weaknesses) to capitalize on opportunities and minimize or exterminate threats. It is also important to understand how organizational culture plays a role in the evolution of a company's strategic identity. For application of the outcomes from the strategic planning process, we look to the experts.

Table 2.2   Facebook through the Lens of Porter's Five Forces

Force	Description
Competitive rivalry within the industry	Innovation, change, and rapid entry of new technology and platforms make this force moderate to high.
Bargaining power of customers	Switching costs to users are low, making it easy to try something new and making the bargaining power of customers high.
Threat of new entrants	Building and marketing new websites/platforms requires significant investment of resources, so barriers to entry are moderate. Change from desktop to mobile device is a threat that must drive innovation and change.
Bargaining power of suppliers	Hardware, software, and mobile apps all benefit from a large account such as Facebook, so bargaining power of suppliers is moderate to low.
Threat of substitute products	New sharing sites may emerge that are more attractive to users; other platforms may solve sharing issues (messaging, videos) that take away from Facebook user experiences. Should Facebook be all sharing to all people?

Note: Adapted from Trevis Team, "Facebook through the Lens of Porter's Five Forces," *Forbes,* November 28, 2014.

Porter's Five Forces: Competing for Profits

Michael Porter examined the landscape from which industry rivals compete. His fundamental premise is that the greater the power of the force, the lower the profitability. Porter describes five competitive forces that define the field parameters that all organizational teams must address in order to develop a winning strategy (Table 2.2).

1. **Threat of new entrants** This force refers to the entry of new competitors to an industry. High barriers to entry protect an industry from new rivals. In industries with high barriers to entry, this force is not a significant threat. In industries where there are low barriers to entry, a plan for dealing with new competition must be built.

2. **Bargaining power of vendors/suppliers** In this factor of competition, the ability of a material supplier is addressed. *Vendors/suppliers* that have multiple customers to whom they may sell their products have a higher degree of bargaining power than firms with only a single customer or group. From a threat

perspective, a company that is reliant on a single supplier may need a backup plan in place should the supplier go out of business or be unable to meet demand. Additionally, the company may need to charge higher prices for its products to compensate for the supplier markup. If supplier power is high, profits will be low because costs of goods will go up.

3. **Bargaining power of firm's customers** Customers can be fickle friends, and their needs drive many strategic considerations. If customers want a higher-quality product, for example, they may be willing to pay a higher price, and a differentiation product strategy makes sense. Powerful buyers will use their collective force to drive prices down, affecting firm profitability.

4. **Threat of substitute products** Substitutes for any product will curb industry profitability overall. Substitutes are not exact replicas of a product or service, but rather a product or service that solves the same or a similar problem. Consider the rise of instant movie streaming from home. Streaming services are a substitute for buying movies, and are a direct rival to DVD manufacturers.

5. **Intensity of rivalry among competing firms** Price competition, new product introduction, and product promotions are just a few examples of activities companies will use to compete with their fellows. If rivalry is intense, businesses will make decisions based on winning, and will erode profits at the expense of the rivalry. Profits diminish either through extreme cost cutting or by increasing the cost to compete with each other.

Porter is also the leader in the generic strategy way of thinking. Instead of companies needing expensive consultants to build and shape custom plans and strategies, Porter argues that there are really only two options: cost leadership and differentiation. Compare a Nissan Versa to a BMW sedan. What is the first difference that comes to mind? If you said price or quality, then you understand these two strategies. Cost leadership is the strategy companies adopt when they want to be the low-priced leader in an industry. The company structure may include large-scale production facilities, *leveraging* suppliers, and focusing on low overhead. HR activities that support this strategy include workforce planning to manage labor costs and training. For example, McDonald's has a global training center—Hamburger University—that teaches franchise owners and employees how to streamline restaurants' efficiencies to keep costs low. In differentiation, a company is seeking a narrower target market, one that creates customer loyalty through high-quality products or high brand name recognition. HR activities in this strategy may include product knowledge and sales technique training, or investment in paying for external talent.

Vendor/Supplier

Service provider, seller

A person or company that sells services and/or products, such as a recruiting firm, financial consultant, or relocation company

Leverage

The ability to multiply the return on an investment

The act of applying a small investment to bring a high level of return

---

Henry Mintzberg

There is so much to say about thought leader and influencer Henry Mintzberg, all of which is amazing. Within the framework of strategic management, Mintzberg brings much to the conversation. In 2007 he cofounded a group called Coaching Ourselves, drawing upon the collective wisdom of experts regarding managing on a global scale. He distinguishes between the words *leader* and *manager*, but not as polar opposites. Mintzberg declares in his video "On Management, Organizations and More" that today's leaders must manage, and today's managers must lead—one is not better or preferred over the other. Additionally, he calls upon management practices and leadership development to be more holistic rather than focusing solely on individual development strategies.

The shift away from personnel management to human resource management also seems to be detrimental to the overall view of employees, managers, and strategic efforts of employers. The term *human resources* positions people as assets to be manipulated, eroding the psychological contract of the past. In order to compete on a global scale, Mintzberg believes that HR and its leaders must become more worldly—a term combining sophistication with practicality, not just by geographic operations.

Piggybacking on Mintzberg's work in his book *Strategy Safari*, here are a few salient viewpoints of strategic management through the lens of Sun Tzu's *Art of War*:

> When ten to the enemy's one, surround him. . . . When five times his strength, attack him. . . . If double his strength, divide him. . . . If equally matched, you may engage him. . . . If weaker numerically, be capable of withdrawing. . . . And if in all respects unequal, be capable of eluding him.
>
> —Sun Tzu, from *The Art of War*

This formula is a way to understand how strategy must be linked to what your competitors are doing. If your competition is a large megafirm with hundreds of employees and unlimited lines of credit, you may want to shrink the target by differentiating a product or service as opposed to trying to outperform a cost leadership strategy.

> Now the elements of the art of war are first, measurement of space; second, estimation of quantities; third, calculation; fourth, comparisons; and fifth, chances of victory.
>
> —Sun Tzu, from *The Art of War*

In forecasting success or defeat, Sun Tzu included two highly relevant factors for comparing yourself to your competitors: "On which side are officers and men more highly trained? In which army is there the greater constancy both in reward and punishment?" Depending on the answers to these questions on internal strengths or weaknesses, your strategy may be to train a stronger workforce or build out a more effective compensation program. It may also identify the need to help supervisors be more consistent in their feedback and discipline.

> According as circumstances are favorable, one should modify one's plans.
>
> —Sun Tzu, from *The Art of War*

A strategic plan may need to change; that is why incorporating milestones into a plan is so important. Businesses that can respond quickly to changing market conditions are better able to control the outcomes—either positive or negative. Engaging in planning efforts that are scenario based, such as "if this, then that," results in a critical guide for employees once the plan is in action.

Edgar Schein

The management philosophies of Edgar Schein lean heavily toward organizational culture and its leaders. Schein, a professor at the MIT Sloan School of Management, describes a model of organizational culture that encompasses three levels:

1. **Artifacts** Artifacts are organizational characteristics that are seen, heard, or felt. HR influences over artifacts include company dress codes and codes of conduct. Management modeling and training are also influenced by the efforts of human resources.

2. **Values** Values are communicated through a company's mission, vision, and goals, as well as by what the company says it will or won't do. Consider safety rules and whether a manager adheres to them.

3. **Assumed values** Assumed values are the unconscious perceptions employees have about what their employer values. These undercurrents may be communicated through management behaviors regarding what gets rewarded and what gets disciplined, the functionality of teams, and the depth of relationships between staff.

These concepts are often taught using an onion model in which layer 1 is easily addressed and changed. The deeper the culture is rooted, the tougher the behaviors are to identify and affect.

Geert Hofstede

A social psychologist by day, Professor Hofstede pioneered work related to the influences of characteristics such as national origin, gender, and social class on individual and organizational behaviors. While both national cultures and organizational cultures may be viewed through the filters of Hofstede's dimensions, he cautions that national and organizational cultures are not the same, but rather share their makeup with a different mix of values, preferences, and practices. HR's understanding of these preferences shapes policies and programs that will have an actual effect on group behaviors. Hofstede's dimensions include:

Power distance *Power distance* refers to the amount of equality (or inequality) between the leaders and the workers, also called the distribution of power. Companies and cultures with low power distance are more likely to have executives, managers, and employees working closely together to achieve business outcomes. In companies with high power distance, one would expect to find traditional hierarchies and greater disparity between executive and individual pay levels.

Uncertainty avoidance Tolerance for uncertainty is higher in some cultures than others. From a workplace perspective, individuals with a high *uncertainty tolerance* will do better in innovative and creative companies that offer support for trial and error. Those with a low tolerance for uncertainty prefer environments with structure, rules, and standard methods of operation.

Individualism versus collectivism Countries and companies with high degrees of *individualism* value the parts more than the whole. Independence, autonomy, and individual rewards are preferred by these groups. Collectivist cultures may value rewards for loyalty and prefer collaborative business environments.

Long-term versus short-term orientation Individuals with high degrees of long-term orientation are big on self-discipline, willing to sacrifice rewards of today in order to achieve the greater things of tomorrow. Short-term-oriented individuals value freedom and thinking for oneself.

Indulgence versus restraint The most recent addition to Hofstede's original four, this dimension was added in 2010. It references the degree toward which countries and companies have a need for immediate gratification as opposed to suppressing gratification in accordance with cultural expected standards of behavior. This dimension is rooted firmly in degrees of control over one's work life and personal outcomes.

Hofstede notes that although cultures remain relatively stable over time, they can shift in response to internal and external forces. This ties directly in with the relevance of the environmental scanning process described earlier. HR professionals must have a strong sense of what is going on both in the HR industry and in the industries of the businesses they serve. Additionally, HR should be aware of and help managers understand the presence of cultural bias, which is based in assumptions that what works in one company or at another location should be a one-size-fits-all solution across any type of border.

Additional work on cultural differences came from Edward T. Hall, an anthropologist. He found that *high-context cultures* are more likely to derive meaning from words and actions, as opposed to *low-context cultures* in which individuals extract explicit meaning from the words of others. High-context organizational cultures are more likely to exist where there is longevity and tenure, as the element of time is a teacher of what to expect when interacting with one another.

Power Distance

The degree of hierarchy

A term Geert Hofstede uses in his cultural theory to describe hierarchical relationships between people in a culture. For example, high power distance means there are strong hierarchical relationships. Low power distance means greater equality and accessibility among members of the population.

Uncertainty Avoidance

The degree of tolerance for risk and preference for clarity

One of Geert Hofstede's cultural dimensions, uncertainty avoidance describes the degree to which cultures accept ambiguity and risk. For example, in cultures with high uncertainty avoidance, people prefer clear, formal rules. In cultures with low uncertainty avoidance, people are comfortable with flexible rules.

(continued)

(continued)

Individualism

Self-reliant, personal independence

Cultural belief that the individual is the most important part of society; one of Hofstede's cultural dimensions, the opposite of collectivism

High-Context Culture

Society that communicates indirectly

A culture that communicates indirectly, through the context of a situation more than through words, and that builds relationships slowly (for example, Japan)

Low-Context Culture

Society that communicates directly

A culture that communicates directly, using words more than situations, and that builds relationships quickly (for example, the United States)

As discussed at the beginning of this section, these leaders serve as guides to help organizations apply the outcomes from the strategic planning process. The aforementioned represent only a handful of the business principles, models, and theories that organizations may draw from to effectively compete, both for market share and for talent. The key is for HR to identify the relevant theories, and guide the employer in the understanding and application of those that will enhance the company brand or performance.

Business leaders may also identify (and drive) the need for an organization to work on the business through organizational development activities. This is the focus of the next section.

Organizational Development (OD)

Organizational development (OD) is a system for change that is both diagnostic and healing. OD is systematic in that it applies tools to identify areas that are barriers to organizational competitiveness, and engages in structured interventions to remove said barriers.

Back in 1969, OD pioneer Richard Beckhard defined organizational development as "an effort, (1) planned, (2) organization-wide, and (3) managed from the top, to (4) increase organizational effectiveness and health through (5) planned interventions in the organization's 'processes,' using behavioral science knowledge." Let's break this down.

1. **Planned** Organizational intervention efforts must be mapped out using a method similar to that of the strategic planning effort. Data must be gathered, current versus future state analyzed, action items identified, plans executed, and results measured.

2. **Organization-wide** OD techniques are generally applied company-wide, but that does not mean only at a strategic level. OD efforts have a very real impact on company operations as well. The focus of OD is on people, processes, and structures across all tiers and boundaries. There are times when the scope of an OD diagnostic and intervention is focused on a division or a department, with the results having an impact on the overall business.

3. **Managed from the top** As with any true organizational change, without executive and management buy-in very little change will actually take root and influence true movement.

4. **Increase organizational effectiveness and health** This element refers to measurable outcomes from the OD effort, which should be identified at the planning stage. What efforts will actually increase the effectiveness of our product, service, people, or technology? How will we know if the OD changes worked? How can we audit the changes going forward to ensure the new processes are being properly maintained? Similar to training objectives, OD efforts must begin with the end in mind.

5. **Planned interventions in the organization's "processes," using behavioral science knowledge** The goal of many OD efforts is to both predict and steer outcomes. This requires sourcing information from behavioral science research and applying the findings through planned interventions.

Organizational Development (OD)

Planned process to improve an organization

Planned process that uses the principles of behavioral science to improve the way an organization functions

The relationships HR develops with individuals both inside and outside the company will have direct influence on the efficacy of HR programs. Calling upon experts to both build and refine strategies ensures that the diverse perspectives are considered and potential conflicts are uncovered. Consulting relevant research studies for insights into the practical implications of OD intervention options will help HR advise executives on what is reasonable to expect before signing off an intervention strategy. Research will also help HR define what is to be measured, a critical step to determine if the intervention produced the desired effect. For example, one study found that using more than one intervention technique is more effective in changing job and work attitudes than interventions that rely on a single OD approach (Neuman, Edwards, and Raju 1989). While both may be relevant to the achieving a desired state, techno-structural interventions will have a different effect than a human/process intervention strategy.

Cross-cultural considerations also affect all aspects of OD interventions. HR should caution executive management against attempts to blindly apply OD interventions strategies that worked in one country to a similar situation in another country.

HR professionals as organizational leaders are looked to as relationship managers. This includes fostering connections with the individual contributors who do the work and will execute strategies, as well as reaching out to subject matter experts for legal compliance and risk management perspectives. HR business partners must trust the process through which decisions are made, and this is best accomplished when the partners take part in making decisions that affect themselves or their team.

In addition to aligning with key individuals, HR takes an active part in aligning the human resource strategic plan with the company's strategic plan. This is to ensure that all HR activities are built or refined to support agreed-upon outcomes and shared goals. Much of the human resource plan will trickle out of the scanning process, developing programs that address any gaps in skills of the current workforce, and coordinating resources to address threats and opportunities. Conducting *feasibility studies* and uncovering *hidden costs* of new equipment or service agreements may also be necessary prior to committing to an intervention.

Out of the strategic plan will come change, and out of change will come projects. This is the focus of the organizational development activities covered in the next section.

Cross-Cultural

Comparing or interacting with two or more groups of people

Involving two or more cultures (such as national, regional, or professional cultures)

Feasibility Study

Investigation, analysis of what is possible

Research and analysis to determine if a project will succeed

> ## Hidden Costs
>
> *Expenses that occur in addition to the purchase price*
>
> Expenses such as maintenance, supplies, training, upgrades, and other costs in addition to the purchase price

Change Management

Change management as an intervention strategy is a near guarantee. The strategic plan will build responses to internal strengths and weaknesses and external threats and opportunities in the form of goals and objectives. In addition to achieving the desired state, the intervention plan must balance the expectations and needs of the organization with the expectations and needs of the stakeholders. Timing, urgency, capacity, and simply ensuring the business continues to function are all important. Unmanaged change can put undue stress on employees and systems. For this reason, human resources is often tasked with managing the change effort.

Out of the environmental scan and competitive analyses, forces for change are discovered. Internal forces may include low levels of job satisfaction, rebranding, organizational design decisions, or a strategy to enter new markets. External forces are often driven by both demands and opportunities, such as customer need for new products or services, and demands from the legal and regulatory environment. Opportunities are often driven by technological advances or by encroachment by the competition that may drive innovation. Cultural events may also influence change via social movements such as environmental concerns or a rising level of consciousness related to the human rights needs of offshored providers. Regardless of the source, relevance, and even urgency for change, many organizations struggle with embracing it. This section takes a look at some of the more prominent change management theories that call upon HR to serve as *change agents* and change leaders utilizing all or part of the various theories of change explored next.

> ## Change Agent
>
> *Something or someone that causes change*
>
> A person or department that deliberately causes change within an organization

Kurt Lewin's Three-Stage Model

HR doesn't have to build change management efforts from scratch. Several models for change exist, most of which evolved out of social psychologist Kurt Lewin's three-stage model for planned change, which explains how to begin, manage, and then anchor the changes as the new norm. The three stages are unfreezing, changing, and refreezing.

Step 1: Unfreezing   Actions at this stage: research such as *benchmarking*, education, employee buy-in, and commitment. *Create openness to the change.*

Unfreezing is all about making the business case for change in which employees are prepped for what is to come, begin to understand what is needed from them, and are given permission to engage in creative problem solving. Think of this stage as gathering employee buy-in through education and commitment.

Step 2: Changing   Actions at this stage: moving from current state to desired state. May include training on new processes, addressing gaps, and consistent messaging through communication. *Make the changes.*

This stage is the most operational of the three, involving the sharing of new information, the development of new processes, and the adoption of new behavior. It's important for companies to stay on message at this stage, reinforcing the underlying need for change and reiterating the goals. Perhaps the change is related to improving the customer experience or adopting new technology. HR is tasked with leading the transition into new technology systems or the addition of service centers. Managers and other individuals will serve as *informants*, helping HR keep track of how the changes are being received within the employee ranks. Staying on message is critical at this stage of Lewin's change model.

Benchmarks

Measures or markers

A basis for judging or measuring something else

Informants

Suppliers of useful information

People who provide business, social, or cultural data to others

---

Step 3: Refreezing   Actions at this stage: backsliding prevention, encouraging social support for change, positive reinforcement. *Make change the new normal.*

Once the new behaviors have been created and implemented, Lewin argues that integration becomes critical. Employees and managers must receive the organizational message that "this is the new normal." Refreezing is an excellent opportunity for HR to engage in positive reinforcement efforts,

Table 2.3   Template for Problem Solving through Change

Forces for Change (Drivers)	Current State (the Problem)	Forces Resisting Change (Obstacles)
Internal		Internal
External		External
Equilibrium interrupted (unfreeze)	*Disequilibrium as changes occur (change)*	*Equilibrium reestablished (refreeze)*

⸻⸻⸻⸻⸻⟶

communicating, coaching others, and modeling behaviors in support of the new behaviors.

Lewin also championed the idea of a "force field" to define problems. This model allows for visual representation of the forces affecting the current business. Table 2.3 shows a sample template to use as a problem identification tool.

MAKING A BUSINESS CASE

Imagine you want to convince your child that he needs to take a course of prescription medicine because something in his little body isn't working. The illness is affecting his ability to go to school and learn. It is keeping Mom home from work, and the doctor visits are expensive. The illness is contagious, so failing to take the medicine may result in others in the home becoming infected. Bottom line, the child really just doesn't feel well, and the whole family's morale is affected. Techniques you may use include calling upon experts such as the doctor, and telling the child that the experts say the medicine is necessary. You may persuade Dad to tell about that one time he had to take medicine and felt better right away. You may share with your child the frequency of doses, noting that once the medicine is gone, he will just have to follow up with the doctor to ensure the medicine worked.

So it is with making a business case for change. Often in a formal, written presentation, making a business case first defines the root cause of a problem along with the symptoms that need to be addressed. A business case will identify the risks both of acting and of not acting upon the proposed changes. The plan will offer courses of action to take, and seek to identify the resources necessary to achieve the desired outcome. In short, a business case is a series of persuasive arguments for a change or project, focused on solving a shared problem.

Systems Approaches

In change management theory, a systems approach does not refer to the implementation of technology, but rather the systems that operate within a certain environment. Think about an ecosystem in which every organism and component has a purpose of interrelatedness to survive; each piece exists to serve the whole. So it is with systems change solutions, which we explore here.

Most systems models of change are built upon the foundation that all change, no matter how small or large, has a trickle-down effect on the entire organization. Changes to the framework, to the people, or to the methods of completing the work will impact the others in ways both large and small. Consider, for example, when an employee is promoted to a supervisory position. That staffing change has an effect on her *peers*, her own performance and learning curve, the gap in contribution left behind, and the chain of command. Consider another example of addressing a culture of hostility and unprofessional behavior that used to be acceptable. The forces for change may be the anti-harassment laws that the company really never paid much attention to. Or it may be driven by a political climate in which inappropriate or unprofessional exchanges were part of the nightly news report that filtered up into offensive watercooler talk at work. Policies will need to be written, supervisors and employees trained, and unprofessional behaviors called out with consistency. There will be some who resist and others who will be relieved that the changes are finally happening. Some employees may be fired, even the highly productive ones. In other words, most if not all of the elements in the model will be affected in some way.

Peers

People equal to each other

People who are similar to one another in age, background, profession, or status

---

Peter Senge

Peter Senge is a world-class champion of learning organizations in which systems thinking is a primary component. He illustrates an organization as a single unit with interdependent components that drive organizational health; if one component is unhealthy, then the entire system is contaminated. This means that any change—small or large—will affect all others.

Senge encourages companies to embrace and seek out changes rather than building a culture that changes only in reaction to crisis. He defines a learning organization as one that regularly changes behavior in response to new knowledge and insights, company successes, and company failures. New information is gathered by constantly engaging in environmental scanning, hiring new talent when new perspectives are required, and investing significant time and financial resources into developing employees.

John Kotter's Eight Steps

John Kotter brought to change theory eight steps, built upon Lewin's unfreeze, change, refreeze model. The steps are:

Step 1. *Increase urgency.* Make the business case for why this change is necessary and important.
Step 2. *Build the guiding team.* Identify and collate the individuals with the authority and influence to lead the change effort.
Step 3. *Get the vision right.* Identify the purpose and targets for change.
Step 4. *Communicate for buy-in.* Create the communication strategy that cascades the message from the top down.
Step 5. *Empower action.* Encourage and reward risk taking, creative thinking, and the removal of barriers to change.
Step 6. *Create short-term wins.* Acknowledge what is working and when milestones are achieved. Celebrate and share the rewards of small successes.
Step 7. *Build upon momentum.* Compound the effect of wins into momentum. Seek to embrace those who have been resistant, and reinvigorate elements that have slowed down.
Step 8. *Root the change.* Reinforce the changes by continued acknowledgment and connection of past to future conditions.

Find out more from the words of the many thought leaders described in this chapter by going online to YouTube. Subscribe to channels such as CoachingOurselves, and search for videos that feature Schein, Senge, Mintzberg, Porter, Lewin, Kotter, and others speaking about their research and experience in strategic, change, and project management.

Many companies make the mistake of reacting to change outside the framework of the strategic planning processes. This competitive disadvantage is often the result of poor quality decisions. For this reason, we explore the psychology of decision making next.

The Psychology of Decision Making

A critical element of leadership that runs throughout all business activities is making decisions—synthesizing all available information and then selecting a course of action using *deductive* reasoning. HR is often charged with coaching others through the decision-making process, helping them improve their performance in this domain. Poor decisions have been at the root of dysfunctional turnover, failed strategies, corrupt business practices that brought down leaders, and even brand annihilation, as was the case with Samsung's Note 7's exploding batteries. For this reason, it is important for HR practitioners to be well versed in the psychology of decision making, both to improve their own skills and to coach managers toward achieving more effective outcomes.

Deductive

Reasoning from the general to the specific

A method of reasoning that forms a conclusion from general information; the opposite of inductive reasoning, where a conclusion is formed from particular facts

---

Decision Making Bias

The existence of bias that influences the perspectives and priorities of employees and managers should also be understood and acknowledged when making decisions. Types of bias include:

Anchoring bias Anchoring bias is the result of giving greater weight to the first piece of information received, or anchoring a decision on specific information. It is characterized by overreliance on a single piece of information when making a decision. One example is in salary negotiations. Applicants who start with a higher number fix (anchor) the amount in the decision maker's mind and establish that number as the starting point for negotiation. Studies have shown that this negotiating technique results in higher salaries for those who use it.

Framing bias Framing bias occurs when a decision maker relies on how a situation is framed or presented. When presented with an option regarding avoidance of risk or realization of gain, most decision makers will select the answer that is framed as a benefit as opposed to the one that is framed as a risk. The classic question of "What's in it for me?" applies well when attempting to gather *buy-in* from employees.

Overconfidence bias When experiencing overconfidence bias, also described as overoptimism, some decision makers are reliant upon forecasts or estimates and push forward into risky situations. Overconfidence puts blinders on decision makers, keeping them from considering response strategies for all possible outcomes. The 2016 American presidential election is an excellent example of when a campaign may have succumbed to overconfidence bias based on incorrect polling data.

Confirmation bias Confirmation bias exists when a decision maker has a hunch or an idea of how something will or should turn out, and then seeks information that will corroborate or confirm the judgment.

Escalation-of-commitment bias Have you ever worked with a supervisor who was determined to push forward with a course of action because he or she was too far into it to turn back? That is an example of the escalation-of-commitment bias, in which a person is unwilling to turn back even when there is evidence pointing to the need to abandon a plan.

Buy-In

Obtaining support

Acquiring backing or sponsorship from a person or group

Evidenced-Based Decision Making (EBDM)

One way to avoid decision making bias is to engage in evidenced-based decision making (EBDM). This is a process of gathering research-based data from the social sciences for use in improving the quality of management decisions. EBDM is a competency as opposed to a theory, meaning that HR professionals actively engage and synthesize data to inform decisions, both as practitioners and as advisors to management. By focusing on what is known and not known, the decision maker is more likely to ask and frame properly the questions necessary to make the right, or a better, decision. As shown in Figure 2.3, after identifying the situation, the

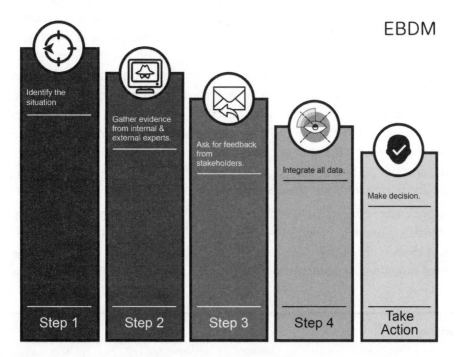

Figure 2.3   Evidence-Based Decision Making
Note: Adapted from Rob B. Briner, David Denyer, and Denise M. Rousseau, "Evidence-Based Management: Concept Cleanup Time?" Academy of Management *Perspectives*, November 2009, 19–32.

process begins by gathering evidence (data) to make all kinds of decisions, from strategy to the day-to-day needs requiring a response.

Problem Solving through Group Decision Making

Often, the process of managing change and tracking projects entangles HR professionals into conflict, not all of which is bad. How a company and its employees approach conflict is often a very real barometer of success. Companies that engage in constructive conflict and creative problem solving are much better at working on the things that matter most. Conflict without trust is politics, and organizational politics is just as destructive as a wrecking ball into the side of the building. For this reason, businesses and employees are best served when HR is an above-average problem solver. While conflict management is discussed in greater detail in the chapter on Employee and Labor Relations, this section focuses on problem solving using groups.

Nominal Group/Brainstorming A creative way to inspire companies focused on innovation, *brainstorming* is the process of getting team members together to discuss a problem along with potential solutions. In practice, facilitators may define the problem on large easel paper, and hand out blank Post-it Notes for participants to write out possible solutions. The group members then stick their ideas to the relevant problem. Now, here is where the nominal technique and a brainstorming session diverge. In a nominal session, the facilitator opens the floor and leads a discussion about the pros and cons of an idea, and the group members evaluate the merits of each idea. In brainstorming, a separate session is used to critique/evaluate the merit of each solution. Note that both the nominal and brainstorming techniques work best in environments where innovation is rewarded and team members are open to new ideas. Rules of engagement are often helpful for a facilitator/group to establish prior to the session opening so the meetings are a productive use of time resulting in reaching a *group consensus.*

The Delphi Technique In the *Delphi technique*, the problem solvers never actually meet. Methods used include online surveys, polls, and questionnaires. The group organizer then gathers the data and sends *briefings* to each group member with additional questions or comments. This process continues until a group consensus is complete.

Brainstorming

A process for producing new ideas and solutions

A method in which individuals or groups spontaneously find solutions to a problem

Group Consensus

Agreement between people

A decision process in which a group of people agree to a decision or come to the same conclusion

Delphi Technique

A forecasting technique

A method of forecasting where a group of experts provide individual opinions, which are later shared in order to reach a more objective decision

Briefings

Instructions or summary

Discussions that provide detailed information

Project Management

A natural result of change management and decision making often is the identification of project needs: activities with clearly defined starts and finishes designed to achieve specific outcomes. Generally, *project management* experts agree that this process includes:

Identifying the project scope A statement of work (SOW) can be helpful in shaping the scope of a project. It involves working backward from stated goals, objectives, and identified time lines that tap into internal and external resources to achieve completion. This includes securing experts, labor, and financial resources while at the same time generating time lines to keep the project on track. HR is tasked with sending out requests for proposals (RFPs) to make the best selection of external resources when necessary. Once the scope is defined and RFPs collected, the action steps may be generated.

Generating action steps The project scope has in varying detail outlined what the desired outcomes are to achieve project completion, including start, project milestones, and finished state. Step 2 defines the specific action steps a company may need to take to get going. Let's assume a project includes generating key performance indicators for each department to be used to build out a company scorecard. An HR professional (HRP) in charge of the project serves as a liaison, meeting with department managers to identify core competencies and review how success will be tangibly measured. From this, the next step is to implement action.

Implementation Getting a project off the ground can generate its own set of challenges. Often, a project manager is identified to champion the project, gain support, and keep things moving in the right direction. This phase of project management includes tracking milestones, identifying and addressing obstacles, and refining behaviors that lead to the project outcomes. As progress is made, evaluation is imperative so a company may respond to issues in real time.

Evaluation The evaluation step begins upon project launch, or "going live." While the implementation phase included noting the achievement of milestones, once a project is complete there are conditions that need to be audited to help prevent backsliding into preproject behaviors. A solid project management plan will identify ahead of time the tools that will be used to ensure that momentum does not get stalled, or, if it does, what options are available to respond. Creating standard operating procedures (SOPs), adding key performance indicators, or including the measurements in the company's scorecard are all viable options.

A word about tracking projects and managing change: technology provides us with many tools to help keep track of the multitude of minutiae necessary in the HR world of today. There are several types of project management software that help a project manager identify and manage the resources necessary to complete OD intervention efforts, and even track adherence to new procedures once launched. The old adage that "what gets measured gets done" holds true for many projects, and evaluation tools are often necessary to make sure the change is embedded into a company culture.

Project Management

Planning and guiding processes

A methodical approach to planning and guiding project processes from start to finish

Liaison

Contact, connection, link

A communication link between people or groups

Organizational Restructuring

Organizational restructuring is an OD intervention that involves eliminating layers of management, changing reporting relationships, and *downsizing* through *layoffs* or early retirement buyouts. Restructuring can be effective when business strategy indicates new (or eliminated) product lines or service offerings, or when a company seeks to remove communication or productivity barriers tied to top-heavy layers of bureaucracy.

Divestitures

Divestitures are another form of organizational restructuring, in which a parent company disposes of a business unit or other investments. One such event was when PepsiCo sold off its company-owned and franchise licenses of KFC, Taco Bell, and Pizza Hut restaurant chains in order to free up resources to focus more on its core beverage brands.

Offshoring and Outsourcing

Offshoring is a strategy used by companies that wish to lower production and manufacturing costs by moving parts of the business out of the United States. Countries such as Mexico, India, and Vietnam all have established manufacturing services. *Outsourcing* assigns internal services to companies with a particular expertise or skill set such as payroll, COBRA administration, and IT services. Both offshoring and outsourcing result in internal staff reductions.

Shared Services

Another form of business restructuring involves *consolidation* of administrative services across business units to avoid redundancies. For example, HR *shared services* is a way to service the similar needs of many business units while reducing the overhead costs of redundant staff at each geographic or global location. This works for other staff positions such as accounting and IT as well. This strategy allows for *cost sharing*, or spreading out the overhead costs of the services across decentralized profit-and-loss statements (P&Ls).

Some companies choose to create *centers of excellence*. These are internal consulting firms made of a team of experts to solve business problems and service the transactional HR needs using global, industry, and company best practices and standards. Centers may operate from company headquarters, or be formed for specific regions to support benefits and payroll services and other HR activities. Corporations may structure this on a fee-for-use basis, serving as an internal revenue source. Business units that are the consumers of the center's services must work with the internal consultants before contracting for outside help.

Contract Manufacturing

Not all business restructuring is the result of organizational decline. Companies with a growth plan may choose to offer private label products through *contract manufacturers* as a way to increase market share or decrease production costs. For example, Winegrapes Australia is a collective of grape growers that sells the product to various wineries for use in winemaking. The company also provides full-service options in which it provides bottle-ready wines for private branding and shipment under a *management contract*.

Mergers and Acquisitions (M&A)

> In the practical art of war, the best thing of all is to take the enemy's country whole and intact; to shatter and destroy it is not so good. So, too, it is better to recapture an army entire than to destroy it, to capture a regiment, a detachment or a company entire than to destroy them.
>
> —Sun Tzu, from *The Art of War*

In some cases, corporate restructuring may be the result of a *merger* or *acquisition*—a competitive decision to shrink the market or leverage resources. A merger occurs when two or more businesses are combined into one. The results of an acquisition are the same as with a merger, but an acquisition happens by the *acquiring company* gaining control over the target company, either in a friendly, collaborative matter or under hostile conditions. As companies began to realize the benefits of running leaner during the recent economic recession, and the economy rebounded, there have been more financial upsides to an M&A strategy, whether desired by the company being acquired or not. Hostile takeovers in 2015 made up 11 percent of the total M&A activity, which was up from previous years. These can happen across borders with *international organizations* as well, making an already complicated process even murkier to manage. Sometimes, it doesn't work, as was the case for Mylan Pharmaceuticals' $26 billion bid to the shareholders of its rival drugmaker Perrigo's in 2015. The unsuccessful attempt ended an antagonistic battle fought over three countries, through an investigation by the U.S. Securities and Exchange Commission (SEC), and past potential board of director conflicts of interest.

The purchasing company in an M&A offers cash or stock in order to acquire the targeted company. HR helps navigate *due diligence*, a process that involves a complete review of the financial and employment practices of the target company, including conducting *economic valuations* of the nonfinancial factors influencing a company's total worth. Compensation practices and employee relations practices are reviewed, along with the employee handbook, *equal employment opportunity* (EEO) compliance records, collective bargaining agreements, and any other relevant conditions that may affect the deal.

HR will also work to help employees deal with postintegration disruptions and uncertainties. Often beginning with a workforce analysis, HR will help map the work being done over the two companies, and identify the resources being consumed for completion. Working with a transition team, decisions about employment are made to address redundancies or gaps in the new work structure. Key talent retention is also a function of HR, and strategies are developed such as offering stay bonuses or negotiating golden clauses for executive contracts. For the long term, HR will need to support company culture initiatives to create a new employer identity that best represents the new business entity, including goals, mission, vision, and values.

> Take a look at the Executive Compensation section in the Compensation and Benefits chapter for more about golden handshakes, golden parachutes, and other executive contract clauses.

Global Expansion

Whether through a merger, an acquisition, or a business strategy, decisions to expand into new global markets have an impact on organizational structure and restructuring needs. Decisions about a global strategy often are made from four factors:

1. The extent of international presence and stages of development
2. The amount of cross-border coordination necessary for successful integration
3. The degree of labor, social, economic, and political influences of the host country environment
4. The complexity of the products, services, and business structure of the multi-national enterprise (MNE) (Galbraith 2014; Tariq, Briscoe, and Schuler 2016)

As referenced at the beginning of the chapter, the complexity of addressing any and all of these four factors will be driven by the existence of subsidiaries, wholly or partially owned operations, joint ventures, and any other type of partnership. Any organizational design attempts to structure from scratch or to restructure a domestic entity into an MNE will take careful planning, resource allocation, control, and coordination.

Downsizing

Reduction in the number of employees

A decrease in a company's workforce to create efficiency and profitability

(continued)

(continued)

Layoff

Loss of employees' jobs owing to business reasons

Temporary suspension or termination of an employee or groups of employees because of business reasons

Divestiture

The sale of a company's asset(s)

Property that an organization sells or gives to another organization (for example, a company's sale of a business unit)

Offshoring

Relocation of a business process to another country

Transferring service or manufacturing operations to a foreign country where there is a supply of skilled and less costly labor

Outsourcing

Contracting or subcontracting noncore business activities

Transferring certain business functions outside of the organization so that the organization can focus on core activities (examples of outsourced functions may be data processing, telemarketing, and manufacturing)

Consolidation

Process of combining, bringing together

Combining separate companies, functional areas, or product lines; in finance, combining the assets, equity, liabilities, and operating accounts of a company with those of its subsidiaries

Shared Services

Business strategy to centralize administrative functions

An operational approach where each country or unit uses administrative services from a central source rather than repeating these services in different locations

(examples of services include finance, purchasing, inventory, payroll, hiring, and information technology)

Cost Sharing

Expenses for a project being divided among those involved

Method of saving money by dividing the costs of a program, project, or business operation

Center of Excellence

An area where high standards produce the best results

A team or division that uses best practices within a specific area to achieve business goals

Contract Manufacturing

Producing private-label goods

A production method in which one company hires another company to manufacture parts or goods under its label and according to its specifications

Management Contract

An agreement to oversee a project or operations

An arrangement in which a person or company operates a project or business in return for a fee

Merger

Two or more organizations coming together to form a new legal entity

Two or more organizations that come together through a purchase, acquisition, or sharing of resources. Usually the new organization intends to save money by eliminating duplicate jobs.

Acquisition

An acquired company

A process in which one organization buys another organization

(continued)

(continued)

Acquiring Company

A company that buys another company

The business or organization that is buying another business

International Organization

A business that operates in more than one country

A company that has operations and services in different parts of the world

Due Diligence

An investigation

The gathering and analysis of important information related to a business acquisition or merger, such as assets and liabilities, contracts, and benefit plans

Economic Valuation

Value given to nonfinancial factors

Giving monetary value to environmental factors (for example, the quality of air and water, which are not normally part of a financial valuation)

Equal Employment Opportunity

EEO

U.S. laws that guarantee equal treatment and respect for all employees

The Role of HR

Human resources is a game of chess. HR professionals are the masters marshaling resources and darting in and out of the maneuvers. Employees are the chess pieces, complete with significant strengths and capacities along with limitations and vulnerabilities. The chessboard is the *marketplace* from which a company competes, and the opponent is everyone else who either can do what the company does or needs the same *human capital* to achieve their own outcomes. Strategies form the playbook from which HR makes the moves. The major difference between the game of HR and the game of chess is that the rulebook is constantly changing. This is due to the introduction and evolution of labor laws, the strengths (and weaknesses) of competitors, the dynamic marketplace, the rapid pace of technology changes, and the company's own goals and objectives.

The role of HR serves many masters, and yet does not directly generate revenue. HR professionals do not build the products or service the customers. HR's tasks are focused on serving the stakeholders who are dependent upon the company being successful. When HR is developed as a company's *core competency*, its value comes from contributing to the *workforce* and strategic plans, forming *strategic partnerships* with people inside and outside the company, improving employee productivity and organizational effectiveness through designed interventions, hiring and developing talent, monitoring and reducing risk, and supporting the real (and perceived) needs of the entire workforce. It requires continuing development, which is discussed in the next section.

Continuing Development

Industry Grouping of economic activity within a particular field, region, or product/service, such as the auto industry or financial services industry.

Profession A disciplined group of working individuals with shared standards, expertise, knowledge, and work experience.

Human resources Professionals and experts working in the areas of human capital management and talent management in roles that further the effectiveness of employees and the organization.

The struggle is real—diminishing the value of HR practitioners as business partners through lack of professional development and industry-specific knowledge happens. It is up to each individual HR practitioner to take up the mantle and champion the value of HR.

As discussed in the introductory chapter, belonging to professional associations, gathering continuing education units and *credentials*, subscribing to trade journals, attending industry-specific training, job shadowing workers, getting professionally *certified*—there are endless ways in which human resource professionals may gather information related to both HR and industry-specific *best practices*—procedures that are accepted as being superior in their fields. Failing to do so threatens the value, both real and perceived, of HR as a whole. Individual HR practitioners who don't keep pace with the evolving nature of the field run the risk of miscalculating the needs of their businesses and/or pursuing the wrong HR strategies and tactics to meet business needs, thus losing credibility and compromising a company's competitiveness. This isn't just a matter of losing a few sales. Hiring wrong, overreaching policies, lack of training and development investment, unequal compensation, failure to manage performance, discriminatory practices—these all contribute to organizational decline.

CEOs pigeonhole HR into activities with tangible outcomes such as payroll or safety because HR often doesn't give them an alternative. Activities such as corporate governance and ethical businesses practices are just two other areas where HR can make meaningful contributions; these are explored in the final section of this chapter.

Marketplace

The geographic area in which business is conducted

A physical or virtual place in which business operates (for example, the global marketplace or the online marketplace)

Human Capital

Knowledge and talents of employees

Employees' knowledge, talents, and skills that add to the value of the organization

Core Competency

Specific expertise

The skills or knowledge that an organization or employee needs to do work

Workforce

Workers, employees

The people working for a single company, industry, or geographic region

Strategic Partnership

An association based on common objectives

A mutually beneficial relationship based on the common goals of people or organizations

Credentials

Certified documents, diplomas

Proof of a person's earned authority, status, or rights, usually in writing (for example, a university diploma or proof of passing a professional exam)

Certification

A procedure to grant an official designation

Confirmation of specific achievements or characteristics given by an authority, usually by issuing a certificate or diploma after a test

Best Practices

Techniques or activities that give the best results

The methods, processes, or activities that have proven to produce outstanding results for organizations' opportunities

Corporate Governance

HR often bears the responsibility for corporate *governance* issues. Just as an employee handbook and code of conduct guide employee behavior, similar tools and practices should be in place to govern corporate behaviors.

As you have seen, a corporation is a legal entity that has obligations to its stakeholders, those with an interest in the company's success such as shareholders, employees, vendors, creditors, and the communities where the company conducts business. These responsibilities are reviewed in more detail next.

Whistle-Blower Protection

Employers are obligated to protect the whistle-blower rights of employees. Enforced by the Occupational Safety and Health Administration and granted by Section 806 of the *Sarbanes-Oxley Act (SOX)*, whistle-blowers who report corrupt or unsafe practices are protected from retaliation by their employer. Affected employees are protected from blackmail, layoff/termination, reduction in hours or pay, and discipline as a result of providing information, assisting others in providing information, or assisting an investigation of violations of securities laws or corrupt business practices.

HR is responsible to ensure that there is a compliant system in place, both for reporting and for preventing retaliatory behaviors from the employer. A defensible system will include a written policy outlining steps employees should take to report unlawful behavior, training for employees and managers on the components of a policy, a process for tracking complaints and record keeping, and a robust investigation procedure if retaliation occurs.

A system for addressing whistle-blower protections is very similar to a system to create an affirmative defense against a claim of harassment: write a policy, train employees and supervisors, investigate claims promptly, and prohibit retaliation.

Fiduciary Responsibilities

While fiduciary responsibility is covered in more detail in the Compensation and Benefits chapter, there are significant reasons why it is an issue of corporate governance. It requires that a company and its leadership make decisions that support the overall financial viability of the company on behalf of its stakeholders. The term has a high legal standard of interpretation as well. For example, a board of directors has a duty of care and a duty of loyalty, acting in the best interests of the company they are charged with governing. The duty of care requires that board members act with reasonable judgment, employing an informed and rational approach to decision making. A duty of loyalty is the obligation of a board member to act in the best interests of the company, without regard for personal gain.

Corporate Citizenship

The concept of *corporate citizenship* revolves around a company's voluntary commitment to the issues affecting the surrounding local and global communities. In *corporate social responsibility*, a company seeks to find ways to protect the physical environment and the people in the communities where it operates. *Environmental responsibilities* may include using materials that are friendlier to the environment, such as diaper companies using the most biodegradable stuffing for their disposable diapers. Another example is Marriott Hotels International, a company leading the way in environmental and *sustainable* business practices, being the first hotel to apply for Leadership in Energy and Environmental Design (LEED) certification. Practices that were evaluated included reducing consumption of energy and water and educating guests through environmental awareness activities, such as shutting off all lights for 60 minutes in March as part of Earth Hour.

Social responsibility initiatives may be assisted by *nongovernment organizations (NGOs)* that work toward improving social and environmental conditions. The Cross Sector Partnership conducted interviews with the staff of 86 companies in 11 countries to identify social engagement opportunities for both private-sector employers and NGOs. Businesses such as BP, Microsoft, and Unilever are tackling solutions to problems such as overpopulation, poverty, unhealthy living conditions, and lack of accessibility to clean water.

HR can help employers by running point on these citizenship *initiatives*, clarifying the goals to avoid conflicts of interest. It is necessary to establish the priorities in these programs to minimize the disruption of competing demands or avoid compromising the general practices of the business.

Governance

System of rules to regulate behavior

System of rules and processes an organization creates in order to comply with local and international laws, accounting rules, ethical norms, and environmental and social codes of conduct

Sarbanes-Oxley Act

A U.S. law that sets specific standards for public companies

A broad range of legal regulations that strengthen corporate accounting controls in the United States.

Corporate Citizenship

Responsibility to employees and to the community

A practice in which organizations take steps to improve their employees' lives and the communities in which they operate

Corporate Social Responsibility

An organization's commitment to improving the community and the environment

A business philosophy in which an organization helps to improve social and environmental problems

(continued)

(continued)

Environmental Responsibility

Concern and care for the environment

The management of products and processes that show concern for health, safety, and the environment

Sustainability

The capacity to endure over time

The capacity to stay, hold, or maintain something, such as a concept, economy, geography, environment, and so on

Social Responsibility

An ethical theory that guides organizations to consider the welfare of society

An organization's voluntary obligation toward the good of the environment in which it operates

NGO

Nongovernmental organization

Any nonprofit, voluntary, and independent organization that is not connected with any government, and that usually works to improve social or environmental conditions

Initiatives

Ideas, programs, projects

Actions related to new ideas or to starting new plans

Business Ethics

Ethics is rarely as simple as deciding a course of action based on whether it is right or wrong, lawful or unlawful. Ethics deals with situational elements that *drive* organizational response. Consider large-scale decisions such as offshoring manufacturing to countries in which human rights violations are prevalent, or the decision of pharmaceutical companies to increase the prices of lifesaving drugs. HR is often tasked with shaping a company's code of ethics, training all employees and managers, and advising the executive team both at the strategic stage of business planning and at the operational stages of implementation.

A company code of ethics establishes and communicates expected standards of behaviors for both the company and the employees. A *global ethics policy* focuses on how the company will behave in its global dealings, especially in areas where bribery and corruption are societal norms. Companies may choose to hire an ethics officer, one who is responsible for complying with internal and external codes of conduct. HR must be careful to craft an independent line of authority to avoid any conflict of interest issues. For example, an ethics officer may report directly to the board of directors as opposed to the CEO or COO.

In addition to ethics policies, HR and the executive team may choose to establish corporate values statements in which to declare their commitment to fundamentals such as honesty, integrity, confidentiality, and workplace privacy issues. Doing so sends a clear message to all stakeholders that the company is committed to holding itself responsible for more than just creating profit. HR must ensure that policies and activities are in line with such statements to avoid direct conflicts of interest, but also to avoid building a company culture of mistrust. For example, a company that commits to behaving in an honest and fair manner should not engage in any practices that are deceptive. Doing so sends a different kind of message to workers that they should "do as I say, not as I do," a strategy that results in an organizational identity crisis, numerous risks, turnover, and counterproductive work behaviors (CWBs)—employee behaviors that do intentional harm to the company's legitimate business interests.

Understanding business principles, participating in the strategic planning process, and leading change/project management efforts are only part of how HR becomes a valued business partner. Trust is fundamental for HR to have true impact. Trust is built upon a foundation of ethical leadership, and it's up to HR to act (and model) ethically responsible behaviors in all functional areas described in the HR BOK. Refer to Appendix B, HRCI's Ethical Standards, for an example of how ethical behavior in the practice of HR serves all behaviors and outcomes.

Drive

Guide, steer

To push or move forward a plan or project

Global Ethics Policy

Company behavioral guidelines

An outline of how a company expects employees to behave around the world, often intended to prevent bribery and corruption

Suggested Study or Organizational Audit Activities

1. Prepare a report for your management team related to organizational culture and Geert Hofstede's work. Include your thoughts on the degrees of characteristics at your place of work, and how the conditions affect company culture.
2. Make a business case for an HR technological intervention to your executive team. How can HR service efficiencies be improved through technology? What types of financial and resource allocations would be required?
3. With a team of two or three other employees or students, work together to design a balanced scorecard or HR scorecard for HR or another business process. Take a look at the Balanced Scorecard Institute online to get started.
4. Does your place of work subscribe to a cost or differentiation strategy? How is this strategy reflected in internal business practices and external competitiveness?
5. Go online to McKinsey & Company and conduct research on emerging workforce trends in a country of your choice. Research how MNEs will need to adapt their practices in the coming year.

References

Drucker, Peter F. 2001. *The Essential Drucker: The Best of Sixty Years of Peter Drucker's Essential Writings on Management.* New York: HarperCollins.

Galbraith, J. R. 2014. *Designing Organizations: Strategy, Structure, and Process at the Business Unit and Enterprise Levels.* 3rd ed. San Francisco, CA: Jossey-Bass.

Hofstede, G., G. J. Hofstede, and M. Minkov. 2010. *Cultures and Organizations: Software of the Mind—International Cooperation and Its Importance for Survival.* 3rd ed. New York: McGraw-Hill.

Magretta, J. 2012. *Understanding Michael Porter: The Essential Guide to Competition and Strategy.* Boston: Harvard Business School Publishing.

Mintzberg, H. 2016. "On Management, Organizations and More." Retrieved from https://www.youtube.com/watch?v=B1YNhr-xeL0.

Mintzberg, H., J. Lampel, and B. Ahlstrand. 2005. *Strategy Safari: A Guided Tour through the Wilds of Strategic Management.* New York: Free Press.

Neuman, G. A., J. E. Edwards, and N. S. Raju. 1989. "Organizational Development Interventions: A Meta-Analysis of Their Effects on Satisfaction and Other Attitudes." *Personnel Psychology* 42(3): 461.

Schrage, M. 2013. "Do Customers Even Care about Your Core Competence?" *Harvard Business Review*, October 17. Retrieved from https://hbr.org/2013/10/do-customers-even-care-about-your-core-competence.

Tarique, I., D. Briscoe, and R. Schuler. 2016. *International Human Resource Management: Policies and Practices for Multinational Enterprises (Global HRM)*. New York: Routledge.

Western, D. (n.d.) "38 Jack Canfield Quotes (Chicken Soup for the Soul)." Wealthy Gorilla. Retrieved from http://wealthygorilla.com/jack-canfield-quotes/.

3 | Workforce Planning and Employment

The Renaissance of Personality Testing at Work

The rise and fall of personality psychology has been occurring for more than 40 years. Scientists of the 1960s such as B. F. Skinner and Victor Vroom believed that employee actions are dependent upon external circumstances, not internal drivers. The dismissing of the effects of personality traits hasn't been only by the academics from 40 years ago. Skepticism of personality psychology continued throughout the 1970s and 1980s, and even drew fire from the evolutionists of the 1990s. Regardless of the noise, there has been progress in building empirical, scientific evidence on which to base best HR practices in the use of personality tests in employment situations.

Trait theories—when used as stand-alone theories—were flawed in that factors such as honesty or friendliness were studied only as *descriptors* of personality differences; they lacked causal relationships to explain behavior (Hogan 2004). For HR this was troubling, because practitioners could not use personality traits to explain, and therefore predict, future behavior on the job. As a result, trait-based personality descriptions in the workplace were viewed as being limited in value and, worse, having low validity.

As the discipline of industrial-organizational (I-O) psychology has become better organized, a renewed effort to understand personality and its effect on the job has emerged. The focus of these efforts has been to expand beyond trait-based assumptions and to link personality traits within other psychological

(continued)

(continued)

functions. Bandura (1997) described personality as an integrated system in which people act in identifiable patterns. This changes the usability of personality tests for HR professionals (HRPs) of today in that individual traits can be viewed as baked into a person's personality type, which may then be used to predict on-the-job behaviors. In functions such as hiring or promoting into leadership roles, the personality trait of conscientiousness has been linked to overall success in any job. Traits such as extroversion correlate to success in positions requiring successful interaction with others, such as leadership, whereas neuroticism is linked to higher levels of job anxiety (Mount and Barrick 1998).

Personality studies and assessments are confirming that people's systems of internal characteristics lead them to both select and influence their environments. A 1999 study by De Fruyt and Mervielde found that extroverts would seek out jobs that have more engaging social settings. Similarly, individuals scoring high in the trait of agreeableness chose roles requiring social interactions. In another study, participants who scored high in neuroticism were less likely to be attracted to work environments that were highly innovative, and conscientious individuals were more likely to be attracted to organizational cultures that were detail and outcome oriented (Judge and Cable 1997). In addition, assessing leaders prior to hiring or promotion can help HR identify those with the necessary skills to achieve strategic outcomes. An organization trying to build a culture of innovation will be less served by authoritarian leaders than by those more open to new things. By successfully linking personality traits to the benchmarks of successful job performance, the assessment's predictive validity is increased. When based on personality constructs linked to the job, the construct validity is improved. This makes the tests more legally defensible than the assessments of old. Personality studies in the current day seek to focus on the use of assessments in employee selection procedures. Tools such as structured interviews, assessment centers, and biodata will continue to have prominence in selection literature, and bear watching for HR application.

References

Bandura, A. 1997. *Self-Efficacy: The Exercise of Control.* New York: Freeman.

De Fruyt, F., and I. Mervielde. 1999. "RIASAC Types and Big Five Traits as Predictors of Employment Status and Nature of Employment." *Personnel Psychology* 52:701–727.

Hogan, R. 2004. "Personality Psychology for Organizational Researchers." In B. Schneider and D. Smith (Eds.), *Personality and Organizations.* Oxfordshire: Routledge.

Judge, T. A., and D. M. Cable. 1997. "Applicant Personality, Organizational Culture, and Organization Attraction." *Personnel Psychology* 50:359–394.

Mount, M. K., and M. R. Barrick. 1998. "Five Reasons Why the 'Big Five' Article Has Been Frequently Cited." *Personnel Psychology* 51, issue 4 (December): 849–857. doi:10.1111/j.1744–6570.1998.tb00743.x.

Introduction

If you didn't show up to work today, would anyone notice? Organizations spend up to 70 percent of their revenue on their people resources, giving HR perhaps the greatest opportunity to demonstrate value as a business partner by effectively managing the interaction between people and the work. How HR professionals perform the tasks found in workforce planning and employment (WPE) will shape whether they are greeted every day with excitement and confidence or are met with dodged phone calls and prepared counterarguments to suggestions. As referenced in the book's Introduction, the value of HR professionals is dependent upon their ability to exist as strategic business partners. In the functional area of WPE, this includes activities that:

- Assess workforce supply and demand to identify current and future talent gaps.
- Understand factors of job design and work structure to improve productivity and employee job satisfaction.
- Manage person-to-job and person-to-organization fit by designing effective recruiting, selection, and on-boarding procedures.
- Align staffing and people management strategies to company goals and objectives.
- Examine business core competencies and make recommendations for outsourcing or third-party management.
- Manage employer risk by understanding labor laws.
- Build relevant compliance programs to protect all stakeholders.
- Advise executive teams using data from internal and external trends and metrics to drive organizational response plans.

Workforce Planning: A Cascading Strategy

A workforce plan is a form of HR strategy that cascades down directly from the company's strategic plan, goals, and objectives. Delivered from a formal *workforce planning* process, the resulting written plan is tied to the company's strategic plan—where one goes, so must the other. Identifying workforce requirements begins by conducting a supply analysis in order to understand the competencies of the current employees. This review is followed by a demand analysis, completed by gathering data related to the current and future needs of the company. Finally, a gap analysis is used to identify the organization's short- and long-term objectives. Working with a desired outcome in mind, goals and objectives typically will trickle down from a strategic plan, and will align with broader interventions designed to maximize internal strengths and minimize weaknesses. This is in pursuit of taking advantage of external opportunities, or reducing competitive threats through staffing activities. A company's *head count* or *manpower* is usually analyzed and addressed through the filter of achieving strategic objectives. A labor surplus or *redundancy* may require *redeployment* of talent or a company-wide *reduction in force (RIF)*. In these cases, employee *mobility* factors must be considered. A labor shortage will require employee training or hiring or other viable staffing strategies such as hiring temporary workers or initiating short-term transfers of talent. Work furloughs are short-term reductions in work hours based on business or economic factors. They differ from layoffs in that furloughed employees continue to work, just on a reduced schedule.

Notice that a company strategy may change from year to year, based on both internal and external forces. In fast-changing industries or innovative companies, HR must be prepared to respond by creating replicable systems where possible. Plan for the plannable, and save reaction for the surprises.

Staffing strategies are highly dependent on many external factors, not the least of which is the availability of talent in the operating area of the business. The information from the supply, demand, and gap analysis will result in a written plan, dependent upon accurate analysis and interpretation of the labor market data. This has been made much easier by the efforts of the U.S. Department of Labor (DOL) over the past decade or so with its creation of a jobs database. The Occupational Information Network (O*NET for short) is a website dedicated to the process of job analysis, which is covered in an upcoming section. For purposes of federal and state data reports, O*NET assigns each job a Standard Occupational Classification (SOC) code, which individual states have adopted to organize their own job databases. This means that if an employer is looking for wage data for a specific job, it can search the O*NET database for the corresponding job title, identify the SOC code, and then search the state and local databases for comparable information.

The DOL assigned SOC code 13-1199.04 to the job of business continuity planner. The national annual median pay for this job is $68,170. In Kansas, the annual median pay is $61,900. In California, the annual pay for a 13-1199 position is $74,490. But if an employer is hiring in the city of San Jose, this position's average median salary is $92,680—a whopping $24,000 difference from the national average, and a $30,000 difference from Kansas. These differences are important to know when making geographic and budget decisions to aid in strategy formulation and development of the workforce plan and budget.

Information such as what is provided on O*NET allows HR to build a business case either for or against a workforce strategy. A business case often will justify the need for change, but will also provide practical information to help a company change for the better. In the case of hiring business continuity planners, a company can more accurately predict the true return on investment (ROI) of the role thanks in part to the continuity between federal and state reports.

There are other helpful government offices on a state level that provide useful information for a workforce plan. Accessing data related to workforce capabilities at a particular location or grouped by industry or occupation provides important information for a workforce plan. *Sourcing* is the practice of identifying the available skill sets of workers. This allows employers to engage in *recruitment* activities that successfully tap into an area's *talent pool.* HR efforts are aided by states and counties, which collect demographic data, including educational levels, work experience, and trends within the local labor market. Other data may identify the availability of transportation resources such as rail or interstate highways. Locations with universities may have specific degree programs for skills that are in high demand, such as in the nursing industry. Grand Rounds Inc., a San Francisco–based Internet medical start-up, expanded to Reno, Nevada, in 2015. The company is relying on graduates from the University of Nevada to achieve its growth strategy from 50 to 200 employees by 2017.

Once the data is collected, HR analyzes it to make recommendations that are directly related to strategic interventions. These recommendations relate to many functions of a human resource department, including the design of programs such as compensation, training, and equal employment opportunity (EEO) compliance. The data also helps predict the efficacy of certain recruitment sources, and forecasts costs related to recruiting or relocating workers. In some cases, the demographic data drives executive decisions on plant locations—decisions that have great impact on successful intervention activities born of competitive strategies.

Workforce Planning

Analyzing the type and number of employees

Identifying and analyzing what an organization needs to achieve its goals, in terms of the size, type, and quality of its employees

Head Count

Number of employees

The number of employees an organization has on its payroll

Manpower

An organization's workforce

The total number of individuals who make up the workforce of an organization

(*continued*)

(continued)

Redundancies

Elimination of jobs

Elimination or reduction of jobs because of downsizing or outsourcing

Redeployment

Moving employees from one location or task to another

A change in an employee's location or task, often to reduce layoffs or to make the best use of employees

Reduction in Force (RIF)

Temporary or permanent layoffs

Loss of employment positions due to lack of funding or change in work requirements

Mobility

The ability to move from one place to another

An HR term that refers to employees and their families who move from one location to another

Staffing

Hiring and firing employees

The act of selecting, hiring, and training people for specific jobs, as well as reducing the workforce when needed

Sourcing

Finding qualified people for a job

Identifying candidates who are qualified to do a job by using proactive recruiting techniques

Recruitment

Process of identifying and hiring qualified people

Process of attracting, screening, and hiring qualified people for a job

Talent Pool

Group of available skilled workers

A group of available skilled workers, or a database of resumes that a company can use to recruit in a particular location

The ability to compete often rests squarely on the deployment of resources at the right time and in the right direction. A company struggling to survive may need to shrink assets by offering only the products and services in the highest demand, or in which the company has an extreme competitive advantage. By shrinking offerings, it may need to reduce the workforce or shut down locations. Companies that are in high-growth mode will need an expansion plan, which HR contributes to by identifying the skill sets of the current workforce and analyzing what is available in the relevant labor market. Demographic shifts, economic forecasts, and the regulatory environment all act with enough force to make or break a company's success if not planned for and executed properly.

The use of third-party vendors may be necessary to address hard-to-fill positions or executive-level skill sets. Executive *placement* agencies (*headhunters*) may be engaged to scour the national market for talent. Staffing agencies may be contracted to help build up a workforce on a *short-term* basis through temporary *assignments*. In some cases, professional trainers may need to come in to set up work processes, or to train on new technology when necessary to meet strategic outcomes where labor supply is lacking. HR supports these efforts by identifying resources and building a business case using metrics such as return on investment or cost-benefit analysis.

Placement

Placing applicants in jobs

Finding suitable jobs for applicants

Headhunter

An employment recruiter

An informal name for an employment recruiter, sometimes referred to as an executive search firm

(continued)

(continued)

Short Term

A brief period of time

Occurring over a brief time (for example, a short-term loan or a short-term assignment)

Assignment

Job or position

A job, usually in a new location

In addition to using data to anticipate the supply and demand of labor, HR may use judgmental forecasts, which use information from the past and the present to predict labor flow. This of course requires that HR has the information from its data collection both from the internal strategic plan and the external labor market demographics. Examples include:

- Managerial estimates, in which managers with a history of addressing work flow are called together as experts to anticipate changes.
- Rule of thumb techniques, in which general guidelines are applied, such as one HR professional for every 80 employees.
- Delphi and nominal techniques, which use groups of experts to analyze data and make projections.

Statistical forecasting is also useful, particularly when HR has a data set to use for source material. Regression analyses are used to identify relationships between variables, in which a single constant is compared to one variable or to multiple variables. A simple linear regression predicts future demand of labor based on a (single) past indicator and represents it in a visual model. A graph shows how the constant variable behaves when other factors are introduced. For example, a retail store that predicts an increase in sales every October for the holiday season may show on a regression model that when sales go up, so do the number of employees. These variables are said to be correlated (co-related) to each other. In multilinear regression, there are more variables present that influence the criterion HR is trying to predict. In the retail store example, holiday sales remain the constant, but the variables introduced can be number of employees, expanded holiday hours, and other conditions.

A simulation model attempts to apply computer-based modeling to real-world scenarios. This method often begins by hypothesizing what-if scenarios such as "What if sales stay flat?" "What if 10 percent of our workforce retires over the next five years?"

Productivity ratios calculate the number of units produced per employee. Employers then may calculate labor needs based on projected sales.

In all of the above, benchmarks are established to define what is normal, and variables are often built up as deviations from standard operating conditions.

As discussed previously, workforce planning efforts must be aligned with company strategy. Actions and interventions that are out of alignment with corporate strategy will result in missed targets and confusing messages. Think of it as a robot that is programmed with a set of instructions that include measurements, outcomes, and error messaging. If the robot's arms and legs suddenly start to act independently, the company may be crippled by the disparities. HR is the central system through which strategy flows, and in the case of workforce planning, it goes straight through jobs and people. These are discussed in the next sections.

Job Design

The process of designing jobs within a company is focused on the need for *formalization*—organizing the work and job structures into coherent sets to meet output and support needs. Tasks, duties, and *responsibilities* must be sorted and grouped into a productive unit of work: the job. These are then grouped into *job families*—similar positions based on skill requirements or other common factors. HR must also take into consideration the structure of the organization to design jobs that are in line with a horizontal, product-based, or matrix structure (described in the Business Management and Strategy chapter). Job design also affects employee performance, particularly when motivation is a factor in productivity. Factors in designing or redesigning jobs include improving worker safety and health or working conditions, identifying the necessary tools and equipment, ensuring that the proper levels of authority are in place, and orienting the work group as individuals or teams. Job restructuring is another form of job design in which changes are made to meet evolving demands. Restructuring efforts include removing responsibilities or building alternative staffing strategies such as job sharing or telecommuting, techniques described in a later section.

Formalization

Structured work roles and rules

The degree to which processes and procedures define job functions and organizational structure

(continued)

(continued)

Responsibility

Duty

A task that is part of an employee's job description

Job Family

A set of related jobs performed within a work group or occupation

Groups of occupations based on the type of work performed, skills, education, training, and credentials

In some cases, a *contingent workforce* may need to be considered, made up of part-time or temporary workers for a fixed period of time. These employees are used to cover entry-level work that is seasonal in nature, or for more skilled positions that are project based. A job that may be critical for only three months out of the year may be designed to include very task-specific responsibilities. In this case, the job design would help HR build an appropriate staffing strategy—including wage/benefit budgets and costs to recruit—into the workforce plan.

Contingent Worker

Part-time or temporary employee

A person who is hired part-time to work under a contract or for a fixed period of time

Many HR staff walk into their roles with preorganized jobs; rarely is there the opportunity to build work processes from the ground up, so the idea of job design seems unnecessary or irrelevant. However, elements of job design and redesign are considered every time a new hire is selected, job performance criteria are created, jobs are added to meet new business, or job descriptions are updated for accuracy. Additionally, simplifying jobs such as when there is a low supply of skilled workers in the relevant labor market may incorporate elements of job design/redesign. At other times, it may be necessary to increase the complexity of the work to satisfy the developmental needs of a high-potential worker. HR is evolving from hiring or changing a person to fit the job to instead focusing on designing jobs to fit the strengths of the talent.

As with many HR activities, there are a few best practice approaches. They include:

Job enlargement Increasing the scope of a job by extending duties and responsibilities, generally without changing pay or status. This strategy is effective when an incumbent desires a more challenging job with different tasks or responsibilities.

Job enrichment A way to motivate employees by giving them greater responsibilities and more variety in their work. This generally involves giving the employee more control over planning and organizing the results.

Job rotation A developmental tool that allows employees to practice skills by moving from job to job. This helps the employer by increasing depth in departmental skills through cross-training.

Job sharing A strategy in which the tasks, duties, and responsibilities of a full-time job are split between two part-time workers.

Another element of job design is the work scheduling. Many organizations are open to flexible staffing techniques that widen their talent pool. For example, *telecommuting* is increasing in popularity, and involves employees accomplishing their work from home or from a virtual office. Issues that HR must prepare for include building out policies that describe expectations and performance measures, as well as accounting for time zone differences where applicable. Other alternative work schedules are also developing. In addition to job sharing and telecommuting, traditional work may be modified by adding shifts, changing start times, and changing the order of the days in which work gets done. HR supports flexible work options such as compressed workweeks by ensuring that laws regarding compensation and overtime are not violated. Performance criteria must also be created that are legally defensible, consistent in application, and clearly communicated.

Insourcing is an HR activity for which job design may need to accommodate. A company that decides to bring in fabrication tasks that used to be done by a third-party vendor will need to make several decisions before integrating the work into production. Options include rearranging existing jobs to take on the new production tasks or adding a new job from scratch.

Telecommuting

Working from home via computer

A flexible work arrangement that allows part-time or full-time employees to work at home via a computer

(continued)

(continued)

Insourcing

Assigning a job or function within a company

Assigning a job to an internal department instead of to an outside organization; opposite of outsourcing

Job Analysis: Characteristics of Jobs

As reviewed earlier, O*NET is built around a systematic *job analysis* process that derives from a *competency model*. These competencies are focused on describing benchmark job content, context, and work styles that are required to perform the work. This information is summarized in the final *job description*, which lists the *essential functions* and *job competencies*. Regardless of the enterprise being conducted, the job analysis, essential functions, and job competencies are used to perform every single HR activity. In selection, it is the building block of hiring criteria. In performance management, it defines the criteria from which employees will be measured. In compensation, the job data forms the benchmarks from which jobs are priced in the relevant market and is used to properly classify employees under the Fair Labor Standards Act (FLSA). In short, the successful execution of an HR department's role within an organization is built upon the information gleaned from a job analysis.

Job Analysis

Review of job tasks and requirements

A study of the major tasks and responsibilities of jobs to determine their importance and relation to other jobs in a company

Competency Model

A description of the skills needed for a specific job

A list of the behaviors, skills, and knowledge needed to do well in a specific job

Job Description

Description of work tasks and responsibilities

Written document describing an employee's work activities

Essential Functions

Required job duties

An employee's main responsibilities or tasks to succeed in a job

Job Competencies

Skills needed for a job

The skills and behaviors that will help an employee succeed in a specific job

Methods for conducting job analysis are dependent upon the type of analysis required. Task-based analysis focuses on the tasks, duties, and responsibilities (TDRs) of a particular job. A task is the most fundamental activity of a worker, whereas a duty is made up of several tasks. Responsibilities are the obligation the worker has to complete the tasks and duties, along with the responsibility to comply with other, more departmental or organizational requirements beyond the specific job outputs. A competency-based job analysis looks more toward the knowledge and skills that are necessary to do the work.

Questionnaires are easy-to-use tools that survey workers about the types of tasks they do, the frequency of the efforts, and to whom they are dependent for task completion. Questionnaires also capture information about the necessary knowledge, skills, and abilities used to perform the work. In some cases, HR may find that one-on-one interviewing is more appropriate to record the data about each job. Employees may also be asked to keep a log of their daily or hourly activities, or to participate in a focus group that evaluates the work content.

Having a system in place to complete the somewhat onerous task of job analysis is critical. Communicating the reasoning behind the effort to both managers and supervisors is the responsibility of HR. Employees may feel apprehensive about the employer's motives, and supervisors may resent the intrusion into their productivity efforts if the reasoning is not clearly explained. Employees tie the importance of their jobs to their own personal worth, which reinforces the tendency toward inflation.

While legal issues are covered more extensively in Appendix A, there are two that are worth mentioning in the context of job analysis (see the following features).

GRIGGS VS. DUKE POWER

In 1971, the Supreme Court decided a landmark case in *Griggs vs. Duke Power* that shaped the use of educational achievement in employment decisions. The court found that seemingly neutral employment requirements must be job related, and not result in adverse impact against a protected class group. Adverse impact occurs when there is a significantly different rate of selection (for hiring, for promotion, or to participate in training) of protected class groups than of nonprotected groups.

Title VII of the Civil Rights Act of 1964 made it unlawful to discriminate against individuals based on their race or national origin. Duke Power had a history of noncompliance with the relatively new law. Duke continued to segregate black workers into the labor department, and hire only white people with high school diplomas for the better jobs in other departments that paid higher wages.

It is also important to note that the diploma and baseline skills testing became a requirement *after* Title VII was passed, preventing African American workers from transferring to better jobs.

Thirteen employees filed suit under Title VII of the Civil Rights Act of 1964, stating that this requirement resulted in disparate or adverse impact against African Americans, as this group at the time had substantially lower rates of high school graduation than whites had.

The Supreme Court agreed. The diploma requirement in and of itself was a neutral hiring tool; however, the impact of this tool resulted in the substantial underrepresentation of a protected class group, rendering the outcome discriminatory.

To find out more about this historic court case, check out an audio version of the oral arguments in the case online at the NAACP's Legal Defense and Educational Fund.

AMERICANS WITH DISABILITIES ACT

The Americans with Disabilities Act (ADA) defined as essential the tasks, duties, and responsibilities that are the reason for the job's existence; they validate the job functions upon which performance needs are measured. Essential functions are determined by considering:

- Percentage of time spent on each job
- The frequency of the task
- How important it is to the overall purpose

Example

> The task "answering calls on a multiline phone system" is clearly essential based on frequency and importance for a receptionist position, but less so for a telecommuting data entry specialist.

Under the ADA, employers may consider the qualifications of a worker in regard to the successful completion—with or without reasonable accommodation—of the essential functions of a job. As jobs and organizations change, the essential functions must be reviewed for continued relevance. Often, job responsibilities morph into a reflection of the incumbent skill set or preferences. This may or may not be conducive to the original job outcomes or needs, and could potentially create a challenge to the necessity of a competency. During any review, HR must document the job analysis process to provide evidence that the job descriptions and essential functions are up to date and valid.

The ultimate output of the job analysis process is the final job description. Understood to be the readable form of all the data collected through the analysis process, it serves as documentation of the specifications and competencies necessary to perform the work. A job description provides a summary of the job and its purpose, along with a listing of the essential duties. The *job specifications* describe the individual knowledge, skills, and abilities necessary to complete the work, the education and work experience requirements, along with the physical and mental duties of the job. A job description will include a summary of those to whom the person reports, the wage classification, and necessary disclaimers to avoid the job description reading as a contract for employment. It should also reserve the right of the employer to make any changes as necessary to the work duties. Be careful, though! The ADA does not consider the statement "other duties as described" to be essential, as it does not meet the standards for importance, frequency, or reason for position existence.

Job Specification

Requirements for an employment position

A description of employee qualifications required to perform a specific job

The outputs from the job analysis process will also be useful in other ways. HR must have the ability to deliver job descriptions with the corresponding job competencies for use in the recruiting and selection process. These efforts will improve the accuracy of hires based on job or organization fit, which also improves the legal validity of selection procedures when all criteria are based on documented job or company requirements. Note that the output from job analysis is not just to hire external candidates. It may also be used to determine internal promotions to identify successor candidates, create developmental action plans for employees desiring to grow in their roles, and help employees see an established career path as they stay with the organization. Strategically, the documented job competencies will aid in the development of the workforce plan, as they may identify the gaps in current organizational competencies to meet future needs.

The process of job analysis is focused on analyzing the work to be done and identifying the tasks, duties, and responsibilities necessary for completion. While the job analysis process also identifies the worker competencies, HR still must be able to screen for the people characteristics. This is the function of recruiting, which is examined next.

Recruiting: Characteristics of People

The business of work is heavily dependent upon worker characteristics. A company's ability to compete is largely dependent upon its ability to attract qualified workers. *Employer branding* is the process of establishing a corporate identity that is communicated to a target audience. Establishing an employer brand is accomplished through the use of systematic and thoughtful approaches to market a company as an *employer of choice* to a diverse local and global market. An employer brand is most often built upon a differentiation strategy: what makes the company different from its competitors. In the case of recruiting, HR's competitors are *every other company* within range that is vying for similar talent. Understanding the transformational and strategic elements of the business such as the mission, vision, and values along with the more transactional details of employment such as wages and benefits all contribute to the *employment branding* effort. HR's goal is to manage the message to create a desire in qualified applicants to come and work for the organization.

Employer Branding

How a company presents itself to the public

The image an organization presents to its employees, stakeholders, and customers

Employer of Choice

An organization highly valued by employees

An organization that people want to work for because it attracts, motivates, and keeps good employees

Employment Branding

Changing how others perceive an organization

Process of turning an organization into an employer of choice

Effective branding techniques will increase the visibility of a company within its market. Strong branding efforts increase the flow of qualified applicants based on the company's reputation. A desirable company with a reputation of being good to its people will attract more talent than one with a reputation as a slave driver. In some cases, targeted branding messages will focus on specific demographics based on the skill sets necessary or in high demand. Regardless of a general or specific target group, the company may communicate its brand by identifying its employer *value proposition*. The HR value proposition is the unique product or service offered to HR's customers. Similarly, the employer value proposition communicates the unique set of offerings, associations, and values that are reasons people should come to work for the company. An effective employer value proposition reflects what the target population desires from an employer, and may be expressed via both tangible and intangible elements.

The HR value proposition is not only about attracting external talent. According to Dave Ulrich, it is critical for HR to demonstrate the right competencies and focus more on deliverables than "doables" to maximize the value of an HR team (Ulrich and Brockbank 2005).

Value Proposition

The benefits of a product or service

The unique benefits, costs, and value that a business delivers to its customers

As with any marketing effort, the key is to control the message. This can be tricky if an employer is not living the brand or the values expressed in its recruiting campaigns. One technique used to communicate the brand that continues to gain popularity is videos. Employee testimonials are a form of digital resume for the company in which brand ambassadors rise up from the ranks of workers. On video, these successful employees describe the working conditions or the workplace values that make the company a great place to belong. *Social media* is another way to embed the employer brand into the community. Sharing company strengths, highlighting efforts that reflect the mission or values, and inviting others to contribute in a meaningful way are all branding techniques used to control the message to the target audience—in this case, qualified applicants.

Social Media

Technology that helps people connect

Technology that lets people communicate over the Internet to share information and resources (for example, Twitter, Facebook, LinkedIn, and podcasts)

The employer brand is a broad effort to deliver a macro message about the general benefits of employment with the company. It is designed to get people in the door, and HR must then have a system in place to—as O*NET describes— identify the enduring traits of workers that influence performance on the job. A *job* *requisition* will often launch the prerecruiting effort of review (or development) of a job description to ensure HR is recruiting for the right qualifications. See Table 3.1 for an example of worker characteristics that O*NET describes as necessary for an HR professional.

> ## Job Requisition
>
> *Request to hire a person for an open position*
>
> A procedure used when a company wants to hire a new employee to fill a position

Once HR practitioners have a shopping list of skill sets, they can begin to accomplish the task of identifying resources from which to source talent.

Internal Recruiting Sources

Investing in internal resources for open job positions serves several positive business outcomes. After an employee has been working with a company for a period of time, the employer has a good sense of the person's capabilities and work style. Promoting from within takes advantage of previous training investments in the worker, giving him or her an opportunity to practice natural abilities and build other skills. Internal candidate promotion sends a message to other employees that there are opportunities for advancement, and that the company is paying attention to their hard work. Employee *relocations*, transfers, and other *workforce rotation* techniques are another tactic in which current workers are moved to a different location on a short- or long-term basis to manage staffing levels, either in the country or as expatriates.

In some cases, internal recruitment is *not* the best source. Bringing in fresh views and different ways of doing things can be motivating for companies seeking to innovate or pace their competitors. When several employees are vying for a particular promotion, competitive conflict may emerge as a disrupter to operations. Internal promotions in which the individual is not completely ready may reduce productivity overall while the employee gets up to speed and other workers fill in the gap left behind. Also, what happens if a newly promoted candidate is failing in the new role? Will the employee have the opportunity to move back if it doesn't work out? These and similar considerations should be identified in a process for promoting from within.

Internal sources for talent may be overlooked when supervisors view certain employees as "too good to lose," which is a flawed short-term strategy. Keeping the strong performers in a single role increases the likelihood that the job will stop being challenging for the worker. Lack of challenging work is one of the top reasons

Table 3.1   O*NET OnLine Report for 11-3121

Human Resource Manager

Abilities	Interests	Work Style	Work Values	Knowledge	Skills
Oral Expression The ability to communicate information and ideas in speaking so others will understand	Enterprising, social, and conventional	**Initiative** Job requires a willingness to take on responsibilities and challenges.	**Relationships** Occupations that satisfy this work value allow employees to provide service to others and work with coworkers in a friendly, noncompetitive environment. Corresponding needs are moral values and social service.	**Personnel and Human Resources** Knowledge of principles and procedures for personnel recruitment, selection, training, compensation and benefits, labor relations and negotiation, and personnel information systems	**Active Listening** Giving full attention to what other people are saying, taking time to understand the points being made, asking questions as appropriate, and not interrupting at inappropriate times

why employees leave. But supervisors have needs, too, and the savvy HR professional anticipates and addresses these needs before a situation becomes a crisis. Building a *leadership pipeline* and identifying the training and development needs of this source for workers is an HR critical task. *Replacement planning* and *succession planning* are tools used to accomplish this, and are reviewed toward the end of this chapter.

Relocation

Changing residence, moving employees

Transferring employees to another location for work

Workforce Rotation

Moving employees when work requirements change

The regular movement of employees from one function, time, or place to another, as needed

Leadership Pipeline

Source of future leaders

The people in a company who will be developed to move into higher levels of leadership over time

Replacement Planning

Identifying employees to fill future vacancies

Using past performance to identify employees who can fill future vacancies (unlike succession planning, which focuses on future potential)

Succession Planning

Determining and preparing for future talent needs

Identifying and developing high-potential employees for the organization's future success

---

Regardless, an internal recruitment strategy will require HR tools for execution. Job posting is the effort by HR to notify internal candidates that a job opening exists. In union organizations, the process is highly formalized and quantified using metrics such as seniority levels. The Internet and company intranets are also useful methods for deploying information about internal opportunities. Job posting is done most often before external candidates are considered, and HR should manage the job posting process carefully to ensure there is clarity regarding application procedures and other issues. For example, are employees obligated to tell their current supervisor that they are applying for another role? Can employees who are under a current disciplinary action be considered for a job promotion or transfer? How long will the job be posted internally before the company turns to external sources? HR will also have to consider the effect a nonselection will have on employee morale.

Another useful tool for identifying internal candidates is a skills inventory, which is used to catalog employee skill sets. HR may refer to a skills inventory to identify candidates with other knowledge, ability, work experience, or education not being used in their current positions. By collecting and organizing the data ahead of time either through a formal intervention project or as a process at the time of hire, HR creates a database of the unknown or forgotten skills of current employees. This enables internal *job matching*, which utilizes the skills inventory to place internal candidates into correct positions.

Job Matching

A process of placing employees in the right positions

The use of objective skill assessment data combined with common sense to determine the best fit for an employee to a specific job

An internal source for candidates with an external orientation is an employee *referral program*. Current workers are well positioned to provide applicants with a realistic *job preview*—an accurate portrayal of the work and work environment. Employee referrals can streamline the recruiting process, unburying the resumes of otherwise qualified candidates that may get lost in the volume of responses to a recruiting ad. Be careful, though—disparate impact may occur if employees refer *homogeneous* groups. Relying only on employee referrals can result in under-representation of protected class groups if employees consistently refer applicants that are similar to themselves in race, age, or gender.

Remember what you learned from *Griggs vs. Duke Power*. Employee referrals are another example of a seemingly neutral employment practice that can become discriminatory in outcome.

An employee referral program is a low-cost way to recruit qualified talent. Current employees are able to provide applicants with a realistic job preview, articulating clearly both the benefits and challenges of the workplace. However, in addition to disparate impact, employee referrals may also run afoul of an employer's *nepotism* policy—the giving of preferential hiring treatment to family members. HR can support compliance by having a clear antinepotism policy in the handbook, and applying consistent practices to all levels of employment. Many policies allow for the hiring of family members, but restrict family members from managing each other or, in some cases, working in the same department.

Referral Program

Using employees to recruit applicants

Recruitment method that rewards employees for recommending candidates

Job Preview

A method that gives applicants an understanding of job duties before being hired

A strategy for introducing job candidates to the realities of the position, both good and bad, prior to making a hiring decision

Homogeneous

The same or similar

Description of a group whose members are all the same or similar (for example, people from the same background and heritage); opposite of heterogeneous

Nepotism

Favoritism shown to relatives and friends

A practice where people of influence appoint their relatives or friends to positions in a business, even though they may be less qualified than other candidates

Re-recruiting is the effort of HR to reach out to past applicants and employees. This practice can save time and improve the quality of the hire, especially when the target is a former employee who left in good standing. This is an excellent example of when job design may influence decision making. A retired worker may be interested in returning to work part-time, opening up an opportunity for job sharing.

Employees who left for other opportunities may be disillusioned if the promise made to entice them to the other company does not come to fruition. For this reason, re-recruiting efforts may be heavily influenced by the nature of the *exit interview* and separation process. If an employee who gives notice is marched off the premises under guard by a security agent or bullied through an exit interview, he or she would be much less likely to consider returning. In highly competitive labor markets, these separation tactics may not serve long-term goals.

Exit Interview

Final interview before leaving an organization

An interview that HR has with an employee to get feedback about the job the employee held, the work environment, and the organization

External Recruiting Sources

External recruiting sources may be both traditional and nontraditional. The use of media outlets such as newspapers, radio announcements, and billboards may still be effective in some markets. Increasingly, however, employers are sourcing external candidates through social media, personal networks, and online job boards. Internet recruiting has many advantages, including lowering the cost per applicant due to high levels of exposure for a single price, and the tendency of people to share job ads via their own *social network*. Applicants often are able to respond quickly by submitting their resume online, with many employers having formal resume databases to sort applicants and store resumes for future openings. In some cases, passive candidates who are not actively looking may come across a job posting or employer brand video that encourages them to consider an employer's openings.

A popular professional networking site is LinkedIn. Employers pay to post formal job ads or simply post openings on their personal or company pages. The ability to upload videos, share news, and describe upcoming events all shape the impression of an organization that many candidates will form even before they decide to apply for job openings. Current employees may also share job openings with their friends on their personal social pages, causing a job ad to get quite a bit of exposure for free and making social media one of the fastest-growing recruiting sources for HR.

Job fairs continue to be fairly popular methods, especially when targeting a specific group such as veterans or a specific industry such as construction. General job fairs may not have a refined enough skill set for all openings, whereas other times they provide a good opportunity to communicate the employer brand for future needs. Virtual job fairs are a type of recruiting campaign in which a web-based link is advertised online and via social media. It can be a quick yet effective way to get the word out about job openings, and to stock an employer's resume database for future job openings.

Universities, trade schools, and high schools can become a continuous recruitment source for local employers. Most schools have career placement services; some are free and others charge a fee. Companies may post their jobs on the university website, or have e-mail blasts sent to alumni with degrees in the desired domain. The relationship with the school should be maintained throughout the year by participating in job fairs on campus, or helping prepare candidates through mock interviews. These activities create depth in the relationship and positions educational institutions as a long-term resource.

Diversity groups such as the Hispanic Chamber of Commerce or Disability Resource Centers are an active way to attract a diverse qualified workforce. Also called minority recruiting, these recruiting activities take a *multicultural* approach to seeking qualified workers. The effort aims for diverse targets that may be under-represented in a work group, or attempts to gather employees with a specific skill set such as language. Other sources for diversity recruiting include advertising at minority colleges and universities, or minority-based trade and professional associations where available.

Social Network

Group of people with similar interests

A group of people who interact because they have a common interest. The group communicates either in person or by using technology (for example, Facebook or Twitter)

Multicultural

Refers to a group of people from several cultures or ethnic groups

Employees of diverse cultures and backgrounds who are part of an organization's workforce

IN REAL LIFE: AUTISM SPEAKS AT SAP

"SAP values the unique skills and abilities that people with autism bring to the workplace." So said Jose Velasco, head of SAP's initiative to hire qualified individuals on the autism spectrum. SAP started by capitalizing on the coveted skill sets of detail orientation and software trouble-shooting required for its products and services that individuals on the autism spectrum often possess. Information technology (IT) positions were the starting point for SAP, which now boasts an international program providing job opportunities for the valuable skills and diverse ways of thinking that are critical to jobs in graphic design, finance, and marketing. Components of the program include a specific recruiting approach to find qualified individuals, many of whom are underemployed. This includes selection procedures that acknowledge some of the social skill difficulties many with autism experience, focusing instead on the professional and technical skill sets of each individual.

SAP is one of many companies that partnered with Specialisterne, a Danish company that prepares individuals with autism and Asperger's syndrome for the workplace. Providing training for these employees is a pillar of the program, as is training for the managers who direct them. Training employees in soft skills and managers on the need to provide clear and precise direction increases the odds of professional and project success. SAP now has implemented the program in Europe, Asia, and South America.[1]

Another source for external candidates is employment agencies. A staffing agency may be sponsored by the state, such as the New Hampshire Employment Security Department. This agency helps employers with the job postings, and also can advise them of tax credits or training reimbursement availability. These types of agencies may also be able to assist employers meet their diversity goals, such as accessing qualified individuals with disabilities or the hiring of veterans.

In other cases, private agencies may be engaged to conduct *headhunting*, seeking to tap into passive job seekers. These services are billed as a percentage of the final wage of a candidate who accepts an employment offer. Most of these agencies have large databases from which they draw applicants. While expensive as a standard form of recruiting, they may reduce the cost of recruiting if the *time-to-fill* rate is low and the candidate hired is the proper fit. As with any outsourced function, conducting the ROI is important before contracting.

Headhunting

Recruiting employees

The practice of recruiting employees from one company to work at another company

Time-to-Fill

Average time to hire people for job vacancies

The average number of days that a certain job position remains open

A professional employer organization (PEO) is a type of employee-leasing company, with the PEO remaining the employer of record after a successful recruiting. For a fee, the PEO handles all of the HR administrative responsibilities of an employer. This includes processing payroll and managing personnel records. In some cases, an employer shifts all of its current or nonessential personnel over to the PEO in order to better concentrate on its core competency and manage shifting overhead costs, with the PEO leasing back the employees to the company. These agreements generally create a joint employer obligation.

See the In Real Life feature for other types of joint employer issues plaguing fast-food giant McDonald's.

IN REAL LIFE: MCDONALD'S AND THE NATIONAL LABOR RELATIONS BOARD

The prospect of joint employment liability is not to be taken lightly. Just look at the headlines targeting McDonald's Corporation and its franchisees. Joint employment was addressed on two legal fronts in 2016, with the logic behind the verdicts just as interesting as the outcomes.

National Labor Relations Board (NLRB)

Unfair labor practices (ULPs) had been filed by unions against franchisee owners of McDonald's fast-food restaurants. The unions filed complaints with the NLRB, charging that the ULP claims should be also held against McDonald's Corporation as a joint employer of the franchisee employees.[2] The NLRB agreed with the unions, finding that McDonald's corporate could be held liable for charges because McDonald's corporate tells its franchisees how to staff restaurants, when to clean the bathrooms, and where partially completed orders should be placed on counters. The NLRB found merit in claims of "discriminatory discipline, reductions in hours, discharges, and other coercive conduct directed at employees in response to union and protected concerted activity, including threats, surveillance, interrogations, promises of benefit, and overbroad restrictions on communicating with union representatives or with other employees about unions and the employees' terms and conditions of employment."

It is telling that the joint employer relationship with regard to franchise owners may also impact rulings on similar associations between employers and their staffing resources as well as in the design of corporate structures. HR in positions of uncertainty should be sure to review the degree of control in any alternative arrangements to help manage these types of risks.

Wage and Hour Disputes

In October 2016 McDonald's agreed to pay $3.75 million to settle a class action wage and hour dispute brought against both corporate and franchise owners in California.[3] This settlement agreement reflects the uncertainty of employers regarding the NLRB's decision to hold McDonald's corporate as jointly liable for employment decisions made by independent franchise owners.

It is important for HR to understand that these recent interpretations and NLRB decisions are new territory in the application of labor law theories in practice. One attorney for the more than 800 class action members was quoted as saying, "We developed legal theories in this case that set the standard and lay the foundation for future litigation against franchisors and other companies that maintain ultimate economic control over the workplaces run by related companies." He was referring to the "ostensible agency" theory. The attorney said that even if McDonald's was not deemed to be a joint employer in the cases, the plaintiffs could have "ostensibly" (appearing as such) believed that they were employees, and that was enough for liability. The attorney said that the company led employees to believe that the franchisee was acting on behalf of McDonald's corporate as their "agent," which was enough to hold the corporate owners liable. In addition, after a conflicting ruling against joint employer vicarious liability in a suit against Domino's Pizza, and in response to another case, the NLRB revised its definition of joint employment to include "indirect control," such as McDonald's providing the computer system for which franchisees calculate overtime.

Independent contractors are another external source for talent. An independent contractor is very strictly defined under the Internal Revenue Service, so it is important that employers are aware of the implications and costs for misclassifying employees as independent contractors. IRS.gov describes independent contractor status as a matter of degree of control. Factors include:

Behavioral control Does the company control or have the right to control what the worker does and how the worker does his or her job?

Financial control Are the business aspects of the worker's job controlled by the payer? (These include things like how the worker is paid, whether expenses are reimbursed, who provides tools/supplies, etc.)

Type of relationship Are there written contracts or employee-type benefits (i.e., pension plan, insurance, vacation pay, etc.)? Will the relationship continue and is the work performed a key aspect of the business?

The IRS goes on to say that there is not one set magic number of conditions under which an employee is either an employee or a contractor, but rather the degree that each factor is present. The key is to document the factors influencing the entire relationship.

Independent Contractors

People who provide goods or services under an agreement

Workers who contract to do specific work for other people or organizations and are not considered employees

Labor unions are an example of an external recruitment source that is industry specific. Many unions have hiring halls where information about employer jobs and worker qualifications may be shared. Hiring halls aren't necessarily brick-and-mortar places; in some cases unions use the Internet to supply job listings online, including Facebook pages and job listings by state. The National Labor Relations Board reminds us that "Unions that operate exclusive hiring halls must notify workers how the referral system works (and of any changes in that system) and maintain non-discriminatory standards and procedures in making job referrals from the hiring hall." Labor unions are covered in more detail in the Employee and Labor Relations chapter.

Labor Union

A trade organization or works council

A group of employees with the same job who join together to ask their employers for things such as better wages, benefits, or working conditions

---

Job analysis identifies the characteristics of jobs. *Recruiting* identifies the characteristics of people. The selection process matches the two to determine fit.

Employer Retention Efforts

The best offense is a great defense, and this cliché holds true with recruiting as well. HR can advocate for resource allocation toward *employee retention* programs, arguing that money spent on *reducing turnover* is a better investment than the cost of recruiting. All of these activities require efforts that engage workers with their jobs, the company, and their peers. Supervisors play a vital role in retaining workers, with many exit interviews showing that employees leave because of their boss, not necessarily the job or company itself. Another common reason for leaving is pay. Many employees report that they are dissatisfied with their levels of compensation in relation to the effort and commitment required to do their jobs. In some cases, employees do not feel valued for their contributions, or they believe there is a lack of diversity and inclusion in the *workplace*.

For HR, conducting periodic surveys that address each issue is a valuable exercise that will provide insight into employee job and company satisfaction. In some cases, HR may conduct *stay interviews*—face-to-face conversations with workers about why employees continue to stay with the company. Collecting this type of data is a critical component of building retention strategies that actually work.

Tenure is another retention strategy often employed in academic settings. It grants a permanent job or position with a contracted worker, in some cases with better employment benefits or leave allocations to encourage employees to stay.

Globally, *brain drain* is a very real problem in which talented individuals relocate from their home country to find work in areas with higher wages, better technology, and more stable living conditions. Because the majority of migration occurs from developing countries to developed countries, there is concern that areas already fighting poverty, unavailability of clean water, and lack of health care services suffer from this loss of talent. For this reason, many employers are well served by investing in *glocalization* efforts to increase awareness and help improve conditions around the world.

Some companies are choosing to reverse the trend of brain drain by exporting work from more developed countries into the less developed countries through the design of joint ventures, subsidiaries, outsourcing, and offshoring efforts. In this way, the business comes to the worker instead of the worker moving to the job.

Take a look at the In Real Life feature about R. Riveter to see how one business builds its workforce specifically based on the mobility of military spouses.

Employee Retention

Keeping employees

Methods of motivating employees to stay with the organization and making sure employees are satisfied and rewarded

Reduce Turnover

Lower the number of unfilled positions

To retain employees and lower the number of vacancies in a company

Workplace

A place where people work

A place, such as an office or factory, where people work

Stay Interview

A method of determining why employees remain with the organization

A retention strategy that helps organizations understand why their employees remain with the organization and how the organization can motivate them to continue their employment

Tenure

Permanent position

Holding a permanent job or position without the need for periodic contract renewals

(continued)

(continued)

Brain Drain

Loss of skilled workers

When smart and talented people leave their own country for better opportunities

Glocalization

A strong local and global presence

Characteristic of a company that "thinks globally, but acts locally"; when a company has a strong presence both in its own country and around the world

---

**IN REAL LIFE: RETAINING A MOBILE WORKFORCE
AS A COMPETITIVE ADVANTAGE—R. RIVETER**

*Permanent change of station (PCS): the movement of an American soldier
and his or her family to another location*

The American handbag manufacturer R. Riveter, named after the World War II poster girl Rosie the Riveter, was launched in an attic by two military spouses determined to find a way to add dollars to their families' incomes despite being PCS'd (moved) several times in just a few short years. The initial effort has grown to encompass a business model of incorporating a mobile workforce as part of the primary manufacturing processes. As many as five Riveters contribute to the sewing of a single handbag made from military uniforms, tents, and other up-cycled textiles, providing a portable career for military spouses and retaining a skilled workforce for the company. The bag components are then sent to the company's central location for quality inspection, assembly, and shipment.

Selection: Matching Jobs to People

Once qualified applicants have been identified through the branding and recruiting efforts of HR, the process of *selection* by differentiating between the competencies of the candidates begins. This is a form of acknowledging the job-related differences between candidates, and using tools that attempt to predict successful performance on the job.

Preemployment Testing

The Uniform Guidelines on Employee Selection Procedures (UGESPs) are excellent resources for certificants and current HR practitioners. These guidelines address an absolute legal right of all applicants to be treated fairly and to be considered only for their job-related qualifications.

Furthermore, any requirement an employer has in the hiring process is considered a test—including an application form that collects *biodata* and interview questions, two examples of *screening tools* that the employer uses to predict future performance. All tools must demonstrate *reliability*, which is a scientific term that means the degree to which a test consistently predicts what the employer thinks it predicts. The UGESPs also outline the *validity* criteria for employment tests that are acceptable to use in employment situations, including those used in *targeted selection* procedures.

The UGESPs provide information for HR about designing legally defensible preemployment tests. The guidelines are built from court *interpretations* of existing law, precedents, and labor law directly to inform employers of the proper use of selection tests in the workplace. They include standards for reliability and validity, and the obligation of employers to ensure that tests are job-related and nondiscriminatory.

Selection

Choosing employees

Method for choosing the best candidate for a job

Biodata

Information about a person

A shortened term for "biographical data": information about a person's education, background, and work history

Screening Tool

An instrument used to assess an employee's suitability for a particular job

An instrument used in employee selection to help assess job suitability (for example, in-basket exercises, psychometric tests, and cultural adaptability inventories)

Reliability

Being dependable or consistent

Having the same results after many tests

(*continued*)

(continued)

Validity

Reliability, true evaluation

The extent to which something is accurate (for example, the extent to which an exam actually measures what it claims to measure)

Targeted Selection

Evaluation of a candidate's abilities based on past behavior

An assessment of job-related behavior from the candidate's previous employment to predict future performance

Interpretation

Explanation of meaning

An explanation of the meaning of something; translating spoken language

There are several types of test validation techniques described by the UGESPs that are used to improve the prediction of outcomes and job relatedness of tests; all seek to measure the link between an employment test and performance. It's useful to know that validity studies rarely result in an identification of causes of performance. Most tests are only able to identify correlations (relationships, either positive or negative) between a test score and performance. They include:

Criterion-related validity A *criterion* is simply a work-related behavior that an employer is trying to predict or measure through the use of a test or assessment. Often built from the job analysis, the study determines whether a test is built upon job-related criteria. The UGESPs give employers a pass from using the job analysis as a basis for assessment if the employer can show that the criteria are important in the employment context. This may include performance related to production and error rates, attendance factors, and length of service requirements. It's helpful to remember that *any* performance measurement is a test subject to the principles of validity. So evaluating an employee's attendance for purposes of a performance review would meet the criterion-related standard for validity. In hiring, if an applicant who scores well on a test also has high performance, the test would be said to be a valid predictor of performance on the job. There are two subtypes of criterion-related validity, and the main difference between the two is timing.

Concurrent validity Concurrent validity is the measurement of a new test against an old test, most likely one that had been previously validated. (It may also refer to two groups of employees or applicants tested at the same time.) For example, a hospital evaluates nursing interns using a practical, hands-on exam via observation, and a computer-generated test with multiple-choice questions. If the interns who score well on the practical exam also score well on the written test, the tests have been concurrently validated against performance on the tests. If, however, a group of students score well on the practical exam but poorly on the written exam, then one or both of the tests may not be valid predictor(s) of performance. The goal is to align the testing criteria so that the results are positively correlated (when performance on one test is high, so is performance on the other; when performance on one test is low, there is also low performance on the other); they have been validated against each other.

Predictive validity If the two tests in the previous example are not given at approximately the same time, but rather are used as a measurement against future performance, then the exam makers are using predictive studies to validate a test. The practical exams given to nurses are conducted within their first 90 days of performance, with the results reviewed and compared to their performance at six months. If the test scores at 90 days are high and the performance scores at six months also are high, the test has been *predictively validated* based on a positive correlation between the test and performance at a future date. Similarly, if an employee scored low on the written test and also received a below-average six-month review, the written test has been positively correlated as well.

Content validity An assessment is said to be content valid if it measures the knowledge, skills, or abilities necessary to perform the work. To be content valid, the test must assess actual work content. For example, in an interview for an HR job a work sample test is administered asking an applicant to complete Form I-9 using information for a fictional new hire. The form must be completed correctly, completely, and with no errors. The interviewer may also ask the applicant a series of questions related to filling out the form to measure the applicant's knowledge of the process.

Construct validity A construct is nonobservable behavior constructed from different mental processes. Often trait based, constructs include intelligence and personality, as well as abilities such as problem solving or teamwork. For example, the American Psychological Association defines the construct of self-efficacy as the degree of belief one has in one's own ability to perform a task. In training, an employer may select participants based on the construct that they must have a high degree of self-efficacy in order to be selected. The instrument (tool) used to measure that construct must be related to the job and must accurately measure that trait in order to be considered valid. Most employers leave construct validation studies up to the professionals. As with many other processes, however, if the professionals make a mistake that HR doesn't catch, the employer is often just as liable as if HR had completed the study in-house.

The Society for Industrial and Organizational Psychology (SIOP) has also adopted standards for selection testing. Titled "Principles for the Validation and Use of Personnel Selection Procedures," these guidelines are useful for employers who wish to develop their own assessments.

You can find more information about these resources online at:

www.uniformguidelines.com
www.apa.org
www.siop.org

Criterion

A standard or rule

A test, standard, or rule on which something is judged or measured

Predictive Validity

Relationship between a test score and a work task

The extent to which a score on a scale or test predicts future behavior

Verifying Applicant Information

Many employers will conduct a *reference check* to help make an informed decision about the work habits and responsibilities of the applicant. Generally HR will contact two or three past employers and ask questions about the employee's work, verifying dates of employment, position titles, and responsibilities in the process. Some employers hesitate to provide information regarding former employees due to privacy laws. A general guideline is that the best defense against a charge of defamation is the truth. As long as the information provided is factually accurate and given in good faith, most states will protect an employer from legal action.

Reference Check

Verification of a job applicant's employment history

Contact with a job applicant's past employers, or other references, to verify the applicant's job history, performance, and educational qualifications

Verifying an applicant's work history is just one type of reference check. Employers may also want to verify an applicant's educational record to confirm information presented on the application for employment. Financial references, such as credit checks, may also be used by the employer to predict future on-the-job performance. The Fair Credit Reporting Act (FCRA) closely governs what employers may collect and how they may use the information. After amendment in 2003 by the Fair and Accurate Credit Transactions Act (FACT), employers must disclose to applicants in writing that a credit report will be obtained, and the candidate must authorize the employer, also in writing, to do so.

A more comprehensive type of employment verification is the *background check*, which includes much of the aforementioned checking, plus a criminal record check. HR often outsources these services to a professional investigative record search company. Any negative information related to convictions of substance abuse, violent crime, or theft should be carefully considered on a case-by-case basis. Safety-sensitive functions or jobs requiring security clearance are allowed to have more restrictive requirements of applicants. When negative information is uncovered, employers should consider the length of time that has passed since the conviction, the age of the applicant when the conviction occurred, the type of risk this conviction may present to customers and coworkers, and, most important, how the behavior is related to the job for which the applicant is applying. Criminal record checks are a type of consumer report, and therefore are subject to the requirements of the FCRA. As a best practice, if an employer decides not to hire an applicant based on the candidate's criminal history, the employer must provide notice to the candidate in writing, and give him or her the time to respond.

Background Check

Process of confirming a job candidate's personal and public information

Gathering data to determine the accuracy of a candidate's experience and records during employment screening (for example, verifying personal data, checking credentials, determining any criminal activity)

Special Issues: Negligent Hiring and Polygraph Testing

Employers may be held liable for the actions of a new hire if they knew or should have known about a person's history prior to hiring that endangered coworkers, customers, vendors, or others. Employers may protect themselves against a claim of negligent hiring by consistently conducting reference and background checks for all new hires within the scope of the laws. Obtaining records related to past employment, driving records, educational achievements, and drug screening are all ways employers may guard against a successful negligent hiring claim.

Polygraph testing is a controversial preemployment check that attempts to verify an applicant's background by asking questions and measuring the truth of the answers. The Employee Polygraph Protection Act of 1988 limits the use of these types of tests to be administered only for employees of federal contractors or subcontractors with national defense, security, or FBI contracts; to applicants for armored security or car services; and to candidates who would have access to the manufacture, storage distribution, or sale of pharmaceutical products. Any polygraph must be administered by a licensed practitioner.

Employee Selection Procedures

HR uses information about the job (job analysis), the company (mission, vision, values) and the management style and needs of the direct supervisor (leadership style, skills gap analysis) to determine proper fit of a potential hire. When done correctly, better person-to-job and person-to-organization fit is achieved and turnover is reduced.

Selection Interviewing

Qualified applicants are invited to the facility for a *face-to-face* interview, of which there are several types. Because interviews are a form of employment test, HR should have a process that is consistently documented and followed. An HR best practice is to have a list of structured interview questions so that the same questions are asked of all applicants for the position. This is because structured interviews have higher validity than their counterparts, unstructured interviews, in which interviewers ask more free-form questions and allow the applicant to guide the conversation. Structured and unstructured interviews are often referred to as directive/nondirective. These types of interviews may take on many forms, including:

Behavioral *Behavioral interview* questions ask applicants to describe how they have handled situations in the past.

Situational *Situational interview* questions ask applicants about how they would handle hypothetical situations that could occur on the job.

Patterned In a patterned interview, also called a targeted interview, a bank of questions is used that focus on specific job-related areas. While the job content area remains constant, the question type will vary. Knowledge questions may be asked of college graduates, whereas practical questions may be asked of the more experienced.

Stress In a stress interview, interviewers take an aggressive approach to candidates to see how they respond. Because this method must be reflective of the job, only highly stressful industries employ this method, including law enforcement and air traffic controllers.

Panel A panel interview is less about the type of questions and more about the number of interviewers. Several individuals take turns asking questions of a single applicant. Notes and ratings are then compared to identify the most qualified applicant.

Face-to-Face

Being physically present with another person

Interacting while in the presence of another person, as opposed to on the telephone, in a webinar, or by e-mail

Behavioral Interview

Job interview method based on past work behavior

Interview process to predict future performance based on how the candidate acted in past work situations

Situational Interview

Technique for assessing a job candidate's problem-solving skills

A method of assessing job candidates' skills by asking them how they would respond to specific work-related issues and problems

As mentioned in the section introduction, interview questions must be tied to job or company capabilities and needs. Unlawful interview questions are those that inquire into a person's protected class characteristics, or characteristics that have no bearing on successful job performance. Questions related to age, gender, family status, arrest records, religion, affiliations, military service, and disability must very clearly link to job outcomes for an interview question or job criterion to be lawful. In some cases, these personal characteristics may be a bona fide occupational qualification (BFOQ), a condition that is reasonably necessary to conduct business operations. For example, religious institutions may make a person's religion a qualification criterion. Or a movie about Native Americans may choose to cast only American Indian actors. The Federal Aviation Administration (FAA) has a minimum age for pilots and copilots, and does not hire individuals over the age of 60.

An HR best practice is to only ask questions directly related to job activities, and only collect protected data such as birthdates after a conditional offer of employment has been made.

Interview Bias

As with any human activity, bias may be introduced and unintentionally influence the ultimate impression the interviewer forms of a candidate and therefore who is selected. Types of bias include:

Average/central tendency This error occurs when an interviewer rates all applicants with about the same score, usually right in the middle of the rating scale.

Stereotyping *Stereotyping* occurs when a rater applies beliefs about the characteristics of groups, such as that women with children prefer not to work. *Generalization* is a similar type of bias in which the raters form opinions of candidates based on what they have observed.

Contrast error Contrast error happens when an interviewer compares all candidates against a single candidate. For example, if the first candidate interviewed is really weak, all subsequent applicants may appear to be stronger than they actually are.

First impression A first impression is formed based on a small bit of information gleaned right at the beginning of an interview. For example, a candidate who appears to be extremely anxious at first, but then calms down as the interview progresses, may be bypassed because of the earlier behavioral anxiety.

Halo effect/horn effect These biases occur when a rater places particular emphasis on a positive trait (*halo effect*) or a negative trait (horn effect) at the exclusion of other candidate criteria.

Question inconsistency A potential legal pitfall, this error occurs when interviewers ask different questions of different applicants, such as asking female candidates to describe their past job weaknesses but asking male candidates to describe only their successes.

Cultural noise Cultural noise exists when a candidate attempts to respond to the interviewer's questions based on what the applicant thinks the interviewer wants to hear, and the rater fails to recognize it.

Nonverbal bias This occurs when a rater is influenced by body language, appearance, or eye contact. An applicant whose leg bounces up and down during an interview may trigger this error.

A strategy to guard against the influences of these biases is to interview with another person and compare notes after the rating is complete. Basing (and documenting) opinions based only on a candidate's person-to-job or person-to-organizational fit is the best defense against charges of interview bias.

Stereotype

Fixed opinion or belief

An oversimplified opinion, image, or attitude that people from a particular group are all the same

Generalization

An objective conclusion

A perception based on observations (for example, "Americans are usually friendly"); different from a stereotype (for example, "All Americans are friendly")

Halo Effect

Transfer of positive feelings

The transfer of the positive qualities of a person or thing to related people or things

Systems Approach

As with many HR activities, a systems approach that is standardized is a best practice for recruiting and selection activities.

Applicant tracking systems (ATSs) help HR keep track of the thousands of resumes and applications for employment that are received. The system documents an applicant all the way through the recruiting process, with a resulting resume database from which employers may draw from for future positions. ATSs can stand alone or be part of a human resource information system (HRIS) in which a person can seamlessly transition from applicant to employee upon hire. A robust HRIS system will have the capability to manage all stages of the employee life cycle from hiring through training and for any other activity related to employment decisions.

ATS

Applicant tracking system

Computer software that helps an organization recruit employees

Negotiations, Offer Letters, and Employment Contracts

Once a selection decision has been made, it's time to develop and extend employment offers, write employment contracts, and, in some cases, conduct negotiations. These are reviewed next.

Negotiating

Once the decision to hire an applicant has been made, an offer of employment is the next step for HR. Many employers make a verbal offer, which is where negotiating begins. During the selection process, HR collects information about what the applicant is looking for from the employer, whether it be a *relocation* package, flexible work hours, *tuition reimbursement*, or vacation time. International employees who don't want to relocate may request an international commuter assignment, along with premiums and covered expenses. When making an offer, HR should address any needs expressed by the applicant, and be prepared to either meet those needs or make a counteroffer by getting approval for how far the employer is willing to go to successfully hire the candidate. Negotiating tools that HR may employ include paying a sign-on bonus to offset lost time off or bonuses a new hire may experience by accepting the offer. HR may also work from a salary range and not offer the highest salary amount the company is willing to pay as a first move. Discretion and balance are critical skills for HR at this stage; if an applicant feels HR is being dishonest, or is not prepared to honor what was discussed during the interviews, he or she may decide not to take the job offer after all.

Offer Letters

Once a verbal agreement has been made, a written offer of employment is drafted by HR. At minimum, an offer letter should include the position title, salary classification, deadlines for acceptance, and any contingencies required prior to beginning work. A statement of employment at will (EAW) should be included in an offer letter. While basic in form, a best practice is to have legal review or prepare an offer letter template to ensure that care is taken to avoid the legal land mines any written document can cause.

Employment Contracts

The intent of a contract is to bind two parties to agreed-upon conditions of employment. An employment contract therefore binds an employer and an

Table 3.2　Difference between an Offer Letter and an Employment Contract

	Offer Letters	Employment Contracts
Written	✓	✓
Position title and duties	✓	✓
Salary classification	✓	✓
Compensation and benefits	✓	✓
Length of employment		✓
Contingencies	✓	✓
Employment at will	✓	
Restrictive clauses, such as noncompete or nonsolicitation		✓
Disability or death of employee clauses		✓
Conditions under which an employee may be fired		✓
Noncash compensation and perks		✓

employee to all of the conditions outlined in an employment offer, but also to a length or term of employment. Whereas noncontracted workers are considered at will, employees with a contract may be terminated only in accordance with the terms of the contract. Much broader in scope than an offer letter, an employment contract typically includes the terms and conditions of employment, restrictive clauses such as noncompete agreements and nonsolicitation agreements, reasons an employee may be terminated plus any severance payment expectations, and base salary and bonuses. One important note: Take care to not list salary in annual amounts, as courts have interpreted this to be a promise of a contract, even if the employee does not complete the year.

Table 3.2 illustrates a few of the differences between employment contracts and offer letters.

Relocation Services

Support provided to transferring employees

Help given to relocating employees (for example, predeparture orientation, home-finding assistance, tax and legal advice, and in-country assistance)

Tuition Reimbursement

Payment for an employee's school fees

A benefit whereby the employer provides full or partial payment for educational courses completed by employees

Employment at Will (EAW)

Understood to be a common law doctrine, EAW is the right of the employer and the employee to terminate the relationship at any time, and for any reason, immediately upon notice to the other. EAW applies to all employment conditions—whether hiring, firing, training, or promotion. This also means that an employee is not obligated to give what is considered the traditional two weeks' notice. However, many court decisions over the past few decades have identified several exceptions to the doctrine of EAW. These exceptions include:

Covenant of good faith and fair dealing exception Employees have the right to be treated fairly in their relationship with the employer. Longevity of service may be a factor in a wrongful termination issue. For example, an employee may have a wrongful termination claim if fired under the doctrine of EAW right before becoming eligible for the employer's pension plan.

Contract exceptions If a written contract exists, employees may be disciplined or terminated only in accordance with the contract conditions. An implied contract may be created by length of service and positive employee reviews. If, for example, an employee has worked for a company for 20 years and has had only positive reviews during that time, the courts have found that the worker may reasonably expect to not be fired as long as the employee continues to do satisfactory work. An express contract may be verbally created when statements are made to employees expressly telling them, "As long as you do your job right, you'll have a job for life."

Public policy exceptions Employees cannot be fired for complying with public policy, or for refusing to break the law for their employer. For example, an employee cannot be terminated for filing a workers' compensation claim or for reporting unlawful employer activity.

Postoffer and Prehire Activities

Most employers use conditional offers of employment at this stage of the hiring process in order to complete additional hiring requirements. Employers may make the job offer contingent on the new hire passing a series of additional tests. The two most common contingencies are explored next.

Preemployment Physicals and Drug Screens

Preemployment physicals are another type of test to give to applicants once they have been identified for hire to ensure the employee is fit for duty. These exams are legal provided they are closely linked to future job performance (are predictive of success on the job), and must be required of all applicants for the same position. Under the Americans with Disabilities Act (ADA), employers may make a job offer conditional on the new hire passing the exam.

Preemployment drug screening is a postoffer activity because not all drugs are unlawful. Many individuals take legal prescription drugs that could be related to a disability. Typical drug screen panels test for the nine most common drugs, including marijuana, cocaine, and methamphetamine. Any positive result is elevated to a medical review officer for confirmation. Urine samples are the most legally defensible type of drug screen, followed by saliva tests. Blood and hair analysis are considered more intrusive and likely to reveal conditions that may not be considered as part of the hiring criteria; therefore, they are considered the riskiest of all drug screening methods.

With the legalization of marijuana in states such as Colorado, Oregon, and California, there has been some concern over applicants who have medical marijuana cards. HR should know that marijuana use remains illegal under federal law. A potential employee with a medical marijuana card who tests positive for the drug may generally be treated in accordance with an employer's substance abuse policy. Note, however, that there are conflicting practices on a state-by-state basis. California allows employers to enforce zero tolerance policies for substance abuse in the workplace. Arizona law expressly prohibits employers from terminating employees for using marijuana under an authorization card. HR practitioners should know their particular state guidelines, and be especially knowledgeable in exemptions to the requirements to accommodate medical marijuana use in the workplace.

E-Verify and Form I-9

E-Verify is a partnership between the United States Citizen and Immigration Services (USCIS) and the Social Security Administration (SSA). The E-Verify system is designed to help employers comply with obligations under the Immigration Reform and Control Act (IRCA) to verify new hire employment eligibility, and to verify employee identity. The E-Verify system electronically compares the information found on documents provided by new hires with the SSA's database. A "match" or "tentative non-confirmation" is returned almost instantaneously. As of 2009, federal contractors are required to use E-Verify if and when they are awarded a federal contract or subcontract in which E-Verify use is a term of the contract. Contracts in excess of $100,000 will require an E-Verify clause, with employers also being obligated to reverify status of existing employees who are assigned to the contract.

E-Verify is voluntary for private employers, and, contrary to federal contractors, private employers may *not* use E-Verify to go back and verify eligibility or identity of existing employees. Form I-9 must still be completed, regardless of E-Verify participation.

Employers are required to complete Form I-9 for all newly hired workers within 72 hours of their first day of work for pay. The form is designed to document an employer's effort to verify a new hire's identity and eligibility to work in the United States. The form is periodically updated, and employers must use the most updated version for employees hired within that period.

IRCA also prohibits discrimination against individuals on the basis of national origin or citizenship. For this reason:

- Form I-9 is a postoffer, prehire document. Employers may not use the informa-tion from the documents presented to make their hiring decisions. This means that Form I-9 and E-Verify should not be given to all applicants, just those to whom offers have been made.
- Employers may not require specific documents from an employee. Instead, they must allow a new hire to present any document from the "List of Acceptable Documents" section of Form I-9.
- Employers must limit access to these documents by storing them separately from an employee's personnel record and to reasonably secure the documents from those who don't need to know an applicant's birthdate or national origin to make employment decisions such as selecting for training or pay raise considerations.

Employers must maintain Form I-9 for the entire term of employment. Upon separation, HR will need to calculate how long to retain the form. Table 3.3 shows the calculation employers should use to determine the proper destroy date for these documents.

Additionally, Appendix D includes an excerpt from the M-274, Handbook for Employers published by the United States Citizen and Immigration Services for reference. You can download a full version from USCIS.gov.

Table 3.3   Form I-9 Retention Calculation

1. Date the employee began work for pay	1. 1/1/2017
A. Add three years to the date on line 1.	A. 1/1/2020
2. The date employment was terminated	2. 3/5/2018
B. Add one year to the date on line 2.	B. 3/5/2019
3. Which date is later, A or B?	3. A
C. Enter the later date.	C. 1/1/2020

Note: The employer must retain Form I-9 until the date on line C.
The employer is required to retain the page of the form on which the employer and the employee entered data. If copies of documents presented by employees are made, those too should be kept with Forms I-9.

Special Issues: Affirmative Action Plans and Record Retention

Affirmative action plans (AAPs) document an employer's intent to address under-represented minority groups in the workplace. These plans are required for employers who contract with the government, and as a court-ordered remedy for employers found to have unlawfully discriminated against protected class groups.

AAPs are not quotas. Employers are specifically prohibited from establishing minimum numbers of certain groups to hire or promote. Rather, an AAP outlines specific actions or strategies employers will use to increase the opportunities for these groups through diverse hiring practices and training.

Government contractors and subcontractors must establish equal opportunity in employment goals through a written plan if they:

- Have contracts in excess of $50,000,
- Have government bills of lading in excess of $50,000 in any 12-month period, or may be expected to total $50,000,
- Serve as a depository for federal funds, or
- Are a financial institution that is an issuing and paying agent for savings bonds/ funds.

Employers may voluntarily create an affirmative action plan as an intervention strategy to increase diversity. Components may include the use of diverse recruiting resources that target a specific protected class group, such as race, age, or gender. A successful plan will account for assessing the needs, establishing the goals, implementing the actions, and measuring results. It is important for HR to help the employer gather data related to the existing workforce, but also the demographics of the communities in which the company operates. A workforce demographic analysis is one tool HR may use to collect information in the communities where the company currently does business or plans to do so. Similar to the SWOT and PEST analysis reviewed in the Business Management and Strategy chapter, a demographics review looks at components such as age, gender, and ethnicity to help employers match/measure diversity staffing levels with the demographics of the communities in which they operate.

More on this topic is found in Appendix A.

Affirmative Action

A process designed to treat all applicants and employees equally

An activity designed to correct previous inequality that may have existed for certain groups or classes of people

---

Additionally, both the recruiting and selection processes generate a ton of paperwork. Even with the use of technology, most employers will have several documents with which to begin an employee personnel file. Regardless of whether the paperwork is stored physically or digitally, there are *document retention* requirements, prompting the need for HR to understand how to legally manage and store files. A *record retention schedule* is the tool many organizations use to keep track of preemployment files, enrollment forms, payroll records, medical files, and training/education documents. Employers have an obligation to their employees to protect sensitive data, including Social Security numbers, medical files, and other confidential information. An HR standard operating procedure (SOP) should identify the system for document control, and what to do if there is a breach. Proper storage requirements should be identified in the procedure, and a system for destroying expired documents should be clearly explained.

Document Retention

Maintaining important employee records

Managing employee data and records as required by the organization or rule or law

Record Retention Schedule

A defined plan for keeping and disposing of documents

A listing of key documents and the length of time that each is required by law to be stored or disposed of by the organization

---

Orientation and On-Boarding

The purpose of orientation and on-boarding programs is to assist new hires in acclimating to their new environment. New hires may be brand-new to the company, or may be existing employees who have been promoted or transferred into their new roles. As discussed at the beginning of this chapter, both programs must align with the company's strategic plan and cultural messages communicated through mission, vision, and values.

Orientation and on-boarding activities will confirm or discount expectations established during the recruitment process and, in some cases, even before an employee decides to compete for a role within the company. Some organizations choose to formalize a realistic job preview during the hiring process. Tools such as "day in the life" videos, tours of the workplace, private interviews with job incumbents, and job simulators all help applicants make an informed decision. Orientation and on-boarding practices build upon these expectations.

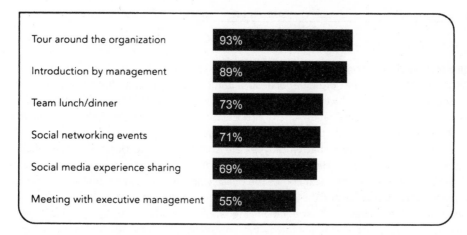

Figure 3.1   Most Commonly Used Practices Supporting the Integration of the New Employee
Source: Top Employers Institute.

HR best practices involve all levels of employees in the process. Executive meet and greets and team lunches are strategies that may be used to help the new hire feel welcome. Formal orientation may include presentations by other departments such as safety, or by C-suite executives describing the company's mission, vision, and values. A specialist may meet with the employee to discuss compensation systems and benefits plans. It is also important to build in a process to follow up with employees on international assignments to see how assimilation is going and to address any concerns. Orientation and on-boarding programs vary quite a bit based on company size. In some cases, an HR department of one will deliver all of these activities! See Figure 3.1 for insight from the Top Employers Institute on the most common methods used by employers to engage a new worker.

Orientation is often referred to as an event, whereas on-boarding is a process, typically lasting from 90 days to six months. Systematizing the on-boarding through an on-boarding schedule can help HR keep track of the desired goals of the program, and measure effectiveness of activities. Training milestones, productivity goals, and enrollment in programs may all be scheduled and managed by the practical HR professional. Do not underestimate the value of following up with new hires; many questions or concerns do not arise until the employee has spent some time on the job. HR should stay connected with new hires, especially because for many employers most turnover occurs within the first year of employment—a costly loss with rippling effects throughout the entire organization. See the feature for an evolutionary look at the on-boarding and orientation practice.

ORGANIZATIONAL SOCIALIZATION

While on-boarding and orientation continue to be the standard by which HR students are tested, recent research shows that *organizational socialization* is being used effectively by more and more companies. Defined by the 1976 *Handbook on Work, Organization and Society* by Robert Dubin, organizational socialization is "the process by which a person learns the values, norms and required behaviors which permit him to participate as a member of the organization." This theory includes the premise that employees are socialized to the business *before* they are actually hired. This supports HR practices related to the employer brand and its effect on the expectations of new recruits. Next comes the phase with which most are familiar. The new hire has joined the organization and the orientation and on-boarding process helps him or her begin to assimilate. In this phase, the expectations the employee had coming into the job are either challenged or supported. This reinforces the importance of using new hire on-boarding to increase the chances of successful engagement and to reduce new hire turnover. Finally, the third phase of socialization is launched, which involves the employee beginning to fully integrate into the company's social norms and values. In this phase, employees have a clear understanding of their roles and responsibilities within their work group, and what is (and is not) acceptable behavior. Behaviors that are either learned or reinforced at this stage include the nonuse of foul language, boundaries regarding meal and rest breaks, productivity expectations, teasing, and the use of social media on the job.

Managers play a critical role in successful employee integration. One study (Cable and Parsons 2001) of newly hired accountants found that the frequency and quality of information obtained in their first six months of employment affected not only their job performance, but also their role clarity and overall socialization into the new environment. This supports the need for HR to coach and model the expected standards of behavior for management.

The Separation Process

Many of the other chapters in this book address everything that happens in between selection and separation. The Human Resource Development chapter deals with managing employee performance through training and development activities, the Compensation and Benefits chapter addresses total rewards, and the Employee and Labor Relations chapter defines disciplinary procedures up to and including termination. WPE is built around many of the processes related to the bookends of selection and separation—what is wound up must wind down. For this reason, the organization's exit and off-boarding processes for both voluntary and involuntary separations are covered next.

Exit and Off-Boarding

Employees rarely voluntarily leave their companies because they simply stop needing to work. There are reasons employees exit, and part of the exit/off-boarding process serves to find out what those reasons are. Data obtained during an exit interview can be used to solve problems and prevent additional turnover. Poor fit may be analyzed and selection procedures refined in response. Lack of work/life balance can be addressed by redistributing some of the workload or by expanding time off policies. Dysfunctional turnover occurs when highly talented performers leave the company, and the off-boarding process must capture the information to diagnose organizational systems that are not supportive of talent.

Functional turnover occurs when poor performers exit, either voluntarily or involuntarily. Compliance becomes a major consideration with these separations, as care must be taken to ensure that the exiting employee is not wrongfully terminated, and is given the opportunity to correct behaviors where possible.

Reductions in Force

Reductions in force (RIFs) in essence are a business strategy to achieve downsizing. It is a form of organizational restructuring that results in a loss of jobs, generally company-wide. In some cases, a single position may be eliminated; in others, entire roles are restructured. HR supports the RIF process long before the pink slips are given. A plan begins to come together as soon as it has been identified as an organizational strategy. Components of the plan should include documenting the business reason for the loss of jobs, and identifying which positions will be eliminated and which positions must be kept. A review of federal, state, and local laws must be conducted to ensure compliance from the start. This may include the need to analyze which employees will be affected to determine if disparate impact may occur. Decisions about how the changes will be communicated, what (if any) severance packages will be funded, and how the workload will be redistributed should all be considered in the planning stage.

A separation checklist is a useful way to ensure that the various steps in a separation process are met. Compliance needs such as COBRA and HIPAA notifications, and coordinating logistical needs such as collecting equipment or deactivating security clearances may all be captured on a single checklist for consistent application.

Metrics

Employers pay in multiple ways for the privilege of employing workers. A *breakdown analysis* is one tool that helps HR sort relevant information, such as attrition rates or staffing levels in categories. This and other tools help employers know which WPE programs are effective, and which perhaps should be refined or eliminated altogether. Metrics that can help HR accomplish this include the following.

Calculating Turnover

The rate of *employee turnover* is expressed as a percentage. A standard should emerge company-wide and at the departmental level. Comparing *separation rates* periodically allows HR to spot potential problems in a business unit, and to investigate to offer support and advice. In some cases, a strategy may be necessary to account for regular high turnover. For example, at a chicken processing plant one department task involves eviscerating chickens. By nature, turnover is high because the job is distasteful to many new hires. In this case, a strategy of continuous recruitment may be necessary.

Turnover is calculated by dividing the number of employees who exited the organization by the average number of total employees. The result is then multiplied by 100 to express it as a percentage. Consider as an example that a company employed 300 employees in 2017, and 50 of those separated in the same time period. Dividing 50 by 300 and then multiplying the result by 100 would calculate the company's turnover rate at 16.67 percent.

Cost per Hire

As a service center, human resources must evaluate its own expenses and resources for efficacy. In some cases, the high cost of recruitment may be justified, as is the case for difficult-to-fill positions. At other times, a high recruiting cost may be unjustified because it is not productive. Knowing an organization's *cost per hire*—and further breaking it down by an average for every position—allows for better budgeting and evaluation. It also prompts recruiters to get creative with their allocated budgets, or know when starting to recruit a traditionally tough hire that they need to spend more early on to attract high-quality talent.

Days to Fill

Calculated per job, *days to fill* is the number of days it took for a position to be filled from the date a job requisition was received.

Full-Time Equivalents (FTEs)

Another calculation HR pros should understand and be able to apply is *full-time equivalents (FTEs)*. Many labor laws are triggered by an employer's total number of employees, and HR needs to be capable of including part-time workers where necessary. This is achieved by dividing the total hours worked in a given period by the number of full-time hours.

Breakdown Analysis

Listing things according to categories

Analyzing and classifying, such as an analysis of revenue sources or a report on attrition numbers

Employee Turnover

The ratio of unfilled positions

The percentage of a company's employees that must be replaced at any time

Separation Rate

The percentage of employees who leave their jobs

The ratio of the number of employees who leave their jobs to the total number of employees in the organization

Cost per Hire

Recruitment measuring tool

The amount of money needed to recruit a new employee, which includes advertising, recruiting fees, referral fees, travel expenses, and relocation costs

Days to Fill

The time it takes to hire someone

The average number of days it takes to hire someone for an open job position

Full-Time Equivalent (FTE)

A ratio of employee hours worked each week

A percentage comparing the number of hours that an organization's part-time employees work to the number of hours that full-time employees work

Succession Planning

One of the most valuable tasks HR may serve employers by is planning for *attrition*, the natural exit of the workforce through planned and unplanned circumstances. The activity of succession planning guides HR toward planning for attrition, the natural ebb and flow of the workforce.

Attrition

Reduction, decrease in numbers of employees

The number of employees who leave the organization for any reason: resignation, termination, end of agreement, retirement, sickness, or death

---

Succession planning is most often leadership oriented, both top-down and bottom-up. It includes planning for executive turnover as the result of voluntary separation, phased retirement, full retirement, contract expiration, or involuntary termination. This focus is often because backfilling C-level roles can be time-consuming, difficult, and expensive. Executive roles and required skill sets are often driven by the strengths and weaknesses of the entire executive team. For example, if the COO is highly operational but lacks interpersonal skills, the hiring of a CEO with counterpoint skills would be smart so as to seek balance. This delicate act is a skill set that senior-level HR professionals must possess.

Senior-level executives aren't the only groups for which succession planning is a best practice. Critical roles within the organization should also be included in a replacement plan, especially those that are served by hard-to-find skills, or, should a vacancy occur, important or essential tasks will go undone. Could you imagine the impact a shortage of air traffic controllers would have on domestic and international flights? Take a look at the In Real Life feature for a glimpse.

IN REAL LIFE: FLYING HIGH AT 14,000

The Federal Aviation Administration (FAA) reports that there are more than 14,000 air traffic controllers in the United States, working 24 hours a day, seven days a week at their flight posts. Responsible for the safe takeoff and landing of more than 2 million passengers per day, these critical jobs would cause a national crisis if left unfilled. Grounded planes and overworked controllers are two examples of why staffing levels of these roles must be kept full. Yet staffing for these vital roles is no easy task. FAA recruiters have several high standards applicants must meet. A successful candidate must:

- Be a United States citizen (BFOQ!)
- Be under the age of 31 (BFOQ!)
- Pass a medical examination

- Pass a security investigation
- Pass the FAA air traffic preemployment tests
- Speak English clearly enough to be understood over communications equipment
- Relocate to an FAA facility based on agency staffing needs

Attention to detail, stress tolerance, and "persistence in the face of obstacles" are just some of the work styles listed by O*NET for the successful candidate. For the potential $127,000 salary, applicants must pass a biographical assessment, which measures the likelihood that a candidate will reach final aviation certification. In 2017, the FAA plans to hire 1,700 air traffic controllers through a continuous recruitment strategy.

Building succession and replacement plans is a process that begins with a needs assessment. This involves identifying the skill sets of the executive and leadership teams, and evaluating the employees who may be groomed for growth. From here, the key roles in which successors must be identified are listed. Talent review meetings are held with relevant employees and managers, and include a review of performance, competencies, developmental needs, and career goals. Development, training, or formal education plans are drafted and refined, with implementation tracked along a time line of milestones. Communication is key to successful succession plans; while the best-laid plans can go awry, the conversations and activities that take place in anticipation of turnover in key roles are much better than waiting to put out a skills gap fire.

Global Workforce Planning

It's a big, big world, with several opportunities to conduct business in the United States, outside of the United States, and on the playing field that is the Internet. Senior-level HR must have a good grasp of the impact planning has on global organization.

An international staffing plan will guide employers in estimating global employment needs. This will aid in creating talent acquisition strategies to recruit and select qualified talent using home country principles, with the added variable of global needs, cultures, and constraints thrown into the mix. In addition to the regular responsibilities the staffing process includes, HR for a multinational enterprise addresses expatriation, repatriation, and relocation services for a mobile workforce.

Industry-specific considerations on a global scale must be accounted for in a staffing plan. For example, the shortage of health care workers across the European Union has had a significant impact on the entire health care system. Issues such as recruiting talent, skills migration, training, and continued professional development have been the focus of joint action committees, resulting in plans such as the Action Plan for the EU Health Workforce. Member states join together to collaborate on solutions across borders, recognizing the benefits of cooperation to find shared solutions.

Some cultural obstacles may exist when staffing international assignments. *Ethnocentrism* is the belief that one culture is superior to another. In a company with an ethnocentric orientation, home country management practices may dominate strategies at the expense of a more localized view. A geocentric business and staffing strategy will take on a more *global mind-set*, one in which the company orients its international practices to best practices around the world.

The management and compliance with labor laws are also a consideration for international assignments. *Extraterritorial laws* may exempt foreign workers from local laws, such as is the case for the United States, which has jurisdiction over U.S. military personnel working overseas. Foreign diplomats also have *extraterritoriality*, where they are exempt from local laws. In some cases, the reverse is true. The *foreign compulsion exception* refers to a home country law that does not apply because it is in conflict with a host country practice.

Ethnocentrism

Belief that one's own culture is superior

The belief that one's own culture is the center of everything and other cultures are less effective or less important

Global Mind-Set

A worldview that embraces cultural diversity

A perspective that helps people understand and function successfully in a range of cultures, markets, and organizations

Extraterritorial Laws

Provisions whereby foreigners are sometimes exempt from local laws

Laws from one country that apply to that country's citizens when they travel or live in countries where they might be exempt from some local laws. Similar exceptions can apply to companies operating abroad.

Extraterritoriality

Being exempt from local law

Being exempt from the laws of the foreign country in which one is living (for example, foreign diplomats)

> **Foreign Compulsion Exception**
>
> *Exemption from a home country's law*
>
> When a law of an organization's home country does not apply because it is in conflict with laws of the country where the organization is doing business

Ethical Business Practices

Competing on an international scale does not perfectly mirror U.S. employment practices. Differences in compensation, leave laws, discrimination laws, and more must all be addressed country by country. *Multinational organizations* that wish to adopt a global ethics policy will find the *Caux principles* to be especially helpful. In 1994 a roundtable was convened to establish principles for responsible business conducted on a global scale. The seven principles are:

Principle 1—Respect stakeholders beyond shareholders Focuses on economic health and viability for all of those affected by the business. This includes acting in an honest and fair manner toward customers, employees, suppliers, competitors, and the community.

Principle 2—Contribute to economic, social, and environmental development Commits global businesses to address the needs of all three components. Economic, social, and environmental needs are dependent upon each other for sustainability; one is not more important than the other. This includes free and fair competition.

Principle 3—Build trust by going beyond the letter of the law Exhorts international business leaders to adhere to both the spirit and the letter of the law through candor and transparency.

Principle 4—Respect rules and conventions Focuses on respecting local customs, cultures, and traditions while staying true to the fundamental principles of fairness and equality.

Principle 5—Support responsible globalization Supports open and fair trade while lobbying for reform where necessary.

Principle 6—Respect the environment Defines responsible business acts as those that seek to maintain the sustainability of the environment and avoid the wasteful use of resources.

Principle 7—Avoid illicit activities All committed global business must not participate in illicit activities such as money laundering, terrorist activity, drug trafficking, and other corrupt practices.

The *Global Sullivan Principles* are another set of guidelines that promote corporate social responsibility. Prompted by the Reverend Leon H. Sullivan, the objectives are to acknowledge the universal human rights of employees, communities, and partners with which business is conducted. Fair compensation, safe and healthy workplaces, and competitive practices that are free from corruption are all principles of integrity promoted by the Global Sullivan Principles.

On a global scale, it is not advantageous to take only an American view of what is right or wrong. Ethical variance may occur as the result of cultural practices. *Ethnorelativism* is the ability to recognize that some behaviors are simply a function of culture, and not universal across countries. This concept suggests that what is right is simply what is acceptable at an individual or societal level. A principled reasoning approach takes into account not only the standards for business ethics, but also the very real consequences of trying to implement standards in societies that are less evolved. Consider countries in which child labor is the norm. For example, a multinational enterprise (MNE) discovers that there are underage workers in its factory, and needs to fire them in accordance with American and international labor standards. However, this solution may compromise an entire family's economic health, or, worse, send the child into a far riskier job such as prostitution. A principled reasoning approach includes taking steps to be ethically responsible using all available information as opposed to only compliance with a labor law.

Multinational companies cannot just look the other way at human rights violations, foreign corruption, child labor, and other fundamentals in corporate responsibility. While an ethical view may guide organizational behavior in this arena, many governments are taking on the task as well. Appendix A discusses in more detail the efforts of international trading blocs and agreements to identify ethical absolutes that should apply across all borders.

Regardless of whether voluntarily or compelled to do so, MNEs should create a global code of conduct that articulates their core values, ethical standards, corporate social responsibilities, and commitment to ethical business practices. In this, cultural sensitivity must be shown as well. Referencing only American law as opposed to the laws of many countries diminishes the likelihood of acceptance. Taking care to recognize the commonalities as opposed to only the differences will help align geographically separated business units with a single company identity.

Multinational Organization

A company operating in many countries

A company that has its headquarters in one country and has offices and operations in other countries; also known as a multinational corporation (MNC)

Caux Principles

Ethical guidelines for international organizations

A set of ethical principles developed for global organizations by the Caux Round Table, a group of global business leaders from around the world

Global Sullivan Principles

Rules for ethics and human rights

A voluntary set of rules to help an organization advance human rights and equality

Ethnorelativism

Understanding one culture in the context of other cultures

The ability to recognize different values and behaviors as cultural and not universal

Global Staffing Strategies

Senior HR professionals must understand how to identify global human capital requirements. Conducting supply, demand, and gap analyses are critical first steps to being a valuable global partner. Once understood, HR takes control of establishing methods for *global staffing* for *transnational corporations (TNCs)*.

With staffing shortages around the world, it is often necessary for companies to outsource, insource, and open source talent. Similar to open source software, this term was coined in the 2006 article "Wikinomics: How Mass Collaboration Changes Everything" by Tapscott and Williams. The authors discuss the influence and benefits of mass collaboration that occurs when employee work teams are connected with external networks. One example is that of user support and forums in which any member may answer a customer question, facilitated by an employee.

In addition to the expected language barriers that exist between nations, HR will need to account for culturally appropriate interviewing methods. In some cases, conducting interviews with both home and host country representatives is the best approach. HR may head a selection committee made up of representatives from the host country, home country, department, and other leadership. Ultimately, the candidate's preference must be considered before placement on an international assignment.

Global mobility refers to the practice of assigning international employees, which has many strategies for implementation. It will be important for HR to understand the length of the assignment in order to address any visa or work permit requirements of various countries to help determine what type of worker to staff the assignment with, and the immigration laws associated with the plan. Some strategies to consider are:

Ethnocentric An *ethnocentric staffing orientation* involves filling important positions in an international organization by choosing new hires from the country where the organization has its headquarters. Key positions are filled by personnel from the home country.

Geocentric An *geoocentric staffing orientation* is the practice of choosing the best employees for a job, regardless of their nationality or where the job is located. Key talent can come from any location.

Polycentric A *polycentric staffing orientation* involves recruiting host country nationals to manage subsidiaries in their own country, and recruiting parent country nationals to fill management positions at headquarters. Key nonmanagement talent is filled by local nationals.

Regiocentric A *regiocentric staffing orientation* focuses on recruitment and hiring of employees within a particular region with opportunities for interregional transfers. Key employees may circulate throughout regions.

Global Staffing

Worldwide employees

The process of identifying the number and type of employees an organization needs worldwide, and searching for the best candidates

Transnational Corporation (TNC)

Organization that operates globally, multinational enterprise

An organization whose operations, production, or service processes take place in more than one country and are interconnected

Global Mobility

International relocation

The transfer of employees from one part of the world to another

Ethnocentric Staffing Orientation

Filling key positions with employees from the headquarters' country

Filling important positions in an international organization by choosing new hires from the country where the organization has its headquarters

Geocentric Staffing Orientation

Management of global talent

The practice of choosing the best employees for a job, regardless of their nationality or where the job is located

Polycentric Staffing Orientation

Hiring citizens of the local country

Recruiting host country nationals to manage subsidiaries in their own country, and recruiting parent country nationals to fill management positions at headquarters

Regiocentric Staffing Orientation

Staffing policy for a particular geographic area

Focus on recruitment and hiring of employees within a particular region with opportunities for interregional transfers

There are several different types of international workers who are used to staff global assignments. They include:

Expatriates Also called *international assignees*, expats are home country nationals who move to another country to take an international assignment. Expats may be placed on short-term or *long-term assignments*, depending on the needs of the employer and the preferences of the employee. On returning home, they repatriate, often into a *permanent assignment*.

Host country nationals Host country nationals are those employees who are citizens working in their own country. They are also called local nationals.

Inpatriates *Inpatriates* are employees who are brought in from another country to work in the headquarters country for a period of time.

Parent country nationals Similar to expatriates, *parent country nationals* are employees who live and work abroad on international assignments.

Third-country nationals *Third-country nationals (TCNs)* are employees who are citizens of a country other than where headquarters or operations are based.

International Assignee

Expatriate employee

A person who moves to a new country to work on an international assignment

Long-Term Assignment

An expatriate job that is more than six months

A job in a different culture that lasts longer than six months, usually three to five years

Permanent Assignment

Regular or usual position

An employee's regular or usual job or position in a company

Inpatriate

An employee on assignment in the country of an organization's headquarters

A foreign employee who is on a work assignment in the country where an organization's headquarters are located

Parent Country Nationals

Citizens of the headquarters country

People who live and work abroad but are citizens of the country where an organization's headquarters are located

Third-Country National (TCN)

An expatriate who works for a company that is foreign in the host country

An expatriate who works for a foreign company that is located in the host country (for example, a French person working in China for a German company)

Once selected, how an international assignee is prepared for the assignment is the responsibility of HR to coordinate. Offering language and cultural training to the employee and family will help them acclimate more quickly to the new environment. Providing a host at the destination to answer questions will help the worker settle into the new culture and routines, increasing the odds of a successful expatriate placement. HR will assist employees with relocation services, helping them find temporary housing where necessary, shipping household goods, and finding appropriate schooling for dependent children where appropriate.

Once placed, having regular follow-up communication with the international assignee will ensure retention in the post. Including expatriates in home country training and development activities and allowing them to return home occasionally for company events where possible will keep them connected with home base.

Repatriation is the process of bringing an expat back to work in the home country or redeploying the worker to another country. In essence, it is an HR practice to successfully reintegrate the worker into his or her professional life, and help the employee and family readjust to living back at home. Repatriation is discussed in more detail in the next chapter, Human Resource Development.

In many cases, best HR practices for global staffing may be a blend of strategies and international assignments. Managing international talent also brings its own need for organizational guidelines. Planning for the intercultural needs of a blended workforce is an activity unto itself, and should not be approached using only American programs. Each culture across the world has its own set of social and behavioral etiquette. In Saudi Arabia, for example, public interaction between men and women is limited and it is polite to accept an offer of coffee or tea when first offered. Businesspeople entering the country will require a Saudi sponsor. The workday is organized around set prayer times five times a day.

Suggested Study or Organizational Audit Activities

- Conduct a job analysis for an existing job within your organization. Use https://www.onetonline.org to search for the occupation, and study the typical requirements. Compare the database information to the current tasks, duties, responsibilities, knowledge, skills, and abilities required. How are they different? What organizational elements are the reasons for the differences? Are they driven by organizational structure components or job design needs?
- Conduct a turnover analysis for each department within your organization. Compare the data to the company-wide turnover ratio. Are there any departments with a higher than average rate? If so, investigate the reasons and recommend solutions within the framework of workforce planning. If not, what does your company do to encourage retention?

- Apply the I-9 retention formula to all I-9s for separated employees within the past five years. Organize the forms by destroy date in a secure file or binder, and schedule for monthly review.
- Log on to www.uscis.gov/e-verify and watch the videos related to the e-verification process for new hires. Review the information through the eyes of employees, and note their rights should a tentative nonconfirmation be returned.
- Log on to the McKinsey & Company website, and search for the term "succession planning." Read through articles related to CEO succession and planning for the next generation of workers.

Notes

1. Jenny Che, "Why More Companies Are Eager to Hire People with Autism," *Huffington Post*, March 29, 2016.
2. McDonald's USA, LLC, a joint employer, et al., National Labor Relations Board.
3. *Ochoa, et al. v. McDonald's Corp., et al.*, N.D. Cal. No. 3:14-cv-02098-JD (N.D. Cal.).

References

Cable, D. M., and C. K. Parsons. 2001. "Socialization Tactics and Person-Organization Fit." *Personnel Psychology* 54(1): 1–23. Retrieved from http://search.proquest.com.portal.lib.fit.edu/docview/220134448?accountid=27313.

Dubin, Robert. 1976. *Handbook on Work, Organization and Society*. Skokie, IL: Rand McNally.

Tapscott, Don, and Anthony D. Williams. 2006. *Wikinomics: How Mass Collaboration Changes Everything*. New York: Portfolio.

Ulrich, D., and W. Brockbank. 2005. *The HR Value Proposition*. Boston: Harvard Business School Publishing.

4 | Human Resource Development

The Deliberately Developmental Organization

A New Paradigm for Twenty-First-Century Greatness

Andy Fleming

HR professionals would do well to look beyond twentieth-century models for guidance in building great organizations for this century and the next.

My purpose here is to briefly consider a widely accepted set of ideas related to people development and to raise two questions: Given the need for an ever-expanding set of capabilities to meet the stream of challenges organizations face today and will encounter tomorrow, how suitable is the twentieth-century model for organizations that aspire to greatness? Is there a new conceptual frame available to HR professionals and leaders in general that can better serve their organizations and people going forward?

The Twentieth-Century Talent Management Playbook

When it comes to growing people in their organizations, most human resources professionals today follow a playbook that we can trace back at least as far as the early 1980s to places like General Electric (GE) under the direction of famed CEO Jack Welch. The basic idea: identify and label a small percentage of your workforce as "high potential" and create special workshops and initiatives, usually including

(*continued*)

(continued)

some form of executive coaching, to accelerate the development of your "hi-po's" and perhaps other key leaders as well.

What are the problems with the core elements of this playbook? First, they provide people punctuated inputs, delivered from time to time rather than continuously. By themselves they may not occur often or intensely enough. Given how daunting the project is to help people grow in fundamental ways, the application of the intervention may be too thin.

Second, they constitute something extra—something beyond and outside the normal flow of work, an approach that raises the vexing problems of transfer and cost. Even if these activities support powerful learning in a context outside work, how do you ensure that employees transfer their new knowledge to the stubbornly durable context of business as usual? And how do you sustain the double costs of external inputs and employees' time away from the job?

Third, these types of programs are provided for only a few, generally 5 to 10 percent of employees, even though the volatile, uncertain, complex, and ambiguous (VUCA) world impacts work and workers at all levels of organizations. How does an organization improve continuously and sometimes reinvent itself without helping everyone grow? What's the impact of writing off the potential of 90 to 95 percent of your workers?

Finally, and above all, notice that the twentieth-century playbook makes the individual, and not the organization, the point of dynamic entry. If the organization wants to significantly impact people's capabilities, it should apparently find something new, outside the organization itself, some additive: give them a coach, a program, a course. The organization itself does not change. We might soup up the fuel through these additives, but the engine remains what it has always been.

The Deliberately Developmental Organization

Is there an alternative to this twentieth-century paradigm for growing people at work? Imagine so valuing the importance of developing people's capabilities that you design a culture that itself immersively sweeps every member of the organization into an ongoing developmental journey in the course of working every day.

Imagine making the organization itself—and not separate, extra benefits—the incubator of capability. Imagine hardwiring development into your bottom line so that, along with asking whether your culture is fostering the other elements of business success (such as profitability or the consistent quality of your offering), you ask—demand—that your culture as a whole, visibly and in the regular, daily operations of the company, be a continuous force on behalf of people overcoming their limitations and blind spots and improving their mastery of increasingly challenging work.

Imagine finding yourself in a trustworthy environment, one that tolerates—even prefers—making everyone's weaknesses public—from the C-suite to the front lines—so that you and your colleagues can support each other in the process of overcoming those weaknesses.

Table 4.1   Growing People at Work: Two Paradigms

	Twentieth Century	Twenty-First Century
Who	"High potentials" and key leaders	Everyone
How	Off-site workshops and executive coaching	Together at work
When	Special times	Every day

You're imagining an organization that, through its culture, is an incubator or accelerator of people's growth. In short, you're imagining a deliberately developmental organization (DDO).

It is beyond the scope of this article to describe the inner workings of such organizations, but they do exist in more than your or my imagination. And the results for the three DDOs that we discovered and researched for our 2016 book *An Everyone Culture: Becoming a Deliberately Developmental Organization* (recently named "Best Management and Workplace Culture Book of 2016" by 800-CEO-READ) speak for themselves. Over the past five years, Next Jump, an e-commerce company based in New York, cut turnover within its largely Millennial workforce from the industry average of 40 percent to single digits while regularly breaking company records for revenue, profits, productivity, and growth rate. Decurion, a Los Angeles–based manager of movie theaters (as well as real estate and senior living facilities) averages the highest gross per screen in the industry. And Bridgewater Associates, a Connecticut-based global investment firm, manages the world's largest and highest-performing hedge fund as measured over the past 20 years.

Since researching and writing our book, we've observed and sometimes worked with a growing number of organizations—in professional services, manufacturing, and high tech, from Atlanta to Silicon Valley to Australia and the Far East—that have also begun the journey toward the DDO idea themselves, perhaps attracted by the promise that organizations and all of their people can become the greatest resources for each other's flourishing.

From aiming to manage the talent of a select few to deliberately growing and unleashing the full capacity of everyone, perhaps a twenty-first-century playbook has already begun to emerge for HR professionals and other thoughtful organizational leaders.

Table 4.1 summarizes two paradigms for growing people at work.

About the Author

Andy Fleming is currently the CEO of Way to Grow Inc. and a contributing author for *An Everyone Culture: Becoming a Deliberately Developmental Organization* by Robert Kegan and Lisa Laskow Lahey (Harvard Business School Press, 2016). Portions of this article were adapted from that book.

Introduction

What if you develop your people, and they leave? The better question is: What if you don't develop your people, and they stay? Failing to address the changing needs of the company's human resources will result in lackluster performance (individual and company) and the loss of talented workers. Similarly, companies that wish to remain competitive must engage in organizational development (OD) activities to respond to the changing landscape of their markets. Overreliance on the status quo leads to stagnation, which leads to decline. The functional area of *human resource development (HRD)* addresses the HR competencies of people and *talent management* while employing OD interventions where appropriate. This includes application of learning concepts at both an individual level and an organizational level. Factors affecting the performance of these competencies include:

- Assessing the current and future skills needs of the organization, assessing the skill sets of the current workforce, and developing a plan to address the gaps
- Applying leadership and motivation theories to improve employee abilities, increase job satisfaction, and meet company goals
- Designing micro and macro interventions that address systemic conditions influencing organizational effectiveness
- Developing training and knowledge management programs that support company short- and long-term strategies
- Designing a talent management system that recognizes, rewards, and manages employee performance while addressing individual development needs and goals
- Integrating repatriation programs into HRD activities to address the needs of expatriates
- Managing knowledge programs and employees to retain key talent and minimize the impact of turnover

HRD

Human resource development

The part of human resource management that deals with training employees and giving them the skills they need to do their jobs both now and in the future

Talent Management

An approach to attract, develop, and keep skilled employees

The process of recruiting, integrating, and developing new workers, developing and keeping current workers, and attracting skilled workers

Employee Training

Training is an intervention strategy designed to impart knowledge, build skills, and change behavior. While not a fix-all, training activities are often an effective way to accomplish several different business objectives.

Training aligned with business strategies involves setting objectives that map directly to organizational goals. For example, a company with rapid growth plans may provide training for its salespeople on how to up-sell products to the existing customers. In other cases, a company may plan to offer new products or services, requiring training for employees on new or updated features and benefits. Some companies choose to compete through their training efforts, offering such to clients and customers and making it a revenue source that provides a regular return on investment (ROI).

Operationally, training is useful to help new hires learn their jobs. It is also an effective response plan for employees who are struggling in their duties and have performance gaps. For customers and third-party distributors, many organizations are providing videos on how to use their products.

Needless to say, any training initiative must spring from a very clear set of defined objectives. Often, this is achieved by starting with employee needs assessments.

Needs Assessments

While *needs analyses* are relevant in every aspect of human resource management, in this functional area this activity is related to identifying and establishing priorities in human resource development activities. *Development* concepts apply to both individuals and organizations. For this reason, a needs assessment may be focused on the needs of the employees, the needs of a job, or the needs of the business.

Employee needs These type of assessments focus on the individual training needs for employees related to the work they are doing in their current positions. Development needs may also be assessed to identify skills or abilities that the employee will have to possess to grow into future positions. Companies may also assess employee needs when deciding whom to select for training. Methods to gather information about employee needs include surveys, face-to-face interviews, formal tests, job records, and simple observation of employee performance.

Job needs In instructional design, a task analysis is conducted to create training objectives by comparing the needs of the job with the abilities of the employees. Depending on the findings, training may seek to impart procedural directions, such as writing and training standard operating procedures (SOPs). Other times the training objectives may focus on organizational structures through job design activities. Tools used for assessing job needs include focus and discussion groups, performance against benchmarks, on-the-job observation, and work instruction reviews.

Company needs Performance targets, dashboards, and scorecards help employers identify what is working and what is not working. Assessments of organizational training and development needs will attempt to target any deficiencies and build on strengths while shaping future needs at a strategic level; identifying the knowledge, skills, and abilities needed for meeting future needs will drive training and development plans. An *HR audit* may be used to take a macro look of the needs of the entire workforce. Other measures such as turnover and retention analysis and studies of employee *absenteeism* rates help employers identify where HR interventions may be appropriate.

Needs Analysis

Assessment to determine next steps

Assessing the present situation to determine the steps necessary to reach a desired future goal

Development

Event, happening, occurrence

Something that happens or has happened, or the act of making or improving something

HR Audit

Assessment of an organization's human resources

An evaluation of the strengths, weaknesses, and development needs of human resources required for organizational performance

Absenteeism

Not coming to work

Not coming to work because of illness or personal problems. Many companies calculate the rate of absenteeism of their employees, which is the average number of days they do not come to work.

At the core of needs assessment are methodologies used to collect and interpret data so that a course of action, called interventions, may be developed. In a training needs assessment, an employer may wish to work backward by first identifying the desired skills, behaviors, or objectives of training, and then designing a program around those needs. A gap analysis is the tool of choice for HR in accomplishing these objectives. Measuring employee, job, or organizational performance against those desired objectives follows next. The third step involves creating an intervention strategy, which addresses the gap between current and future states. This third step is where exploring solutions and calculating costs are very important tasks. From these first three steps of a needs analysis, HR should be prepared to recommend a course of action for approval, implement the intervention, and establish tools to measure program success.

Needs That Motivate

There are many theories on how employees can be motivated to perform at their optimum levels; these theories are covered in greater detail shortly. At the heart of many motivational theories is the ability to truly understand employee and company needs. Needs as a training benchmark also increase *employee engagement* in training outcomes. Compare this to a salesperson pitching a product to you. Successful salespeople identify first what you are looking for, and then seek solutions that meet your needs. When this occurs, you feel satisfied and happy with the exchange. When it doesn't occur, you may feel that the salesperson completely ignored your needs. In some cases, such as compliance training, this approach isn't possible. But any sort of development activity should seek to build outcomes that are customized solutions for employee success. Instructional designers know that the "What's in it for me?" question must be answered for training to have impact.

Other factors such as individual internal drivers, external conditions, and the type and quality of work being performed should also be taken into consideration when seeking to influence the employee performance through training and development activities. Similarly to hiring for fit—where HR attempts to match the characteristics of a person to the characteristics of the job—leaders must make the effort to tap into the internal and external needs of their employees when designing HRD programs.

> One of these things is not like the other: A patient goes to his eye doctor complaining that he can't see. The eye doctor takes off his own glasses and hands them to the patient, saying, "There, that should be better." This, of course, is ineffective, simply because the need of the patient is not identical to the need of the doctor. The employment relationship is similar: HR leaders must understand the unique needs of both the employee and the company, and then tailor development activities toward maximizing employee or organizational performance. In some cases, an assessment may discover that training is not the proper intervention strategy.

> **Employee Engagement**
>
> *Level of satisfaction with work*
>
> A measurement of employees' involvement, satisfaction, happiness, and loyalty with their employment (how hard they work and how long they stay with their organization)

HRD takes into account all of the aforementioned, and then some. Human resource professionals (HRPs) must be able to apply insights from information and conduct activities that develop/select and implement employee training programs. We start from the top by looking at the unique needs of company leaders.

Leadership Development

Leadership is a discipline in which managers must influence and direct the efforts of others in order to get things done. Leadership is a people-relationship activity in that it requires followers in order to achieve outcomes. In order to gather followers, one must understand what people need, share the vision, take personal responsibility for outcomes, and, most important, be able to lead change efforts.

> **Leadership**
>
> *A management ability*
>
> The ability to influence other people or groups to achieve a goal

Leadership Theories

Whether leaders are born or made has been the subject of psychology and the social sciences for hundreds of years. In this context, a few of the better-known theories about what makes great leaders tick are the following:

Great man The great man theory of leadership is built upon the belief that there is a biological predisposition to leaders: leaders are born, not made. Embedded in literature and history as traditionally male heroes, the great man theory has been applied to the likes of Abraham Lincoln and Julius Caesar. This type of leadership theory in general is not widely accepted any longer due in large part to the evolution of research on the subject.

Trait-based Trait-based theories of leadership sought to identify a certain set of characteristics that leaders had in common. Searching for correlations between leadership ability and traits such as intelligence, optimism, or self-confidence, these theories eventually concluded that there was not a single set of predictable characteristics to apply to the identification of leaders.

Behavior-based Emerging from the early attempts at leadership trait identification came the behavior-based theories. In these theories researchers began to look at what leaders do as opposed to who they are. These theories suggest that anyone can be a leader if they simply adopt certain behaviors.

Contingency/situational *Contingent* means dependent on, so in the case of contingency theories, a leader's behavior is driven by situational variables. These theories emphasize that there is no one trait or set of behaviors that will define leadership effectiveness, but rather that effective leaders learn to adapt their responses to what is necessary at the time.

The Leadership Grid

Blake and Mouton of the University of Texas provided leadership theories with a measurement tool called the Leadership Grid. It is built on two criteria: the concern for people and the concern for production (results). The grid is built as a 9×9 matrix with 1 indicating low concern and 9 reflecting high concern. There are five possible combination scores using the grid:

    1/1—low concern for production, low concern for people
    1/9—low concern for production, high concern for people
    5/5—moderate concern for production, moderate concern for people
    9/1—high concern for production, low concern for people
    9/9—high concern for production, high concern for people

HR can plot managers and create development strategies based on their strengths and weaknesses, and design training and development plans in alignment with company needs. Take a look at Figure 4.1 for a sample.

Leadership Styles

Different types of organizations require different types of managers. With the evolution from production-based manufacturing to more relationship-driven services, there is a place for every leadership style. However, an improper fit can create challenges that ultimately affect outcomes, such as employee job satisfaction, productivity, quality, and even a hostile work environment. For this reason, HR must understand the company culture, the nature of the work, and the leadership

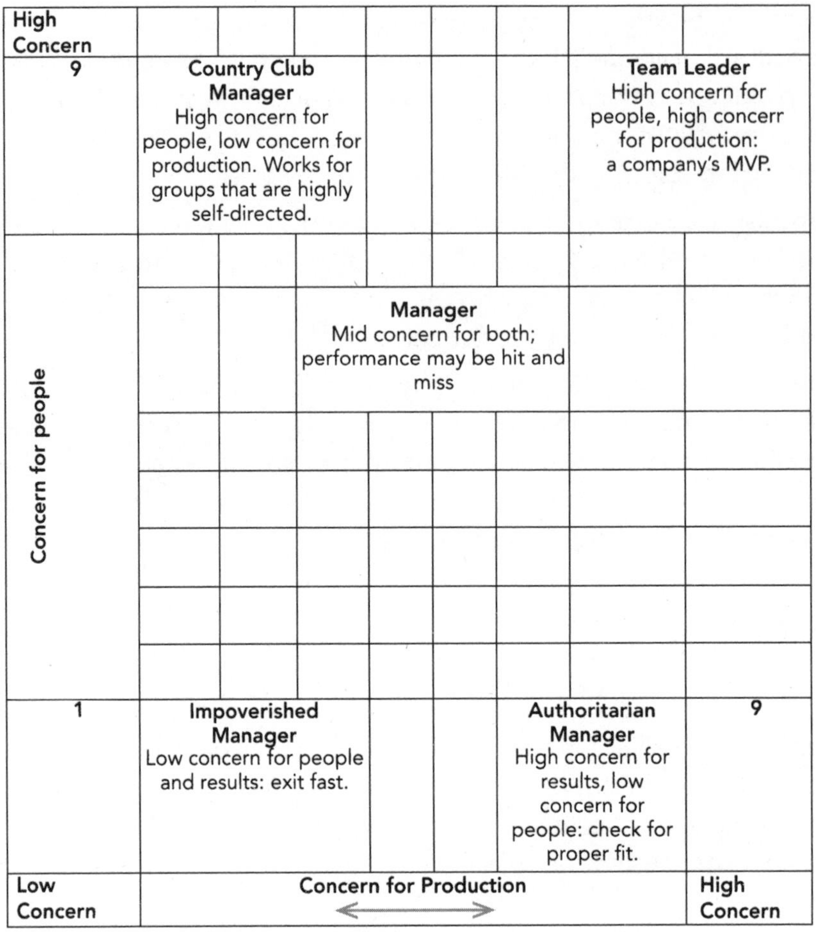

High Concern								
9	**Country Club Manager** High concern for people, low concern for production. Works for groups that are highly self-directed.					**Team Leader** High concern for people, high concern for production: a company's MVP.		
			Manager Mid concern for both; performance may be hit and miss					
1	**Impoverished Manager** Low concern for people and results: exit fast.			**Authoritarian Manager** High concern for results, low concern for people: check for proper fit.				9
Low Concern			Concern for Production ←——————→				High Concern	

Concern for people (vertical axis label)

Figure 4.1   Mapping Board for Blake and Mouton's Leadership Grid
Source: Adapted from Robert Blake and Jane Mouton, "*The Managerial Grid*, 1964," in S. Crainer (Ed.), *The Ultimate Business Library* (Hoboken, NJ: John Wiley & Sons, 2003).

styles of individual managers. While company culture and job context are covered in other chapters, leadership styles include:

Authoritarian Authoritarian leaders are effective in situations in which there is a high level of insecurity or critical decisions that must be made and followed quickly. If productivity goals are the highest priority, an authoritarian leader may be the best solution.

Laissez-faire The term *laissez-faire* roughly translates from French to English as "let do." These types of leaders let their people operate in large part without them. This leadership style is effective in environments where the employees are highly skilled, motivated, or self-directed. Its success is highly dependent on a job design that allows for a great degree of autonomy.

Transactional This leadership style focuses on getting the job done using "this for that" or "do this to avoid that" exchange techniques. Transactional leaders look for what is not getting done, and engage in reward and punishment activities to achieve outcomes.

Transformational These types of leaders are more focused on the people relationships. Effectiveness of these leaders is often built upon a shared vision, with the manager facilitating and leading the effort necessary to accomplish the objectives.

Leadership development and coaching should be aligned to elements of the business strategy, including the mission, vision, and values. This helps HR put the right leaders in the right roles for maximum effectiveness. Factors that influence both motivation and leadership are discussed next.

Global Leadership and Organizational Behavior Effectiveness (GLOBE)

It's interesting to note that as globalization of the workforce has evolved, the Western leadership models just discussed may not be as relevant. The GLOBE study on leadership was aimed at identifying global leadership characteristics to help multinational enterprises (MNEs) manage across cultures. The original 2004 study used more than 200 researchers across 62 countries; in 2014, 70 researchers collected data from a variety of industries in 24 countries. Consistent to both findings were the impact a society's culture has on the effectiveness of leaders, and the need for senior leadership styles to match the expectations of the cultures within which they perform. Additionally, the transformational leadership style works across cultures, with the most important characteristics being visionary and inspirational leadership, acting with integrity, and a strong performance orientation. The GLOBE research supported the hypothesis that a better fit of the CEO to societal expectations correlated with stronger firm performance.

These findings are very instructive for international HR management practitioners. They show that the need to conduct leadership assessments along with coaching leaders on assignment in a different culture is imperative for successful organizational outcomes.

Additionally, being selected for an international assignment is attractive as a development opportunity for many employees. Building development criteria for a competent global HR professional should include a 50,000-foot view of global market trends and a clear idea of the business strategy for the relevant assignment location. On a more operational and individual level, transnational competencies should include the ability to effectively interact with a diverse group of people, and having a natural curiosity about life and business in general.

Intrinsic versus Extrinsic Motivators

Recall the concepts in Chapter 2 related to strategic planning. One of the activities supported by HR is the analysis of internal and external forces that act upon an organization, prompting movement. So it is also with individual behavior. Forces from within, also called intrinsic motivators, will cause a person to move in a certain direction. Extrinsic forces may also apply performance pressure to an employee, driving actions. *Intrinsic rewards* come from high levels of job satisfaction, *empowerment*, and a sense of purpose that is the result of the work the employee is accomplishing. *Extrinsic* motivators are served by salary bumps and titles. Both are served well when a manager provides *instant awards* and sincere performance feedback.

Leadership Development

Activities that enhance leadership performance

Investment in programs to help current leaders become more effective and to build future leaders

Intrinsic Rewards

Nonmaterial satisfaction

Nonmaterial motivation that comes from personal satisfaction (for example, job status, job satisfaction, or human interest)

Extrinsic Rewards

Measurable recognition

Work or actions where the motivating factors are material and are measured through monetary benefits, grades, prizes, and praise

Empowerment

Authorized to make decisions

The ability for employees to manage their work, share information, and make decisions without close supervision

Instant Awards

Immediate employee recognition

Rewards for employees that are provided immediately after the desired behavior is produced

Locus of Control

The term *locus* means point or location. People's locus of control is the point or location of their beliefs about how well they can control what happens to them. Individuals with an internal or high locus of control believe that their actions determine what happens to them—they are large and in charge. Employees and managers with a low or external locus of control believe that what happens to them is the result of luck, chance, or other outside factors—they believe they have very little effect on the world around them.

Attitudes and Leadership/Motivation

Before we get to the next section's review of the most widely accepted theories of motivation, one theory belongs in this leadership section. Developed by Douglas McGregor, Theory X and Theory Y explain the differences in leadership beliefs about employees. Theory X managers believe that as a general rule employees are lazy and unmotivated and do not like to work. The only meaningful motivation techniques are fear, direction, and punishment. Theory X managers tend to be more task-oriented than people-oriented. Theory Y managers are the exact opposite. They expect employees to fundamentally want to do their best, and that they—the managers—really need to give them a reason to care about what they do. Theory Y managers are more likely to be people-centered.

It may be appropriate to mention here that HR has a responsibility to match leaders to the right role within the organization. Factors such as personality, attitude, and task versus people orientation are all to be considered when hiring, retaining, and coaching leaders. An operational role may be better suited for individuals who are highly task-oriented and where direct control over processes or people is necessary to get the job done. Collaborative roles are better suited to leaders who must rely on others, such as in a matrix organizational structure described in the Business Management and Strategy chapter. Still others may excel in leadership roles in which advisory responsibilities are most important, such as human resource managers. In this role, people skills and the ability to influence outcomes through knowledge, integrity, and excellence are the characteristics of successful leadership. Emerging theories such as what is described in Rath and Conchie's book *Strengths Based Leadership* build on the idea that effective leaders focus on strengths—their own and their employees'. By focusing on strengths, work can be framed around what employees do best, rather than trying to train, coach, or discipline an employee to use less developed skills

(*continued*)

> (*continued*)
>
> or aptitudes. In many cases, leadership coaching will be required to help supervisors transition from the more traditional, authoritarian methods of managing employee performance to the twenty-first century's strengths-based, employee-owned skill and career development practices of today's workplace.

Leadership Coaching

HR is responsible to provide *coaching* to managers and executives on how to manage their people resources using leadership concepts and applications. Executive coaching is a formal system to counsel managers and new supervisors regarding the skills necessary to perform well. Different from employee coaching, management coaches are typically sourced from outside the company. Generally beginning with a leadership assessment (often including a 360-degree assessment), a coaching program seeks to build outcomes that meet the unique needs of those with high degrees of responsibilities. Topics such as strategic thinking, change leadership, leadership style, interpersonal skills, and working through others for results are common topics for executive coaching sessions.

Motivation theories and leadership theories are closely linked, as getting employees to successfully perform and follow the leader requires advanced skills that may be learned. In order for HR practitioners to help develop managers, they must understand and be able to apply the different theories of leadership to development efforts. In addition, HR may need to teach managers about these theories to help them begin to understand the people they are responsible for supervising. For this reason we explore theories of motivation next.

Coaching

Guiding, giving information, or training

A method of developing specific skills in which a coach gives information and objective feedback to a person or group

Theories of Motivation

Understanding how adults are motivated to perform is critical information for leaders seeking to accomplish work through others. Traditional methods of authoritarian leadership are no longer relevant in many organizational designs. Companies of today have a highly diverse workforce with motivating needs varying from money (see the Compensation and Benefits chapter) to recognition, career opportunities, development (Human Resource Development), interesting work (Workforce Planning and Employment), personal risk factors (Risk Management), and the psychological influence of personality characteristics. A one-size-fits-all approach to motivating employees simply does not work. This section introduces fundamental principles of *motivation* techniques designed to influence supervisor success, employee productivity, and overall job satisfaction.

Motivation

Inspiration for action

Reasons or influences that lead to specific desired behavior such as commitment to a job or continuing efforts to achieve a goal

Scientific Management—Frederick Taylor

To the sciences we go! In this theory, Taylor believed that people could be managed by using principles of engineering such as work design. Standardizing and breaking jobs down into their simplest forms for completion by the human machine could drive productivity. Building out clear work instructions and training employees could reduce the margin of error. Many also consider Taylor's work as the origin of employee meal and rest breaks. During Taylor's observations of his workers, he realized that if given the opportunity to physically rest, the employees came back and were more productive than before.

Other observations led to an understanding that an employee's working conditions could be motivators. This meant that it was in the employer's best interest to provide things like safety, lighting, and the availability of proper tools and equipment. See the feature to review an interesting social experiment that took place at the Chicago plant of Hawthorne Works that expanded upon Taylor's theories.

THE HAWTHORNE EFFECT

Between 1924 and 1932, the social scientist Elton Mayo conducted a series of experiments in which employee working conditions were manipulated. The goal was to put Frederick Taylor's theories on scientific management to work. What Mayo found was that, indeed, when better lighting was installed, employee productivity improved. However, when the experiment ended, so also did the increased productivity, even though the better conditions remained. This was later dubbed the Hawthorne Effect when researchers realized that it was the effect of

(continued)

> (continued)
> management paying attention to employees and the awareness of the employees that they were being studied that drove the behaviors. This is relevant in coaching managers on how to motivate workers by giving them time and attention, and also in the context of job analysis and design methods discussed in the Workforce Planning and Employment chapter. Employees who know they are being observed will modify their behaviors.

Job Characteristics Model—Hackman and Oldman

In 1975, Hackman and Oldman built upon prior work that described the influence of the job on employee levels of productivity. These researchers found that how the work is organized and the dimensions of job characteristics had a direct influence on employee performance. The characteristics included:

Task identity Employees who know the whole as opposed to operating in a vacuum of parts seem to experience higher levels of job satisfaction. It offers a sense of achievement when people have the opportunity to complete a task from start to finish and have a line of sight to how they contribute to the bigger picture.

Task significance Employees who feel good about what they put in eight hours producing have a sense of contribution that can be a strong motivator of performance. The impact that work has on other people, such as that performed by nurses, nonprofit employees, and educators, can have a significant impact on employee fulfillment.

Skill variety The ability to use multiple skill sets in work contributes to a sense of jobs being meaningful and important.

Note that these first three skills all contribute to employees feeling they are engaged in meaningful work. These next two job characteristics give employees a sense of responsibility and ownership over the outcomes:

Autonomy The extent to which employees are allowed to use independent judgment gives them the sense that management trusts them and believes in their talent.

Feedback Feedback gives employees the information they need to improve performance, or keep on doing what they are doing. Some employees and personality types require more feedback than others do.

The job characteristics model states that employee productivity is a function of job design more than of internal or external motivators. This theory was supported by a 2012 U.S. Merit Systems Board study of federal employees. The study found that all five of Hackman and Oldman's job characteristics directly influenced the motivation and productivity levels of federal workers.

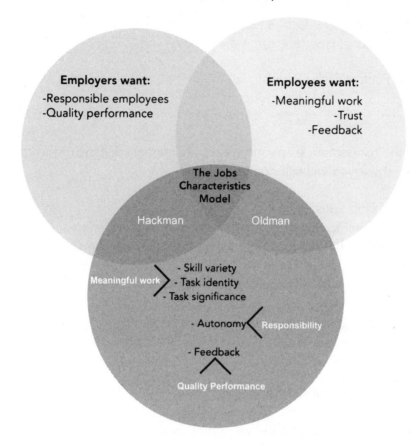

Figure 4.2   Hackman and Oldman's Job Characteristics

Figure 4.2 describes in more detail the characteristics and the relationships between these five factors.

Frederick Herzberg—Motivator Hygiene Theory

Beginning with a 1950s study of jobs, this two-factor theory of motivation worked from the hypothesis that the causes of job satisfaction would be the opposite of the causes of job dissatisfaction. For example, if high-paying jobs are satisfiers, then low-paying jobs must be dissatisfiers. Herzberg's studies disproved this hypothesis, finding that job satisfaction and job dissatisfaction are not opposites and are not on a continuum; they are independent of one another. This means that remedying job dissatisfiers will not lead to job satisfaction, and adding causes of job satisfaction will not eliminate dissatisfaction.

Building upon the work of Taylor, Hackman, and Oldman, Herzberg found that motivators result from intrinsic factors such as recognition, achievement, and personal growth; hygiene factors result from extrinsic factors such as pay, benefits, and work conditions. Here are some examples:

Hygiene Factors (Job Dissatisfiers)
- An employee is being harassed at work.
- An employee is being paid low wages.

Even if the harassment stops and wages are increased, if the motivators are not present the employee will still not be satisfied.

Motivators (Job Satisfiers)
- An employee is recognized for her contributions and effort.
- An employee has access to professional development opportunities.

If an employee loves the work but is treated poorly, the employee will not be satisfied.

So, the ultimate goal in a work environment is to eliminate job dissatisfaction by removing hygiene factors and increasing job satisfaction by introducing motivators.

B. F. Skinner—Operant Conditioning

Skinner's operant conditioning theory of motivation was centered on the idea that individual behavior can be shaped and anticipated through reward and punishment actions. This was based on his experiments in which he either created or reversed a behavior through scheduled interventions of reward (recognition, food, money) and punishment (removal of a desired condition, strong consequences). In the context of worker productivity, this means that an organization should seek to institute a program of response that goes beyond the basics of a paycheck and discipline. Regular feedback, either negative or positive, is one example.

To help understand this concept, consider how you would behave in a public parking lot if the ticket kiosk failed to deliver the required parking permit—when you push the button for the stub, nothing happens. Because you have been conditioned to expect a certain reward for pushing the button, you push it again, perhaps harder this time. If that doesn't work, you might pound on the button with increasing force. In other words, the absence of the expected reward initially causes an increase in the frequency and force of behavior, and no small amount of stress about what to do next. Skinner would suggest that in order to "reprogram" this behavior, the absence of the reward must be consistently delivered.

In the work context of change and motivation, employees rarely change behavior on demand; they must instead be reconditioned to behave in a certain way through either reward, punishment, or the avoidance of punishment. Concepts to understand in operant conditioning include:

Positive reinforcement An act by the employer in which rewards are used to influence employee behavior. An example would be pay-for-performance programs.

Negative reinforcement An act by the employee in which he or she behaves in a certain way to avoid an unpleasant consequence. An example would be an employee showing up to work on time to avoid discipline.

Punishment An employee in training receives a sharp reprimand for holding side conversations during the facilitator's presentation.

It's important to understand that these early scientific theories of motivation and job design such as Taylor and Skinner were driven by research and observation of the prevalent industries of the times—manufacturing, production, and coal energy. Many of these jobs were easily organized into repetitive tasks with countable outputs. As the economy and industries have shifted and changed, the social sciences, industrial-organizational (I-O) psychology, and sciences related to organizational behavior have responded. Research related to employee needs such as managing expectations and change, the desire for a sense of belonging and meaningful work, and the need for personal growth are all areas that have proper scientific theories behind them. A few of these are explored next.

Maslow's Hierarchy of Needs

The pyramid of needs represented by Abraham Maslow has its roots in humanistic psychological principles. Maslow's hierarchy reflects that all human beings have needs, and suggests that certain needs must be met before other needs will be consciously or unconsciously considered. The base of the pyramid is physiological needs. This implies that people's hunger or thirst needs must be satisfied before they will seek to satisfy the next level of need, which is safety. Safety needs include the need for shelter from both physical and emotional harm. From safety, the pyramid moves up into the social needs of belonging and acceptance by peers or managers. This is followed by the need to satisfy the esteem needs in which people wish to feel as though they are valued and respected. Finally, when other needs are satisfied, an employee may seek to satisfy the need for self-actualization, or a sense of purpose and fulfillment through their own actions and choices.

David McClelland's Acquired Needs Theory

McClelland's theory of motivation centered on the premise that individuals are motivated by three characteristics: achievement, affiliation, and power. Figure 4.3 describes sample behavior of employees within each category. Note that some

Achievement	Affiliation	Power
• Has a strong need to set and accomplish challenging goals. • Takes calculated risks to accomplish goals. • Likes to receive regular feedback on progress and achievements. • Often likes to work alone.	• Wants to belong to the group. • Wants to be liked, and will often go along with whatever the rest of the group wants to do. • Favors collaboration over competition. • Doesn't like high risk or uncertainty.	• Wants to influence others. • Likes to win arguments. • Enjoys competition and winning. • Enjoys status and recognition.

Figure 4.3   McClelland's Acquired Needs Theory

employees may share characteristics of combined categories. For example, one employee may be highly achievement oriented but also enjoys the feedback and esteem of her peers. She would map more toward the right side of the achievement column, closest to the affiliation column. Similarly, an employee who demonstrates a strong need to be in charge but knows he must get work done through others may present to the left side of the power column, closest to affiliation.

McClelland's theory seems to be in direct contrast to Skinner's in that McClelland believed individuals are motivated from within (intrinsic), whereas Skinner believed that employees are motivated by external factors (extrinsic).

Victor Vroom's Expectancy Theory

Vroom, a professor at Yale University, is credited with the development of the expectancy theory of motivation. His work is built upon the premise that employees *choose* to behave in a certain way, dependent upon their expectations. The level of effort (motivation) an employee will apply depends on the expected outcome and whether the employee believes the outputs are worth the inputs. The three terms used to explain his theory are:

Expectancy People's belief that if they work hard, their performance will be high. It is the degree of effort that drives the outcome.

Instrumentality Performance is considered instrumental when it leads to a certain outcome; the performance is the instrument used to achieve an outcome.

Valence The term *valence* can be related to the meaning of the term *value*, in that employees perform well when they highly value an outcome, and perform less well when an outcome is less valued. Valence is different for every employee, as employees have different needs.

PUTTING THE THEORIES TOGETHER IN THE WORKPLACE

Most people are much too complex to assume that a single theory can explain their behavior. Let's suggest that a sales employee who is paid on commission is asked to attend classroom training on harassment prevention. Normally, the employee enjoys the opportunity to engage with his coworkers as he is motivated by McClelland's affiliation need to engage with others. While the training is on an interesting topic and is required by company policy, the employee also needs to be on the phone or out in the field selling or he will not make the rent payment on his apartment. In this case, the employee's security needs reflected on Maslow's hierarchy will not allow him to be highly motivated to attend and participate in training. It may take an intervention from Skinner's theories to either reward him for attending or discipline him for not showing up to actually drive his behavior to attend and, more important, have an attitude that allows him to learn from the training.

Instructional Design

A systems approach to training programs is at the core of instructional design theories. Designing effective training programs from the ground up can be daunting, especially if the needs are not clearly understood. Instructional design methods address all of the moving targets present in training programs: the needs of the people, the needs of the company, and the training sessions themselves. Put all together, formal methods and academic theories of program design, development, delivery, and evaluation can be studied, all in the pursuit of a *transfer of learning*.

Transfer of Learning

Sharing knowledge and information from one person or place to another

The continuous exchange of information, knowledge, and skills from one context to another

The ADDIE Model

The development of training programs is a critical skill set for all HR professionals, and it goes beyond simply conducting the training sessions. Instructional design models, such as ADDIE (analysis, design, development, implementation, and evaluation), are tools HR may use to guide design efforts. The stages of assessment, design, development, implementation, and evaluation are explored next.

Analysis

The needs analysis techniques reviewed in an earlier section—including a review of leadership skills to identify training and development needs—describe the knowledge, tasks, and tools for this stage of the *ADDIE model*. The information gathered through careful data analysis gives HR the information necessary to begin designing an effective program that addresses root causes of employees' and leaders' behaviors. In some cases, an assessment of the potential *trainees* may uncover special participant needs. Language barriers requiring material *translation*, shift schedules needing accommodation, technical skills gaps that have to be addressed first, and reading and writing levels all may be identified at this stage. The needs assessment is all about gathering and analyzing information through interviews, observations, documentation, and simply asking the employees what they need.

An effective assessment may also discover that training is not the proper intervention technique.

ADDIE Model

A training design technique

A process for designing training programs that has five steps: analysis, design, development, implementation, and evaluation

Trainee

A person learning skills for a certain job

A person who is learning and practicing the necessary skills for a particular job

Translation

Interpreting text from one language to another

Changing a message from one language to another while keeping the meaning

Design

Think of the design stage of a new home. The decision to start shopping for a new house is usually driven from need: the need for more bedrooms, the need to live in a safer area, or the need to be close to good schools. Once the decision to build a new home is made, an architect may be selected to draw up plans. These plans include the layout of the new home, the size of garage desired, and any specialized services that need to be subcontracted. Cost estimates are researched and compared with options submitted for final consideration and approval.

The design stage of ADDIE is a planning stage that builds out training objectives in direct relationship to the findings of the needs analysis. Once the training objectives are identified, delivery methods, target markets, vendor selection, and cost comparisons are made. HR may be asked to research the engagement of a professional instructional designer. HR may also need to research off-the-shelf products, or to tailor programs with a little bit of original material and a little bit of best practice sources. *Licensing* and issues of *proprietary* ownership must be evaluated and respected.

The focus of any training program is on the transfer of training, so a wish list of job tasks or responsibilities, people skills, or abilities is created at this stage for mapping in the next stage: content development.

Customized training is content that is built from scratch to address specific learning outcomes. *Tailored* training is existing or off-the-shelf content that is modified for a better fit.

Licensing

Giving permission to use, produce, or sell

A written contract in which the owner of a trademark or intellectual property gives rights to a licensee to use, produce, or sell a product or service

Proprietary

Relating to an owner or ownership

Rights of property ownership relating to key information, materials, or methods developed by an organization

---

Develop

This is the phase in which curriculum is built and training materials such as manuals and facilitator's guides begin to take shape. Off-the-shelf products are evaluated for objective fulfillment and degree to which the product can be customized. Time and other resource commitments are evaluated. Metrics, such as pretests and posttests, participant surveys, the use of control groups for results comparisons, and on-the-job results, are considered in the development of program deliverables.

Using the house-building analogy, program delivery mechanisms are identified that will serve as conduits that carry the training material to the participants. There are several *training methods* to select from, and all have merit:

Classroom-based In a more traditional method of delivering training, participants gather together outside of their department in a classroom. The room is set up with the relevant tools of the training trade: audiovisual equipment, whiteboard, easel, projector, and screen. Tables and chairs are organized to improve learning outcomes. Classroom training is best for smaller groups made up of participants who all need the same training, such as harassment prevention training that is legally compliant with the Civil Rights Act of 1964 and state laws.

Self-paced programs You will learn in a few pages about how adults learn, and one element is that adults are generally self-directed. This is because their focus is problem centered as opposed to concept centered. Self-paced programs give participants a sense of control over when they complete the training. It allows their minds to focus on what is most important to them while taking in the whole content through to completion.

Virtual classrooms Technology has greatly contributed to the rise and convenience of virtual classroom environments. Ranging from databases housing information for access by employees as needed to highly interactive computer simulations, this type of training program delivery has received a lot of attention in recent years. A virtual classroom uses collaboration software to engage the instructor with students, and the students with other participants, often using *distance learning* techniques. Virtual classrooms are characterized by discussion boards, videos, simulation exercises, case studies, and PowerPoint slides. *Synchronous* training occurs in real time with the instructor and participants all online at the same time. *Asynchronous* training is when the student and instructor are not in the virtual classroom at the same time, such as in a self-paced online program. Sometimes, these programs are accessed online, a form of *e-learning* without the need for additional software.

Microlearning Characterized by short bursts of content delivery, often through the use of videos, microlearning seeks to narrowly target learning objectives for maximum effect. An advantage of building microlearning videos is that an online training library may be built for employees (or customers) to access at any time. Modifying training content is logistically easier as well, as a short, 3-minute video should be easier to refine than a mixed-content 30-minute training session.

Training Method

A way of helping people learn

A way of communicating skills and knowledge (for example, classroom training, distance learning, online training, and on-the-job training)

Distance Learning

Remote teaching method

A method of education that uses TV, audiotapes or videotapes, computers, and the Internet, instead of traditional classroom teaching where students are physically present with their teacher

Synchronous Learning

An online teaching method

A type of e-learning in which participants interact without a time delay, which requires them to attend at specific times

Asynchronous Learning

An online teaching method

A teaching method where the students and teachers are online at different times

E-Learning

Online training or education

A method of education where students attend classes on a computer or on the Internet

Blended programs In blended programs, a combination of methods may be used to deliver training. The benefits of *blended learning* include reinforcement of the key concepts over time and in multiple modes using *distributed training* methods. Blended learning outcomes can be adapted for time, with part of the curriculum done digitally while the instructor is working with others, or prior to the classroom session. From a training evaluation perspective, training delivered at least partially online or via software allows for better data collection using both pretests and posttests that can be consistently delivered to all participants and compared over time.

On-the-job training (OJT) Some training programs make the most sense to be conducted on the job. Training participants *job shadow* a worker who is performing the tasks needing to be learned. This can be particularly useful when standard procedures must be followed. Challenges to OJT include trainees learning poor habits from the trainer, so HR should be sure to follow up to evaluate the efficacy of this training method.

Blended Learning

A mix of different types of learning

A learning method that combines face-to-face teaching with online learning

Distributed Training

A method of instruction over time and distance

A method of training that allows instructors, students, and content to be located in different places. This type of training can be used together with a traditional classroom, or it can be used to create virtual classrooms.

On-the-Job Training (OJT)

Receiving instruction while working

Acquiring knowledge, practical skills, and competencies while engaged in daily work

Job Shadowing

Observing another person's work practices

Learning a new job by watching another employee work

Implement

It's now time to build the house. This stage involves delivering the training that was developed in the previous step to the target audience identified during the planning stage. Activities involved at this stage may include preparing the trainer, preparing the learner, and preparing the selected environment.

Evaluate

All HRPs tasked with training delivery and design should be familiar with standard evaluation methods referenced earlier, such as gathering employee feedback about the training, and using the design stage of ADDIE to bake in components that can be measured, such as pretests and posttests of training content.

Other Instructional Design Models

While ADDIE continues to be a reliable instructional design model, the multitude of variables associated with successful training design suggests that the one-size-fits-all assumptions of ADDIE may no longer be sufficient. For this reason, project-based methods have emerged to address the ever-changing environments affected by factors such as e-learning, collaboration, and a global audience.

In the article titled "Methodology Wars: ADDIE vs. SAM vs. AGILE," the author describes the AGILE (align, get set, iterate and implement, leverage, and evaluate) model as one that focuses on "sprints," where design teams collaborate to build silos of learning content that are completed prior to moving on to the next training module (Russell 2015). The approach is repeatedly applied to chunks of content as opposed to using it once to map out an entire learning system.

The Successive Approximation Model (SAM), designed by Allen Interactions, was formed in response to the e-learning needs of clients and is based on repeated small learning steps. Working from the bookends of performance, SAM progresses through three phases:

Phase 1 This is the information gathering stage where training or project needs are identified.

Phase 2 In this stage, design participants engage in collective brainstorming to identify performance outcomes through project planning, design, prototyping, and review.

Phase 3 In phase 3, content is designed, developed, and analyzed, with real-time changes made as needed.

Many instructional designers are adapting their own design methods to incorporate elements of all three models for maximum effect.

Learning

The acquisition of knowledge or skills is the goal of any training program, and forms the basis for learning. This can be achieved through discussion and lectures such as in academic settings, or on the job through experience and practice. Regardless of how learning is done, there are a few basic concepts an HR practitioner must know and be able to perform on the job. These follow in the next sections.

Learning Curves

The purpose of all training sessions is for the participants to learn something: gain knowledge, master a skill, or heighten an ability. Each individual operates at a different *learning pace*. A *learning curve* is a graphical representation of the pace of learning. They include:

Negatively accelerating Defined by early performance improvement with a slowing as time goes on.

Positively accelerating Characterized by a slow rate of performance improvement at first with increased performance improvement as the skill is practiced.

S-shaped In an S-shaped learning curve, considered a blend of negative (decelerated) and positive (accelerated) curves, the rate of performance improvement starts out slowly, takes off as the skills are practiced, and then begins to decelerate over time.

Plateau A plateau occurs when an individual starts out with a rapid acceleration of performance and then the rate flattens out over time.

Learning Pace

How fast a person learns

The time it takes for a person to understand and retain information

Learning Curve

The rate at which a person acquires new skills and knowledge

The time it takes for a person to acquire new information and skills and to perform successfully

Adult Learning and Learning Styles

The science of how adults learn is called andragogy, whereas how children learn is called pedagogy. This is relevant because research has shown that there are significant differences between how adults learn and how children learn. This means that the principles of education that may be effective for the under-18 set may not transfer well to adult learners. The major differences are built around research that shows that what adults are learning is both practical and skills oriented as opposed to the transfer of academic knowledge that is a typical objective for elementary, secondary, and high schools, as well as colleges. Surveys have also shown that most adult learners, when asked why they engage in educational activities, say they do so for job-related purposes. If you are tasked as an HR professional with the design or development of training, these principles suddenly become important. Malcolm Knowles delivered fundamental research that distinguishes between the characteristics of adult learning and the characteristics of adolescent learning. His findings concluded that:

- As a person ages, his or her self-concept moves from dependence and direction from others to independent, self-directed learners.
- Adults accumulate both work and life experience, which they call upon to use for learning.
- The readiness of adults to learn is closely related to the needs of their social role, as in the case of their role on the job.
- There is a shift from gathering knowledge from learning to apply at a future date to an immediacy of use based on practicality or need. Did you ever say to your parents, "I'm never going to use algebra in real life"? Adults orient toward learning focused on problem solving; adolescents are taught to orient toward general subject matter.

Additionally, Knowles found that:

- Internal motivators are more powerful than external motivators.
- Adults want to know why they need to learn something.

Now that you have reviewed *why* adults take on learning activities, what about *how* adults learn? Adult learning styles describe the biological factors that shape the ways people learn and how they process information. There are three widely accepted learning styles:

1. **Auditory learners absorb and retain information through their sense of hearing.** They respond best to information that is presented through verbal discussions or audio presentations such as recordings or narrated videos. Interestingly, auditory learners learn best when they hear material presented in their own voices. Auditory learners use more than just what is presented at face value. They are adept at interpreting verbal cues of tone, inflection, pitch, and speed. Facilitators may unwittingly transfer meaning to training sessions if they talk super fast (as though they just need to get it over with) or are flat with their delivery (as if bored). Example: When trying to memorize a phone number, an auditory learner will repeat it out loud several times.

2. **Visual learners need to use their eyes to absorb and retain data.** They also pick up on nonverbal cues such as crossed arms, rigid posture, and facial expressions. If a new policy is rolled out accompanied by supervisor eye rolling, the policy is immediately undermined. Visual learners tend to draw, sort, and organize information into graphs, charts, and Venn diagrams, looking for the relationships between ideas. Visual learners appreciate handouts, presentations, guides, and pictures. Example: When trying to memorize a phone number, visual learners will write it down or take a picture of it with their phones so they can see it in their mind's eye when they try to remember it.

3. **Kinesthetic/tactile learners, also known as hands-on learners, prefer to learn by touch.** Trainers can spot tactile learners in the audience because their knees are jumping, their pencils are tapping, or they tend to get up and stand in the back of the room during training sessions. Practice sessions that engage the learner are best for these individuals. Example: When trying to memorize a phone number, these learners prefer to type it into their phone contacts, pushing the buttons as a means to store the information in their brains for future recall.

These principles of adult learning are so significant that they must be considered for all participants attending a training session. This may be very difficult, particularly if HR is charged with designing training for a large group or doesn't have the budget or time to inventory every single worker. The best solution in these cases is to develop training content that incorporates something for everyone—audio components, visual tools and graphs, and hands-on practice or activities—to ensure that no student is left behind.

Techniques for Training and Instructional Methods

Think about the best training you ever attended. What made it so? Was the instructor engaging and an expert in her field? Were the materials and training content relevant to your job? Did the presentation and the group exercises capture your attention? The effectiveness of training may be compromised if the proper instructional method is not selected with the audience and materials in mind. The three main methods to choose from are:

1. *Passive training* methods include presentations, lectures, videos, or computer-aided content that requires little or no audience interaction. It is incumbent upon the trainer to keep audience attention. *Didactic* methods focus on theories and information sharing.
2. *Active training* methods are a bit more lively, and generally are led by a facilitator as opposed to a subject matter expert. The facilitator will need to have presentation and problem-solving skills, as well as familiarity with the training materials being used during the session. In this Socratic method of teaching, Q&A formats are popular, asking participants to use critical thinking skills to apply training

content. Classroom exercises may be used, including role playing, case study analysis, and discussion questions. Simulation or vestibule training is also a form of active training in which participants learn in an environment similar to where they will be working. Picture an inventory clerk being taught how to enter purchase orders. If the clerk is asked to practice on the live system, the consequences would be of nightmarish proportion! It is better to have a simulated version of the inventory system in which the clerk may gain skills through practice.

3. *Experiential training* is led by a person with the knowledge, skills, and expertise to train the worker. It may include a form of demonstration in which the instructor shows a worker how to do a task and then allows her to practice on her own under the expert's guidance. This type of training focuses on practicing a new skill using structured exercise, so it benefits from delivery to smaller groups or one on one, depending on the need.

Additionally, *webinars* attempt to blend components from the various training methods. Held online, a webinar features a live instructor or facilitator who uses a combination of presentation and Q&A to impart information. Technical difficulties can plague webinars, as can the absence of body language cues that all learning styles learn from. Without the need for direct eye contact or participant interaction, it is also very easy for trainees to stay muted during the session, losing focus and potentially missing key points to the training content.

The location and method of delivery should be considered when designing the training to address costs, time frame, specialized equipment needs, and the target audience.

Cultural factors also influence learning styles and expectations, on both a macro and an individual scale. Learners from different cultures have different expectations of training design and content. For example, Asian cultures view learning as a formal endeavor, expecting their teachers to be experts deserving of high levels of respect. Role playing and simulations may be more accepted in countries such as Switzerland and Canada, whereas didactic methods such as lectures and demonstrations are preferred in Venezuela and Turkey (Tarique et al., 2016Tarique, Briscoe, and Schuler 2016; Tyler 1999).

Didactic

Instructive, teaching

Intending to teach or demonstrate

Webinar

Meetings, training, or presentations on the Internet

An interactive seminar on the Internet (usually a live presentation)

Classroom Configuration

Training can be held just about anywhere, and that is both fortunate and unfortunate. Which participants would be most eager for training to end: those being taught in a beautifully decked-out training room with all the latest technology and as much bottled water as desired, or training delivered in a poorly lit corner of a warehouse with insufficient seating and no climate control? Training is already often perceived as disruptive and inconvenient, even under the best of conditions. Just ask any employee or manager who has to stop production or stay after work to log their training hours. However, training as an intervention strategy is valuable, and the right classroom environment can go a long way toward easing the pain and keeping participant attention focused squarely on the learning objectives. The environment where training is held is a measure of employer commitment to the training outcome, and should not be underestimated. Seating arrangements contribute to learning outcomes and training delivery. The most common seating arrangements are reviewed next, and sample configurations are shown in Figure 4.4.

Theater Set up as a movie theater, all participants are facing the front of the room in anticipation of a lecture, video, or presentation. This style is useful when a large group of people are being trained, the curriculum requires very little interaction between participants, and note taking is not required.

Classroom Similar to the theater style, the classroom setting has tables in front of chairs so that participants may take notes or review handouts, guides, or other materials requiring a table.

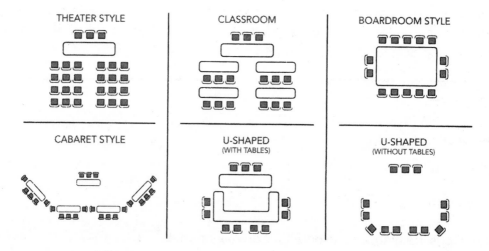

Figure 4.4   Training Seating Styles

U-shaped Most often seen in conference room, this configuration is best when collaboration is necessary or the facilitator needs to interact with the group.

Boardroom style Similar to the U-shaped style, the boardroom style may be closed off in a rectangle or have added audience seating for observers, such as those seen at small shareholder or board of directors meetings.

Cabaret/banquet style Have you every attended an HR networking workshop held in the banquet room of a local hotel? It was probably set up cabaret style. This style is useful for small group interactions where participants are working independently of the whole group (or if food is being served). Note that if a presentation will be included, some participants will have their backs to the front of the room with this configuration.

Chevron This seating style can accommodate large groups and be used with or without tables. All participants can face the front of the room or be on both sides of the tables if the training requires interaction.

Technology in Training

The ability to reuse learning content—especially custom content—and deliver it to new hires and for retraining has been improved tremendously by technology. The ability to sort and order, deliver, and track training program content can result in a high return on the investments such systems generally require. Many human resource information systems (HRIS) have training *modules* specifically for the purpose of tracking participants. Stand-alone *learning management systems (LMSs)* are a good choice in the absence of an existing solution in-house. LMSs also provide expanded solutions for tracking employee development activities, and self-service learning for growth.

The Internet has delivered very credible options for employee learning. *Learning portals* are websites that store a database of relevant training topics that employers may purchase access to for a fee. Learning portals may be the most cost-effective solutions for companies with fairly standard training content needs, or those without the budget for in-house, customized training. *Open sourcing* has emerged in recent years, especially through academic institutions. Massive open online courses (MOOCs) have popped up on topics such as business, finance, and first aid, to name just a few. How-to videos on YouTube offer training for software programs such as Outlook or Excel and many other topics.

With the technology of today, employee skill development can be formal or informal, on virtually any topic, and priced from free to thousands of dollars—all the more reason HR must lead the effort of creating clear training outcomes, and sourcing the most cost-effective training options to deliver success.

Module

A unit or segment of an educational program

One section of a training program that is presented alone or as part of a series of other units

Learning Management System (LMS)

Computer software for employee development

Computer software that administers, tracks, and reports on employee development opportunities such as classroom and online events, e-learning programs, and training content

Learning Portal

Website for learning

Internet site where employees can use educational resources

Open Sourcing

Freely sharing

Made available for others to use or modify

Talent Management

This section addresses the need for HR professionals to build and evaluate a robust talent management system. Talent management is about much more than *performance reviews*. Talent management extends beyond human resource development and will vary in its elements from organization to organization. While some organizations may include talent identification and acquisition in the mix, most organizations include on-boarding, talent development, talent review and mobility, performance management, leadership development, succession planning, career pathing, and the retention of *high-potential (hi-po) employees*. An HR best practice is to have a documented system for capturing the varying needs of employees as they perform throughout the talent management life cycle.

Performance Review

Formal evaluation of an employee's work activities

A documented discussion about an employee's development and performance that involves managers, HR, and the employee

High-Potential (Hi-Po) Employees

Employees identified for advancement owing to their talents and skills

Employees who have the capacity to grow into higher levels of leadership in the organization

Performance Management Systems

In order to truly add value to organizations in the realm of *performance management*, HR must approach the process as a system of interconnected activities that address strategic people goals. A *performance management system* is built upon a feedback foundation delivered through formal and informal channels.

As with most HR activities, managing performance should be in direct alignment with the company's strategic goals and objectives, and begins with a basic understanding of the expectations of the tasks, duties, responsibilities, and priorities of the job. For this reason, managing performance begins at the time of hire and extends through the employee life cycle.

Performance Management

Supervising employees

The process of setting goals, measuring progress, and rewarding or correcting performance of employees

Performance Management System

Process of creating a productive work environment

The process of helping people perform to the best of their abilities, which begins by defining a job and ends when an employee leaves the organization

On-Boarding and Orientation

In the context of performance management, effective techniques at the beginning stage of managing employee performance include communicating the job and behavior expectations and explaining to associates the *performance standards* of the organization. New hires are given information related to the expectations of the job (job description) along with information related to company expectations (employee handbook). Employment benefits plans are reviewed, and paperwork is completed to form the basis of the personnel file. In addition to the compliance training required by many federal and state laws, the orientation/*on-boarding* process is an opportunity for the employee to become *assimilated* to the new organization, its environment, and the culture. This highlights the need for HR to build on-boarding activities that identify the goals and objectives of the company through the company mission, vision, and values.

Evaluating the efficacy of recruiting and on-boarding efforts is an important step at this stage; it helps HR practitioners reflect upon their own performance in the delivery of these services. An emerging metric is that of employee retention rate, in which HR looks at how many employees stayed, as opposed to how many left. Another metric used is the new hire turnover rate, which measures the percentage of new hires within the prior six months who left the organization.

In the month of January a company hired 50 workers. Twelve of them separated within the first 90 days. Calculate the new hire turnover rate by taking the number terminated and dividing it by the number of total hires in the same period.

$$\frac{\text{Number of terminations after 90 days (12)}}{\text{Number of new hires in January (50)}} \times 100 \text{ (to convert to a percentage)}$$

Turnover rate for that batch of hires = 24%

The topics of employee orientation, on-boarding, and socialization are reviewed more in depth in the Workforce Planning and Employment chapter.

After an employee has been integrated into the new environment, more traditional methods of performance management begin to be administered. These are explored next.

Performance Standards

Expected behaviors and results from employees

The behaviors and results that management expects employees to achieve on the job

On-Boarding

Training and orientation of new employees

The process of helping new employees learn the organization's policies, procedures, and culture in addition to their job responsibilities

Assimilation

A process of integration

The process of becoming a member of a team, organization, or culture

Performance Appraisals and Reviews

Companies generally use employee *performance appraisals* to do two things: (1) provide feedback to employees about how well or how poorly they are doing and (2) create plans for development.

Performance feedback of the formal sort is generally scaled over a period of time. For example, in the first 30 days of an employee's tenure, it would be difficult to justify discipline in response to performance deficiencies since the employee is just learning the job—areas for improvement are expected. Instead, feedback within the first 90 days should be focused on training and developing the necessary skill sets for baseline performance; the feedback is designed to get the worker up to speed with the job requirements. As time goes by, the supervisor will give periodic *progress reviews* to let the employee know how he or she is doing toward achieving goals, or to address concerns the worker may have.

Often, performance reviews will include goal setting, a review of the job competencies, and development planning. Typically, performance reviews are conducted at midyear and end of year if on a business calendar year cycle, or are tied to an employee's anniversary date.

The value of an annual performance review continues to be challenged. The diversity of the workforce along with the fluid nature of jobs requires an evolved approach to providing feedback. Companies are shifting toward giving real-time feedback on performance rather than relying on an annual or biannual summary. Additionally, companies are evolving to seek feedback from all stakeholders rather than only providing one-directional feedback from the supervisor to the employee. Employees are encouraged to be actively engaged in their career development, often leading the discussion about their own strengths and weaknesses. This ownership mentality gives employees a sense of control over their careers, while giving supervisors clarity on how to structure jobs around employee development needs where possible.

After the introductory period, feedback from supervisors is often given on the job, providing direction and redirection so the employee gains *on-the-job experience*. The feature offers the perspective that how supervisors provide this feedback makes a difference.

Performance Appraisals

Evaluations of employees

A method of measuring how effective employees are

Progress Review

Evaluation of an employee's performance

Formal or informal evaluation of an employee's progress toward goals and recommendations for improvements and development

On-the-Job Experience

Skills and knowledge gained through work

The skills and knowledge a person learns from day-to-day work experience

---

QUALITY INFORMAL FEEDBACK

Have you ever heard of the 80/20 rule? In HR and management, it refers to the premise that 20 percent of employees take up 80 percent of HR's time. This is relevant in terms of providing feedback, as most managers find that they are putting out the fires caused by low-performing workers more often than investing and supporting the employees who are getting the job done properly. HR can help supervisors develop the communication skills necessary to deliver *both* positive and negative feedback. Remind supervisors that the quality of the comments matter. Comments such as "You're doing great" are less effective than "I noticed how you handled that difficult customer this morning—you were very professional, and I think it made a difference." The first approach is vague and doesn't encourage repeat behavior. The second comment tells the employee that her professionalism is noticed and having an effect.

When supervisors must redirect employees, statements such as "You're doing it wrong" are interpreted as condescending and disrespectful. Instead, a statement such as "Feed the boxes sideways into the machine so there is no chance of your fingers getting caught" provides direction and attaches meaning to the process.

While day-to-day, informal feedback is ongoing, most employers have a formal method for performance *appraisals*. Many employers use a combination of methods when designing their reviews.

Comparison method As the title implies, this method involves comparing employees to one another. Common tools used to do this include:

- *Ranked performance* is a method in which supervisors rank the employees based on highest to lowest performance.
- Paired comparison involves comparing one employee's performance against all others in the group.
- *Forced distribution* uses a bell curve to visually represent employees who are high, low, or average performers. This technique may also be built into other methods as part of an overall calibration process to increase accuracy.

Narrative method This appraisal method requires managers to write descriptions about individual employee performance as opposed to using a rating scale or checklist. A critical incident review asks supervisors to keep track of notable events over a specific rating period, and report them during the review. Both positive and negative events should be tracked. An essay method requires managers to write a short description of employee behaviors. The essay method can use prescribed questions in which the supervisor must respond, or be more free-form to improve flexibility.

Rating method This review method incorporates tools and checklists to aid managers and ensure consistency between employees. A Likert scale (named after the gentleman scholar Rensis Likert, who developed it) may have any range of responses from "Strongly agree" to "Strongly disagree." A scale may also be numerical, such as 1 being low performance and 5 being high performance. A challenge to this method of performance appraisal is that the ratings are highly subjective. Objectivity and consistency are increased when evaluators are provided with definitions and behaviorally anchored examples of the rating scales. Some managers don't believe anyone can ever "exceed expectations." Particularly when a company ties annual raises or bonuses to a performance rating, this can be exceedingly frustrating for employees (the best employees, especially!).

BARS A behaviorally anchored rating scale (BARS) requires the use of anchoring statements. While scaled in format, a BARS appraisal provides additional detail about what constitutes outstanding or unsatisfactory performance. BARS must be customized for each job within the organization, built up from standardized job descriptions. The anchoring statements for a salesperson will be different from those for a shipping and receiving clerk.

Checklist A checklist is another form of rating method. It involves the rater checking boxes to statements such as "Always completes work on time" or "Has poor follow-through on projects." While easy to use, it is somewhat limiting in terms of providing meaningful feedback that will change behaviors. For this reason, some employers choose to use *graphic rating scales*, which have a continuum of low to high in the job duty being measured. The graphic rating scale is a hybrid in that it allows raters to include commentary on performance in the relevant descriptive category along with numeric or other scaled ratings.

MBO Management by objectives (MBO) is the process of setting goals directly between the manager and the employee. These goals should cascade down from an organization's strategic plan for maximum alignment. Also known by other names such as target coaching and performance objective setting, it nonetheless follows the same goal setting process:

- Review the job description for agreement.
- Develop measurable standards of performance (there is a difference between "answer the phones" and "answer the phones in a professional manner").
- Create realistic objectives.
- Agree to both formal and informal progress checks.

Some companies use the MBO format to pay for performance outcomes—an employee agrees to the objective and is paid a bonus if it is achieved.

360-degree feedback Few jobs impact only a single department; *360-degree feedback* methods seek out comments from relevant stakeholders affected by employee performance. Performance insights are solicited from customers, coworkers, and other departments to provide the employee with meaningful feedback on how performance is perceived. This method is also used to rate managers by asking employees and others for their views on how the boss is performing.

Self-assessment Asking employees to rate their own performance is the premise of *self-assessments*. Some employees report disliking this method as they are unwilling or unable to document their weaknesses for fear of retribution. For this reason, employee self-assessments are more beneficial for use to identify development opportunities. This takes the fear out of an honest self-review of employee strengths and weaknesses. In an organization where employee ownership of work achievements and career development is at the heart of the company's performance philosophy, self-reviews form the core of a feedback system.

Appraisals

Evaluations

Assessments of the value or performance of something (for example, job appraisals)

Ranked Performance

A method of evaluating employees

Rating employees from best to worst against each other according to a standard measurement system

Forced Distribution

A rating system for evaluating employees

A performance measurement system that ranks employees against each other on a bell curve and according to predetermined categories such as high, low, or average

Graphic Rating Scale

Method of evaluating employees

A method of giving employees a numerical rating for having certain traits (for example, being reliable or honest)

360-degree feedback

Method of appraising job performance

Employee appraisal data gathered from internal and external sources (such as peers, subordinates, supervisors, customers, and suppliers); also known as multi-rater feedback

Self-Assessment

Evaluating one's own performance

Evaluation of one's own performance, abilities, and developmental needs

Legal Issues with Performance Appraisal Tools and Methods

There are legal issues associated with all of the methods and tools described in this section. As with any other employment action, a performance appraisal must be based on job-related characteristics, not the protected class characteristics defined by various laws, including Title VII of the Civil Rights Act of 1964. This is important because by nature some of these performance tools are *asking* supervisors to discriminate between employees and their performance (such as the comparison methods). As a reminder, not all discrimination is unlawful; in fact, it can be part of a supervisor's job. Discrimination becomes unlawful when it is based on non-job-related criteria such as a person's age, race, or disability status. The following criteria should be considered in administering legally defensible performance appraisals:

- There is evidence that the appraisal is a valid review of behavior.
- The appraisal tool is applied consistently, without discrimination based on any factor other than job-related criteria or varying standards between employees in similar jobs.
- The tool is objective.
- The review is evidenced-based in that it includes documentation of employee performance.
- The rater has a work relationship with the employee and is in a position to evaluate performance.
- The more subjective the criteria, the more difficult to prove job-relatedness. Seek to tie performance objectives to tasks, duties, and responsibilities.

Rater Errors

There are other errors in addition to legal mistakes that can be made by raters in the administration of performance reviews. These errors are common for any HR task in which bias may influence a rater's decision. Bias includes a rater's predisposition toward behaviors such as stereotyping and generalizations. Consider previous chapters that discussed interview bias and decision-making bias; errors in perform-ance ratings are very similar:

Central tendency, leniency, strictness A form of rating pattern in which the appraiser rates all employees either down the middle (*central tendency*—all employees are average), as low performers (everyone needs improvement), or as high performers (*leniency error*—we're all doing our best).

Similar to me/different from me This error occurs when appraisers are influenced by similarities to or differences from their own performance. A new supervisor just promoted may hesitate to call out a subordinate on certain negative work behaviors, mainly because the supervisor used to do the very same thing before being promoted.

Primacy The *primacy error* occurs when an appraiser forms—and adheres to—a first or early impression of performance. This is particularly pervasive when a newly hired employee's performance starts out roughly, and the supervisor makes a snap judgment of the employee's skills.

Recency The *recency error* occurs when a rater weighs the most recent levels of performance instead of employee behavior over the entire rating period. This often happens because the rating period is too long, and supervisors can remember only so far back (or the worst incidents—see the horn effect). Employees are often aware of this form of bias, so performance improvements are made just prior to their appraisal times.

Halo/Horn Ever had an employee who has the best performance of the work group, but is often late? Supervisors may be reluctant to address the tardiness because of fear of losing a high producer. This is an example of the *halo effect*, when competence in one area serves as the benchmark for ratings in other performance areas. Conversely, the horn effect occurs when weakness in one area pervades other results.

The upcoming Employee and Labor Relations chapter has an opening research review of the study of conflict at work. In HRD, conflict avoidance is one reason supervisors may hold back on giving truthful feedback. The supervisor may worry about the employee's reaction, or fear a loss of an otherwise high-performing worker. HR can help minimize these errors through supervisor training and education. It helps if the managers are on board with the general performance feedback system, so a root cause analysis may be the first thing HR attempts when addressing high incidents of rater errors. Other tools to help supervisors become great at giving performance reviews are discussed next.

Central Tendency

Average value of a data set

A measure of the middle of a statistical distribution of data

Leniency Error

Favoritism in performance evaluations

Rating employees higher than their actual performances deserve

(continued)

(continued)

Primacy Errors

Incorrect assumptions or judgments

Incorrect conclusions where the first impression of someone or something continues despite contradictory evidence

Recency Errors

Inaccurate assessments based on recent behavior

Incorrect conclusions due to recent actions that are weighed more heavily than overall performance

Halo Effect

Transfer of positive feelings

The transfer of the positive qualities of a person or thing to related people or things

Training for Reviewers

Senior HRPs must also engage in training reviewers in the proper way to conduct activities in the realm of performance management. Both supervisors and employees alike report low levels of satisfaction with the performance rating system. Supervisors complain about how time-consuming the process is. Apathetic employees report the feedback as having little impact on their job satisfaction, and there is lack of clarity as to how their performance contributes to the company strategies. Some supervisors feel that "no news is good news," whereas some employees simply need to know if they are on the right track. With all of these moving parts, it is unfortunate that many companies have yet to figure out how to make performance feedback the center around which a department gathers. A properly built system gives the employees the feedback they need to achieve business goals. It also gives supervisors a neutral tool in which to offer feedback. Training of those who are performing the appraisals can help alleviate some of the problems. Training of evaluators should involve:

Describing the process This first step in the training of evaluators should include information related to the company mission, vision, and values and ways in which employee performance can have an impact on business results. A performance appraisal process is most valuable when it serves the overreaching reason for existence with business relevance, and relates the organizational mission with the department mission, goals, and objectives.

Communicating expected standards of behavior As with any training, evaluators should understand how to conduct themselves before, during, and after the meeting. Giving them information about the forces affecting performance appraisals such as customer criteria, industry ratings, and the regulatory environment can all help supervisors behave in a way that meets business outcomes and manages risk.

Sharing daily practices Performance feedback should be given on a daily basis, using job-related, nondiscriminatory methods that are focused on job outcomes. Tools include the use of progress reviews, success plans, and short- and long-term goal setting.

Special Focus: The Appraisal Meeting

Helping supervisors prepare for employee reactions is critical. Accusations of bias, harassment, and preferential treatment are not uncommon from employees who are receiving a below-standard appraisal. Therefore, employers may want to advise supervisors to conduct evaluations with HR or another manager (often second-level) in attendance. Giving appraisers training in conflict management and how to deliver negative or critical messages may also be helpful, including reminding them on the expected standards of professional behavior regardless of employee reactions to the feedback. Reviewer training must also help appraisers focus not only on the negative performance, but on what the employee is doing right, and how the manager will support the worker's development.

General guidelines to give to training evaluators include:

- Use specific examples of behaviors over the entire rating period as opposed to vague statements that are recency or primacy biased.
- Focus on development and support activities, as opposed to focusing on authoritarian tactics. Remind managers that a review is not a disciplinary session.
- Teach managers to ask questions (*upward communication*) as well as provide feedback (*downward communication*). Communication should flow both up and down.
- Target job-based behaviors as opposed to personal failings.

Upward Communication

Flow of information from subordinates to superiors

Information that is conveyed by employees to upper management

Downward Communication

Flow of information from superiors to subordinates

Information that is conveyed by upper management to lower-level employees in the organization

Employee Development

A very important part of a performance management system is employee development—helping employees expand their knowledge and skills for future application in their careers. As with the design of most HR programs, a needs assessment is the perfect starting point for this process.

Assessing Talent

Before attempting to plan for employee development, it is necessary to identify where the employee is and where he or she wants to be. There are several different types of tools available to conduct this type of gap analysis, and many can be found in an assessment center. Outcomes from the assessments form the basis of training plans, career paths, and simply building an increase in self-awareness.

Assessment Centers

An *assessment center* is not a physical place (although it can be), but rather a collection of tools, exercises, and resources that are used to diagnose employee development needs. Assessment centers are also used to administer preemployment tests to help employers select the most qualified candidate. In addition, centers are useful to identify an employee's readiness for *promotion*.

In HRD, assessment tools are used to help employees understand their strengths and weaknesses. An exercise called an *in-basket* (work sample) is based on typical work issues the employee may see in the course of the workday. Assessment activities may include role playing, case studies, observation checklists, group discussions, a set of online questions, and computer-based simulations to assess where the employee is at professionally. Assessment tools are designed to measure *interpersonal skills*, emotional intelligence, oral/written communication, *cognitive abilities*, application of skills/abilities, work styles, and personality. An expert administrator or certified HR practitioner will need to be trained and on hand to administer some of the assessments and guide the employee through the exercises, interpret the results, and make recommendations.

Assessment Center

A method of selecting personnel

A system of tests and interviews that evaluate employee performance and help companies select the right people for job positions

Promotion

Job advancement

Advancement of an employee's rank, usually with greater responsibility and more money

In-Basket Exercise

A method of evaluating candidates

A test used to hire or promote employees to management positions that measures the candidate's ability to prioritize and respond to daily tasks

Interpersonal Skills

Traits for effective social interaction

Effective social qualities for communicating and building good relationships with different people

Cognitive Ability

Intelligence

Thinking skills and mental abilities

Developing Employees

Development efforts should always focus on specific needs of each individual employee—rarely is there a one-size-fits-all approach. In addition to the tools described in the assessment section, there are other techniques that may be applied to develop the workforce of tomorrow. Coaching is one such technique. In *coaching*, a supervisor advises employees on development and growth opportunities outside the context of discipline or rewards. Coaching relationships require trust, and an employee may not be willing to reach and fall short if she knows that she will be reprimanded for her failures. Development activities are focused on behaviors that must be learned or acquired, as opposed to current job performance. In formal coaching programs, both internal and external resources may be identified. The use of *mentors* may be beneficial when a more neutral approach is desired. As always, HR must model and communicate the expected standards of behaviors for the coaches, help identify the desired outcomes from the coaching intervention, and communicate the value of the program to the executive team.

Apprentice programs are a formal method for establishing benchmark job skills and knowledge. More commonly found in the trade industries, apprentice programs have a very clear path to certification and expertise that is guided by skilled professionals.

Another technique that is effective in developing people is *job rotation*. This involves *cross-training* employees in multiple roles to improve their skill set overall. While it can be cumbersome to track and administer, the long-term value of having a cross-trained workforce can work to the advantage of an organization, particularly in the realm of knowledge management.

Stretch assignments are those that require the employee to learn something new or apply different critical thinking skills. These can be the result of special projects, or an increase in job responsibilities for practice. HR can support these types of exercises by identifying opportunities, recommending employees for consideration, and evaluating performance, working in tandem with the developing employee's direct supervisor.

Resources for developing employees may also occur off-site. Continuing education through certification programs offers professional credentials that have been linked to positive employment outcomes. Seminars are useful for a focused view on specific topics, especial labor laws. Outdoor training or adventure camps have also been used, with varied results. Leaves of absence or *sabbaticals* give employees the freedom to expand their knowledge or skill set, often in alignment with company goals. The key to effectiveness—and return on investment—of these off-site experiences is to link them to professional or organizational goals and outcomes.

Employee development is not the only focus of HR activities. Companies may also seek to be certified in industry best practices. Take a look at the In Real Life feature for an example of how one company excelled and was recognized for its HRD programs.

IN REAL LIFE: DHL AND THE TOP EMPLOYERS INSTITUTE

Source: DHL Global Press Release, 2016.

The Top Employers Institute exists to recognize, well, top employers by applying rigorous certification and validation standards. Employers apply for the recognition by submitting to a best practices survey. The survey asks employers about their HR best practices in areas such as strategy, communication, and employee development. Companies that are rated in the highest ranking of international standards are awarded the Top Employer designation for the year. One example is DHL, which in 2016 was just one of eight companies that successfully certified on a global scale. Examples of excellence include the company's employee on-boarding program, a system of interconnected activities that links a new hire plan with executive meet and greets, team lunches, and a posthire assessment. DHL's approach is a lesson in practical HR best practices for multinational enterprises.

The company scored particularly high for talent strategy, leadership development, performance management, and learning and development. Examples of systems in place at the time of the designation include actions throughout the career plan scale. With DHL offering internships, graduate development programs, job rotation, and soft skills training, many employees continue to learn both on and off the job.

Regine Buettner, Executive Vice President, HR Global & Europe, DHL Express had this to say about the designation: "... it is our motivated people who define great service in the eyes of our customers, and it is our motivated people who ensure that we stay ahead of the competition. We have put in place a comprehensive range of initiatives and measures—from regular, small gestures of appreciation for frontline employees to spectacular employee of the year recognition events—that engage employees at all levels in our business and enhance our appeal as an employer."

Practically speaking, the lesson is that HR best practices can be scaled for any size business, in any type of organizational structure. By creatively problem solving and working from a playbook of goals, HR can design the necessary combination of the best practices celebrated by the Top Employers Institute. The trick is to simply get started.

Coaching

Guiding, giving information, or training

A method of developing specific skills in which a coach gives information and objective feedback to a person or group

Mentoring

Helping a person learn

When an experienced person shares knowledge with someone who has less experience

Apprentice

A person learning a skill, trade, or profession

A person learning a trade or skill from a qualified person for a specific length of time

Job Rotation

Changing work assignments

A way to develop employees by giving them different jobs to perform

(continued)

(continued)

Cross-Training

Learning new skills beyond one's current job responsibilities

Teaching employees the skills and responsibilities of other positions in the company to increase their effectiveness and to provide greater staffing flexibility in the organization

Sabbatical Leave

Paid time off for a predetermined period

A benefit provided by some organizations that allows eligible employees paid time off during a specific time period for study, rest, or travel

Career Pathing

Assessment tools such as those just described can help employees translate their interests and aptitudes into satisfying and rewarding careers. *Career development* is built upon the belief that a satisfying career is not an accident. It utilizes strategic *career planning* to gain work experience (such as with *career ladder promotions*) and knowledge. For example, many human resource professionals "just fell into" their role and all its glory, but may experience *career plateaus* due to lack of planning. While some are lucky and the job fulfills their natural aptitude or talents, others keep a weather eye on other job opportunities (or early retirement). A career is a series of linked positions within the framework of an industry or discipline.

Career decisions are often made based on age. For example, early career professionals may be concerned with acquiring new skill sets and gaining experience. Midcareer professionals are concerned with balancing work/life obligations, and late career individuals may begin to mentor others or plan for career exit. While generalized based on stage of life, it is important to note that career interests and paths are highly dependent on lifestyle issues as well as ability or skill set. To design approaches that address the unique needs of a diverse workforce, some companies are moving away from traditional career paths in favor of broader, more situational activities that focus on building transferable skills and engaging in experiences rather than traditional position titles or educational programs.

A portable career path is another view of *career management* adopted from the U.S. military. A portable career path may be built upon knowledge, skills, and abilities that can be used across industries and sectors. It is often applied to those who must relocate frequently, but is certainly applicable to the building of foundational skills. Figure 4.5 reviews the portable career path in more detail.

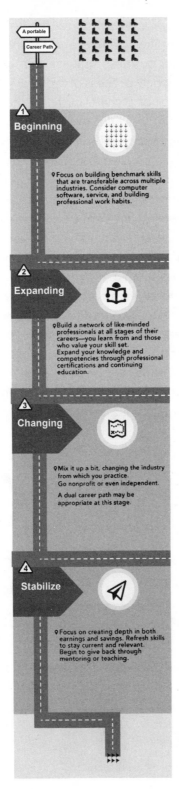

Figure 4.5   Portable Career Path

The other side of this coin is how organized a company is toward identifying career progression opportunities. These are the result of natural attrition, in response to growth and other business strategies, from short- and long-term labor forecasting, and from the practical process of replacement planning. In the absence of strategic plans and organizational charts outlining the natural progression of jobs, supervisors may assign meaningless titles to employees who have been around for a while. Or the company may create jobs that aren't necessary or are potentially redundant to satisfy an associate's desire for career growth. HR leads the efforts in shaping the playbook from which employees will build their careers. Without this, employers wind up grooming employees right out the door.

Dual career ladders in recent years have become more of a jungle gym than a ladder. Lateral moves are attractive when employees have the opportunity to develop new skills or gain new knowledge. Dual career ladders are also useful for talented employees who don't necessarily see management as the next step in their careers. In a dual career ladder, a path is identified that is rich in expertise and cross-training. Employees master two traditionally disparate roles, and then move on to the next phase. These approaches create a cross-trained staff with high degrees of flexibility to respond to changing needs of the companies they work for.

The traditional approach to career pathing is taking on new shape as it goes beyond the more linear approach of the past. The emerging philosophies consider a portfolio of experiences that form a career journey, as illustrated in Figure 4.6.

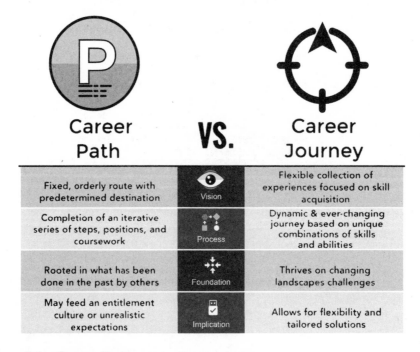

Career Path		Career Journey
Fixed, orderly route with predetermined destination	Vision	Flexible collection of experiences focused on skill acquisition
Completion of an iterative series of steps, positions, and coursework	Process	Dynamic & ever-changing journey based on unique combinations of skills and abilities
Rooted in what has been done in the past by others	Foundation	Thrives on changing landscapes challenges
May feed an entitlement culture or unrealistic expectations	Implication	Allows for flexibility and tailored solutions

Figure 4.6   Career Path versus Career Journey
Source: Used with permission from Karla J. Kretzschmer, Karla K Enterprises, LLC.

Issues that arise with having such well-trained workers are those of knowledge management. This is discussed in detail next.

Career Development

Progress in a job or profession

An employee's progress through each stage in his or her career

Career Planning

Managing professional goals

Taking steps to improve professional skills and create new opportunities

Career Ladder Promotion

A structured job advancement

Job advancement through a series of defined positions, from lower level to higher level

Career Plateau

No possibility for advancing in a career

Inability of an employee to advance further in the company due to mediocre performance or lack of opportunities

Career Management

Planning and controlling the professional development of an employee

Preparing, implementing, and monitoring the career path of an employee, with a focus on the goals and needs of the organization

Knowledge Management

Knowledge management programs are formal systems built by HR to capture and store the information needed to conduct the business of work. Knowledge management is important for two reasons:

1. Many companies are competitively dependent upon knowledge workers. Technology and health care are two industry examples of when intelligence is the raw

Table 4.2   Practical HR Tools for Knowledge Management

	People	Process	Structure
Succession plans			X
Career plans	X		
SOPs		X	
Centers of excellence			X
Job analysis			X
Training program content	X	X	
Gap analyses	X	X	X
Cross-training	X	X	
Technology		X	X
Continuous learning	X		
Industry trends (political, economic, social, technology)			X
Strategic plans			X

material from which a company performs and is measured. Sharing knowledge becomes a strategic advantage.
2. Tribal knowledge (unwritten information that only a few people within the company have) is a form of risk that HR must manage.

Voluntary and involuntary separations or information hoarding by key subject matter *authorities* is debilitating to a company that relies on information to operate. All companies rely on information to some degree, and knowledge management programs seek to capture this data from the *key talent* who have mastered a subject. Key activities for HR to understand in this area include facilitating the extraction of information from subject matter experts, formally documenting processes through standard operating procedures or reference guides, leading training and cross-training efforts, and protecting the company's *intellectual property* where appropriate. *Competency models* may be used to launch the process of cataloging and ordering the critical information that must be retained through knowledge management efforts.

Table 4.2 shows a few practical tools HR may use to help the company compete on the knowledge of workers, and retain the knowledge for future performance and growth.

Knowledge Management

Organizing information to improve business performance

The process of gathering, documenting, and sharing important information to improve the performance of employees and the organization

Authority

Expert or person in control

Someone with extensive knowledge of a specific subject; a person in a superior position

Key Talent

Important and valued workers

Employees that perform extremely good work and are highly valued by the organization

Intellectual Property

Creations or inventions protected by law

An original invention or something created by the mind, which is usually protected by patents, trademarks, or copyrights

Competency Model

A description of the skills needed for a specific job

A list of the behaviors, skills, and knowledge needed to do well in a specific job

---

High-Potential Employees

If HR practitioners want to maximize the return on investment of coaching efforts, they should focus on their high-potential (hi-po) employees. Coaching low performers may move the needle up toward average performance. But put the high-po's in coaching and career development, and they will engage and connect through natural motivation. Managing the talent of these individuals is not just about pay increases and title changes. These individuals need to feel that their employer is invested in their success and trusts them enough to give them meaningful responsibilities. Opportunities to make a difference, learn new skills, and mentor others are all techniques employers may use to retain and support this talented group.

Targeting only high performers, however, may serve to decrease the morale of other workers who may view their career options as limited. Some employees may simply need some baseline life skills training to get them moving in the right direction. The question for HR becomes deciding what behaviors classify some employees as having higher potential than others, and ensuring that the HRD programs meet the unique needs of the entire workforce. This was addressed at the beginning of this chapter, "The Deliberately Developmental Organization."

Organizational Development

Companies may also be in need of strategic and operational development interventions. The study of *organizational development (OD)* focuses on behavioral, social, and psychological sciences to understand the business of work. While the Business Management and Strategy chapter discusses the role of HR in organizational change management, and the Workforce Planning and Employment chapter focuses on OD interventions-related workforce structures and job design, HRD focuses the intervention efforts of OD on process and people orientations.

OD adopts a macro approach to organizational change. It must link to the company's strategic plan, and be delivered in a series of planned steps that make up an entire intervention activity.

Quality initiatives

Quality efforts are focused on developing both people and processes. *Total quality management (TQM)* is a strategic system designed to achieve process targets such as improved customer satisfaction and waste management. There are four main theories of quality that should be understood:

1. **The TQM guru: W. Edwards Deming** Believed to be the pioneer of TQM, Deming established the baseline for understanding this approach in the organizational setting. Deming developed a 14-point system for managing both productivity and quality outcomes, two conditions that often were seen as being at war with each other. Deming believed that quality is defined by the consumer, and he held top management accountable for products that were flawed.

2. **The trilogy: Joseph Juran** The Juran trilogy builds upon Deming's work in that the process stays firmly rooted in customer needs and expectations. The trilogy attempts to translate customer desires into the language of business in three areas: quality planning, quality control, and quality improvements. Quality planning focuses on building quality into the design stage of products or services. Quality control transfers the quality initiatives into the production process. Quality improvements are used to address deficiencies as they occur through adjustments in people and process interventions as needed. Waste reduction is a primary goal for all TQM efforts and should be built into all three stages.

3. **Six Sigma** Developed by Motorola, this quality strategy is most commonly understood through the DMAIC (define, measure, analyze, improve, control) model, as follows:

   Define What is the problem from the customer's perspective? What does the customer need?

   Measure How often are the defects occurring? What are the established benchmarks being used for comparison?

   Analyze Where are the gaps between current and desired conditions?

   Improve What solutions will be most effective to address the root cause of the defects?

   Control How can backsliding be prevented?

   Six Sigma is a team-based approach to quality management. A quality leader is identified and team members are formally trained to implement and manage the DMAIC process for any quality issues at the company. Process owners are also appointed—individuals who are responsible for the specific processes identified as the focus of a quality management intervention.

4. **A focus on analytics—Dr. Kaoru Ishikawa** One of Dr. Ishikawa's most valuable contributions in the quality movement was through the development of analytical tools. The Ishikawa diagram is perhaps the most famous. Also called the fishbone diagram and the *cause-and-effect diagram*, the visual aid is used to diagnose the contributing factors to defects. People, processes, equipment, material, the environment, and management are all explored for root cause analysis. From this, quality intervention efforts may be developed.

Check sheets are another analytical tool used to diagnose quality defects. The simplest of all tools, the template takes stock of the quantity of occurrences to track where the defects are originating. From this, a *histogram* may be built showing patterns from which HR may help design interventions.

Vilfredo Pareto contributed to Ishikawa's work when he developed the *Pareto chart*, a visual representation of the 80/20 rule. This chart demonstrates that 80 percent of quality problems are attributed to 20 percent of causes. By focusing on the top 20 percent, the majority of defects may be eliminated.

A *scatter diagram* takes on a visual representation of two variables, with data sourced from check sheets or other methods for documenting quality deviations.

Organizational Development (OD)

Planned process to improve an organization

Planned process that uses the principles of behavioral science to improve the way an organization functions

(continued)

(continued)

Total Quality Management (TQM)

Continuous improvement

A method for improving the organization by continuously changing its practices, structures, and systems

Six Sigma

Business management strategy

A strategy to improve current business processes by continuously reviewing and revising them

Cause-and-Effect Diagram

A tool used to examine quality factors

A visual tool to organize factors that contribute to certain outcomes; also called a fishbone diagram

Histogram

A bar graph showing frequency distribution

A bar graph that shows the upper and lower limits in a set of data

Pareto Chart

Chart that shows most frequently occurring items

A vertical bar graph in which values are plotted in decreasing order of frequency, from left to right; often used in quality control

Scatter Diagram

Chart that shows relationships between variables

A graph with a vertical axis and a horizontal axis with dots at each data point; also called a scatter plot or dot chart

Metrics

Measuring HRD efforts is both a subjective and an objective activity. Quantifiable data may be gathered and analyzed for retention rates for high-potential employees, or decreasing time to fill for leadership openings. A reduction in recruiting costs may also be attributed to HRD efforts, as are costs associated with quality defects.

Prior to selecting a training program, a cost-benefit analysis (CBA) should be conducted to determine whether training is the proper intervention activity. More on this approach is covered in the Business Management and Strategy chapter.

Measuring the return on investment of any training program is important to help executive decision makers understand the true value of training cost per employee. ROI should measure the direct costs, such as hourly rates and materials costs, but should also be used to measure the transfer of training on the job. Take a look at the case study "Measuring Return on Investment in HR: A Global Initiative for HR Strategy" at the end of this chapter for a comprehensive look at the big-picture strategic outcomes of ROI at work.

CBA, ROI, and training evaluation may all be part of a larger *learning effectiveness model*, used to measure and link training and development programs to strategic goals.

Learning Effectiveness Model

Method of assessing results of development programs

Measuring the impact of employee training and development programs on business goals

---

In addition to all of the aforementioned metrics, there are two specific objectives in the area of HRD that senior-level HR candidates must thoroughly understand: special programs that meet the rapidly changing needs of employees and organizations and the process of managing repatriation of employees returning from international assignments.

Special Programs

When change is happening, an organization and its HR delegates must be in a position to respond with special services, programs, or different ways of solving new challenges. The changing needs of the workforce may drive special HRD programs, or the need may be a direct descendant of the company's strategic plan. Regardless of the impetus, these programs are generally in response to some level of change going on within the organization. Special programs include:

Telecommuting Understanding and effectively managing the benefits this alternative staffing arrangement may have on company and individual needs requires thoughtful planning. Telecommuting can have a direct effect on employee *work/life balance* while reducing overhead expenses for a company that is embarking on an expense-reduction journey. Outside of the initial overhead expenses of setting up laptops and other equipment, employees who work from home are not on-site using office space, lights, phone lines, and so on. Telecommuting may also benefit a company that has many jobs requiring difficult-to-find skills. By removing geographic barriers, the applicant pool and subsequent available skill sets are made much larger. For companies with high turnover, telecommuting has been shown to increase retention because of the flexibility it offers workers. Consider the portable career path discussed earlier. If a spouse of a military employee is forced to relocate, telecommuting may be a viable option to retain the knowledge and skill set of the employee, who would otherwise be forced to resign.

Diversity *Diversity* is another special program seasoned HRPs should be prepared to address. Employee and manager training is often a large component of a diversity initiative. Training may be compliance driven, such as through antiharassment and retaliation policies, but may also be focused on the benefits of diversity in a collaborative, customer-centered environment.

Many managers base diversity on the protected class characteristics identified by various labor laws, including race, ethnicity, or religion. *Cultural coaching* efforts are employed by HR to help managers and employees better manage relationships with coworkers and develop *cultural intelligence* and competencies. HR's diversity efforts should focus on much more than cultural components. Varying educational levels and work experiences showcase many different ways of accomplishing outcomes. In these cases, an HR professional may design training that includes information regarding the value of constructive conflict. This type of conflict embraces the process of collaborating through differences in order to find the best possible solution to a problem or course of action.

Other types of diversity training may focus on specific needs, such as increasing the awareness of workplace diversity, or providing basic reading and writing skills to workers who need them. These efforts demonstrate an employer's commitment to giving everyone the opportunity to apply their unique skill set to the effort of work. Finally, diversity initiatives may roll down from the organization's strategic plan to align with local and regional practices, in which training is but one element of action.

Other reasons companies may take a strategic approach to manage diversity include the need for a cultural change within the organization. Perhaps a toxic supervisor or executive has recently been replaced, and the company needs to engage in repair efforts. Or perhaps the recruiting numbers show that the organization is not attracting talented individuals from certain cultural groups. There may be an element of risk management driving the efforts in order to prevent inappropriate or harassing behaviors from occurring, and response planning should anything of the kind happen. Regardless of the reasons, diversity is absolutely within the framework of responsibilities of a senior-level human resource professional.

Work/Life Balance

The time allocated to the work and to the personal parts of one's life

The ability to effectively manage time at work with the time spent on life demands, leisure, or with family members

Diversity

Composed of different elements

A combination of various types of people working together, often with differences in culture, race, generation, gender, or religion

Cultural Coaching

Guidance to help a person interact to achieve greater success with other cultures

Giving support and suggestions to help employees achieve greater success with different cultures

Cultural Intelligence

Measure of competence in culturally diverse situations

A person's ability to function in multicultural situations and to interact appropriately with people from different backgrounds

Training Evaluation

As discussed previously, the "E" in the ADDIE model relates to evaluating the effectiveness of employee training programs.

One of the most accepted methods used to evaluate training comes from Donald Kirkpatrick's four levels of training evaluation. They are:

Level 1, Reaction This level measures the participant's reaction to the training, most commonly administered via evaluation forms. Data regarding the instructor knowledge, environment, and a content review to gauge job relevance are collected and used to refine future training designs. Other tools include surveys, checklists, and interviews with participants within a short period of time after the sessions.

Level 2, Learning The learning level evaluates the degree to which knowledge is gained as the result of the training. Measurement tools include pretests and posttests.

Level 3, Behavior Level 3 is focused on the application of the knowledge, skills, or abilities learned in the training session. Tools used to measure behavioral outcomes are applied while the employee is working, such as simulations, observations, and performance tests.

Level 4, Results This level evaluates whether organizational or individual goals were met as the result of training. This is often measured by comparing target performance prior to the training and when a period of time has passed after the training.

In addition to Kirkpatrick's four levels, Jack Phillips added a fifth element: training ROI. This level seeks to evaluate learning in the context of return on investment. It compares the tangible financial outcomes of the training to the cost to provide the training to measure value.

> The case study at the end of this chapter reflects the global HR processes advanced by Jack and Patti Phillips at the ROI Institute.

Expatriation and Repatriation

Supporting the needs of all employees—not just those who work at corporate headquarters—is necessary for senior-level HR pros. It's often easy to get caught up in the day-to-day needs of the workforce that shares geographic space with the HR team, but HR at a senior level must focus on the entire workforce. For this reason, international staffing issues are explored in three chapters: Workforce Planning and Employment, Compensation and Benefits, and here.

In the context of HRD, in order for an *expatriate assignment* to be successful there must be a process to manage the placement. As with any selection, the first step is to establish the criteria for hire. Many employees may have the necessary skill set to perform the duties of the job, but may not be well suited for the change of location. Addressing the needs of an *assignee's* family may also be necessary for a successful international assignment. Offering language and cultural training is also a component of successful expatriate experiences. *Commuter assignments* require special attention in the selection and management of a successful placement; not everyone is suited for the lifestyle. The ability to shift between different cultural norms and to apply local management practices may require extensive training and ongoing support. Global assignees should be evaluated for very specific cultural competencies appropriate for the assignment location.

Repatriation is all of the above but in reverse. Repatriation involves reorienting an employee who had been working abroad back into the home country.

Repatriating workers is much more than supporting relocation. HRD efforts may need to include a review of compensation, particularly if working in another country causes the employee to miss out on promotion opportunities. Helping the employee and the family deal with *reentry shock* by reintegrating families into schools, providing job search support for the spouse, and transitioning the employee back into the economy through tax or housing needs are all methods of repatriation support.

Professionally, the repatriate may need to ease back into the home country pace of work or ramp up depending on where the international assignment was. Repatriates have a strong desire to apply what they learned on the international assignment to the work flow of the home country location, usually with mixed results if improperly managed. HR can help integrate these workers and their new skills in a systematic way, encouraging them to find opportunities to use their talent regularly, to mentor or train other international assignees, or to participate in OD interventions to provide an alternative viewpoint. A combination of customized strategies will help increase the retention of the repatriate, and encourage the acceptance of a future deployment when appropriate.

Expatriate

A citizen of one country who lives in another country

An employee who has been transferred from the person's country of citizenship (home country) to live and work in another country (host country)

Expatriate Assignment

A job outside the home country

A position in one country that is filled by a person from another country who moves there to live and work

Assignee

Expatriate, transferee

A person who is on (or will go on) an international work assignment

(continued)

(continued)

Commuter Assignment

A type of expatriate position requiring frequent travel between two countries

An international job that requires an employee to live in one country and work in another country, and to travel regularly between them (for example, an expatriate who lives in Bahrain and works in Saudi Arabia)

Repatriate

To return to the country of origin

To return home from an international work assignment

Reentry Shock

Culture shock upon repatriation

The transition challenges that a person experiences when returning to his or her home country after living in another culture

---

Suggested Study or Organizational Audit Activities

- Find and take a free or low-cost leadership style assessment online. What is your leadership style? How has your style positively affected you on the job? When has your leadership style put you at a disadvantage? Share you leadership style with your own manager, or someone you trust. Discuss ways in which you can be a more effective leader.
- Prepare a training session for a group within your organization. It may be your own HR staff, the management team, or the executive team. Select an HRD topic that you feel would be of most use at your place of work. Suggestions include leadership styles, theories of motivation, and rater bias in performance reviews.
- Create an employee satisfaction survey that focuses on the performance appraisal process at your place of work. Create one for all employees, and one for just supervisors. Evaluate the feedback, and brainstorm with your team on methods you may use to improve or enhance the assessment process.

CASE STUDY: MEASURING RETURN ON INVESTMENT IN HR

A Global Initiative for HR Strategy

Jack Phillips, PhD, and Patti Phillips, PhD

ROI in Action

ROI has been growing as an important tool for the HR team. Here are three scenarios that illustrate just how much ROI is being used as a tool to connect HR to the business.

Top Executive Support

Twenty-three HR professionals convened at a downtown hotel near company headquarters for an all-day briefing session. They were joined by a variety of executives, including the Chief Financial Officer (CFO). On the agenda was a presentation of eight ROI studies conducted by the HR team. These studies showed the impact, including ROI, of a variety of initiatives such as improving work climate, absenteeism reduction, language training, project management solutions, and leadership development. The presentations were professional, on track, and full of information. The presenters were sharp, but a bit nervous. The audience raised many questions, often stirring up debate among participants and the executives. At the end of the day, the studies were a smashing success, and this was the final step for 12 of the presenters becoming Certified ROI Professionals. After the presentations, the group adjourned to company headquarters for a presentation by the company's CEO, congratulating the HR professionals for their work and their achievement with an eye toward the next 12 participants coming behind them. Certificates designating these HR professionals as Certified ROI Professionals were presented by the chief financial officer.

Building Capacity

In the second scenario, 25 senior HR executives with the titles of senior vice president, group HR head, or executive vice president of HR convened in an airport hotel to focus on one critical topic: building key competencies to conduct ROI studies. These executives were learning how to measure the impact of a variety of programs such as Performance Management System, Leadership Development, Reducing Lost Time Accidents, Executive MBA, Building Manager Effectiveness, and Employee Retention. For five days, they tackled assignments, discussed applications, and prepared for presentations. Homework was a standard item on the agenda. The groups practiced presenting ROI studies to the top executive team and developed specific plans to conduct an ROI impact study, which was required to become a Certified ROI Professional.

Tackling the Issues

In the third scenario, a group of 22 HR managers met at the conference center of a major organization that served as a host for a five-day ROI Certification Workshop. These managers were eager to tackle the subject and were enthused about being there. For many of them, this was a long-awaited program. Finally, they were learning how to show their contribution—to make a difference in their organization. Their projects and issues explored were diverse. At the

(continued)

(continued)

beginning of the session, the participants detailed the concerns they had about ROI. Thirteen key issues were identified by the group as they tackled the ROI concerns. One by one, the group tackled each of these issues as they learned more about ROI and how to use it in their respective settings. Ultimately, the goal was to develop the capability to conduct ROI studies routinely after they achieved ROI Certification.

Key Issues about ROI

1. Selecting projects for ROI studies
2. Using ROI data to gain respect from management
3. Justifying the HR budget
4. Ensuring that the ROI methodology is credible
5. Forecasting the value of a project in advance of implementation
6. Measuring ROI for soft programs
7. Ensuring that the ROI process is consistent from one study to another
8. Keeping the ROI process as simple as possible
9. Integrating ROI with other processes in the organization
10. Isolating the effects of HR from other factors
11. Sustaining the use of ROI over a period of time
12. Getting managers involved in the process
13. Building management support for ROI

A Global Issue

No, these sessions were not in New York, Chicago, or San Francisco. No, this is not some type of human resources fad or gimmick. These situations represent what is quietly taking place around the globe. The first scenario took place in Santiago, Chile, and involves Codelco, the world's largest copper mining company. The President and CEO, José Pablo Arellano, and the Senior Vice President of Finance, Francisco Tomic, expressed their support for the use of ROI as it is used to show the impact of human capital in the organization.

The second scenario was in Mumbai (formerly Bombay), India. The executives were attending with an eye to implement the ROI methodology within their organizations to show the senior executives and other stakeholders the value of human capital. These senior executives at the top of the HR function represented some of the most impressive companies in India. They were willing to devote an entire week to make sure they understood the process completely before taking the time and effort to implement it throughout their organizations. Imagine the head of HR of a major U.S. company participating in a workshop for a week to learn how to conduct ROI studies.

The third scenario took place in Johannesburg, South Africa. The participants represented a broad range of organizations, including government agencies, the rail system, postal services, telecommunications, electric utilities, banking, manufacturing, as well as mining companies. They were the elite, well-known, and respected organizations in South Africa and neighboring African countries. For example, one of the executives in the room was head of HR for Safaricom, a telecommunications company in Kenya. Ultimately, he sent additional HR managers to Washington and London for the same training to implement the ROI process in their organization.

These scenarios and others like them are being repeated globally in more than 60 countries as the ROI methodology becomes the new tool for the HR executive. HR executives are frustrated with the lack of respect for HR. They are concerned about the image and contribution of HR and are determined to do something about it. These executives are involved because they want to be involved. They have taken a proactive approach to show alignment, contribution, and results from HR using a process that has been evolving since the 1970s.

Why ROI?

Calculating ROI has been a valuable measurement tool for a long time—it is not the latest management fad. A century ago, ROI was the emerging tool to place a value on the payoff of capital investments. In the 1920s, the *Harvard Business Review* proclaimed ROI as the principal tool to measure results. In recent years, the application of the concept has been expanded to all types of investments, including human capital investment. This reflects the growing demand for evidence of positive returns on investing in people and in HR programs. Today, key clients—those funding HR initiatives—require critical evaluation data, and measuring ROI can be a valuable tool for communicating the positive impact of HR's work on the organization.

For an ROI process to be feasible, it must balance many issues, including feasibility, simplicity, credibility, and soundness. The ROI methodology described in this article meets these challenges.

The ROI Methodology/Approach

To develop a credible approach for calculating the ROI in HR, several pieces of an evaluation puzzle must be solved and integrated. This puzzle comprises five key elements of the ROI process:

1. An evaluation framework is needed to define the various levels of evaluation and types of data.
2. A process model must be created to provide a step-by-step procedure for developing the actual ROI calculation. Part of this process is the isolation of the effects of the program from other factors in order to show the monetary payoff of the HR project.
3. A set of operating standards with a conservative philosophy is required. These guiding principles keep the process on track to ensure successful replication. The conservative standards also build credibility with executives in the organization.
4. Successful case applications are critical to show how ROI actually works in the organization. Users of the ROI process are encouraged to conduct a case study quickly for an immediate application.
5. Finally, the necessary resources should be devoted to implementation issues to ensure that the ROI process becomes operational in the organization. ROI implementation addresses issues such as responsibilities, policies, procedures, guidelines, goals, and internal skill building.

Together, these five elements are necessary to solve the ROI puzzle and develop a comprehensive evaluation system that contains a balanced set of measures, has credibility with the various stakeholders involved, and can be easily replicated. Here's a closer look at these five essential pieces.

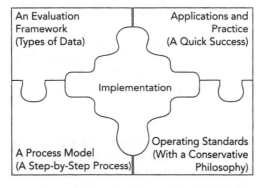

(continued)

(continued)

The Evaluation Framework

There are seven types of data used in the ROI process. Although these data types can be considered separately, they are inevitably woven together and their meaning lies in relationship to one another. The graphic shows these types of data and our progress with collecting and analyzing them.

Level	Measurement Category	Current Status*	Goal*	Comments about Status
0	**Inputs/Indicators** Measures inputs including the number of programs, audience, costs, and efficiencies	100%	100%	This is being accomplished now
1	**Reaction** Measures reaction to experience, content, and value of the program	100%	100%	Need more focus on content and perceived value
2	**Learning** Measures what participants learned— information, knowledge, skills, and contacts (what they need to know to make the program successful)	30–40%	80–90%	Must use simple learning measures for most programs
3	**Application and Implementation** Measures progress post-program— the use of knowledge, skills, and contacts (what they have done to make the program successful)	10%	30%	Need more follow-up
4	**Impact and Consequences** Measures changes in business impact variables such as output, quality, time, and cost-linked to the program—the business success of the program	5%	10%	This is the connection to business impact. The influence of the program is isolated from other factors.
5	**ROI** Compares the monetary benefits of the impact measures to the costs of the program	1%	5%	The ultimate level of evaluation

(Chain of Impact spans levels 2 through 4, shown in the left margin)

*Percent of programs evaluated at this level.

A chain of impact should occur through the levels and types of data as the skills and knowledge learned during the HR program are applied on the job as implementation takes place to produce business impact and drive a positive ROI. It is recommended that data be collected at all levels when planning an ROI evaluation.

The Process Model

Represented by the model in the following graphic, the ROI process has been refined and modified over many applications. As the figure illustrates, the process is comprehensive as data are developed at different times and gathered from different sources to develop the seven types of measures. Each part of the process is outlined next.

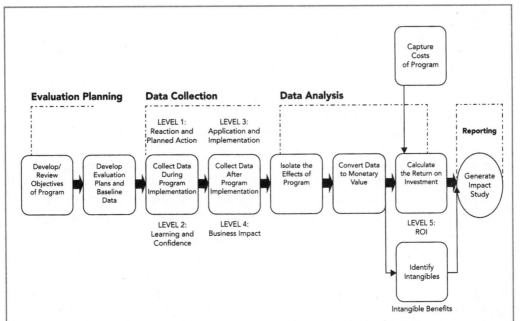

Evaluation planning The first two parts of the ROI process focus on critical planning issues. The first step is to develop appropriate objectives for the HR initiatives. These range from developing objectives for reaction to developing an objective for the ROI. A specific program should have multiple levels of objectives.

With the objectives in hand, the next step is to develop two important planning documents. A data collection plan indicates the type of data collected, the method for data collection, data sources, the timing of collection, and the various responsibilities for collection. The ROI analysis plan details how the HR initiative is isolated from other influences, how data are converted to monetary values, the appropriate cost categories, the expected intangible measures, and the anticipated target audience for communication.

Collecting data Data collected during the launch of the HR program measures reaction and learning to ensure that adjustments are made to keep the program on track. The reaction and learning data are critical for immediate feedback to make early changes. Sometimes postprogram data are collected and compared with preprogram data and expectations. Both hard data and soft data are collected. Data can be collected using a variety of methods.

Isolating the effects of the HR program An often overlooked issue in most evaluations i s the process of isolating the effects of an HR program. This step is essential because many factors will influence performance data after an HR program is implemented. Specific strategies in this step will pinpoint the amount of improvement directly related to the HR program. The result is increased accuracy and credibility of the ROI calculation. A total of 10 strategies have been used to address this important issue. Here are the three most common strategies:

1. A pilot group of participants in an HR program is compared with a comparison (control) group not participating in the program to isolate program impact.

2. Trend lines are used to project the values of business impact data, and projections are compared with the actual data after an HR program.

3. Participants/stakeholders estimate the amount of improvement related to an HR program; when estimates are used, the values are adjusted for error.

(continued)

(continued)

Converting data to monetary values To calculate the return on investment, business impact data need to be converted to monetary values and compared with HR program costs. This requires a value to be placed on each unit of data connected with the HR program. Ten strategies are available to convert data to monetary values.

Tabulating the cost of the HR program The denominator of the ROI formula is the cost of the HR program. The typical cost components are: initial analysis and assessment, development/design cost for the HR program, participant/stakeholder time for the HR program, implementation costs, maintenance costs, administration costs, and evaluating and reporting costs.

The conservative approach is to include all these costs so that the total is fully loaded.

Calculating ROI The return on investment is calculated using benefits and costs. The benefit/cost ratio (BCR) is the monetary benefits of the HR program divided by the costs. In formula form, it is:

$$BCR = \frac{HR\ program\ monetary\ benefits}{HR\ program\ costs}$$

Sometimes this ratio is stated as a cost/benefit ratio, although the formula is the same as the BCR formula—the return on investment uses the net benefits divided by costs. The net benefits are the program benefits minus the costs. In formula form, the ROI becomes:

$$ROI\ (\%) = \frac{HR\ program\ costs}{Net\ HR\ program\ benefits} \times 100$$

This is the same basic formula used in evaluating other investments where the ROI is traditionally reported as earnings divided by investment. The BCR and ROI formulas present the same general information but with slightly different perspectives. Here's an example that illustrates the use of these formulas:

An absenteeism reduction program for city bus drivers produced savings of $581,000, with a cost of $229,000. Therefore, the benefit/cost ratio is:

$$BCR = \frac{\$581,000}{\$229,000} = 2.54\ (or\ 2.51{:}1)$$

As this calculation shows, for every $1 invested, $2.50 in monetary benefits is returned. In this example, net benefits are $581,000 – $229,000 = $352,000. Thus, the ROI would be:

$$ROI = \frac{\$352,000}{\$229,000} \times 100 = 154\%$$

This means each $1 invested in the program returns $1.54 in net benefits, after costs are covered. The benefits are usually expressed as annual benefits for short-term programs, representing the amount saved or gained for a complete year after the program has been implemented. Although the benefits may continue after the first year, the impact usually diminishes and is omitted from calculations in short-term situations. For long-term projects, the benefits are spread over several years. The timing of the benefits stream is determined before the impact study begins, as part of the planning process. For a complete copy of this study, contact info@roiinstitute.net.

Identifying intangible benefits During data analysis, every attempt is made to convert all data to monetary values. However, if the conversion process is too subjective or inaccurate and the resulting values lose credibility in the process, the data are listed as intangible benefits with the appropriate explanation. For some programs, intangible, nonmonetary benefits have extreme value, often commanding as much attention and influence as the hard data items. Intangible benefits may include items such as improved public image, increased communication, improved customer satisfaction, increased employee engagement, reduced stress, and improved teamwork.

Reporting results A final operational step of the ROI process is to generate an impact study to document the results achieved by the HR program and communicate them to various target audiences. A variety of different reports and formats are used to disseminate the information, ranging from the complete impact study described earlier to a one-page summary for clients who understand the process.

Standard Guiding Principles

To ensure that each study is developed in the same way, consistent processes and operating standards for the measurement and evaluation process should be implemented. The following 12 guiding principles should be used as operating standards when implementing the ROI process:

1. When conducting a higher-level evaluation, collect data at lower levels.
2. When planning a higher-level evaluation, the previous level of evaluation is not required to be comprehensive.
3. When collecting and analyzing data, use only the most credible sources.
4. When analyzing data, select the most conservative alternatives for calculations.
5. Use at least one method to isolate the effects of the program or project.
6. If no improvement data are available for a population or from a specific source, assume that little or no improvement has occurred.
7. Adjust estimates of improvements for the potential error of the estimates.
8. Avoid use of extreme data items and unsupported claims when calculating ROI calculations.
9. Use only the first year of annual benefits in the ROI analysis of short-term solutions.
10. Fully load all costs of the solution, project, or program when analyzing ROI.
11. Intangible measures are defined as measures that are purposely not converted to monetary values.
12. Communicate the results of the ROI methodology to all key stakeholders.

These guiding principles will ensure that the proper conservative approach is taken and the impact study can be replicated and compared with others. More important, the principles build credibility with, and support from, clients and senior managers who review and scrutinize results.

Applications and Practice

Another major element of the ROI methodology is application. As with any new change or process, there must be a speedy application to ensure that what was learned is used properly. Because this methodology is user friendly, valid and reliable, and CEO/CFO friendly, it has become the most used evaluation system in the world. Participants involved in ROI Certification are required to conduct an ROI study before they achieve certified ROI status. The types of projects undertaken vary and represent any type of project, program, event, or initiative in the talent management and HR function.

(continued)

(continued)

Implementation

The best tool, technique, or model will not be successful unless it is properly utilized and becomes a routine part of the HR function. As with any change, it will be resisted by the HR staff and other stakeholders. Some of the resistance will be based on realistic barriers, while much of it will be based on misunderstandings and perceived problems that may be mythical. In both cases, specific steps must be taken to overcome the resistance by carefully and methodically implementing the ROI process. Implementation involves several issues, including assigning responsibilities, building the necessary skills, and developing the plans and goals around the process. It also involves preparing the environment, team members, and support staff for this type of comprehensive analysis.

The greatest challenge is fear. Some HR staff members do not pursue ROI because they perceive the ROI as an individual performance evaluation process instead of a process improvement tool. A planned implementation will help to overcome these barriers and meet the challenges.

Benefits of ROI Use

With the ROI process, the HR staff and the client will know the specific contribution of an HR program, with data not previously developed or in a language understood by the client. Measuring ROI is one of the most convincing ways to earn the respect and support of the senior management team—not only for a particular HR program, but also for other HR projects as well. The client who requests and authorizes an HR program will have a complete set of data to show the overall success of the process. Throughout the cycle of HR program design, development, and implementation, the entire team of stakeholders focuses on results. Because a variety of feedback data are collected during the HR program, the comprehensive analysis provides data to drive changes in HR processes and make adjustments during program implementation. If a program is not effective and the results are not materializing, the ROI process will prompt changes or modifications.

Outlook

While the ROI methodology has enjoyed success, it has just reached the tipping point in the HR world. Although the benchmarking results vary by country, it is estimated that in most countries only 10 to 15 percent of HR functions are using this methodology. Yet the same benchmarking shows that as many as 75 to 80 percent of them plan to use ROI. They wish they were using it now. This huge gap between "actual use" and "wish we were using" creates a great opportunity, but also some great challenges. The payoff, in terms of building support for programs, improving programs, and increasing funding for HR, is huge. As more organizations understand the success that can be achieved with this methodology, more will embrace it.

References

Allen Interactions. n.d. "Iterative eLearning Development with SAM." Retrieved from www.alleninteractions.com/sam-process.

Elkeles, Tamar, Jack J. Phillips, and Patti P. Phillips. 2017. *The Chief Talent Officer.* 2nd ed. New York and London: Routledge.

Jones, Marshall (Ed.). 2010. *Psychology of Leadership: Theory and Practice.* Mason, OH: Cengage Learning.

Kirkpatrick, James D., and Wendy Keyser Kirkpatrick. 2016. *Kirkpatrick's Four Levels of Training Evaluation.* Alexandria, VA: Association for Talent Development.

Knowles, Malcolm, Elwood F. Holton III, and Richard A. Swanson. 2015. *The Adult Learner: The definitive classic in adult education and human resource development.* New York and London: Routledge.

Phillips, Jack J., and Patti P. Phillips. 2012. *Proving the Value of HR: How and Why to Measure ROI.* 2nd ed. Alexandria, VA: Society for Human Resource Management.

Phillips, Jack J., and Patti P. Phillips. 2015. *High-Impact Human Capital Strategy: Addressing the 12 Major Challenges Today's Organizations Face.* New York: AMACOM.

Phillips, Jack J., Patti P. Phillips, and Kirk Smith. 2016. *Accountability in Human Resource Management: Connecting HR to Business Results.* 2nd ed. New York and London: Routledge.

Rath, T., and B. Conchie. 2009. *Strengths Based Leadership: Great Leaders, Teams, and Why People Follow.* New York: Gallup Press.

Russell, Lou. 2015. "Methodology Wars: ADDIE vs. SAM vs. AGILE." Association for Talent Development, April 8. Retrieved from https://www.td.org/Publications/Blogs/L-and-D-Blog/2015/04/Methodology-Wars.

Tarique, I., D. Briscoe, and R. Schuler. 2016. *International Human Resource Management.* 5th ed. New York: Routledge.

Tyler, K. 1999. "Offering English Lessons at Work." *HR Magazine,* December, 112–120.

5 | Compensation and Benefits

(*continued*)

Organizational justice perceptions consist of three primary dimensions, distributive, procedural, and interactional justice, each associated with important organizational outcomes (Bies and Moag 1986; Colquitt et al. 2001). Distributive justice refers to the appraisal of the fairness of outcomes, such as pay, given in an organization (Colquitt and Greenburg 2003). These distributive fairness appraisals are based on subjective perceptions of equality, equity, and need (Colquitt 2001). Distributive justice perceptions of economic outcome distributions in particular (such as pay) are thought to be fostered when organizations base decisions for distribution on varying levels of employee performance or contributions (Cropanzano, Bowen, and Gilliland 2007).

Procedural justice refers to the perceived fairness of processes that result in outcome decisions and allocations (Thibaut and Walker 1975). This dimension of organizational justice can be achieved through adhering to fair and ethical process criteria and by allowing employees to have an influence in decision making processes and/or a voice during the decision making process. Finally, interactional justice focuses on the treatment received when processes are implemented, and includes interpersonal aspects of respect and propriety as well as informational aspects of truthfulness and justifications (Bies and Moag 1986). More specifically, interactional justice involves the human side of organizational processes, including the treatment individuals receive when procedures are implemented (Cohen-Charash and Spector 2001; Colquitt et al. 2001). Interactional justice may be fostered through treating people with respect and through thorough and timely explanations of reasons for decisions (Colquitt 2001).

Studies have shown that examining justice perceptions in the workplace is valuable due to their effects on important job attitudes and behaviors. For instance, organizational justice perceptions have been found to relate to several important outcomes, such as trust in decision makers, outcome satisfaction (e.g., satisfaction with pay), organizational commitment, helping behaviors, and better performance (Colquitt et al. 2001). Additionally, low perceptions of organizational justice have been associated with various negative consequences, such as retaliatory behaviors (e.g., Skarlicki and Folger 1997) and withdrawal behaviors (e.g., turnover, absenteeism; Colquitt et al. 2001). Although all aspects of organizational justice are important to maintain, perceptions of justice are expected to interact in a way where the negative impact of injustice can be mitigated (at least partially) as long as at least one form of justice is perceived (Cropanzano, Bowen, and Gilliland 2007).

Ultimately, organizational justice is an important topic area for human resources as HR professionals can take an active role in influencing employee perceptions of justice through their involvement in fair employment practices, such as wage and promotion distributions, and through guiding and training supervisors on how to communicate and discuss these practices with employees (Folger and Cropanzano 1998). The following case studies highlight events that impact justice perceptions in performance management contexts.

Case Study 1

Company A

A retail company in the Northeastern portion of the United States recently conducted its annual performance reviews and accompanying raises. This year, employees all received a 2 percent raise. Each employee was given a notification letter of the percent increase in pay, which stated the following:

Dear [Employee Name]:

This letter notifies you of an increase in wage in the amount of 2 percent of your base pay. The effective date of this increase is October 1, 2016, and the increase in pay will appear in the pay received on October 10, 2016.

We hope this increase will act as an incentive for your continued performance put forth for achieving business goals and future objectives.

The day after the last performance review meeting was held, a high-performing employee reached out to her supervisor to inquire about her raise. She expressed to her supervisor that she had heard that other noticeably lower-performing employees received the same amount increase as she did. In reply, her supervisor simply stated, "That's just the way it is this year" and "We didn't want to make any waves."

Company B

A small Southeastern distribution center recently conducted its annual performance reviews. Employee raises ranged from 0.5 percent to 3 percent. During the annual performance reviews, Michelle, the distribution center manager, went over performance appraisals and accompanying performance and developmental goals with each employee. At this time, Michelle also distributed raises, which were directly tied to employee performance ratings.

At the end of each performance review, Michelle asked the employee if the person had any questions or concerns. During this time, one employee, Allison, voiced her frustrations with her raise amount. She expressed that she was hoping for a higher raise than she had received the previous year because of her increase in responsibilities and her achievement of various performance goals. After listening to Allison, Michelle stated that she completely understood Allison's concerns and reiterated how valuable Allison was to the company. Michelle explained how Allison's raise was a direct result of specific performance aspects, which were also identified in her performance appraisal. Michelle then gave Allison specific strategies to help her improve her performance ratings, and thus her raise, for next year.

Case Study Questions

1. Compare and contrast the organizational justice elements of Companies A and B.
   a. What dimensions of organizational justice were present or deficient in each company?
   b. Describe strategies to increase perceptions of organizational justice in the performance review process.
2. Describe potential benefits and/or consequences that these perceptions of organizational justice could have in each company.

Instructor Answer Guide

1. Companies A and B differ on the distributive justice dimension of organizational justice. Although Company A has an equal distribution of raises (2 percent), this outcome is not equitable. In other words, the employee raises and quantitative performance appraisal results do not correspond to their differences in contribution to the company. Therefore, Company A's employee perceptions of distributive justice are likely to be low for those who feel as if they contributed more to the company than their coworkers who received

(continued)

(*continued*)

the same raise amount. Alternatively, Company B's distributive justice perceptions may be more likely to be high, as its raises, although different, are equitable in that employees with greater company contributions received higher outcomes than employees with smaller company contributions (based on the information that they were tied to the performance appraisal results). Although distributive justice perceptions are often subjective in nature (e.g., what employees think is equitable may depend on the social comparisons they make), each company can foster these perceptions by basing distributions of pay and raise amounts on varying levels of employee contributions.

Companies A and B differ on the procedural justice dimension of organizational justice. Company A lacks a clear performance management process for determining pay raises, whereas Company B bases raise amounts on the results of annual performance appraisals. Thus, there is a clear process in place for determining employee raises in Company B, which should result in higher perceptions of procedural justice than in Company A. Perceptions of procedural justice in both companies may be increased if employees are able to have a say in or voice their opinion on the criteria used to determine raise distributions. This may be achieved through an open discussion of performance appraisal criteria at the beginning of each performance review cycle where employees are allowed to express any concerns about the criteria, and by allowing employees to have input in establishing the criteria and/or jointly setting performance goals.

Companies A and B differ on the interactional justice dimension of organizational justice. Managers at Company A did not provide clear justifications or information regarding how raises were determined. Alternatively, the manager at Company B displayed inter-personal consideration by listening to employee concerns and showing appreciation for the employee. Further, the manager provided thorough explanations for raise-related deci-sions. Ultimately, the respectful interpersonal treatment and clear information presented in Company B should result in higher perceptions of interactional justice than in Company A. Perceptions of interactional justice may be fostered in these settings by respectful and empathetic treatment toward all employees and through timely and adequate explanations of how raise amounts are determined and linked to performance appraisal ratings.

2. Various outcomes may be listed. For example, Company A may have a greater likelihood of outcomes such as increases in lateness, absenteeism, and turnover, and lower satisfaction with pay. Company B may be more likely to have greater employee trust in the company, greater satisfaction with pay, higher employee commitment, and increases in organizational performance and helping behaviors.

Case Study 2

Applied Science Tech (AST) is the research division of a training company in the American Northwest. Among other employees, AST employs 12 research analysts, two project managers, and a director. The managers have a fairly hands-off approach when it comes to overseeing day-to-day work. Typically, employees work well together in strategizing and planning to accom-plish business goals. However, in the past several months, performance has been declining and morale seems to be at an all-time low. The director of AST has asked an organizational climate consultant, Lisa, to investigate why these changes have occurred and to suggest strategies for improvement.

Lisa begins her investigation by conducting one-on-one interviews with the research analysts. She interviews James, who is a relatively new research analyst and was recently told that he would be the lead on a new effort to develop a training program for workplace diversity and inclusion (D&I) initiatives for organizational leaders. While James never wants to decline an opportunity, he is unsure why he was selected for this role. Although he is not the lead on any current project, he is a vital and active member on other efforts of the company, which gives him a fairly heavy workload. Taking on this opportunity means that he will have to take a less active role in the other efforts, which may cause their progress to suffer. Additionally, he knows that his coworker, Christa, has expertise in D&I and would potentially be a better match for leading this initiative.

When speaking to the other research analysts, Lisa learns that they don't know how management makes decisions but assume that they're made arbitrarily. One analyst expressed that he guesses management often distributes opportunities based on who they think is due for a lead role rather than considering current individual workloads and expertise. All of the analysts express their ongoing frustrations with this issue. One coworker divulged that she lacks motivation to perform to her highest potential because it ultimately does not result in any recognition in terms of additional opportunities. Lisa inquired about whether anyone has expressed this to the managers. The analysts state that they have tried but their managers fail to offer clear explanations and often sidestep the issue.

Case Study Questions

1. Based on your review of Case Study 2, identify the dimensions of organizational justice that are deficient at AST. Explain your rationale.
2. What should Lisa tell the director of AST for strategies to increase perceptions of organizational justice of the research analysts?

Instructor Answer Guide

1. Although each analyst seems to be given opportunities to lead a project, the process for deciding who gets which opportunity is very unclear. The opportunities don't seem to be based on each analyst's expertise or contributions; thus, perceptions of distributive justice may be low. Not having clear processes in place (procedural justice) or explanations for how outcomes are determined (interactional justice) has resulted in the analysts drawing their own conclusions about managerial processes, leading to feelings of frustration and a lack of motivation.
2. Lisa could advise the director of AST to ensure that management takes into account each analyst's area of expertise, current workload, and developmental goals when distributing opportunities to lead projects. These practices should help each analyst perceive an equitable distribution of outcomes. To increase perceptions of procedural justice, management should inform all analysts that decisions are based on these factors, as well as any other criteria management finds important (such as performance), and allow analysts opportunities to provide input on the criteria. Additionally, for analysts to feel heard and respected (aspects of procedural and interactional justice), managers should be coached on how to actively listen to the analysts when they bring up concerns, and acknowledge and address concerns as appropriate. Further, upon giving analysts opportunities, the rationale for why each opportunity was given should be explained. All interactions between management and analysts should be conducted in a respectful manner.

(continued)

(continued)

References

Bies, R. J., and J. F. Moag. 1986. "Interactional Justice: Communication Criteria of Fairness." In R. J. Lewicki, B. H. Sheppard, and M. H. Bazerman (Eds.), *Research on Negotiations in Organizations*, Vol. 1, 43–55. Greenwich, CT: JAI Press.

Cohen-Charash, Y., and P. E. Spector. 2001. "The Role of Justice in Organizations: A Meta-Analysis." *Organizational Behavior and Human Decision Processes* 86(2): 278–321.

Colquitt, J. A. 2001. "On the Dimensionality of Organizational Justice: A Construct Validation of a Measure." *Journal of Applied Psychology* 86:386–400.

Colquitt, J. A., D. E. Conlon, M. J. Wesson, C. O. L. H. Porter, and K. Y. Ng. 2001. "Justice at the Millennium: A Meta-Analytic Review of 25 Years of Organizational Justice Research." *Journal of Applied Psychology* 3:425–445.

Colquitt, J., J. Greenberg, and C. Zapata-Phelan. 2005. "What Is Organizational Justice? A Historical Overview." In J. Greenberg and J. Colquitt (Eds.), *Handbook of Organizational Justice*, 3–56. Mahwah, NJ: Erlbaum.

Cropanzano, R., D. E. Bowen, and S. W. Gilliland. 2007. "The Management of Organizational Justice." *Academy of Management Perspectives*, 34–38.

Cropanzano, R., and S. M. Discorfano. 2007. "Organizational Justice." In S. G. Rogelberg (Ed.), *Encyclopedia of Industrial and Organizational Psychology*, Vol. 2, 570–574. Thousand Oaks, CA: Sage.

Folger, R., and R. Cropanzano. 1998. *Organizational Justice and Human Resource Management*. Beverly Hills, CA: Sage.

Skarlicki, D. P., and R. Folger. 1997. "Retaliation in the Workplace: The Roles of Distributive, Procedural, and Interactional Justice." *Journal of Applied Psychology* 82:434–443.

Thibaut, J., and L. Walker. 1975. *Procedural Justice: A Psychological Analysis*. Hillsdale, NJ: Erlbaum.

Introduction

Raise your hand if you are paid what you are worth. If you didn't move a muscle, you aren't alone in your belief! Many employees tie their personal value directly to the amount of their paychecks, making this an important management function for the HR professionals of today. The functional area of compensation and benefits (CAB) addresses the operational activities of paying employees and the more strategic themes of attracting and retaining key talent all while maintaining a competitive position in the marketplace. The CAB efforts led by human resource professionals include:

- Establishing and maintaining CAB programs for all employees
- Creating pay structures that maintain internal and external equity
- Designing compensation and benefits programs that reward and engage the workforce
- Building and communicating legally compliant total rewards programs

- Identifying global best practices in international compensation and benefits programs and administration

Strategic Compensation

Similar to job analysis, an employer's *total reward* system impacts all other areas of HR. Pay rates and benefits offerings affect individual decisions to apply for open jobs. *Performance-based* and *variable pay systems* have a direct impact on employee productivity levels. Many American labor laws have compliance elements related to *compensation* and benefits, and international compensation practices must be accounted for in a robust global total rewards program. The decisions around a company's *total compensation* strategies are critical for HR performance across the board. This requires regular planning and program refinement as the needs of the workforce—both internal and external—are continually identified.

Total Rewards

All the tools available for attracting, motivating, and keeping employees

Financial and nonfinancial benefits that the employee sees as valuable

Performance-Based Pay

Earnings based on merit or how well the employee meets goals

Pay linked to how well the employee meets expectations; better performance results in more pay.

Variable Pay Plan

Compensation that is less predictable than standard base pay

Profit sharing, incentives, bonuses, or commissions that align compensation with performance

Compensation

Salary and benefits

Everything that an employee receives for working, including pay and nonmonetary benefits

(continued)

(continued)

Total Compensation

Complete pay package

An employee's complete pay package, including cash, benefits, and services

Compensation Philosophies

There are several questions employers must ask before embarking on a process of pricing jobs, but the most important is to establish their compensation philosophy. For some, an entitlement philosophy in which employees are given pay increases to reward loyalty is preferred. Examples include automatic annual increases calculated as a percentage of overall pay, seniority-based pay, and *cost-of-living adjustment (COLA)*. In other cases, a *pay for performance* system in which part of an employee's monetary wages are at risk makes more sense. Examples include *merit increases* linked to performance targets and bonuses for goal achievement. The primary difference between these two philosophies is that employees expect pay increases in entitlement-oriented companies whereas employees know their pay is tied to outcomes in the other.

Note that the examples all refer to how pay increases are calculated. When establishing compensation for new jobs, or during strategic planning, HR supports the job pricing process by conducting market surveys. A company with an entitlement orientation will calculate pay using industry comparisons of wages only. In a company with a performance orientation, the company will cast a wider net to make broader industry comparisons and collect data related to variable pay plans, bonuses, and other types of incentive pay. Internationally, HR will address pay philosophies to create an appropriate blend of compensation and benefits based on the practices of the countries where employees are based.

The second question that is addressed during the philosophy discussions is "Will we lead, lag, or match the labor market?" Employers must define their strategic approach to paying for positions in their relevant labor markets. It is not unusual for some positions to be paid below the market rate, particularly those with an abundance of available workers. For other positions, there may be a need to pay above market rates to attract the highest-quality talent. The decision to lead, lag, or match markets is fundamentally about supply and demand and is tied directly to the workforce planning efforts covered in the Workforce Planning and Employment (WPE) chapter.

The market data collected will serve as the baseline for wage and salary scales. The scales may then be used to account for individual differences in education, experience, or other job competencies or location variables. Figure 5.1 further illustrates this competitive strategy.

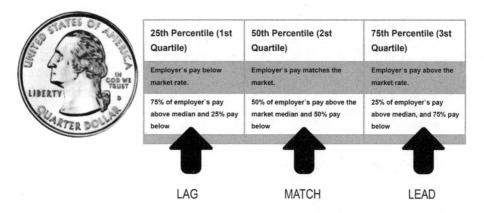

25th Percentile (1st Quartile)	50th Percentile (2st Quartile)	75th Percentile (3st Quartile)
Employer's pay below market rate.	Employer's pay matches the market.	Employer's pay above the market rate.
75% of employer's pay above median and 25% pay below	50% of employer's pay above the market median and 50% pay below	25% of employer's pay above median, and 75% pay below
LAG	MATCH	LEAD

Quartile Compensation Strategies

Figure 5.1 Quartile Compensation Strategies

HR must also help companies avoid pay compression, which occurs when the pay levels of current employees do not increase at pace with the external market. When pay differences between incoming workers and incumbents become small, pay compression has occurred. HR tools to avoid this demotivating effect include conducting regular wage surveys and advocating for market-based pay increases while still balancing the need to contain overhead costs. See the feature for a special issue regarding pay compression.

Cost-of-Living Adjustment (COLA)

Pay change due to economic conditions

An increase or decrease in pay based on changes in economic conditions in a geographic location or country

Pay for Performance

Salary based on merit or on meeting goals

A payment strategy where management links an employee's pay to desired results, behaviors, or goals   (*continued*)

(continued)

Merit Increase

Pay raise for meeting performance goals

An increase in wages for meeting or exceeding the performance goals of a job

---

PAY COMPRESSION AND STATE MINIMUM WAGE INCREASES

Many states are adopting higher minimum wage standards than called for by the Fair Labor Standards Act (FLSA). As these laws are passed and step increases occur each year, employers must also consider increases for their current workforce. For example, a California employer currently paying a customer service representative with 10 years' incumbency $17 an hour will be forced to pay new staff a minimum wage of $15 in 2021. By then, the incumbent will have 15 years invested with only a $2 hourly differential. HR can help by building in performance-based opportunities for the incumbent to raise his or her total pay rate while still helping the employer balance the rising cost of labor.

Pay Equity

As highlighted in the introduction, many employees do not feel that they are paid what they are worth. It is up to HR to help employees understand that jobs are priced using a *competency-based pay* approach—pay based on job tasks, duties, and responsibilities (TDRs). A range may also account for knowledge and experience, but only as they relate to the needs of the position.

However clear and objective a competency-based approach may be, there are still very legitimate fairness issues that must be addressed via an employer's compensation strategy. The perceived fairness of the amount of employee effort when compared to the reward for said effort is at the heart of compensation justice issues. Procedural justice is the perceived fairness of the processes used to calculate pay rates and increases. Addressing procedural justice concerns of employees is why HR should share with workers the data used to price jobs as a means of achieving *internal equity*. Distributive justice is the perceived fairness of how rewards are distributed throughout the workforce. In an entitlement-oriented company, if all employees receive the same across-the-board increase at the end of the year, the higher performers will feel aggrieved that employees with attendance or attitude problems received the same pay treatment.

External equity issues are just as important to consider, especially in labor markets that tightly compete for certain employee skill sets, such as nursing and technology. High turnover and low job satisfaction levels are just two examples of negative outcomes for employers that fail to price jobs comparable in the relevant market. In addition to retaining key talent, an employer's ability to attract qualified applicants is very often founded upon the employer's total reward system.

The degree of pay transparency behaviors of the employer is another area where HR lends expertise. Closed systems are those in which employees are discouraged from discussing their pay or benefits. However, many states as well as court interpretations of the National Labor Relations Act make it unlawful for employers to prohibit employees from discussing pay information. This includes a prohibition of policies that identify disciplinary action for employees who share their pay rates, or requiring employees to sign a document in which they agree to not disclose pay information.

See the feature for a special issue related to antitrust laws and recruitment practices in the tech industry.

SILICON VALLEY "NO COLD CALL" AGREEMENTS

Between 2010 and 2013, class action lawsuits were filed against several prominent Silicon Valley tech companies by the Department of Justice (DOJ) and other private entities. Charges against high-profile companies such as Apple, Google, Intel, and Pixar claimed that the companies' "no cold call" agreements—agreements in which each firm agreed not to poach via telephone tech talent from competitors—amounted to collusion. The suit also described practices in which the companies agreed that "when offering a position to another company's employee, neither company would counteroffer above the initial offer." This in effect suppressed market wages, a clear violation of Section 1 of the Sherman Antitrust Act. According to the DOJ, "The complaint alleges that the companies' actions reduced their ability to compete for high tech workers and interfered with the proper functioning of the price-setting mechanism that otherwise would have prevailed in competition for employees."

Most of the suits have since been settled.

Competency-Based Pay

Salary based on demonstrated skills and knowledge

Pay based on the skills and knowledge that make an employee valuable to an organization

Internal Equity

Fairness in pay and benefits for similar jobs

Making sure that employees with jobs of similar value to the organization receive equal compensation

Budgeting for Compensation and Benefits

Compensation and benefits (CAB) budgets are reviewed on an annual basis, often during the company's strategic planning process or as part of the annual budget preparation activities. CAB budgets account for current salaries plus projected increases in wages and benefits costs. Adjustments in accordance with external market conditions are also factored in.

Top-down budgets are set by the executive team, and individual departments must take steps to meet the budget requirements. These steps may include hiring freezes, layoffs, or job task blending when a CAB budget is low or unchanged.

Bottom-up approaches to budgeting build upon department forecasts for labor needs, and are a less reliable method as there are no cost control measures built into the CAB budgets.

Federal, state, and city laws do have requirements for paying the *prevailing wage*—the obligation of employers to pay a wage above minimum where required. Prevailing wage laws most often apply to jobs with federal contracts or subcontracts, whereas living wages are required in some cities with a higher cost of living. HR practitioners must know when these laws apply to their employers and incorporate them into annual budgets where possible.

Prevailing Wage

Usual wage paid to workers in an area

The hourly wage, usual benefits, and overtime that most workers receive in a certain location

Internal Revenue Service

Employment tax obligations exist on the part of both the employer and the employee. Social Security taxes, Medicare taxes, and state taxes such as disability are all types of employment-related taxes that have to be paid (either by the employer, by the employee, or shared). While these programs are discussed in more detail in Appendix A, they represent the influence the IRS has on employer pay systems. Any time employers plan to make changes to their pay systems, they must be sure to understand any tax or reporting requirements. In some cases, a private letter ruling may be requested from the IRS to find out what the tax implication of any change may be.

Fiduciary Responsibilities

HR has a fiduciary responsibility to comply with government reporting requirements, but also to hold itself to high standards of ethical compensation practices. HR could breach this obligation by creating programs that serve self-interests, and must address conflicting duties by making data-driven decisions whenever possible. HR managers must not profit from the information they have access to, such as using salary survey information to position themselves for a higher pay rate. These types of activities erode trust and compromise the advisory nature of HR's role in CAB management.

Controlling Costs of CAB Programs

The cost of payroll and benefits is hands down one of the most expensive line items on a company's profit and loss statement. While high salaries may attract and retain qualified workers, they can diminish a company's ability to compete with other businesses offering similar products for less. As with any employee program, HR is responsible to help employers balance employee needs for benefits with the need for employers to control costs. Strategies such as the use of employee copayments, changing *eligibility* time lines, and the increase in the use of managed care programs all may help defray the increasing costs of many programs.

Technology has greatly contributed to an employer's cost containment tool kit. Using direct deposit for paycheck processing or autodelivering pay statements and benefits summaries are two examples of how technology may streamline the costs associated with payroll and benefits administration. The savings brought by these types of systems range from simple reduction of the amount of paper necessary to print various documents, all the way to meaningful reductions of hourly worker time to administer.

Employee self-service technologies have grown in popularity. Using personal identification numbers to give employees access to personnel documents related to pay and benefits reduces the amount of time HR must invest in meeting the more simple of employee needs. Items such as changing the number of dependents claimed on tax forms, home address changes, autoenrolling during open enrollment when no changes are necessary are just some examples of the types of services employees may conduct on their own behalf. A word of caution: The use of technology comes with its own price tag. From the initial investment of software, training costs for employees, setting up files for workers to access, and then maintaining said files can really add up. Bank fees, user subscriptions, and help desk support also come with their own fee structures. For this reason, HR should be clear on the return on investment (ROI) of the initial costs and ongoing fees to balance out any potential savings.

With the continuing uncertainty of state and federally mandated health insurance, employers know one thing for sure—health insurance costs have continued to rise over the past several years. As a result, many employers have chosen to increase the amount of burden employees must bear for their health insurance deductibles and/or *premiums*. Other employers have shrunk the offerings of employer-sponsored health programs, or eliminated ancillary options such as dental or vision programs that are underutilized by employees.

HR is responsible for driving employee health and wellness programs to improve the overall well-being of workers. Programs include rewarding employees for losing weight or stopping smoking. Companies may offer healthier options in the employer cafeteria or eliminate soda pop from the on-site vending machines. HR may also partner with its insurance broker or occupational health clinic to educate workers on healthy behaviors, offer annual flu shots, or pay for early-detection/preventive procedures to create a healthier, more productive workplace.

HR can help employers contain the cost of CAB by establishing pay ranges that are built from market data. A manager who is given discretion within a range can make hiring or salary increase decisions that are appropriately controlled. It also allows HR to properly forecast based on anticipated hiring needs. HR may also develop pay for performance or shared rewards programs in which employees are paid when the company achieves its goals.

HR must also keep up with the changing landscape of benefits administration. This includes monitoring the political, economic, and social forces shaping the benefits of today. One relevant example from the past is the Social Security Act of 1935. Passed under President Roosevelt, this security benefit program sought to address the economic pressures brought on by the Great Depression. It addressed social responsibility needs to older and disabled Americans. The program was met with political skepticism and obstruction from those who were against forced savings and those who did not want the government to tax businesses more than it already was doing.

By understanding the political, economic, and social pressures of today, HR may not only respond to but also anticipate ways in which employers must build their programs. Political strategies to control costs include educating employees on the advantages of health savings accounts. Social cost containment strategies may include allowing leave-sharing programs, in which employees are allowed to donate personal paid time off to help a coworker in need. Economically, HR can direct employer resources toward benefits that are most desired by employees (such as paying 100 percent of an employee health insurance premium) and offering nonsponsored options for the less used (such as having a retirement plan that the employer does not match).

Eligible

Qualified

To be qualified to participate in a program or apply for a job

Premiums

Payments or incentives

Payments for insurance; also, payments employees receive for meeting goals by a certain time

Communicating Total Rewards

Compensation and benefits programs can have a significant effect on employee engagement and retention, but only if the employees know about the value of the programs and how to best take advantage of the offerings. Many employees do not understand the value of their total rewards. Lack of clarity regarding compensation programs also inhibits an employer's ability to attract and retain talent. Employers that are conducting regular employee surveys are more likely to have the data about what employees expect from their compensation programs. This increases the likelihood that a company's pay practices are hitting the right targets.

Having *one-on-one meetings* with employees is a personalized way to help them understand their compensation and benefits programs, and provides them with resources for questions they may have. Meeting one-on-one gives HR the opportunity to connect the dots between compensation and performance, or give written FAQs about program eligibility time lines, health insurance, or leave benefits.

Never underestimate the value of training. Small groups are best when communicating about total rewards so specific questions can be answered where possible. Holding brown bag meetings, where experts are available during employee lunch breaks, is an informal way to make compensation programs more visible and increase the degree of transparency an employer has about pay practices. Technical training for self-service systems will also benefit the portion of the workforce that is less computer savvy than peers.

External resources such as the company's insurance broker, financial adviser, or tax planner is another way to engage employees with their total rewards, increasing the likelihood that they will understand and take advantage of program components.

HR should take steps to communicate the company's compensation philosophy so employees know what to expect regarding salary rates and other pay decisions.

Sharing market wage surveys with management and employees helps them see that the company is competitive. If a company's base pay is not competitive, the employer may compile a total rewards statement that shows the employee the total value of the compensation program as opposed to only the base salary. This is a useful tool, especially when an employer offers generous health insurance benefits, a 401(k) matching program, or above-average leave benefits that help employees balance work and life responsibilities.

Many employees are concerned about job security. While employers must avoid making lifetime statements about employment, they can communicate with the workers the company's vision and plans for the future and create programs that clearly tie compensation factors to the achievement of goals and objectives. This allows employees to see how their performance and rewards connect directly to the company's momentum, and helps ease any business security concerns that may be lingering from the global economic instabilities of the past several years.

One-on-One Meetings

Direct interaction between two people

Person-to-person communication, such as a conversation between an HR manager and an employee

---

Designing Pay Systems

Employers (translation, HR) must design a comprehensive system to reward employees for their hard work. Components of these systems most often include:

Direct compensation Payments made to employees to include *base salary*. Direct pay includes *exempt* (employees who are exempt from overtime wage laws) and nonexempt (hourly paid) workers, and may be tied to *minimum wage* laws and other regulated components of direct pay programs.

Indirect compensation All other rewards not associated with direct pay, including *incentives*, *inducements*, time-off benefits such as sick time or holiday pay, and pension plan payments.

As discussed in the WPE chapter, a job family consists of a group of jobs with similar tasks, duties, and responsibilities. Pay structures are often built for each job family, and may be organized by hourly versus salaried, administrative, executive or professional, clerical, production, sales, or any other grouping that makes business sense. These job families make up the structure of an employer's pay system from which decisions about pay can be made.

Base Salary

A fixed amount of money paid for work performed

Compensation that does not include benefits, bonuses, or commissions

Exempt-Level Employee

Employee whose position is not bound to hourly job rules

A U.S. term that describes employees who work however many hours are necessary to perform the tasks of their position. They do not receive overtime pay, unlike hourly workers.

Minimum Wage

Least amount paid for work

The lowest hourly, daily, or monthly salary that employers must legally pay to employees or workers

Incentive

Motivation, inducement

A monetary or nonmonetary reward to motivate an employee (for example, a bonus or extra time off)

Inducement

Incentive

A benefit that management offers to employees as motivation for producing specific results

Job Evaluation

Pricing jobs is a complex process that requires dedication and skill. There are a few widely accepted methods HR may draw upon to complete the task with confidence:

Point method This method depends upon the identification of compensable factors shared by jobs in a job family and assigns a weight (point) to each factor.

These points have an assigned value based on skill, responsibility, effort, working conditions, knowledge, degree of problem solving, levels of importance, or any other *job-content-based* factor. The purpose of the point system is to quantify individual elements of a job.

Ranking The *job ranking* method of evaluation places jobs in order of importance from highest to lowest. The most important job has the highest salary.

Classification In this method of evaluation, job classes are created by grouping positions with common characteristics. The job classes are then graded, with a minimum and maximum pay *range* established for employee salaries. The job classifications are then referred to as grade 1 or grade 2, with shared educational or experiential characteristics defined and valued.

Factor comparison This model is a complicated hybrid of the ranking and point job evaluation methods. It involves ranking each job using compensable factors, and then assigning a monetary value to each factor to build a pay rate for each job.

Note that each of these methods is used to price jobs according to their worth *within* the company: How valuable are the tasks, duties, and responsibilities to an organization's competitive ability? A *market-based job evaluation* uses external comparisons to properly price jobs within a company. Market pricing is successful when jobs for comparison are good matches with external job classifications. This goes beyond simple job titles, and must include geographic boundaries, profit versus nonprofit status, and company competitive strategies.

Job evaluation helps employers make objective decisions about how to pay their people, and helps employees understand that pay rates are established based on job worth, not personal worth. Systems that don't place enough emphasis on knowledge, skills, abilities, and other job characteristics may be less legally defensible. Market-based pricing in an organization that fails to keep pace with external conditions can unintentionally contribute to a lagging compensation philosophy. Regardless of the selected approach, HR must carefully draw from both internal factors, and external market conditions to equitably price jobs at work without compromising an organization's ability to remain competitive.

Job-Content-Based Job Evaluation

Method to decide an employee's salary

A way of estimating how much people should be paid based on what they do

Job Ranking

A way to compare all jobs based on their value

A job evaluation method that compares jobs to each other based on their importance to the organization

Range

The difference between the most and least

The amount covered, or the amount of difference (for example, a salary range is the difference between the lowest and highest amount paid for a particular job)

Market-Based Job Evaluation

Comparison of current salaries for a specific job

An evaluation that compares the salaries for particular jobs offered on the external job market

Pay Ranges and Comparisons

Salary ranges set the minimum, *midpoint*, and maximum base pay rates for a pay grade. Both internal equitability and external competitiveness are important, so HR must use the data collected during the job evaluation process plus external pay information to build each grade. HR does this by conducting or commissioning a *market salary survey*. Often, employers establish the *wage band* using the minimum rate for a position at 80 to 85 percent of the midpoint, and the maximum rate for the position between 115 percent and 120 percent. This allows for some flexibility when hiring or promoting someone into a role with varying qualifications and capabilities.

Internal and external data are also used to help HR identify pay equity issues. A comparison of internal pay rates to external market rates is done using a *compa-ratio* (comparison ratio) formula: dividing the pay rate by the midpoint, and then multiplying the number by 100 to get a percentage. For example, a job paying $75,000 per year with a salary midpoint of $95,000 has a compa-ratio of 79 percent.

Similarly, an internal comparison can be made by auditing an employee's *range penetration*—where an incumbent's pay is when compared to the range. Someone with 100 percent penetration would be at the top of the range, whereas someone with 20 percent penetration would be 20 percent above the minimum level for the job. This is calculated by:

$$\frac{\text{Pay} - \text{Range minimum}}{\text{Range maximum} - \text{Range minimum}}$$

The result must be multiplied by 100 to calculate the percentage.

Finally, HR will calculate the range spread, which is the difference between minimum and maximum salaries in a range. This is done by subtracting the range minimum from the range maximum, and then dividing it by the minimum. The spread may vary for different job classifications. For example, executive positions may have a range spread of 60 percent or more, whereas hourly workers may have a range of only 40 percent.

Once these activities are complete for all jobs being compared, the positions may be mapped on a chart or by using a matrix structure to look for any pay equity issues, or to talk with employees about their room for salary growth. This information is frequently used to make decisions about pay adjustments, which are discussed in more detail next.

Salary Range

Wage band, pay scale, compensation rate

The lowest and highest wages paid to employees who work in the same or similar jobs

Salary Midpoint

The center point of the middle range paid for a certain job

The amount of money halfway between the highest and lowest amount paid for a particular job

Market Salary Survey

Research summary of fair wages

Review of median pay for specific positions in the same labor market

Wage Band

Salary range, pay scale, compensation rate

The lowest and highest wages paid to employees who work in the same or similar jobs

Compa-Ratio

Math formula for comparing salaries

A number comparing a person's salary to other salaries for the same job; the comparison ratio is calculated by taking a person's salary and comparing it to the midpoint of other salaries (if a person earns $45,000 per year in a job where the salary midpoint is $50,000 per year, the compa-ratio is $45,000/$50,000 = 90%).

Range Penetration

An employee's pay compared to the total pay range

An employee's pay compared to the total pay range for the same job function

Pay Adjustments

There are several conditions under which employee pay adjustments may be necessary. As illustrated previously, internal and external equity issues may drive the need to make changes, often based on an organization's decision to lead, lag, or match market rates.

Once a pay range has been established, HR must identify where each person within the range is placed, and make salary recommendations where appropriate. In one method, green-circled employees are those whose pay rate is below the range minimum, whereas red-circled employees have pay rates above the range maximum. Frequent base pay increases may be necessary to bring green-circled employees into range; freezing a red-circled employee's pay increases may be used until the range catches up to the incumbent's pay. Rarely would HR recommend that a red-circled employee's pay be reduced, but HR can advocate for small lump-sum increases or a bonus structure to continue to reward employee contributions without increasing base pay.

Other pay adjustment needs are dependent upon company strategy. In a performance-oriented environment, HR may help craft policies to give pay *raises* when an employee completes training or obtains a degree. *Piece rate* programs may be used to reward individual output, provided they meet minimum wage standards. In an entitlement-oriented environment, seniority systems are often used to calculate pay increases. Cost-of-living adjustments (COLAs) are increases tied to an external economic indicator like the consumer price index (CPI). COLAs are calculated as a percentage of an employee's base pay; for example, let's assume that all employees will receive a 2 percent COLA increase. An employee with an annual salary of $45,000 will receive a $900 increase per year, whereas a $90,000 employee would receive an $1,800 increase per year. COLAs' main disadvantage is they fail to reward employees for individual performance. An advantage is that they help employers keep pay rates current over time.

For a company trying to control expenses, *lump-sum* increases may be a better way to go, as they do not increase an employee's base pay. This strategy slows the progression of pay range increases over time, and has an impact on other programs calculated on an employee's base pay such as *overtime* and pension contributions. A lump-sum strategy may be used to pay out a COLA or any other type of pay increase.

Another cost-saving strategy is to hire *per diem* workers in industries where work flow is less predictable and thus it is difficult for employers to plan (and compensate) a full-time staff. This of course can quickly become an expensive route if HR does not conduct a cost-benefit analysis to ensure that the increased costs and *reimbursements* for per diem workers do not offset the savings from a pay-as-you-go employment situation.

As with any strategy affecting the absolute right of worker payment, HR must understand any relevant legal issues under the Fair Labor Standards Act or union contract obligations. Pay adjustments must also be accounted for in an employer's payroll management system, which is covered next.

Per diem translates into "day rate." This term may apply for a type of worker, or as an employee *allowance* for company-paid travel expenses associated with meals and lodging.

Raise

Salary increase

An increase in salary that an employee receives, often for good performance

Piece Rate

Payment determined by the amount produced

A wage system in which the employee is paid for each unit of production at a fixed rate

Lump-Sum Compensation

A single payment made at one time

An extra amount of money paid at one time rather than on a regular basis (for example, an expatriate may receive a lump-sum payment to cover the extra costs of the assignment related to housing, taxes, dependent education, and transportation)

Overtime

Time worked in addition to regular paid work hours

Extra time worked beyond the normal hours of employment or the payment for extra time worked

Per Diem

Daily expenses or reimbursements for an employee

The amount of money a person receives for working for one day, or the amount an organization allows an employee to spend on expenses each day (for example, meals and hotels on a business trip)

Reimbursements

Compensation paid for money already spent

Payments made for money already spent (for example, a company pays an employee for the cost of travel or supplies after the employee has spent his or her own money)

Allowance

Amount of money

Money for a specific purpose

Managing Payroll

The operational and administrative nature of payroll-related tasks has a significant impact on an organization as a whole and HR as a department. Companies need HR to build and manage a payroll system with activities that include:

- Maintaining and storing accurate timekeeping records
- Integrating technology with other company software programs
- Complying with federal and state laws
- Completing tax collection and payments
- Processing pay adjustments
- Protecting employee confidential information

Employees need HR to get their paychecks processed on time and accurately.

Inefficient or inadequate payroll systems will have a negative effect on all of the aforementioned activities, so this section takes a look at payroll best practices for program administration and management.

Get the Right Hardware

A computerized payroll system's usefulness is significantly dependent upon the selection of the right hardware. Depending on an employer's need, the system may be as simple as inputting employee time into a packaged software program such as Quickbooks. Larger organizations may choose to have a networked or online system as part of a larger human resource information system (HRIS) or enterprise resource planning (ERP) system. Still others choose to partner with payroll or business process outsourcing groups to perform some or all of the pay-related tasks, requiring timekeeping system installation and reports management. With so many technological options for this important task, HR must help the company navigate the choices, lead the implementation efforts, and train affected employees in the system's use.

Know How to Complete a Paycheck

Experienced HR professionals know that getting an employee paid on time and accurately is a function with many, many steps. Fundamental to the process is calculating gross earnings, which includes all regular wages from base pay, overtime, cash incentives, paid time off, and shift differentials.

Voluntary deductions may also be required to be processed on behalf of employees. These include payments for health insurance premiums, union dues, and contributions to retirement plans. Involuntary deductions, like garnishments, are court-ordered deductions from an employee's pay. Employers must comply with the orders, and do not have the authority to alter them in any way.

Tax calculations are fundamental to processing paychecks. From employee withholding to employer payroll taxes, calculating Social Security and Medicare taxes, calculating an employer's match obligations—all require a working (and current) knowledge of the changing requirements of the Internal Revenue Service (IRS). The finance and tax components of payroll have created debate within the HR industry as to whether payroll is a true human resource function or a function of accounting. When questions such as these arise, HR must take steps to find out the goals, needs, and skill sets of the workers to determine how to best integrate this critical function into operations.

The paycheck stub is also of interest to HR for compliance purposes. Federal laws such as the Fair Labor Standards Act do not currently require an employer to provide a paycheck stub to employees, whereas various state laws do. That being said, the FLSA and other laws do have strict regulations regarding payroll record keeping. Many of these are covered in the labor law appendix at the end of the book (Appendix A).

Employee Benefit Programs

A total rewards *benefit program* includes both direct compensation and indirect compensation in the form of employee *benefits*. Framed as an advantage for working for an employer, these programs serve to attract qualified workers and keep employees from leaving. They also serve the more culturally sensitive goals to help employees live longer and have more balanced lives through health benefits, leave benefits, and other work/life balance programs. Strategically, benefits are a means for employers to differentiate themselves from their competition. They serve employees as well in terms of tax advantages, as a dollar paid in benefits is not taxed the same as a dollar offered in compensation. These are the objectives covered in the next section.

Benefit Programs

Compensation in addition to wages

Workers' entitlements in addition to base salary (for example, health insurance, life insurance, disability pay, retirement pension, and so on)

Benefits

Noncash compensation provided to employees

Compensation that the employee receives in addition to a base salary (for example, health insurance, company housing, company meals, clothing allowance, pension, and gym membership)

Needs Assessments

Many *employee benefits* are voluntarily offered by employers, so it makes sense that they should understand what their people need if they hope to satisfy those needs. Additionally, some benefits are mandated by federal and state governments, which means HR must know what is required in order to achieve compliance. Other benefits are negotiated via the collective bargaining process with labor unions or works councils. For these reasons, a benefits needs assessment is often the first step to designing employee benefits programs.

Benefits benchmarking is the act of comparing current or possible benefits with what other employers are offering in the relevant labor market. This data may be collected independently, or as part of a wage survey. Note that HR should help employers choose industry-specific or geographically oriented wage survey data in order to ensure that the data being compared are relevant to their needs.

Asking employees what they need is another effective method to use when designing benefits programs. Using employee surveys, HR may collect data about what is most valuable to the workforce, and seek to design a program that best represents those components.

Managing employer risk is also a focus of conducting a needs assessment. This includes complying with both federal and state laws regarding minimum wage, overtime, and what time must be compensated, such as time to change into a uniform if required.

Both benchmarking and employee surveys can help HR spot trends based on past use and future needs. Taking into consideration what the relevant labor market is offering will help HR craft programs that are competitive while incorporating what employees are asking for. It will also help employers comply with laws mandating certain types of benefits.

Benefits Offerings

As discussed earlier, an employer has many reasons for offering *employer-paid benefits*, including attracting a qualified workforce, retaining key talent, matching host country CAB practices, and complying with labor laws and union contracts. Whether *voluntary* or *mandatory*, paid or unpaid, it is very likely that an employer's program has some sort of legal compliance component that HR must manage. For example, employers are not required by law to offer *fringe benefits* such as 401(k) retirement plans to employees, but if they do, the plans must be compliant with the highly complex rules of the Employee Retirement Income Security Act (ERISA) and Securities and Exchange Commission. Regulations regarding who may be designated as *beneficiaries* and guidance for employers regarding *blackout periods* are just two examples of areas about which HR must have some understanding.

Voluntary benefits are those that employers may choose to offer to their people. *Statutory benefits* are those mandated by laws. Types of benefits include:

Social and Security These are the most common types of mandated benefits. Retirement security such as Social Security program participation, *health care benefits* such as Medicare programs and offerings under the Patient Protection and Affordable Care Act, and workers' compensation insurance are examples of employee security benefits.

Financial While not mandated by any particular labor law, once an employer chooses to offer financial benefits they tend to be regulated. Examples include life insurance, credit unions, and financial counseling.

Personal and Family Family-style benefits may be both voluntary and involuntary. Offering unpaid leave under the Family Medical Leave Act (FMLA) and the extension of eligibility to domestic partners are two examples of family laws required by laws. Voluntary programs such as *employee assistance programs* are offered to help employees who are struggling with personal challenges or challenges within their families.

Time off Often highly valued by employees, time off benefits serve to both comply with labor laws and enhance employee work/life balance. Employers are required to provide employees with protected time off to serve a military commitment or to vote, but may choose to offer additional time off because of the death of a loved one or to observe various holidays.

Medical benefits Health insurance is coveted to some degree by most employees at all stages of life and in all areas. Managed care program premiums are set by providers based on use, similar to the experience rating in workers' compensation insurance. These include programs such as health maintenance organizations (HMOs) in which the focus is on preventive care and use of a gatekeeper to determine when individuals may need to see a specialist. Preferred provider organizations (PPOs) are a type of managed care plan in which a network of health care providers is contracted to provide services to member employees, with out-of-network or premium pricing being paid by the patient. Note that multinational firms may have to offer specialized insurance for expatriates, particularly if home country insurance policies have territorial clauses.

Employee Benefits

Compensation in addition to salary

Payments or allowances that organizations give to their employees (for example, medical insurance, Social Security taxes, pension contributions, education reimbursement, and car or clothing allowances)

(continued)

(continued)

Employer-Paid Benefits

Something extra that employees receive in addition to salary

Benefits that an organization gives its employees in addition to salary (for example, medical insurance, payments to retirement funds, and allowances for cars or clothing)

Voluntary Benefits

Programs offered to and paid by employees

Extra benefits or discounted services offered to employees with little extra cost to the employer (for example, additional life insurance, gym memberships, and concierge services)

Mandatory Benefits

Laws that require certain benefits to protect workers

Laws that outline benefits to provide economic security for employees and their dependents

Fringe Benefits

Payments other than, or in addition to, salary

Payments that the employee receives other than or in addition to a salary, such as for health insurance

Beneficiary

Receiver of benefits

A person who is eligible to gain benefits under a will, insurance policy, retirement plan, or other contract

Blackout Period

Temporary denial of access

A brief period in which employees cannot access or change things about their retirement or investment plans

Statutory Benefit

Employee benefits that are required by law

Employee benefits mandated by federal or local laws, such as Social Security and unemployment insurance

Health Care Benefits

Medical support plans provided to employees

Company-sponsored medical plans that help employees pay for the cost of doctor visits, hospitalization, surgery, and so on

Employee Assistance Program

Services and counseling that employees receive to help them solve problems that could affect their work productivity

Examples include counseling for drug or alcohol problems or family issues

Leave Benefits

Employers are required to protect workers' jobs when they take time off to vote, are called to jury duty, have a pregnancy-related disability, or are called back to active duty in the military. None of these are currently required to be paid, although states such as California have more strict requirements.

In addition to leave rights granted by law, such as the Family Medical Leave Act (covered in Appendix A on legal issues), employers may offer voluntary benefits to their workers needing to take time off for various reasons.

Standard paid time off for sick time, vacations, holidays, and bereavement is still commonly offered by employers. Trends in time-off programs by companies such as Netflix and Salesforce have made recent headlines. In 2015, Netflix announced "unlimited time off" for new parents in the first year after birth or adoption. Other programs such as those at Salesforce offer partial pay while on leave, gradual return to work schedules, sabbaticals, and time off to volunteer. These programs are increasing in popularity in order to retain critical talent and satisfy the work/life balance needs of a 24/7-connected workforce.

Retirement Benefits

Pension programs to help employees save for retirement are still a popular benefit used by employers as part of a strategic total rewards plan. In a contributory plan, both employers and employees may make contributions to these voluntary programs. In noncontributory plans, only the employer pays into the retirement accounts. Employees do have vesting rights, in which they become owners of any employer contributions after a certain period of time has passed. Once employees are vested in their accounts, they have portability rights in which they can take their money with them if they change jobs.

A *defined benefit plan* is a pension program that the employer funds where the employee receives a set payment amount upon retirement (lump sum or regular payments); the benefit amount is defined based on age and years of service. Many of these plans have been replaced by defined contribution plans because of the complexity of appropriately funding defined benefit plans. Under a defined contribution pension plan, the employer makes an annual contribution to the employee's pension account, usually calculated as a percentage of employee earnings.

Employers may offer a *deferred compensation plan* to workers as well, helping them take advantage of U.S. tax laws that may be more beneficial to them when their income is lower during retirement.

Individual retirement accounts (IRAs) and 401(k) plans remain popular for employees, particularly if an employer chooses to match employee contributions to these tax-deferred retirement savings accounts. A Roth IRA differs from a 401(k) and other IRAs in that the employee is taxed in the contribution year as opposed to when the funds are withdrawn at retirement.

With all pension programs, HR must reach out to subject matter experts to help an employer craft a legally compliant plan.

Defined Benefit Plan

A retirement plan with predetermined payments

A retirement plan that tells participants exactly how much money (lump sum or regular payments) they will receive on a specific later date (usually the day they retire)

Deferred Compensation Plan

An employee pension program

A pension program that allows an employee to contribute a portion of income over time to be paid as a lump sum at retirement when the employee's income tax rate will probably be lower

---

Compensation and Benefits Outsourcing

Let's face it—sometimes the best advice from HR to executive management is to outsource a complex or time-consuming practice. Payroll is one of the most commonly outsourced functions by companies, and for good reason. Cost savings by leveraging size, decreasing errors, and improving processing times are just a few of the advantages of outsourcing employee payroll. The decision to outsource payroll services still requires time, attention, and maintenance. The use of technology to capture time data, combined with reporting and documentation requirements are important elements of a legally sound and compliant outsourced payroll function. Most employees depend on their paychecks to be delivered accurately and as promised. Many do not have the ability to wait for mistakes to be corrected, making payroll a significant link in employee-employer relations and trust. It is important that HR selects a third-party payroll administrator with care, and offers regular oversight and audits to ensure vendors are delivering quality service to all stakeholders.

The detailed notification requirements and complexity of the Consolidated Omnibus Budget Reconciliation Act (COBRA) makes COBRA administration another popular CAB outsourcing function. Tracking notification time lines, sending notices, reinstating eligible workers, and helping employees understand their rights are just a few of the headaches managed by expert COBRA administrators.

Technical tools may also be provided by third-party vendors. Employee recognition providers will track employees' anniversary dates and then offer a variety of rewards they may choose from on the company website.

As with any other outsourcing activity, employers are not off the hook if an error is made. Care must be taken to ensure that all practices conducted on behalf of the employer are legally compliant and ethically sound, and balance the rights and responsibilities of both the employer and the employee. Failing to comply with COBRA regulations, for example, can cost employers upwards of $100 per day, or long-drawn-out and expensive lawsuits for improper administration. For these reasons, written contracts reviewed by corporate attorneys for any third-party administrator are recommended.

Expatriate Compensation

Expatriates are citizens of one country working on assignment in another country for their home country employer. Properly compensating expatriates is a function of an experienced HR professional, but generalists should have a basic understanding to offer support.

The traditional model for expatriate compensation plans is the *balance-sheet approach*, which attempts to equalize any cost differences between what an expatriate would be earning at home versus while on the international assignment. The goal of balance sheet approach is to keep the expatriate "whole" when abroad—the incumbent neither gains nor loses, but is able to maintain an equivalent standard of living while on assignment. Under this model, employees continue to receive home country compensation and benefits programs, and are given additional allowances for differences in cost of living, housing, and taxes, as well as other allowances such as annual home leave trips, children's schooling costs, and relocation expenses. Some organizations follow a *localization compensation strategy* where they will include expatriates in the local compensation program of the country where they are on assignment, often with additional pluses such as housing and tax assistance. In *split pay practices*, the employer agrees to pay the expatriate partly in the currency of the home country and partly in the currency of the host country.

Deciding how to pay international assignees and at what rate can be difficult, especially because pay and benefit practices and scales vary so widely around the world. Accessing competitive wage data can be achieved through the U.S. Department of Labor, which publishes the International Labor Comparisons. HR may also purchase wage data for larger markets through companies, such as AON's Total Compensation Center. The Hay Group is another credible source for information related to international compensation, including a bank of videos from which practitioners may begin to understand the complex nature of this HR function.

International models to determine COLAs exist as well. A goods and services allowance may need to be built into an expat's total compensation package to give the assignee time to adjust to the buying power of the currency and lack of familiarity regarding host country items. An allowance may be granted at the time an assignment begins, and subsequently adjusted using the Efficient Purchaser Index (EPI) as the assignee acclimates to the new location. The EPI may also be factored into the overall compensation prior to assignment to avoid the perception of a decrease and to communicate clear expectations for both the multinational enterprise (MNE) and the employee.

Balance-Sheet Approach

A model for international compensation

A way to set the salary and living allowances for employees on international assignments

Localization Compensation Strategy

Expatriate salary based on the salary structure of the host country

Salary for an international assignee that is the same as the salary that a local employee receives for a similar job

Split Payroll

A method of paying expatriates

A method of paying expatriates that gives part of their salary in the currency of the home country and part in the currency of the host country

Tax Issues

There are special tax considerations for employees agreeing to be staffed as expatriates. While HR practitioners must be careful to never position themselves as tax experts, it is still necessary to understand a few of the basic concepts. At minimum, this knowledge may be used to select subject matter tax experts to advise on how to address expatriate tax issues.

A *tax equalization policy* attempts to compensate for any variance on an employee's global *tax bill* that would result in the expatriate paying more in taxes than if he or she had stayed in the home country. This addresses *territorial rules*, which require expatriates to follow the tax rules of the host country. Depending on the countries, a *totalization agreement* may be in place that limits the amount of social tax payments to the host country only, helping the expatriate avoid double social taxes.

Tax Equalization Policy

A policy ensuring that the expatriate assignment is tax-neutral

A policy that makes sure that expatriates' combined home and host taxes are no more than they would have paid if they remained in their home country. The expatriate's company pays for any additional taxes.

Tax Bill

Amount of money owed for taxes

A document that lists the tax money owed to a government or legal body

(*continued*)

(continued)

Territorial Rule

A tax law

A rule that employees must follow the tax laws of the country where they are working

Totalization Agreement

Arrangement to avoid double social taxes of expatriates

An agreement between countries that says an expatriate needs to pay social taxes to only the country in which he or she is working

Pay Premiums

Other international compensation program elements revolve around the unique challenges of sending expats to other countries. A *hardship premium* is frequently paid to expatriates assigned to locations where living conditions are difficult and challenging, creating *hardships*. A *danger premium* may be paid as additional compensation to employees who are assigned to highly risky global locations. The U.S. Department of State describes these locations as those with civil unrest, terrorism, or war conditions that threaten physical harm.

Recruiting for expatriate talent, especially at a senior level, often requires creative compensation strategies. A *foreign service premium* may be added to a total rewards offer to make the assignment more attractive to key talent. Similarly, a lump-sum *mobility premium* may be used to encourage employees to accept out-of-country positions.

Hardship Premium

Extra compensation for difficult living conditions

Extra payment or benefits that an expatriate receives on assignment in a country where the living and working conditions are challenging

Hardships

Difficult living or working conditions for expatriates

Situations in a country that cause political or economic uncertainty that make it challenging for expatriates to live and work there. Often, expatriates receive extra hardship pay.

Danger Premium

Additional pay for high-risk work

Extra pay that employees receive for working in dangerous jobs or places (for example, environments that are hazardous or politically unstable)

Foreign Service Premium

Financial reward for moving to a foreign country

Extra pay that an employee receives for accepting an international work assignment

Mobility Premium

Financial benefit for expatriates

Extra salary paid to expatriates to encourage them to move to a new country

It is important to note that international compensation and benefits laws and practices vary from country to country. For example, the prevalence of labor unions in Europe has a significant impact on the pay practices of companies doing business there. Policies that integrate expatriates into local pay and benefits programs must account for these variances.

Executive Compensation

Few employment issues have received more attention than the gap between executive and worker pay across all industries. In 2015, the median compensation for the 200 highest-paid executives at public companies was estimated at $19.3 million per year compared to average worker pay of less than $85,000. But are executives to blame? Many argue that it is the responsibility of the compensation committee and board of directors to act with *moral absolutes*, applying standards of reasonableness and fairness when building total reward packages for executives. Committees will have access to reliable data soon: beginning in 2017, the SEC will require that public companies disclose the ratio of executive pay to median worker pay, allowing for a glimpse into the pay practices of some of the world's largest enterprises. Additionally, many local governments are considering plans that tax a business for executive compensation ratios that unreasonably exceed worker pay. In Portland, Oregon, publicly traded companies will have to pay an additional 10 percent in taxes if executives' pay is greater than 100 times that of the median pay of their workers, and an extra 25 percent for pay ratios greater than 250 times the median pay. These executive pay surcharges will be added to what a company owes for a business license tax, generating an additional $2 million to $3 million per year for the city's general fund. Critics charge that these types of programs will cause companies to move out of areas to more business-friendly environments, causing loss of jobs. Proponents suggest that communities will benefit, as the general funds are how police and firefighters and other critical services are funded.

How to compensate C-suite executives (CEO, COO, CFO, etc.) is a very real activity for human resource departments around the world. In some cases, such as at Fossil, the CEO claims $0 in annual salary, preferring to benefit from the increased stock price that is a benchmark of the CEO's performance. While Fossil notes that the CEO has refused all of the more traditional forms of executive compensation, stock ownership represents equity-based compensation practices that can be highly lucrative. For this reason, HR must understand the individual components of executive pay packages.

Employment Contracts

HR is responsible for administering executive employment contracts. This includes gaining the necessary approvals from a board of directors, legal counsel, or the CEO directly regarding base pay, *perquisites (perks)*, incentives, and benefits. These written contracts outline the general terms and conditions of employment that are discussed in more detail in the WPE chapter.

Other Executive Contract Clauses

In addition to base pay, incentives, and terms of separation, there are a few unique clauses related to executive contracts. These include:

Golden handshakes These provisions confirm in writing the terms of a *severance* agreement should the executive voluntarily or involuntarily separate from the company.

Golden parachutes Used to minimize the risk of an executive losing his or her position in the event of a change of control such as a merger or acquisition.

Golden handcuffs Used to ensure a length of service from an executive by making it difficult to leave the company without a significant loss of earnings.

Golden life jackets Offered to an executive after a merger to entice him or her to remain with the reorganized company.

Clawbacks These provisions allow a company to take back payments made to executives under certain conditions, such as fraud or accounting errors.

Moral Absolutes

Beliefs that are right or wrong

The idea that there is a clear definition of what is right and wrong

Perquisites (Perks)

Benefits and special treatment

Special nonmonetary privileges (such as a car or club membership) that come with senior job positions; also called executive perks or fringe benefits

Severance

Separation payment

An additional payment (other than salary) given to an employee when employment termination occurs

Base Salary

An executive's *remuneration* generally has some portion of it that is secure. Base salary is negotiated for a period of time and is not dependent upon specific performance outcomes of the individual or the company. In some cases, CEOs and other top executives forgo a base salary or take $1 (or even $0) per year in exchange for equity compensation. In other companies, executives' salaries may make up 90 percent of their total rewards packages. HR's role is to undertake *remuneration surveys* and present the data to decision makers in order to make compensation decisions regarding current executives, and to make competitive offers in recruitment and selection activities.

Remuneration

Pay or salary

Money paid for work, including wages, commissions, bonuses, overtime pay, and pay for holidays, vacations, and sickness

(continued)

(continued)

Remuneration Surveys

Gathering information on salary and benefits

Surveys that gather information on what other companies pay employees and what kinds of benefits they provide

Perks

Perquisites, or perks, are executive compensation elements that include nonmonetary rewards such as housing, company cars, club memberships, and first-class travel accommodations. These are attractive to high-level workers not only for status, but for the tax advantages they may provide.

Executive Benefits

In addition to the benefits plans offered to all workers, supplemental benefits may make up a portion of an executive's total compensation. Key person life insurance in which both the company and the executive's family are paid in the event of the executive's death are growing as a risk management tool. Estate planning and tax planning are also options to offer to highly paid workers with complex tax or financial circumstances.

Incentives

Both discretionary and performance-based incentive programs may be used in total rewards planning for senior talent. With an average CEO tenure of just seven years, there is much discussion of the true ROI of executive incentive plans. Short-term incentives such as quarterly bonuses can help with some of the challenges that rewarding highly paid workers brings to the budget. The key is to understand what the company needs and to design incentive programs that motivate senior talent to perform. Hybrid plans that attempt to link executive pay to outcomes over multiple periods of performance are more complicated. There is a growing belief, however, that these multiperiod, dynamic plans more accurately reflect the real impact that the leaders of a company have on organizational outcomes.

Stock Options

Employee stock ownership plans (ESOPs) are designed to give selected employees equity ownership in the companies they work for. The underlying strategy to offering ESOPs is to help employees develop an ownership mentality in their work, which in turn improves performance, which in turn increases stock value. While a publicly traded company may offer *equity compensation* to all employees, it is more often than not a portion of an executive compensation package.

Under some *stock option* plans, employees are given the opportunity to purchase company stock at the strike price—the price of the stock when the option was granted. This opportunity is available within a specified period of time, and is favorable if the stock value increases over time.

Restricted stock is granted to employees as actual shares, not as opportunities to purchase. It carries the value of a real wage that is executed over a period of time defined by a vesting schedule. Once the employee is fully vested, he or she may choose to sell the stock or hang on to it to see if it increases in value over time.

Phantom stock is used by companies to give employees the benefit of stock ownership without actually granting equity. Also following a vesting schedule, executives are granted "shares" that follow a company's performance. For many companies, phantom stock is a good solution when they don't want to increase the number of shareholders they are accountable to, but still want to tie payments to market performance. For employees, it is a way to financially benefit when the company's market performance is high.

A potential benefit to executives is the favorable tax treatment of some of the stock purchase plans. Incentive stock options may also have some favorability, but require companies to navigate a complex set of rules by the IRS. HR best serves the company by resourcing tax experts to ensure that a plan is properly developed and executed.

Reporting

Complying with the Securities and Exchange Commission (SEC) creates special issues, particularly for employers with employee stock ownership and executive reward programs. The SEC requires that companies annually report the compensation for the top five executives, including cash compensation such as wages and bonuses, long-term or deferred awards, and information about executive pensions. Additionally, these companies must provide to their investors a description of the compensation objectives, the existence of employment or severance agreements, and share ownership guidelines for executive pay.

ESOP

Employee stock ownership plan

A tax-qualified benefit plan with defined contributions that allows employees to own shares in a company

Equity Compensation

A type of payment that gives employees an ownership interest in a company

Noncash payment that represents an ownership interest in a company (for example, stock options and restricted stock)

Stock Option

An employee's right to buy or sell shares in the company

A benefit that gives employees the right to buy or sell stock in their company at a certain price for a specific period of time

Restricted Stock

Stock with rules about its transfer

Stock with rules about when it can be sold (restricted stock is usually issued as part of a salary package, and has a time limit on when it can be fully transferred)

Phantom Stock Arrangement

An employee incentive plan

A technique in which a company gives its employees the benefits that come with owning stock, including dividends, but does not actually give them stock in the company

Global Executive Compensation

On a global scale, organizations may adjust different components of a total rewards package to account for the pay customs and the competitive landscape of the particular countries where executives are employed. It is up to HR practitioners to help their companies research relevant data to build executive compensation plans for each country that reflect the importance of senior roles but also reflect the company's mission, vision, and values, as well as the social mores of the host country.

For expatriates, agreement on choice of law codes may also be necessary for employment contracts. This clause allows the parties to agree on which laws—home or host—will apply should a contract dispute arise.

Metrics

As stated earlier, compensation and benefits account for one of the largest overhead costs of employers. For this reason, quantitative data collected by HR can help employers identify trends and forecast future needs. Among the most popular are:

Compensation as an percentage of operating expense Calculated by dividing the total cost of compensation (base, variable, and deferred) by the total operating expenses company-wide. When multiplied by 100, a percentage can be reviewed during workforce planning and budgeting activities.

Benefits as a percentage of operating expense Similar to the preceding calculation, the benefits percentage is calculated by dividing the total cost of benefits offerings by total operating expenses. Many employers find that benefits account for a large portion of employee compensation, so calculating the total cost of benefits as a percentage of payroll per full-time equivalent and by employee group may be of value in decision making.

Utilization review An audit of health care provider services and costs to ensure accurate billing.

Employee burden The total cost of having an employee, including salary, benefits, and taxes, to calculate actual employment cost. Generally communicated as an hourly or annual rate, this allows HR to forecast the true cost of adding or replacing staff.

Hidden paychecks A communication tool delivered as an annual statement to employees that identifies the total value (beyond base pay) of an individual's employment when taxes, benefits, training, and other perks of a job are factored in.

Suggested Study or Organizational Audit Activities

- Select three key positions at the organization for which you work, and conduct salary surveys using O*NET online or any other state or federal resource. Establish a pay minimum that is set at 85 percent of the midpoint, and a pay maximum of 115 percent of the midpoint. Plot all three positions, and compare for internal and external equity.

(continued)

(continued)

- Using the Fair Labor Standards Act definitions of exempt and nonexempt workers, conduct an exemption audit of an entire class of workers. What data did you use to measure eligibility? What changes would you recommend to your employer? How would you communicate any changes to the employee?
- Write or audit an existing standard operating procedure to comply with a wage garnishment order received from the courts. Investigate applicable legal issues, and work with accounting to formalize the process. Where would you store these orders?
- Conduct research online for companies that offer COBRA management services. Write a request for proposals that outlines what services would be provided and addresses potential liabilities.
- What are the priorities of executive compensation programs at your place of work? How have these priorities been represented at your or another's place of work? What equity and transparency issues had to be addressed?

6

Employee and Labor Relations

Conflict at Work

There is a lot of information and research related to managing conflict at work. Fundamentally, however, it is not the *absence* of conflict that makes for a positive work environment, but rather the *nature* of the conflict itself. Functional conflict can result in better ideas and issue- or client-centered problem solving. Dysfunctional conflict causes high turnover, increased absenteeism, and burnout of a skilled workforce. One study by Brinkert (2010) reviewed the causes and pervasive impact of conflict in nursing. Of the respondents, negative social interactions with others accounted for 75 percent of the work situations described as "detrimental"; the other 25 percent were interpersonal issues. The good news is that the researchers found that sources of conflict can be managed through interventions such as normalizing conflict and building systems for managing it (Brinkert 2010). This includes training in conflict management for all employees and supervisors along with the building of advanced communication skills. Leaders will need to have the courage to address interpersonal and relational conflicts that are destructive, and to commit to a culture of workplace civility. Most important, management must model the expected standards of behavior.

Additionally, labor law requires that employers are prepared to address workplace conflict that escalates beyond simple disagreement. Harassment prevention and the emergence of abusive conduct (bullying) prohibitions

(continued)

287

(continued)

reinforce the need for HR expertise in managing conflict. Bullying can occur in any social environment, on the job or online. A 2014 Workplace Bullying Survey reported that 65 million people have been affected by bullying at work. The survey conducted by the Workplace Bullying Institute (WBI) defined bullying as "abusive conduct that is threatening, intimidating, humiliating, work sabotage or verbal abuse" (WBI 2014). The study found that 72 percent of employers try to deny or rationalize bullying conduct with statements such as "It doesn't happen here" or "Bullying is necessary to be competitive." For reasons like these, the State of California in 2014 passed AB 2053, which requires employers with 50 or more employees to include abusive conduct prevention training in their unlawful harassment programs. Bullying differs from harassment in two important ways: (1) it occurs four times more often than harassment (Hocker and Wilmot 2014) and (2) it is status-blind, meaning it does not rely upon protected class characteristics to be unlawful.

HR will need to lead the prevention efforts as more and more states adopt healthy workplace laws similar to California's and for companies with multistate facilities to ensure consistency. It may soon become more than just a best practice. The WBI survey reported that 93 percent of all adult Americans support a law against abusive conduct at work, so becoming educated in this area is an emerging HR competency.

References

Brinkert, R. 2010. "A Literature Review of Conflict Communication Interventions in Nursing." *Journal of Nursing Management* 18:145–156.

Hocker, J. L., and W. W. Wilmot. 2014. *Interpersonal Conflict.* New York: McGraw-Hill.

Workplace Bullying Institute (WBI). 2014. 2014 WBI U.S. Workplace Bullying Survey. Retrieved from www.workplacebullying.org/wbiresearch/wbi-2014-us-survey/.

Introduction

When called to the HR department, many employees wonder: "Am I in trouble?" This is unfortunate, as the heart of employee and labor relations (ELR) is about much more than the process of discipline and terminations. ELR activities focus on understanding and managing relationships in the workplace, seeking balance between the needs of the employee and the needs of the company. In some cases, this balance is negotiated via union representation.

Elements explored in this chapter regarding the relationship between the employee and the employer include:

- Establishing and communicating employee and employer rights and responsibilities
- Managing grievances in response to decisions made about the employee

- Promoting employee fairness through company programs and procedures
- Disciplining and terminating employees in accordance with legal guidelines to manage risk
- Coaching and counseling employees where appropriate
- Employing positive employee relations strategies to enhance company climate and culture
- Conferring with employee representative groups such as labor unions, works councils, and joint action committees.
- Managing the process of union organizing and collective bargaining

Managing the Employee-Employer Relationship

Managing the employee experience affects all other functions and outcomes of human resource management. There is a need for HR to effectively create a positive workplace culture by employing industrial relations strategies and *employee relations* programs built upon best practices. Knowing which HR and business best practices to apply requires HR practitioners to engage in problem solving and critical thinking efforts to meet the unique demands of their people, and, for this, assessments must be completed.

Employee Relations

Interaction between employees and the organization

Interaction between employees and an organization (for example, communications, conflict resolution, compliance with legal regulations, career development, and performance measurement)

Climate and Culture: Assessing Attitudes

Organizational culture is an emerging discipline that has received much attention over the past several years. While Geert Hofstede described the dimensions of culture on a global scale (see the Business Management and Strategy chapter), and diversity management efforts address culture-based individual differences (see the Human Resource Development chapter), *corporate culture* is something else. A *psychological contract* exists between an employee and the company. The company in this contract serves as an independent entity, a whole system that acts and behaves as though it were an independent being. The culture is a collection of the values, beliefs, behaviors, and norms that an employee comes to expect from the organism. In the psychological contract, employees expect the company to provide competitive compensation and career development opportunities. The employer expects employees to commit to continuous skill improvement and to do their best when acting on behalf of the business. Psychological contracts can be strengthened through positive employee relations strategies, so HR must become proficient in methods to assess the organizational climate.

Tools in the HR kit include the use of employee satisfaction and engagement surveys. Designed to measure exactly what the titles suggest, these surveys can help measure employee feelings related to their pay, their boss, their job responsibilities, and company leadership. These surveys often identify the warning signals of turnover or the stirrings of union organization. Having this data allows HR to intervene at the first signs of *red flags*, before the negative environment starts to have an impact on company success. Satisfaction surveys should be anonymous to encourage honest feedback.

Focus groups may be convened on narrow topics, such as diversity management or career development. In one-on-one interviews, HR may seek to extract the same kind of information as the aforementioned techniques, or larger town hall–style meetings may be held in which executives respond to questions from employees. Social media monitoring is another way to gauge the temperature of what employees are feeling and the overall morale of the people.

Stay interviews are another feedback tool that has gained popularity. Defined by HRCI® as a retention tool to identify why employees stay with the company, it may also be used to ask questions about what motivates employees to perform. These and other types of one-on-one engagement efforts using *active listening* techniques are useful for HR to employ in measuring job and individual employee satisfaction.

The humble staff meeting is an ideal opportunity to gather information regarding the organizational climate. Ranging from the weekly standard where some HR managers ask questions such as "What went well on your job this week?" to more formal town hall forums with Q&As for the company president, these meetings are effective ways to get a general sense of contentment or malaise. A skip level lands in the middle of this climate assessment range. It involves managers meeting face-to-face with subordinates one or two levels down from them, giving employees the sense that their direct supervisors have *accountability* measures to their performance just like the employees have. While time-consuming to administer, when properly managed it can create a positive sense that there is parity in the group as opposed to an "us versus them" dynamic.

Finally, metrics such as turnover rates, the number and types of employee grievances, the number of claims filed with regulatory agencies, and benefits program participation rates may all provide clues to how employees are feeling about their partner in the psychological contract.

Special attention should be given by HR to protect the confidentiality of employees who share honest feedback where possible. Third-party vendors such as skilled facilitators or survey managers can help accomplish this. In addition, the company needs to be ready to hear what the employees have to say; otherwise, the effort is wasted and employees feel that their opinions don't matter. What to do about the data collected is decided on a case-by-case basis, but, where possible, positive strategies to respond to the assessment findings should be the priority.

Corporate Culture

The beliefs and behaviors of an organization

The values, language, rules, procedures, expectations, and processes that affect how employees of an organization think, act, and view the world

Psychological Contract

Beliefs that influence the employee-employer relationship

An unwritten agreement of the mutual beliefs, perceptions, and informal obligations between an employer and an employee, which influence how they interact

Red Flag

A warning signal

An indicator of a problem, or something that calls for attention

Active Listening

Checking for understanding

A communication method that a listener uses to interpret and evaluate information from a speaker

Accountability

Responsibility

An obligation to accept responsibility for one's actions

Positive Employee Relations Strategies

Employee relations strategies that promote a positive organizational culture are those that are aligned with corporate strategy while serving employee needs. For example, a company seeking to build a learning organization would not be served well by strict policies that discipline mistakes and subvert innovation. A company seeking to promote honest and meaningful communication to aid in problem solving may write an open door policy, but should also be certain to avoid the hiring of authoritarian supervisors who don't listen.

HR is responsible for creating behavioral guidelines for all members of the workforce, and for seeking constructive ways to solve conflict. As the opening research shows, effective conflict resolution skills are a must for HR professionals seeking to support a positive corporate culture, as pervasive conflict affects outcomes such as employee engagement, morale, and commitment. Fair procedures to make decisions about promotions and eligibility for training, as well as for making compensation-related decisions should be developed and communicated.

Participative Management

Participative management techniques are appealing on many levels to help improve the relationship between an organization and its people. This is a process where employees are included in making decisions that affect their work. It may include goal setting, problem solving, and change management. The key to participative management success is to clearly communicate the objective of the efforts, and these objectives (of course) should be aligned with the company's strategies objectives. The change management approach of "run, fix, change" focuses first on running the business, then fixing elements that aren't working, and, finally, changing the processes or people that are out of alignment with stated goals. The fundamental element to this approach—and that of participative management techniques—is the use of employees as experts regarding what they do each and every day. Advocates of these types of approaches believe that employee satisfaction increases, as does organizational commitment. HR must lead cultural intervention efforts to gain acceptance of this management approach. It may start as a strategic objective, but will require thoughtful analysis and a series of planned interventions for people and leaders to help execute.

Work Teams and Task Forces

Self-directed work teams are another method employers may implement to improve employee relations. These structures are built upon autonomy in all functional areas, from hiring and selecting team members to measuring perform-ance and rewards. Members of these teams have two roles: their work role and their team role. The team members together plan and schedule work, make decisions based on consensus (or at least to disagree but commit), and work together to solve problems. Although these teams may not have leaders, diversity is important to ensure that all perspectives are considered.

Work teams don't necessarily have to be self-directed; in some cases it may be necessary to follow a more formal hierarchy. These are evident in both functional teams and cross-functional teams in which labor resources are shared along lines of department functions, specific customers, or particular brands.

A *global team*, sometimes referred to as a cross-border team, consists of individuals working together from different locations, connected through robust technology. These types of teams require a shift from managing people to managing results, and training leaders to understand the nuances of remote work. Additionally, trust between team members is not often fostered across a virtual-only platform; it may be wise to get team members together for face-to-face interaction every three months or so for team building, problem solving, and celebration of successes.

A task force is a special kind of temporary team that is formed to address a specific need. Task forces are a good *ad hoc* strategy to give high-potential workers who crave career development the opportunity to apply their talents to meaningful outcomes. Calling upon them in unplanned circumstances sharpens their focus and taps into areas of skill that perhaps go unused in the course of day-to-day work outcomes. Task forces also empower work groups to take ownership of problems or situations, which research has shown promotes a positive organi-zational culture.

Global Team

Group of employees from different countries who are working on a project together

A group of employees who are working on the same project but who are located in different countries or come from different cultures

Ad Hoc

Not planned, for a specific case

A solution to a specific problem that is not planned, or cannot be used in other situations

Labor-Management Cooperative Strategy

You'll see in an upcoming section that the relationship between employers and unions has an antagonistic history. Labor-management cooperative strategies seek not necessarily to remedy, but at least to have a different go-forward approach in today's global world. The strategies recognize that constant battles and unreasonable demands compromise the competitiveness of organizations. Parties taking a cooperative approach seek to form partnerships as opposed to adversarial relationships. A growing trend noted by the U.S. Department of Labor (DOL) supports this view in that many collective bargaining agreements are now including cooperative provisions.

> Saturn—part of General Motors (GM), one of the big three U.S. automakers—and the United Automobile Workers (UAW) have taken a unique approach in that union members are allowed to participate in decision making and in the determination of management bonuses. The DOL finds that pacts like these, which involve a full exchange of information between union and employers, help to build trust and cooperation for shared responsibilities and shared rewards.

Positive employee relations programs serve many outcomes, not the least of which are reduced turnover, improved attendance, union avoidance, and customer satisfaction.

Directly tied to the achievement of these outcomes are rewards and recognition programs. Employees are motivated when they receive feedback and believe the rewards for their efforts are equal to their inputs. HR can support employee satisfaction and motivation by designing rewards and recognition programs that seek to (1) sincerely acknowledge the employees' efforts and (2) reward said efforts in both monetary and nonmonetary ways. HR can best achieve these outcomes by first asking employees what rewards they prefer, and then persuading management to respond by aligning the rewards to organizational outcomes.

Codetermination strategies and *works councils* are formal involvement strategies used in some countries to involve employees in decisions that affect themselves and their coworkers. In codetermination strategies, employees may have voting rights to elect board members, and in other cases sit on company boards themselves. Works councils have similar levels of involvement but come about it in a different way. In Germany, for example, labor agreements are negotiated on a national level, and then trickle down to employees to make local modifications. Nonunionized employers may also use works councils, often appointed by a board of directors, to decrease conflict and improve employee satisfaction.

Codetermination

A management structure involving employees

An organizational structure in which employees share responsibility for the operation of a company

Works Councils

Groups that represent employees

Organizations that function like trade unions and represent the rights of workers, most commonly found in Europe and the United Kingdom

Special Issues

In some cases, concentrated intervention programs may be necessary to resolve ongoing issues that are barriers to a positive corporate culture. For example, a culture of inclusiveness in which employees are valued for their individual contributions will not be supported through hiring practices that are exclusive or discriminatory. Finding creative ways to accommodate disabled individuals and focusing on attracting military veterans are examples of hiring practice interventions that ensure companies are making the effort to support a diverse workforce.

Another issue that may need a targeted intervention is that of *grievance* resolution. As you will read in the section on unions, happy employees are both more productive and less likely to organize as a union. HR may need to intervene when there is a changing of the guard, such as the removal of toxic, dysfunctional leadership. When this occurs, a new *grievance procedure* built and focused on more positive solutions may need to be a concentrated HR effort. This will include the rebuilding of trust through consistent responses and the modeling of positive behaviors by management.

Grievance

Serious complaint

A cause of distress that can lead to an official complaint (for example, difficult work conditions)

(continued)

(continued)

Grievance Procedure

The method used by employees to address problems at work with their employer

The steps that employees must follow when they want to express their concerns about work-related issues to their employer

Employee Communication and Feedback

The business of work is conducted by people. This statement seems simple, but even with automation and technology, the need to manage the relationships at work takes up a large portion of an HR professional's time and is not to be underestimated as a primary role of HR departments today. The key to managing any relationship is communication and feedback.

Organizational behavior is strongly identified by the way the employer communicates with the workers, and the way coworkers communicate with each other. With the ever-increasing diversity of the workplace, it is worth understanding how group characteristics influence communication styles.

Linguistic Styles

Directness or indirectness, a sense of humor, pace of speaking, and frequency (or lack) of apologies are all examples of linguistic styles that are culturally learned. Referencing back to Hofstede's work covered in the Business Management and Strategy chapter, different cultures use linguistic cues to interpret meaning from social and professional interactions. In this way, organizations also establish learned behavior in their workers. If work meetings are characterized by interruptions and swearing, employees learn that this is how the culture communicates and are likely to adopt aggressive behaviors.

Generational Differences

In addition to verbal and behavioral cues, generational differences influence the flow of information at work. Today's workplace has up to four generations working together, with an age spread of over 45 years. It is then worth understanding the patterns of each generation in order to effectively navigate any challenges—real or perceived—that may serve as obstacles to communication.

Millennials continue to be the largest cohort of employees in the workplace. Some estimates show that this generation will make up close to half of the workforce by 2020. Millennials have not grown up in a world without technology, computers, e-mail, and virtual meetings. ComScore, a digital world measuring service, reported that 234 million Americans over the age of 13 used mobile devices as of 2011, with more than 70 million of these devices being smartphones. Of this market, Google, Android, and Apple made up over 80 percent. These statistics characterize this generation's work style preferences for digital communication, and the need for skill development in the basics such as business writing and etiquette.

The Generation X cohort has had to evolve their workplace communication skills. Beginning their careers when many programs and practices were conducted on paper, they were in the workforce when computers became mainstream. Starting with pagers, faxes, and shoebox-size cell phones, this generation has had to be the most adaptable in terms of communicating at work.

Baby boomers came of age in an environment where analog and manual inputs were the norm, and have had to adapt and learn many iterations of technology as it has developed. This generation makes up much of the management ranks, being responsible for their employees, the millennials, who have an entirely different technological and communication skill set. Millennials are more mobile than the boomers, changing jobs often to the disapproval of the more job-stable boomers. For every 1.5 millennials entering the workforce, a boomer retires,[1] meaning that the generational gaps between these twin labor powerhouses must be systematically managed.

Gender Differences

Communication differences between men and women have been well researched and documented. The social role theory is based on the idea that men and women learn how to communicate by modeling those around them at a young age. Research from this perspective has found evidence that girls learn conversational habits focused on relationships, whereas boys orient toward conversations based on negotiation and competition. Other research has found that women are more likely to share credit for success and to give moderate feedback to avoid offense, whereas men give more direct feedback and are less likely to ask questions or appear to ask for help. While many may find these studies to be based on participant regurgitations of outdated stereotypes, practical HR management uses the information where appropriate to improve communication across genders and within the workplace.

Supporting All Groups

Here again is an opportunity for HR departments to demonstrate their value. HR leaders can have a significant impact on improved communication by clearly defining dos and don'ts for all generations, genders, and styles. While each company has different sets of needs, general guidelines include:

- Asking employees not to text or e-mail during meetings.
- Establishing communication standards, such as listening without interrupting.
- Requiring employees to speak and act with professionalism.
- Encouraging courtesy, dignity, and respect in all employee and management interactions.

HR is responsible to set the tone for the communication style of the organization, modeling the behavior of and in some cases coaching managers (and executives) on how their communication style is affecting the workplace. Conducting training sessions on e-mail etiquette, including the use of acronyms, slang, and emojis, and the appropriateness of other digital habits can go a long way toward integrating the diverse mix of communication styles present in the workplaces of today.

Employee Handbooks

An *employee handbook* helps a company organize and distribute expectations that the employer has of the worker, and describe what the employee may expect from the organization during the course of employment.

A handbook serves many purposes, including acting as a manual for employee reference on the behavioral expectations of the employer, often in the form of a *code of conduct* or work rules. A handbook serves to communicate to employees what they may expect from their place of work. This includes a review of health insurance benefits or time-off options. *Compliance* with various labor laws through written policies and procedures is another reason employers have handbooks. For example, written polices prohibiting harassment are one step in proving an affirmative defense should an employer be charged with unlawful harassment, because a harassment-free workplace is an employee right. An employee's responsibility in this area is to report any harassing behavior, either to a supervisor or to HR. In this way, a handbook helps an employer comply with antiharassment laws while describing both employee rights and responsibilities. Other policies about expected work behaviors, such as *moonlighting* or requesting time off for *planned absences*, are also examples of what may be included in a handbook. Categories used to organize handbooks may vary from company to company, but often include sections related to:

- Introduction, including equal employment practices
- Time of hire information, including definitions of employee classifications and job duties

- Wages and hours information, including timekeeping expectations and definition of the workweek
- Benefits, both mandatory and voluntary
- Time off, such as leaves of absence and personal time
- Employee relations, including the use of company property, social media, discipline, and termination
- Health and safety, such as a code of safe practices and injury reporting
- Confirmation and acknowledgment forms

One other important aspect of an employee handbook that HR must manage is to ensure that a handbook does not unintentionally become an employment contract. A statement of at-will employment at the beginning of the handbook, along with a definition of who may alter the at-will relationship, can help avoid creating an express or implied contract. More on this is discussed in other chapters.

Employee Handbook

A reference document for workers in an organization

A manual that contains information about an organization's policies, procedures, and benefits

Code of Conduct

A set of principles and behavioral expectations

A written description of the principles, behaviors, and responsibilities that an organization expects of its employees

Moonlighting

Working for more than one company at the same time

To have a second job in addition to full-time employment

Planned Absence

Scheduled time away from work

Missing work after asking permission in advance, such as for a vacation or a medical appointment

Employee Operational Guides

As just discussed in the handbook section, many employer policies are described in the employee handbook, and are generally used for informational purposes. Employers may find that they need additional written guides that are more operational in nature. These are described next.

Procedures are descriptions of a work process, often written as step-by-step instructions. Known also as standard operating procedures (SOPs), these guides are used for training purposes and to provide performance feedback. They help ensure that consistent practices are followed so that quality, customer service, or other positive work outcomes are achieved.

While most employees are conscientious about their behavior at work, rules help to define the framework within which employees are expected to act. Examples of common work rules include safe work behaviors, ethical conduct, and professional performance standards. When an employee is underperforming, there may be a need for discipline or termination. This aspect of managing the employee relationship is covered next.

Discipline and Terminations

One of the main support functions HR can offer to an organization is successful interventions into the behavior of underperforming employees. There is just no getting around it—the words *policy* and *police* have similar connotations. HR addresses employee performance that is out of compliance with policies, procedures, or work rules through a series of both positive and negative interventions. When positive strategies such as coaching or mentoring do not work, or for a single seriously egregious event, HR will manage the discipline process.

Employee Discipline

Discipline is a form of conditioning that seeks to change employee behavior. Behavioral scientists such as B. F. Skinner (covered in an earlier chapter) believed that behavior that is rewarded is strengthened, and behavior that is punished (or not rewarded) is extinguished. Discipline seeks to weaken undesirable behaviors in two ways: through punishment (there is an unpleasant consequence when an employee misbehaves) and avoidance learning (the threat or experience of punishment is enough to drive behavior).

Many employers have a discipline policy, which serves to identify standards of behavior and provide for corrective action when necessary. Goals of a policy should also include giving supervisors a resource to call upon when faced with an event. This will help managers respond consistently to similar behaviors of employees. Fundamental to a discipline policy is *due process*. Similar to the right of all U.S. employees to a fair trial, due process gives employees the chance to explain their actions before a consequence is applied. Due process is one component of having a discipline policy that does not discriminate and helps employers avoid a future charge of wrongful discipline or termination. Employees who are disciplined should understand the *appeals* process should they disagree with the judgment.

Finally, HR must live or die by the adage "If it isn't documented, it never happened." HR must train and model the expected standards of documentation of *reprimands* for the employee files. From a simple date-stamped e-mail up to a formal incident report, HR is instrumental in training managers in how to legally document employee conduct. Helping managers write unemotional accounts of incidents, link negative employee behaviors to job or policy standards, and acquire conflict management skills are all efforts that will help defend against a wrongful discipline or termination lawsuit.

Due Process

The way a government enforces laws

In the United States, the way a government enforces its laws to protect its citizens (for example, guaranteeing a person a fair trial)

Appeal

A request to a higher authority

To challenge an official decision (for example, in court)

Reprimand

Formal warning or scolding

A warning given to an employee who violates an organization's rules and that may result in dismissal

Special Issues with Discipline

As with any other employment action that is based on a protected class character-istic, a discipline policy that is not related to the job can cause problems for an employer.

Written policies that are progressive in nature may form an implied contract, forcing the employer to proceed through each step in the discipline process. Properly worded discipline policies include a statement of at-will employment, and remind the employee that the employer reserves the right to proceed directly to termination under certain conditions.

Employee Terminations

Unfortunately, discipline does not always result in the necessary behavior modifi-cations. For this reason, competent HR pros will be able to create and administer a legally defensible termination process for both voluntary and involuntary separa-tions. As touched on in the preceding special issues section, terminations are fraught with legal land mines for which HR must prepare. These include:

- Complying with mass layoff regulations, including the Worker Adjustment and Retraining Notification Act (WARN). This act was designed to protect employees and the communities in which they worked from the effect of mass layoffs without notice. Passed in 1998, the act requires employers with 100 or more employees to give 60 days' notice for plant layoffs or closings. The act also requires that employers notify local government offices that may be able to offer assistance to the displaced workers.
- Managing the risk of constructive discharge, which occurs when an employer makes working conditions so unpleasant that an employee feels he or she has no option other than to quit.
- Maintaining the employment at-will relationship, or, in the event of an employ-ment contract, ensuring that the contract is not breached by either party.
- Reducing the risk of unlawful discrimination or disparate impact by ensuring that due process is followed (covered in the chapter on Workforce Planning and Employment).
- Administering postemployment efforts such as complying with COBRA rights, final paycheck mandates, and other federal and state notification requirements.

Coming up in another section is information related to collective bargaining agreements, a form of employment contract that covers a group of employees and is negotiated by their union representatives. These contracts generally outline the terms and conditions under which an employee may be disciplined or terminated. Because the agreement is a contract, HR will need to help determine if the employee was disciplined or terminated for cause. In accordance with policy and contract rules, questions about warnings (and a review of related documentation) will be necessary. HR will need to at minimum participate in and, at times, lead an investigation into the behavior in question and the subsequent response to determine if the discipline or termination is in line with the collective bargaining agreement.

Once termination has been decided on as the appropriate course of action under any circumstances, HR will lead the participants through the process. Regardless of whether a separation is voluntary or involuntary, a single occurrence or a mass layoff, there are several moving parts to a termination process that HR must lead, coordinate, or audit:

- A final review of related documentation for clarity and to manage any potential legal issues
- The creation of a severance agreement or package that is in compliance with the Older Workers Benefit Protection Act and the Age Discrimination in Employment Act
- Participating as a witness or scheduling a witness during the termination meeting(s)
- The coordination of outside resources for risk management, including a documentation review, exit interview, and legal counsel before and after the session(s), and possibly also managing third-party vendors such as COBRA administrators to ensure compliance
- The ability to work with government agencies and other local employers to coordinate placement assistance where appropriate
- Reviewing final pay and benefits payments to ensure they are given within the time requirements of federal and state laws
- The collection of company property and security clearances, including cell phones, laptops, passwords, or security codes
- Strategizing on how coworkers and others will be notified of the separation

Dispute/Grievance Resolution

An ounce of prevention is always better than even the best of reactions, so HR may support and train managers on how to have a true open door policy. In some cases, employees may be encouraged to talk to any member of management about their concerns. HR will need to ensure there is a strong relationship between department managers built on a foundation of trust in order to avoid conflict that may arise with this type of open door policy. If speaking to their direct supervisor or any other member of management does not work, a formal grievance process will address how employees may escalate their concerns. In some cases, HR will set up a confidential 800 number. In other cases, it may be an escalation to a regional director or to the HR manager. When these efforts are unfruitful, alternatives will need to be available.

Alternative Dispute Resolution (ADR)

Alternative dispute resolution (ADR) involves a neutral third party who is engaged to hear employee complaints. HR will have to have set up an ADR agreement in which the employee agreed to this form of complaint resolution, usually included in time-of-hire paperwork or in a collective bargaining agreement. *Mediation* and conciliation are types of ADR in which a counselor attempts to open the flow of communication and reach a successful outcome. Mediation is not binding. *Arbitration* is designed to be a substitute for the courts. Arbitration can resolve a dispute more quickly than the courts and is less expensive. The process also allows for *conflict resolution* without a union resorting to a strike or the employer resorting to a lockout because of disagreements. Employers may find qualified arbitrators through the American Arbitration Association, a private organization founded in 1937 (a peak time for union membership). The Department of Labor also maintains a list of arbitrators through the Federal Mediation and Conciliation Service. Regardless, HR staff is often tasked with both writing the ADR process and managing the necessary resources at each stage.

In some cases, disputes come in litigated or already filed with a federal agency, meaning the opportunity for ADR is limited or gone altogether. Complaints from federal agencies may include safety violations filed with the Occupational Safety and Health Administration (OSHA), claims of discriminatory treatment filed with the Equal Employment Opportunity Commission (EEOC), contract exceptions filed with the Office of Federal Contract Compliance Programs (OFCCP), unfair labor charges filed with the National Labor Relations Board (NLRB), not to mention state-specific agencies.

HR must have the capability to participate in an investigation by a federal agency, including preserving documents, complying with requests for documentation, making employees available for interviews, and implementing any required solutions upon resolution.

If HR professionals have done their jobs well and trained supervisors and executives, much of their prevention efforts will bear fruit when a formal complaint is received. Quality documentation and compliant supervisor behaviors will reduce the chance of losing a harassment charge filed with the Equal Employment Opportunity Commission. Properly classifying employees in accordance with the Fair Labor Standards Act will reduce the odds of losing a wages and hours claim. Having a social media policy that does not violate employee rights to engage in protected concerted activity will help form a response to a charge from the National Labor Relations Board (see feature). In these and similar cases, anticipating the risk and formulating policies, training programs, and system audits will make investigating and responding to a claim more likely to be successful, as opposed to telling the CFO that he or she needs to write a check with several zeros at the end of the amount.

THE NLRB AND SOCIAL MEDIA POLICIES

The National Labor Relations Board protects the rights of workers to engage in protected concerted activity—acting together to address conditions at work. These protections exist while at work, in the company parking lot, at the local bar, over the phone, and now online as well. Employer social media policies that are too strict violate an employee's rights under the NLRB. In response to these issues, NLRB reports have underscored two main points:

1. Employer policies should not be so sweeping that they prohibit the kinds of activity protected by federal labor law, such as the discussion of wages or working conditions among employees.
2. An employee's comments on social media are generally not protected if they are mere gripes not made in relation to group activity among employees.

As with any policy, it is useful for HR to get a sign-off from the legal department to ensure that the policy does not inadvertently subjugate employee rights.

ADR

Alternative dispute resolution

A method for resolving a disagreement without going through formal legal procedures

Mediation

Helping others negotiate

An attempt to help other people or groups come to an agreement

Arbitration

Resolving a dispute

The process of coming to an agreement about something without using a judge or court

Conflict Resolution

Process of negotiation, arbitration

A method of negotiating agreements or solving problems

Managing Risk and Responding to Complaints

Many of the efforts of human resources are aimed at preventing risk, and a labor attorney will often attempt to make employers "bulletproof" through strict policies and behaviors. But the truth is that HR spends valuable time simply trying to shrink the target. In other words, HR cannot prevent current workers, job applicants, and past employees from filing charges against an employer or complaints against each other, but HR can drive the effort to build in protection of strong policies, procedures, rules, and documentation requirements to respond effectively.

Internal Investigations

The HR desk is the place where complaints of any sort land, so it makes sense that HR should be prepared to launch investigations where appropriate. These investigations are looking in the rearview mirror, meaning it is too late to make any changes to the actions that preceded a charge. HR may only carefully analyze root causes of problems and initiate a sequence of response events aimed at reducing threats and preventing similar occurrences. Steps to an effective internal investigation are:

- Remain a neutral investigator, saving opinions and determinations for when all data has been collected.
- Know which laws are relevant to the behavior, and ask specific questions to decide if a violation has occurred.
- Interview all relevant employees while using discretion and a need-to-know-only approach to sharing information.
- Look for facts that can be corroborated through documentation, e-mails, or witnesses.
- Identify environmental causes such as policies or work conditions, and behavioral causes such as leadership and employee conduct.
- Focus solutions on the causes, not the symptoms.

As with many HR functions, investigations may be outsourced to a professional group to maintain the integrity of both the process and the findings.

Managing the Union Relationship

Many of the aforementioned employee relations strategies are used when employers have a direct connection to their people. When a third party such as a labor union is in place, the employer manages the relationship with the people through the union, an overview of which is the focus of this section.

Union Labor Law

There are three major federal acts related to unions and employers, and they each serve a distinct purpose.

The National Labor Relations Act (NLRA) was passed in 1935 to protect the right of workers to organize and bargain collectively. The NLRA, also known as the Wagner Act, also established the National Labor Relations Board (NLRB) to oversee and enforce the Act. This includes responsibility to address employer unfair labor practices.

The Labor-Management Relations Act (LMRA) was passed in 1947 as an amendment to the NLRA, in part to balance the rights of the employers. Also known as the Taft-Hartley Act, its primary impact was limiting workers' right to strike. In 1941 one of the largest strikes had occurred when more than 4,000 workers walked off the job at the North American Aviation plant in California. With American involvement in the World War II war effort about to get seriously under way, President Roosevelt imposed martial law by executive order and sent the military to California to intervene in the walkout. After the attack on Pearl Harbor in December of that year, the larger unions agreed to a no-strike pledge in the defense industries. The pledge ended with the end of the war, and strikes were back in play. The LMRA of 1947 gave the president of the United States the authority to order an 80-day cooling-off period when national security is threatened, requiring striking workers to go back to work. George W. Bush most recently used this in 2002 when he halted employers' lockout of 10,500 West Coast longshoremen and ordered them back to work at more than 29 ports that were vital to military operations.

While the NLRA protected workers' right to strike and the LMRA protected the rights of businesses, the third major legislation protected the rights of union members from their union. The Labor-Management Reporting and Disclosure Act (LMRDA) of 1959 sought controls for internal union operations. It granted workers a majority vote before a union could increase member dues, and created a member Bill of Rights. The LMRDA, known also as the Landrum-Griffith Act, guarantees to every union member:

- Equal rights and equal privileges within the union to nominate candidates for union office, to vote in elections or referendums, and to attend union meetings
- The right to exercise freedom of speech and assembly
- The right to be free from arbitrary increases in dues, initiation fees, and assessments
- The right to sue and participate in administrative and legislative proceedings
- The right to procedural due process in disciplinary proceedings within the union

Union Organizing

As discussed earlier in the chapter, managing activities in employee and labor relations is predicated on understanding employer and employee rights and responsibilities. The National Labor Relations Act granted employees the right to organize a union without interference. A union is a formal labor organization that is authorized to act on behalf of a group of employees. This section covers rights related to union representation, as well as the various responsibilities that go along with them.

Why Employees Organize

This chapter's title, "Employee and Labor Relations," suggests, correctly, that many employees choose to organize because their relationship with management is unsatisfactory, and they want to authorize a union to act on their behalf. This may occur for several reasons, but the most common ones seem to be employees' desire for higher wages, desire for better health or retirement benefits, or a general dissatisfaction with management. Some workers feel that management treats them unfairly, needs are not met, and their opinions are not respected. One response to this dissatisfaction is an attempt to organize a union.

The Union Organizing Process

The National Labor Relations Act gave employees the right to organize, and also developed the process for doing so. It generally begins when a disgruntled employee contacts a union, but a union can also target a specific employer or industry. Interested employees form an organizing committee with the help and education of a union representative. The goal of the committee is to gain support for union representation and to begin an authorization card campaign. This step in the organizing process is important, because before the union can demand recognition or request an election, at least 30 percent of the employees in the targeted group must sign authorization cards.

Other terms to know related to this stage of campaigning include:

Leafleting The union hands out pamphlets to persuade employees to sign authorization cards.

Salting The union sends qualified applicants who are being paid by the union to apply for open positions and who, if hired, begin to organize immediately from within.

Bannering The union places obvious signs (banners, trucks with union logos) outside the organization to advertise a message to the public and to employees about business practices.

Picketing The union and its representatives gather outside the employer's premises with hand signs and chants—it's bannering with human sign holders.

Organizing Activities at Work

Employers cannot prohibit employees from organizing. Employers can, however, prohibit the distribution of pamphlets, the use of company equipment, and organizing on company time. Many employers have nonsolicitation policies for this very reason, and companies should be sure to enforce this consistently for all forms of solicitation at work, not just union collateral. The company cannot prohibit union organizing activities while on break or before or after work hours. Many unions have websites and chat rooms to which interested employees can go for information, but the process of distributing leaflets and holding face-to-face meetings with workers after hours continues to be a popular method for gathering interest.

Card Campaigns

The goal at the card campaign stage of the organizing process is to get as many employees as possible to sign authorization cards. While the union only needs 30 percent of employee signatures from the bargaining unit they wish to represent, organizers often seek to gain above 50 percent. This allows the union to demand voluntary recognition by the employer. In terms of pending legislation and issues to watch, unions have been trying for years to get a law passed in which employers must automatically recognize a union if they receive a high percentage of authorization cards signed. The Employee Free Choice Act would eliminate the secret ballot election if more than 50 percent of employees sign authorization cards, but has not been passed by Congress. It is important to note that some states have already adopted these types of laws for public-sector unions. Currently, if a union does receive 50 percent + 1 signed cards, the union may ask the employer for voluntary recognition. If the employer refuses, the union files a petition for an NLRB-supervised election.

Bargaining Units

Understanding the term *bargaining unit* is important at this stage of the organizing process. A bargaining unit is a group of two or more employees that will be exclusively represented by the union. Another way to look at it is the group of employees who will be bound by a single employment contract. Employees covered in the bargaining unit must be a community of interest, defined as those with the same or substantially similar interests concerning wages, working conditions, and hours. The NLRB will consider a bargaining unit based on a history of collective bargaining, the desires of the employees concerned, and the physical location, as well as groupings by industry classifications. Once the bargaining unit has been defined, a bargaining representative is selected by a secret ballot election and a petition to the NLRB for representative certification is requested.

Special Issues with Bargaining Units A *supervisor* may not be selected to serve as a bargaining representative. The term *supervisor* is defined by more than just a title; job responsibilities matter. A supervisor is an individual who has the authority to hire, fire, demote, transfer, lay off, suspend, assign, reward, or discipline employees on behalf of the employer.

Supervisor

A person in charge of other employees

Someone who oversees employees in a department or business unit to assign tasks and make sure work is completed, among other duties

---

Unfair Labor Practices (ULPs)

The union and the employer may commit unfair labor practices both during the organizing process and while working under the collective bargaining agreement. Examples of employer ULPs during organizing include withholding wage increases that would have occurred had the union not been on the scene, or photographing employees participating in peaceful union organizing. Once the election petition is filed, the employer is restricted as to the information it shares with employees. Most experts agree that the easiest way to remember the types of ULPs at the organizing stage of unionization is to use the acronym TIPS: employers cannot threaten, intimidate, promise, or spy. Table 6.1 shows a few of the ULPs defined by Section 8 of the NLRA.

In addition to the ULPs listed in the table, the following are also considered ULPs:

Hot cargo agreements When a union and an employer agree to not require union members to handle so-called hot cargo—goods or materials coming from a nonunion employer or subcontractor.

Featherbedding When a union tries to require the employer to use more labor than is necessary for a job.

The Election

If the union members are successful in their campaigning, they will petition the NLRB for a supervised election and provide evidence of a show of interest, usually in the form of the signed authorization cards. A consent election is held when a

Table 6.1   NLRA Section 8 ULPs

Union ULPs	Employer ULPs
Restraint and coercion of employees such as physical assault or threatening employees with job loss if they don't support the union activities.	Employer interference, restraint, or coercion directed against union or collective activity such as threatening employees with loss of jobs or plant shutdown if they support the union.
Restraint and coercion of employers in the selection of a bargaining representative, such as refusing to meet with the employer's attorney.	Employer domination of unions such as forming a fake union, getting the organization started, and deciding how it will be set up and what it will do, and management taking part in decision making at the meetings.
Causing or attempting to cause discrimination such as prompting an employer to discharge union members because they made speeches against a contract.	Employer discrimination against employees who take part in union or collective activities such as firing workers who support the union or demoting workers who circulate union petitions.
Refusal to bargain in good faith such as meeting at reasonable times, or insisting on illegal provisions.	Employer retaliation for filing unfair labor practice charges or cooperating with the NLRB.
Engaging in prohibited strikes and boycotts, such as inducing or encouraging a work strike or boycott.	Employer refusal to bargain in good faith with union representatives, such as designating a representative without the authority to bargain.

regional NLRB representative meets with the employer and union to measure the amount of agreement on issues such as bargaining units and voter eligibility. If there are no issues, they may waive the right to a formal hearing for rulings. A direct election is an election ordered by the NLRB representative when the employer and the union are not able to agree on issues. In order to make this more clear, consider this stage of the organizing process as being when both the employer and union consent to an election to be held once any issues have been resolved. Once the NLRB receives an election in petition and issues are resolved, an election can be scheduled.

If a simple majority (50 percent + 1) of the *employees who vote* selects "yes" for union representation, the union is certified. It is important to understand that the number of affirmative votes does not have to be a simple majority of the entire bargaining unit. If a unit is made up of 100 employees but only 20 show up on voting day, the union needs only 11 votes to win the right to represent all 100 bargaining unit members. For this reason, employers want to encourage all members of a bargaining unit to vote on election day.

Within seven days of consent or direction of an election, the employer must provide the names and addresses of all employees in the bargaining unit to the NLRB. This is called an Excelsior list.

Election Bars

The NLRB may also bar a petition to an election under certain conditions. These bars include:

Statutory bars When a valid election has been conducted (usually by another union) within the past 12 months, another union cannot petition to represent the same bargaining unit.

Contract bars When a valid collective bargaining agreement covering a period of three years or less exists, it will bar an election for the contract period.

Blocking bar If an unfair labor practice charge is pending and thus holding up certification, another election will not be allowed by the NLRB.

Collective Bargaining

Once a union wins the right to represent a bargaining unit, the process of negotiating terms of the employment contract—the collective bargaining agreement—begins.

The process requires the employer and union representatives to meet at reasonable times, act in good faith, and put any agreement reached in writing. Both parties have a duty to bargain, and failure to do so may result in a ULP charge. Bargaining in good faith does not obligate either party to concede, but rather to engage in the process of coming to an agreement. HR practioners may support these efforts by helping to coordinate meeting times and dates. They may also be called upon to collect data and perform wages and hours costing and modeling to aid in decision making. This information will help represent the employer's needs and serve as negotiating points throughout the bargaining process.

Bargaining Subjects

There are three main bargaining subjects:

1. *Mandatory subjects* are directed by the NLRA, which compels employers and unions to come to terms on certain contract provisions. These include wages and hours issues such as overtime and paid holidays as well as issues related to seniority arrangements and the grievance resolution process.

2. *Permissive subjects* are those that the union and employer may choose, such as dress codes and the recording of negotiating sessions. Either side may refuse to bargain on permissive subjects.
3. *Illegal issues* are those prohibited by the NLRA, and include bargaining for closed-shop security agreements and limiting concerted activity of the employees and other unlawful behaviors.

Typical Items in a Collective Bargaining Agreement

- Purpose of Agreement: Preamble and Recognition
- Statement of Nondiscrimination
- Management Rights
- Wages and Incentives, Leave Entitlements
- Discipline and Termination
- Seniority
- Training
- Pension and Insurance
- Safety
- Grievance Procedure
- Strikes and Lockouts
- Term of Agreement

Bargaining Impasse

If the union and employer fail to reach an agreement, a bargaining impasse is said to have occurred. HR may need to activate the mediation or conciliation services at this stage to try to achieve resolution. This is a strategy designed to achieve the organization's desires prior to making its final offer.

The Rights of Employees

The NLRB enforces two main types of employee rights under Section 7 of the NLRA. In addition to the right to self-organize, join a union, and collectively bargain, the NLRA specifically discusses union security agreements and the right to strike. These are discussed next.

Union Security Agreements

Union security agreements are formed between the union and the employer and require the employees to make payments to the union in order to keep their jobs. These types of agreements cannot require applicants to be members of a union in order to be hired, and an agreement may not require employees to join or maintain membership in a union in order to retain their jobs. These arrangements may allow individuals to become dues-paying nonmembers. If nonmembers object to their dues being used to fund nonrepresentational costs (such as political efforts), the most that can be required of them is payment of their share of costs related to activities such as collective bargaining, contract administration, and grievance adjustment. Employees who have religious objections to either becoming a member or paying dues may be exempt from dues and initiation fees. Other fees may still apply.

The Right to Strike

Another right granted by the NLRA is the employees' right to strike, but with some limitations. The lawfulness of a strike may depend upon the purpose or object of the strike. Most lawful strikes are either economic strikes, which occur for purposes of contract negotiations, or unfair labor practice strikes. The purpose of an economic strike is to force the employer to make a concession about higher wages, shorter hours, or better working conditions. While strikers retain their employee status and cannot be fired for striking, the employer may replace them. If the employer hires legitimate, permanent replacements for the striking workers, the striking workers may not be reinstated.

Unfair labor practice strikers may not be discharged or permanently replaced. Absent serious misconduct, the strikers must be reinstated to their jobs even if replacement workers must be fired as a result.

See the Twinkie time line in Figure 6.1 for another view of the job losses of striking workers.

Special Issues: Unlawful Strikes

The NLRB also may declare a strike unlawful (and thus strikers subject to termination) under the following conditions:

- Strikes to compel an employer to commit a ULP
- Strikes that violate no-strike provisions in a contract
- Misconduct by the strikers, such as physical blocking or assault

Union Decertification

Similar to certifying a union, an election must be held to decertify a union from representing a bargaining unit. A decertification election must be requested by

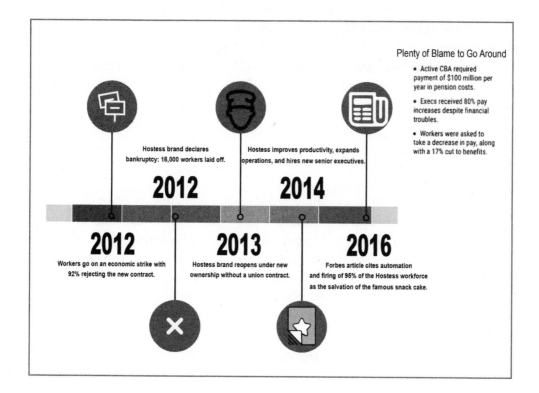

Figure 6.1   Death (and Resurrection) of a Twinkie
Source: Tim Worstall, "What Saved Hostess and Twinkies: Automation and Firing 95% of the Union Workforce," *Forbes* Online, July 6, 2016.

employees, and cannot be encouraged or compelled by an employer. The NLRB will process a petition to decertify if at least 30 percent of employees in the bargaining unit indicate their desire to do so.

Union Avoidance Strategies

In 2015, the NLRB adopted procedural changes that substantially shrank the time between an election petition being filed and the election event. The changes include the ability to file petitions electronically, with a regional NLRB director setting up the preelection issues hearing about eight days after the petition is received. In addition, an election will not be stayed if there are preelection objections, as parties may now wait until after an election is held to file a request for review. Voter lists, including personal phone numbers and e-mail addresses, must be submitted within two days of the consent or directive election.

All of this contributes to the union benefiting from any momentum gained during the campaign process, and reminds HR that employers should not rely on antiunion campaigns that begin after a petition to hold an election is filed. While employers may not interfere with an individual's right to organize, there are several steps they can take to help limit the success of an organizing campaign. This section discusses those strategies.

Organizational Structure

It is easier for unions to successfully organize smaller groups of employees, so it is beneficial for employers to structure larger departments made of employees with shared job duties or responsibilities. For example, a manufacturer with production workers, shipping and receiving workers, and quality assurance inspectors may reasonably structure them into one work unit or wage band, such as production.

Positive Employee Relations Strategies

Happy, satisfied employees typically do not vote for unionization; communication is often at the root of positive relationships. Train managers in problem-solving techniques, and promote open door policies that encourage the discussion of employee concerns. Survey employees periodically, and be sure to address any issues right away to avoid small issues festering into poisonous feelings. Conduct stay interviews, as opposed to waiting until an employee exits, for real-time opinions of how employees are feeling about their jobs, supervisors, wages, and working conditions. Remind employees of the benefits of an open relationship with the company, and the non-wage-based perks built into their salaries like time off and coverage of health insurance premiums.

Early Intervention and Response Planning

There are often signs when employee thoughts about organizing change over into actions, so an HR professional who is paying attention can often advise employers when early intervention efforts may be necessary. Indicators of organizing may be misread as normal operational issues such as high turnover or increased employee complaints. There may also be more obvious signs such as discarded union pamphlets in the break room. Regardless, employers should have a union response plan that addresses both early and late issues signaling pending organization.

Suggested Study or Organizational Audit Activities

- Approach your management team and ask for their thoughts on what types of employee input would be most valuable for their decision making. Discuss the advantages and disadvantages of focus groups and employee surveys, and note the concerns of management. If they were resistant, find out what their concerns were. If they preferred one data collection method over another, go deep into their reasoning.
- Create a training session for supervisors that address one of the ELR responsibilities described in this chapter. Suggestions of particular value include training them on the company discipline policy, and how to avoid disparate impact or a charge of harassment or discrimination.
- Go online to the American Arbitration Association or other ADR website, and research the advantages and disadvantages of ad hoc arbitration.
- Do you know the advantages of remaining union-free? Are you aware of the best practices related to union avoidance strategies? Task yourself with writing a union avoidance policy for your current or a past employer.

Note

1. From live stream video between HRCI and Gabrielle Bosché on YouTube, December 14, 2016: https://www.youtube.com/watch?v=PkmMtgcURd4.

7 | Risk Management

319

(*continued*)

lack of high-quality studies within this HR domain, particularly from the perspective of the injured worker. In fact, only 13 of the 29 studies originally sourced were included due to lack of validity issues. Areas to consider for future research include a review of employee satisfaction, quality of life after an injury, and the impact that a workplace injury with a subsequent RTW program had on lifetime earnings potential.

That's not to say that more current research doesn't exist, particularly in the context of RTW for non-work-related disabilities. A study in Norway was prompted by a national absenteeism rate of over 40 percent, and near 50 percent disability rate by people with reported non-work-related musculoskeletal disorders such as fibromyalgia. The researchers found that the well-crafted RTW programs of employers changed the way off-work employees were thinking, and gave them a more optimistic view of the future. Returning to work gave them back a sense of being part of a community. The researchers reported that many participants "expressed they had changed their focus from what they struggled with to what they managed." The study also found that six months after a completed RTW program, the injured individuals had a better idea of their own responsibilities to stay at work as opposed to missing time due to their disability (Hamnes, Rønningen, and Skarbø 2015). Other studies found that 49 percent of employers with more than 10,000 employees already had RTW programs for non-work-disabled individuals, with 22 percent of other companies planning to add these programs in the near future. This may be in large part due to the competing demands of the variety of nonoccupational injury leave programs HR must manage for the organizations of today. The downside: the employers who have more robust RTW programs for non-work-related disabilities are grading the programs at a C+. The reasoning of one executive in the study was the frustration employers felt at trying to monitor the effectiveness of RTW programs in general (Harrison 2015).

We can learn both from the older summary studies of occupational RTW programs and the more recent studies of emerging RTW efforts for nonoccupational disabilities. We must recognize that it is difficult for HR to successfully argue the merits of RTW programs due to the lack of clear, evidence-based support. Employers may learn from industrial best practices, and through their own trial and error. A solution is for HR practitioners to keep track of their own metrics to see how the numbers look at their places of employment. By conducting internal research such as comparing the total cost of injuries between RTW and non-RTW employees and tracking the amount of time the HR department is spending on managing leaves of absence, HR can make a business case for an RTW program that—for now—appears to be a valuable risk management tool.

Best practices in large companies such as Kaiser Permanente involved the union to help with the build-out of return to work and stay at work programs. Other companies have sought to standardize the interactive process to comply with legal requirements, but also to encourage creative problem solving to keep their talent working. Changing the structure of an HR or benefits department may also be necessary to create depth in expertise of the oft-competing laws on managing leaves of absence, and provide focused services to employees struggling with any type of disability. HR may find that the true discussion with executives is whether to completely internalize RTW management or to outsource the management of these programs. This growing trend may shift the day-to-day burden of administrative oversight and allow HR to engage in the more personal approaches to achieve a satisfactory blended approach.

References

Hamnes, B., A. Rønningen, and Å. Skarbø. 2015. "'I Am So Much More than My Work': Qualitative Study of Experiences after Participating in Return to Work Programs for People with Rheumatic Diseases." *Annals of the Rheumatic Diseases* 2015 (74:Suppl 2): 177. doi:10.1136/annrheumdis-2015-eular .5181.

Harrison, Sheena. 2015. "Return-to-Work Programs Expand beyond Workers Comp: Action on Disability Claims Can Reduce Employers' Costs." *Business Insurance*, March 22, 0020.

Krause, N., L. K. Dasinger, and F. J. Neuhauser. 1998. "Modified Work and Return to Work: A Review of the Literature." *Journal of Occupational Rehabilitation* 8:113. doi:10.1023/A:1023015622987.

Introduction

How do you like your toast? Lightly crisped to caramel-colored perfection, or dark and coarse with burned bits for flavor? Regardless, you may have to prepare it at home because many employers of today are adopting employment practices that ban small appliances such as toasters, tea kettles, and portable heaters at work. This is just one example of the seemingly never-ending HR tasks of interpreting and applying the various safety standards required in the workplace.

Protecting workers from identified job hazards (and themselves) is not the only focus of an employer's *risk management* efforts. While fire risks and personal safety are important, HR is also called upon to:

- Promote employee health and well-being
- Protect organizational assets from loss and liability
- Identify and comply with the laws that apply to their business
- Focus on preventing risk to all stakeholders
- Design health and safety programs that meet the diverse needs of international human resource management
- Develop policies that communicate both employer and employee rights and responsibilities, and procedures to protect physical, financial, and human assets

- Train and communicate with the workforce on policies and identified hazards in the workplace
- Work with internal and external resources to plan and respond to disasters and emergencies
- Comply with record-keeping and notice requirements

Risk Management

Assessing and preventing threats

The process of analyzing potential threats and deciding how to prevent them

A Focus on Compliance

Many of the risk management efforts of the past have placed a heavy emphasis on complying with the standards established by the Occupational Safety and Health Administration (OSHA). Covered in more detail in the labor law appendix, OSHA continues to consider and adopt various safety standards designed to prevent incidents in the workplace (see Figure 7.1).

The National Institute for Occupational Safety and Health (NIOSH) exists to study trends, patterns, and the science of workplace safety. NIOSH often makes recommendations to OSHA for standards that should be adopted. State and local governments and unions play a part in obligating employers to worker safety. For example, in the Central Valley of California, where summer temperatures frequently exceed 100 degrees, agricultural workers were experiencing high incidents of heat illness, heat stroke, and death. The problem became so severe that California adopted a Temporary Emergency Standard for employers, bypassing the regular process for approving new safety standards. In order to comply, affected employers must provide training for employees, and access to water, shade, and rest under hot conditions.

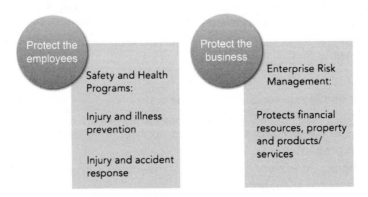

Figure 7.1   Focus of Risk Management Responsibilities and Knowledge

The European Union also has adopted a framework for occupational safety and health standards. The European Agency for Safety and Health at Work issue OSH directives (EU-OSHA). Similar to the American OSHA standards, these directives provide guidance to employers in the areas of evaluating, avoiding, and combating safety and health risks to employees and the company. Unions and works councils also take responsibility for designing and enforcing workplace safety provisions.

For countries without legal regulations governing employment safety and health programs, international HR practitioners will need to adapt practices in areas of health and safety that are culturally relevant to protect both the workers and the employer from risk and liability. Dealing with outdated equipment and a poorly trained workforce often is addressed through an international health and safety management program.

Regardless of the existence of laws governing employer safety requirements, the prudent HR professional has in place steps to address workplace risk. As with most other HR activities, these steps are the result of a needs assessment.

Risk Assessments

How do we know what laws apply to our organization? What clear and present dangers lurk in the figurative cubicles of our facilities? What is the root cause of injuries at our workplace? Who is at risk for global illnesses, and how do organizations prevent them? How can HR prove to legal agencies that the organization is taking steps to prevent injuries and accidents from occurring? The answers to these questions can be found by doing the all-important HR task of conducting needs analyses, conducting risk assessments, or conducting threat assessments. Regardless of what the process is called at your company, there are a variety of tools and resources available that you need to know about in order to accomplish this task. These are covered next.

Self-Inspections

A safety self-inspection documents an employer's effort to identify hazards and take corrective steps. The goal of these efforts is to correct hazards and prevent incidents. For this reason the findings may be used to:

- Communicate new hazards to affected employees
- Coach employees on safe work practices and procedures
- Discipline individuals for unsafe acts or for failing to follow safety procedures
- Document unsafe conditions and abatement efforts
- Identify the need for new safety procedures or rules

- Recommend personal protective equipment
- Prepare for a formal inspection by a government agency, customer, or insurance provider

OSHA has on its website a self-inspection checklist that employers may modify to fit their individual needs. From a general perspective, OSHA recommends that employers review the following:

Processing, receiving, shipping, and storage Equipment, job planning, layout, heights, floor loads, projection of materials, materials handling and storage methods, training for materials handling equipment.

Building and grounds conditions Floors, walls, ceilings, exits, stairs, walkways, ramps, platforms, driveways, aisles.

Housekeeping program Waste disposal, tools, objects, materials, leakage and spillage, cleaning methods, schedules, work areas, remote areas, storage areas.

Electricity Equipment, switches, breakers, fuses, switch boxes, junctions, special fixtures, circuits, insulation, extensions, tools, motors, grounding, national electric code compliance.

Lighting Type, intensity, controls, conditions, diffusion, location, glare and shadow control.

Heating and ventilation Type, effectiveness, temperature, humidity, controls, natural and artificial ventilation and exhausting.

Machinery Points of operation, flywheels, gears, shafts, pulleys, key ways, belts, couplings, sprockets, chains, frames, controls, lighting for tools and equipment, brakes, exhausting, feeding, oiling, adjusting, maintenance, lockout/tag-out, grounding, work space, location, purchasing standards.

Personnel Training, including hazard identification training; experience; methods of checking machines before use; type of clothing; personal protective equipment (PPE); use of guards; tool storage; work practices; methods for cleaning, oiling, or adjusting machinery.

Hand and power tools Purchasing standards, inspection, storage, repair, types, maintenance, grounding, use and handling.

Chemicals Storage, handling, transportation, spills, disposals, amounts used, labeling, toxicity or other harmful effects, warning signs, supervision, training, protective clothing and equipment, hazard communication requirements.

Fire prevention Extinguishers, alarms, sprinklers, smoking rules, exits, personnel assigned, separation of flammable materials and dangerous operations, explosion-proof fixtures in hazardous locations, waste disposal and training of personnel.

Maintenance Regular and preventive maintenance on all equipment used at the worksite, recording all work performed on the machinery, and training personnel on the proper care and servicing of the equipment.

Personal protective equipment Type, size, maintenance, repair, age, storage, assignment of responsibility, purchasing methods, standards observed, training in care and use, rules of use, method of assignment.

Transportation Motor vehicle safety, seat belts, vehicle maintenance, safe driver programs.

First aid program and supplies Medical care facilities locations, posted emergency phone numbers, accessible first aid kits.

Evacuation plan Establish and practice procedures for an emergency evacuation (e.g., fire, chemical or biological incident, bomb threat); include escape procedures and routes, critical plant operations, employee accounting following an evacuation, rescue and medical duties, and ways to report emergencies.

Employer self-inspections should be conducted on a regular basis. For example, you could do a daily walk-through of the facility to ensure that no immediate hazards exist such as blocked emergency exits or slip/trip hazards. On a monthly or quarterly basis you may want to complete a full-scope inspection, such as the one recommended by OSHA. On a semiannual or annual basis, it may be prudent to work with your insurance carrier, fire department, building inspector, or other external resource to ensure your workplace remains free from notable hazards.

Job Hazard Analysis

OSHA defines the term hazard as "the potential for harm." A job hazard analysis is a tool used to evaluate hazards that are job specific. By evaluating these hazards, employers can take steps to control the exposure and thus reduce the likelihood of an injury, illness, or accident. As with most assessments, a focus on prevention will include:

- Communicating hazards to employees
- Training affected workers on safe work practices
- Developing control and response plans
- Selecting personal protective equipment (PPE)

In order to complete a job hazard analysis, it is important to involve the employees who are doing the work. Employees understand best the potential risks associated with the environment or equipment relevant to the job tasks. Their

Figure 7.2   Effective Hazard Controls

supervisor is also a good resource, as he or she may have a unique perspective to contribute on how a hazard may be eliminated. If a hazard cannot be completely eliminated, ask the supervisor and employees for solutions related to the hazard controls found in Figure 7.2.

Deciding which jobs to evaluate may seem a daunting task to the HR professional working at a company with hundreds of job classifications. A best practice is to analyze injury and accident records to look for jobs that have higher incidents of injury. Along with frequency, look for which body parts are most commonly affected. Sort the data three ways—at the organizational, department, and individual levels. Next, identify high-hazard jobs in which fire or chemicals are used. Review positions that involve risk taking, heights, or ladder use, paying special attention to environments in which employees work in extreme heat or cold. These are all excellent places to start the job hazard analysis process. Don't forget to review near-miss reports as well.

OSHA has identified the following questions to ask when conducting a job hazard analysis:

- What can go wrong?
- What are the consequences?
- How could the hazard arise?
- What are other contributing factors?
- How likely is it that the hazard will occur?

A sample job hazard template is found in Table 7.1.

Injury and Accident Data

Investigating all incidents—injuries, accidents, and near misses—is a practical way for HR to identify the threats and exposure to all workers.

Incident investigations are an important component of any organizational safety program. Often conducted by an individual supervisor or member of a safety committee, these investigations focus on determining if an unsafe act or unsafe

Table 7.1 Sample Job Hazard Form

Job Location	Analyst	Date
Food Distribution Warehouse	Safety Sandy	

Task Description
Warehouse employees drive an electric pallet jack to place boxes of soda syrup onto a pallet for loading onto a delivery truck to customers. The syrup weighs between 30 and 50 pounds per box.

Hazard Description
The product is stored on a 12-tie pallet that is loaded four boxes high. When received, the pallet is stored flush up against a warehouse wall. When employees deplete the first row of boxes, they must reach across the tie and pull the product toward them, and then stack it onto the jack by hand. Hazards include:

1. The weight of the product combined with the excessive reach may lead to lower back or shoulder problems.

2. If an employee drops a box, it could cause severe injury to the foot or toes.

Hazard Controls
Engineering
Pull the storage pallet away from the wall so the employees may access the product on all sides.

Administrative
Conduct safety training in proper lifting techniques, including safe reaching.

PPE

1. Change the type of protective gloves to ones that allow for a better grip.

2. Require the wearing of steel- or Kevlar-toed work boots.

---

condition has caused an injury, accident, or near miss. The unsafe act or unsafe condition is known as the indirect cause of the accident. The direct cause is the "unplanned release of energy, or hazardous material." See Figure 7.3 for a visual representation of this concept from OSHA. When investigating injuries, it is important to identify both the direct and indirect causes of harm. This information is used to ensure that any future preventive efforts address the fundamental element(s) that contributed to a safety incident. Prevention efforts may be focused on eliminating an unsafe condition (see previous discussion of hazard controls) or addressing an unsafe act committed by a worker. Addressing employee unsafe acts is most commonly achieved through training, coaching, and/or discipline. A word of caution when using discipline, especially if an employee was injured: The discipline must address the employee's unsafe behavior, not discipline the employee for

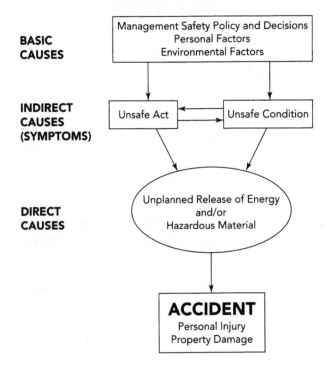

BASIC CAUSES

Management Safety Policy and Decisions
Personal Factors
Environmental Factors

INDIRECT CAUSES (SYMPTOMS)

Unsafe Act ⟷ Unsafe Condition

DIRECT CAUSES

Unplanned Release of Energy and/or Hazardous Material

ACCIDENT
Personal Injury
Property Damage

A detailed analysis of an accident will normally reveal
three cause levels: basic, indirect, and direct.

Figure 7.3   OSHA's Analysis of Incident Causes
Source: Occupational Safety and Health Administration (OSHA).

getting hurt. The discipline may be interpreted as an act of retaliation against an employee for getting hurt or reporting an injury. Employee morale is also affected when injured workers are disciplined. See the "In Real Life" feature example.

IN REAL LIFE . . .

Joshua was a commercial driver for SodeCo, a food distribution warehouse in New Jersey. His daily responsibilities included delivering products to the fast-food establishments on his route. Many of his customers were open 24 hours, so Joshua usually was dispatched around 12:00 a.m. At his second stop of the morning it was still dark outside. Joshua was hand-carting in product while wearing earbuds and listening to music, even though SodeCo's code of safe practices specifically prohibited nonmedically necessary ear wear. According to the restaurant video feed, a robber came up behind Joshua and slammed the butt of a gun into the back of his head, rendering him unconscious. A restaurant employee who witnessed the incident followed procedure and barricaded himself in the walk-in refrigerator while dialing 911. Joshua was taken by ambulance to the nearest hospital and diagnosed with a concussion and severe contusions, receiving several stitches as a result. In this case, the direct cause of injury was Joshua's head being hit with a gun butt. The indirect cause of the injury was Joshua's failure to follow company safety standards.

Joshua's coworkers were outraged and worried about him when they heard the news. The incident elevated driver concerns about the security risks associated with early-morning route stops. One driver declared that he was going to start carrying his gun on his route. Another insisted that his guard dog be allowed to ride shotgun in the cab of his truck. Still others demanded that all early-morning and key card stops be staffed with two workers. Amidst of all of this, human resources was faced with the need to potentially discipline Joshua for his unsafe act and violation of the code of safe practices.

Investigative Steps

Steps to an appropriate incident investigation may go as follows:

- *Investigate the scene of the accident.* Observe the conditions that were present, including the time of day, weather, lighting, and floors. Look for the presence of machine safety guards and observe if equipment appears to be well maintained. Take pictures or video of the surrounding area. Make note of any unusual or seemingly out-of-place objects. In this step, you are the detective seeking to find any environmental (unsafe) condition that may have caused or contributed to the accident.
- *Interview involved employees and witnesses.* To avoid contamination, it is important to separate individuals as soon as is reasonable following an incident. Ask for statements regarding what was observed, allowing each person to explain it without prompting and in his or her own words.
- *Document findings.* Many employers find it useful to have an incident report for documentation purposes. This is in addition to documents required by your insurance carrier or OSHA. The incident report is a tool for internal use. It allows for the collection of consistent information for comparison of hazards. It often serves as the primary reference point for HR or the safety committee to determine both direct and indirect causes, along with any contributing factors.

First Responders

The first priority when responding to the scene of a workplace accident is to secure the area so nobody else gets hurt. The second priority is obtaining care for any injured party. In many cases, achieving both of these outcomes may require the designation and training of first responders. The depth and scope of first responder responsibilities may vary. A risk assessment will help the proactive HR professional determine the need, define the responsibilities, establish the procedure, and train the workers.

Historical Data

Another way to identify risks associated with the business of work is to review historical data. When looking at past incidents, patterns tend to emerge. This bears out even at a national level, and trickles down through industry statistics and geographic clusters. Take a look at the feature to practice interpreting data.

INCIDENTS BY THE NUMBERS

On a national scale, OSHA collects data pertaining to the most commonly violated standards by employers (see Table 7.2). Construction workers are considered at high risk for workplace fatalities—in 2014, one in every five workplace fatalities occurred in the construction industry. Through trend analysis, OSHA has identified the "Fatal Four," those workplace injuries that account for more than 60 percent of the construction industry fatalities. These are falls, electrocution, being struck by an object, and being caught in-between.

As an experienced HR professional, what trends do you see in the construction industry data found in the table? What steps would you take to eliminate these hazards? If you're not sure, go online and search for OSHA's "Construction Pocket Guide: Worker Safety Series." Find and read the section "Hazards and Solutions" for a review of recommended abatement activities for the hazards. What suggestions does OSHA offer that are engineering controls? Which are administrative controls? How many of the solutions include personal protective equipment?

Table 7.2   Top 10 Most Frequently Cited OSHA Standards Violations, FY 2015

General Industry Standards	Construction Industry Standards
#2 Hazard communication	#1 Fall protection
#4 Respiratory protection	#3 Scaffolding
#5 Lock out/tag out	#7 Ladders
#6 Powered industrial trucks (forklifts, etc.)	
#8 Electrical, wiring methods, components and equipment	
#9 Machinery and machine guarding, general requirements	
#10 Electrical systems design	

Incidence Rates

Calculating incident rates is another way an employer may identify the needs of a workplace safety and health program. OSHA defines an incident rate as the number (frequency) of injuries, illness, or lost workdays per 100 full-time workers. Rates are calculated using the formula:

$$N \times 200,000 \div EH$$

where:

> N = number of injuries and illnesses, or number of lost workdays
> EH = total hours worked by all employees during a month, quarter, or fiscal year.
> 200,000 = base for 100 full-time equivalent workers (working 40 hours per week, 50 weeks per year)

After an employer has assessed the types of risks to its employees and company, the next step is to design programs and plans for prevention and response.

Injury and Illness Prevention Programs

An injury and illness prevention plan or program (IIPP) is part of an overall safety management program designed to reduce or eliminate workplace injuries and illnesses. Employers with 10 or fewer employees are not generally required to have a written plan in place. In order for an IIPP to be successful, OSHA recommends that:

- There is top-level commitment from senior management, and employees are encouraged to participate in workplace safety and health efforts.
- The company regularly engages in workplace hazard analyses.
- There is a hazard prevention and control program in place to address identified hazards before an injury or illness occurs.
- The company regularly holds safety training meetings to communicate hazards and educate the workforce on safe behaviors.

Workplace Injuries and Illnesses

The work-relatedness of injuries affects inclusion of the event in the incident rate calculation, recordability for OSHA record-keeping purposes, and compensability under an employer's workers' compensation insurance. For an injury to be work-related, the employee had to have been injured or become ill while acting within the scope of his or her job. For example, let's say a receptionist is driving to the post office as part of her regular duty to pick up mail. She is in a car accident and breaks her foot. This injury would be considered to be work-related because she was acting on behalf of her employer at the time of the event. Compare this example with an employee who is driving to work as part of her normal commute and is in a car accident, also breaking her foot. This latter incident would not be work-related, as she was not acting on behalf of her employer at the time.

These distinctions are important, particularly when complying with OSHA's record-keeping requirements. Most employers with 10 or more workers must complete the OSHA 300 log for any recordable illness or injury, and post the summary from February through April.

Employers are not required to record first aid—only events. OSHA defines first aid very specifically:

- Using a nonprescription medication at nonprescription strength (for medications available in both prescription and nonprescription form, a recommendation by a physician or other licensed health care professional to use a nonprescription medication at prescription strength is considered medical treatment for record-keeping purposes).
- Administering tetanus immunizations (other immunizations, such as hepatitis B vaccine or rabies vaccine, are considered medical treatment).
- Cleaning, flushing, or soaking wounds on the surface of the skin.
- Using wound coverings such as bandages, Band-Aids, or gauze pads, or using butterfly bandages or Steri-Strips (other wound-closing devices such as sutures or staples are considered medical treatment).
- Using hot or cold therapy.
- Using any nonrigid means of support, such as elastic bandages, wraps, nonrigid back belts, and the like (devices with rigid stays or other systems designed to immobilize parts of the body are considered medical treatment for record-keeping purposes).
- Using temporary immobilization devices while transporting an accident victim (e.g., splints, slings, neck collars, back boards, etc.).
- Drilling of a fingernail or toenail to relieve pressure, or draining fluid from a blister.
- Using eye patches.
- Removing foreign bodies from the eye using only irrigation or a cotton swab.
- Removing splinters or foreign material from areas other than the eye by irrigation, tweezers, cotton swabs, or other simple means.
- Using finger guards.
- Using massages (physical therapy or chiropractic treatment are considered medical treatment for record-keeping purposes).
- Drinking fluids for relief of heat stress.

See Figure 7.4 for the decision tree of when to record an injury or illness that occurred at the workplace.

Electronic Reporting

In 2017, a new rule took effect requiring some employers to submit their injury data electronically. OSHA will analyze this information for use in trend identification and prevention efforts. The information may also be posted on the OSHA website to "encourage employers to improve workplace safety and provide

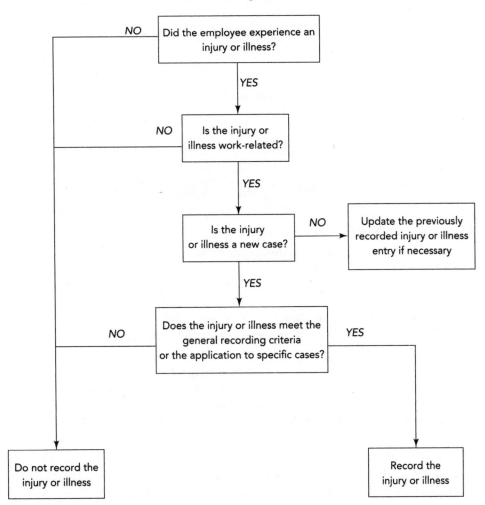

Figure 7.4   When to Record an Injury

valuable information to workers, job seekers, customers, researchers and the general public." See Figure 7.5 for the compliance schedule.

Compensation Insurance

Employers have a responsibility to return injured workers to their preinjured state, or to compensate injured workers if they cannot be rehabilitated. This is an absolute right of all employees, and employers are therefore required to carry workers' compensation insurance (paid for by the employer) as part of an overall safety management program. Things you should know about workers' compensation insurance include:

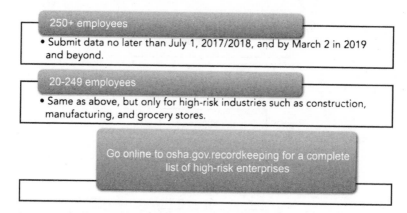

Figure 7.5   OSHA Electronic Reporting Schedule
Source: Occupational Safety and Health Administration (OSHA).

- Compensation plans are state run. Requirements will vary state by state.
- Insurance coverage often provides categories of care. Continuing medical treatment and rehabilitation are well-known benefits of workers' compensation insurance. Wage replacement income owing to lost time is also covered, as is future earnings replacement in the event of a permanent disability. In the case of a fatal injury, survivors benefits are paid to the worker's family.
- Workers' compensation is experience rated (the rating is often referred to as the experience modifier or "ex mod"). Similar to auto insurance, the premium amounts are correlated to use: the more claims administered, the higher the premium. Workers' compensation insurance premiums have a baseline that is based on industry trends. For example, a service-oriented company that employs only office workers will have a lower ex mod than a mining company with confined-space workers.

▌ The higher the ex mod, the higher the premium.

Crisis Management Plans

Business travelers and expatriates have unique needs for an employer's health and safety programs. Employers have a global duty of care to keep international assignees safe. A crisis management plan takes into account factors such as language barriers, access to medical services, availability of emergency response, and infrastructure components that will drive the ability of an employer to respond to an international threat or industrial accident. International HR practitioners should know and communicate to assignees the proper agencies to contact, such as the Bureau of Consular Affairs of the U.S. Embassy, and who the employee should contact internally in the event of an emergency.

Kidnap and ransom insurance is another practical tool employers may use to assure international assignees that the employer takes the risk of hazardous assignments seriously. Brokers who provide this type of policy are available to help organizations create a crisis management plan, and partner with resources abroad to provide communication, negotiation, medical, and emergency travel service when needed.

Kidnap and Ransom Insurance

Protection for employees in high-risk areas

Policies that reimburse employees' losses due to kidnapping or extortion in high-risk areas of the world

---

Return to Work Programs

A return to work (RTW) program is the effort by the employer to help injured or ill employees get back to work in a transitional capacity until they are able to return to full-duty work. RTW is not only for those with a work-related injury. These programs can be built to respond to the many types of disabilities that may keep some people from getting back to work at all.

RTW programs benefit both the employer and the employee. For example:

Employer Wage replacement is often paid for through the company's workers' compensation insurance carrier. This adds to the overall cost of the injury, and thus affects the employer's experience modifier on which annual premiums are calculated. An RTW program finds tasks, duties, and responsibilities that accommodate an employee's limitations, and the employee is thus paid through regular payroll rather than collecting an insurance payment while on lost time. For non-work-related injuries, bringing people back to work in a restricted capacity has been shown to lower the overall lost time, keeping work flow, customer, and morale disruptions to a minimum.

Employee For the employee, workers' compensation and disability insurance law has built in maximum payment amounts. In New York, for example, the maximum amount injured workers may earn while off work is two-thirds of their average weekly wage. This may cause financial hardship for the employee. In an RTW situation, an employer may choose to pay the employee's full wage to incentivize the employee to come back to work so the employer gains the benefit of a reduced total claim amount. In some cases, however, the employer may be able to lower the injured worker's wages to account for the lighter duty. This is a strategic consideration for discussion when planning an RTW procedure.

An important member of a return to work program is the licensed physician. The doctor diagnosing and treating the injured worker must have access to an objective summary of the employee's regular tasks, duties, and responsibilities on the job in order to accurately determine restrictions. This allows the physician to provide clear instructions to both the employer and the employee on what work may be done in a modified capacity, or not at all. For this reason, HR should be prepared to send over a current, accurate job description describing the essential functions, physical requirements, and mental abilities that are part of regular job duties.

In some cases, there is a discrepancy between what employees think they are able to do and what the doctor says they are able to do. In these cases, an independent medical exam (IME) may be necessary. Performed by a neutral third-party physician, the IME is used to provide an objective view of the employee's condition.

Reasonable accommodation is the process of the employer working within the restrictions conveyed by the doctor. It has legal implications under the Americans with Disabilities Act, in which employers are obligated to engage in an interactive dialogue to determine if the employee is qualified to work.

A Focus on Prevention

Despite all the different ways employees can be injured at work, employers can take very effective steps to reduce exposures. These steps begin with planning. The most valuable output from the planning process is not always the written plan. The process of assessing risk, talking with employees, and reaching out to the experts serves to create depth in organizational behaviors for managing risk. For this reason, HR should not be locked in the back office filling in the blanks on a template in response to a consultant's urging. HR must advocate for thoughtful, engaged action to produce effective programs that have management and employee support. Detailed plans, policies, and procedures allow employers to demonstrate compliance with various labor laws, communicate expected standards of behavior to employees, and develop prevention and intervention procedures where appropriate.

Disaster Preparation and Continuity Planning

Natural and man-made disasters occur in all parts of the world, and present very real threats to employee well-being and business survival. Acts of terrorism, acts of workplace violence, and natural disasters such as hurricanes have prompted companies to expand the role of human resources to prepare for disasters.

Ready.gov is a website developed by the Department of Homeland Security (DHS) that has several excellent examples of plans and actions employers may take to be ready in a crisis.

The threat assessment in this planning competency relates to identifying business impact. As described by the DHS, HR must consider and analyze the tangible and intangible impact of:

- Physical damage to a building or buildings
- Damage to or breakdown of machinery, systems, or equipment
- Restricted access to a site or building
- Interruption of the supply chain, including failure of a supplier or disruption of transportation of goods from the supplier
- Utility outage (e.g., electrical power outage)
- Damage to, loss of, or corruption of information technology, including voice and data communications, servers, computers, operating systems, applications, and data
- Absenteeism of essential employees

Figure 7.6 shows the four main steps described by the DHS to take to prepare a business continuity plan:

1. *Conduct a business impact analysis.* Every employer has unique conditions affecting the needs of continuity. Factors such as geographic location, availability of response resources, industry, and specialized needs of customers will all drive plan components.
2. *Create recovery strategies.* Working with internal and external experts, HR will drive the brainstorming sessions to identify strategies in response to the business impact measures identified in step 1.
3. *Develop the plan.* More than a written plan, this step involves the coordination of all resources and tools to use should a disaster event occur.
4. *Practice the plan.* This step involves training trainers and conducting drills to evaluate both what worked and what still needs to be perfected.

See Table 7.3 to review OSHA's requirements for emergency response and fire prevention plans.

The FBI describes some disaster events as "media-intense." For example, the highly visible post office shootings in the 1980s and 1990s prompted the pejorative phrase *going postal* to reference a disgruntled employee. The terrorist attack on September 11, 2001, was the largest incident of workplace disaster in American history. In the event of a disaster, a response plan should explore how any media inquiries will be addressed.

The post office and 9/11 references are both examples of disasters classified as workplace violence. These are covered next.

Business Continuity

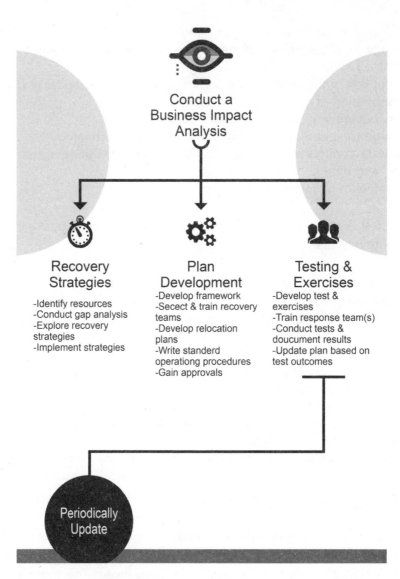

Figure 7.6   Business Continuity

Table 7.3 OSHA Response Plan Requirements

All of OSHA's safety standards have emergency action plan requirements. Following are examples from the General Industry Standards for emergency action plans and fire prevention plans:

Emergency Response Plan	Fire Prevention Plan

1910.38 (a) through (f)
Emergency action plans:

a. **Application.** An employer must have an emergency action plan whenever an OSHA standard in this part requires one. The requirements in this section apply to each such emergency action plan.

b. **Written and oral emergency action plans.** An emergency action plan must be in writing, kept in the workplace, and available to employees for review. However, an employer with 10 or fewer employees may communicate the plan orally to employees.

c. **Minimum elements of an emergency action plan.** An emergency action plan must include at a minimum:

1. Procedures for reporting a fire or other emergency;

2. Procedures for emergency evacuation, including type of evacuation and exit route assignments;

3. Procedures to be followed by employees who remain to operate critical plant operations before they evacuate;

4. Procedures to account for all employees after evacuation;

5. Procedures to be followed by employees performing rescue or medical duties; and

6. The name or job title of every employee who may be contacted by employees who need more information about the plan or an explanation of their duties under the plan.

a. **Application.** An employer must have a fire prevention plan when an OSHA standard in this part requires one. The requirements in this section apply to each such fire prevention plan.

b. **Written and oral fire prevention plans.** A fire prevention plan must be in writing, be kept in the workplace, and be made available to employees for review. However, an employer with 10 or fewer employees may communicate the plan orally to employees.

c. **Minimum elements of a fire prevention plan.** A fire prevention plan must include:

1. A list of all major fire hazards, proper handling and storage procedures for hazardous materials, potential ignition sources and their control, and the type of fire protection equipment necessary to control each major hazard;

2. Procedures to control accumulations of flammable and combustible waste materials;

3. Procedures for regular maintenance of safeguards installed on heat-producing equipment to prevent the accidental ignition of combustible materials;

4. The name or job title of employees responsible for maintaining equipment to prevent or control sources of ignition or fires; and

5. The name or job title of employees responsible for the control of fuel source hazards.

(continued)

Table 7.3   OSHA Response Plan Requirements (*continued*)

Emergency Response Plan	Fire Prevention Plan
d. **Employee alarm system.** An employer must have and maintain an employee alarm system. The employee alarm system must use a distinctive signal for each purpose and comply with the requirements in §1910.165. e. **Training.** An employer must designate and train employees to assist in a safe and orderly evacuation of other employees. f. **Review of emergency action plan.** An employer must review the emergency action plan with each employee covered by the plan: 1. When the plan is developed or the employee is assigned initially to a job; 2. When the employee's responsibilities under the plan change; and 3. When the plan is changed	d. **Employee information.** An employer must inform employees upon initial assignment to a job of the fire hazards to which they are exposed. An employer must also review with each employee those parts of the fire prevention plan necessary for self-protection.

Source: Occupational Safety and Health Administration (OSHA).

Workplace Violence

Workplace incivility can very quickly lead to harassing and bullying behaviors. Rude coworkers and lack of courtesy contribute to an overall environment of tension and strain. In a climate where incivility and disrespect are the norm, negative interactions and conflict can quickly escalate into hostile, bullying, or violent behaviors.

Workplace violence plans and programs should be primarily focused on taking proactive steps to minimize the likelihood of a violent incident on the job, and plan for a coordinated response should an event take place. The first step is to create and encourage a company culture where professionalism and courtesy rule all interactions, and managers are trained in conflict deescalation when necessary.

In order to be effective and taken seriously, top management must support prevention efforts. In some cases this means taking serious steps to drive culture changes in a toxic environment. A lack of trust within a company may also require top-level intervention to avoid workplace violence. Organizational cultural issues such as abusive managers will act as barriers to any practical efforts of HR to address and, most important, prevent workplace violence issues.

An example of the practical efforts of an HR professional to address workplace violence threats is to help select and develop a program. A threat assessment is one tool that may be used to accomplish this effort. In addition, working with local law enforcement agencies or professional threat assessors will educate HR on the needs of the organization. These professional resources are able to offer advice on how best to deal with escalated events characterized by weapons, hostage situations, or terrorist threats. Gathering legal advice and concerns regarding potential loss and liability will also be an important step in developing the company prevention and response plans. Legal resources that will be charged with defending any policy or program should also be part of the planning or review process.

Preventive steps include written policies, employee training, and response planning to minimize the effect of an incident.

A written policy should be in place that defines the behavioral expectations for all employees. This includes a list of prohibited conduct, such as:

- Threatening physical or aggressive contact
- Threatening an individual or his or her family and friends
- Harassing verbal or written communications
- Stalking
- Veiled threats or intimidation

Domestic Violence

Domestic violence is another area that should be addressed in a policy. The Centers for Disease Control (CDC) refers to intimate partner violence (IPV) as physical, sexual, or psychological harm by a current or former partner or spouse. The CDC estimates that victims of severe IPV lose thousands of days of paid work each year as the result of violent episodes.

An employer may choose to address the threat of workplace violence through a statement of zero tolerance in its handbook. The policy may establish how the employer will respond if an employee is convicted of a crime of violence, reserving the right to discipline/discharge workers under certain conditions. An effective policy will define the reporting procedure for employees who believe they have been victims of workplace violence, the investigation procedure, the rights and responsibilities of affected employees, and a description of how the employer will deal with issues of confidentiality and privacy.

Employee Training

Training offers many opportunities to employers who wish to have a comprehensive workplace antiviolence program. Training teaches employees about acceptable and unacceptable workplace behaviors. A training session should review warning signals that often precede violence, and teach the employees how to report their concerns.

Supervisor training is an important component of an employer's violence prevention efforts. Teaching supervisors how to manage and deescalate conflict may reduce the likelihood of a situation getting out of control. Educating supervisors on the legal liability issues associated with workplace violence—including personal liability should they become a harasser—can help communicate why they are critical to an organization's prevention efforts. Helping supervisors recognize warning signs of violence gives them the ability to intervene early, while giving them a clear, supportive procedure to guide their efforts.

All training should encourage employees to report suspicious behavior, or behavior of their coworkers that seems out of character or escalating in frequency or force. The employees need to know when to report and what to report, and be assured that the company takes their concerns seriously. Finally, employee training should make clear that employees who report concerns will not be retaliated against. Often, a combination of the employer's own policy and code of safe practices along with an external resource such as a professional training program is effective for communicating the workplace antiviolence program elements.

Signs of Violence

Despite an organization's best attempts, workplace violence incidents unfortunately still occur. An employer must be prepared to respond to a crisis, whether it is related to domestic issues, an escalated workplace conflict, disgruntled former employees, or terrorism. For this reason, taking the lead in response planning is a critical function of human resources.

In 2015, an active shooter/attempted bombing situation took place in San Bernardino, California. The shooter was an employee who targeted his coworkers at an office holiday party, killing 14 and seriously injuring another 22. This and other tragedies leave many wondering whether these situations can be predicted. The surprising answer is that sometimes they can indeed be foreseen. There are consistent behavioral signals that may indicate a problem is escalating; OSHA notes that it is often more likely that a pattern or multiple indicators will be present. These may include:

Attendance problems Excessive sick leave, excessive tardiness, leaving work early, improbable excuses for absences

Adverse impact on supervisor's time Supervisor having to spend an inordinate amount of time coaching and/or counseling employee about personal problems, redoing the employee's work, dealing with coworker concerns, and so on.

Decreased productivity Making excessive mistakes, poor judgment, missed deadlines, wasting work time and materials

Inconsistent work patterns Alternating periods of high and low productivity and quality of work, inappropriate reactions, overreaction to criticism, and mood swings

Concentration problems Easily distracted and often has trouble recalling instructions, project details, and deadline requirements

Safety issues More accident prone, disregard for personal safety as well as equipment and machinery safety, needless risks

Poor health and hygiene Marked changes in personal grooming habits

Unusual/changed behavior

- Inappropriate comments, threats, throwing objects
- Evidence of possible drug or alcohol use/abuse
- Evidence of serious stress in the employee's personal life
- Crying, excessive phone calls, recent separation
- Continual excuses/blame
- Inability to accept responsibility for even the most inconsequential errors
- Unshakable depression
- Low energy, little enthusiasm, despair

The presence of one or more of the indicators does not necessarily mean a violent act will occur. An employee may be suffering from a physical or mental illness or other personal problems. However, knowing the signs allows human resources to design intervention services. Examples include employee assistance programs, staff nurses trained as mental health advisers, a referral agency, or even just the ear of a sympathetic supervisor—these may all serve to defuse an act before it occurs, and offer the employee help at a time when it is clearly needed.

Some of the more notable acts of workplace violence seem to be around workplace homicide. But a far greater percentage of violent incidents take the form of damage to company property, verbal abuse or aggression, and concealing or brandishing a weapon.

Again, these examples are a matter of degree, and should be framed in the context of other behaviors. However, direct threats should always be taken seriously.

Other Preventive Efforts

Taking preventive steps within the scope of other functional areas may also serve HR's priority on prevention. Consider background checks to screen out any potentially violent new hires, a function of Workforce Planning and Employment. Or conduct employee surveys as part of an employee labor relations strategy to identify any unknown threats. Management coaching using techniques defined in the Human Resource Development chapter may be appropriate. And finally, workplace violence incidents are more likely to be caused by workers under the influence of drugs or alcohol. This means that an employer's protective efforts must include a substance abuse program.

Substance Abuse

Another plan HR must prepare is a *substance abuse* plan. There are many reasons why an employer should have plans and policies in place to address substance abuse in the workplace. The U.S. government has found that more than 70 percent of substance abusers have jobs, making this relevant across industries and states. Substance abusers tend to have lower productivity, increased absenteeism, more accidents, and higher health care costs.

Many employers start with a policy that addresses the use of both legal and illegal substances that affect work performance. Considerations include notifying the employee that the employer reserves the right to search employee belongings if an employee is suspected of possessing alcohol, controlled substances, or illegal drugs. It is also necessary to address the accommodation of an employee who is seeking treatment or rehabilitation for an addiction. A plan may define what steps an organization will take, including discipline expectations, referral to an employee assistance program, or time off from work to seek treatment.

Supervisors and managers should be trained to identify the signs of an employee who may be under the influence. In some cases training is required, such as the reasonable suspicion training under the Department of Transportation rules governing commercial drivers. Specifically, the Federal Motor Carrier Safety Administration requires:

> . . . supervisors of commercial motor vehicle drivers who operate vehicles that require a commercial driver license to take 60 minutes of training on the symptoms

of alcohol abuse and another 60 minutes of training on the symptoms of controlled substances use (120 minutes in total). The purpose of this training is to teach supervisors to identify circumstances and indicators that may create reasonable suspicion that a driver is using or under the influence of alcohol or drugs, supporting referral of an employee for testing.

—49 CFR 382.603

Signs and symptoms covered in training include:

Physical symptoms Slurred speech, flushed face, staggering, fatigue, rolling or red eyes

Behavioral symptoms Poor job performance, irritability, aggressiveness, missed work or tardiness

Psychological symptoms Depression, emotional instability, anxiety

Employer drug and alcohol testing policies include language related to post-offer, postinjury, and reasonable suspicion, sometimes called fit-for-duty testing.

Substance Abuse

Excessive use of drugs, alcohol, or other addictions

Use of habit-forming drugs or substances that impair behavior

---

Physical Asset Protection

Security audits will identify the types of physical hazards present at a place of work. Calling upon the expertise of facilities managers and HR, along with third-party experts looking for vulnerabilities, will produce a to-do list of meaningful tasks. Factors such as access, lighting, and traffic patterns are evaluated and assessed against potential risk.

Taking this step is important not only for employee protection, but also for company image. Wal-Mart has taken a beating in the media for having multiple layers of security against store theft, but paying lackluster attention to securing the stores' acres of parking lots. Several attacks on customers have been featured on the news, forcing Wal-Mart to defend its security priorities. HR is usually responsible for collecting requests for proposals (RFPs) for security services to help guard facilities if necessary.

Risk to a company's cash flow can be controlled specifically through its inventory levels. For example, $100,000 worth of cooling unit compressors lining the warehouse racks represents $100,000 of a noncash asset. For this reason, steps should be taken to help control the variability of purchasing and to moderate cash flow. While not an HR task per se, it may be necessary for HR to work with employees to develop plans and procedures to regulate the process.

Cyber Vulnerability and Liability

"Password1." Look familiar? It might, because a 2015 Trustwave Global Security report identified it as still the most common password in use today. This and other findings are troubling in the context of data security.

Industries such as retail and fast food remain high on the list of targets; specifically, criminals attempt to gain access to the information stored on the magnetic strip of a credit or debit card used for customer purchases. The Trustwave report found that 50 percent of the victims targeted were in the United States, followed by 24 percent in Australia and 14 percent in the United Kingdom. It's obvious that in a world of business being conducted more frequently online, employers have to pay attention to cyber liabilities.

The first step to reducing liability is to have a written policy clearly outlining the terms of acceptable use of all sensitive information. Data classification policies direct employees on what information is most sensitive, and allows them to follow proper procedures to protect it. Asking employees to sign confidentiality agreements is a paper defense against stolen trade secrets and other proprietary information. Technical solutions such as tiers of access can be a simple, effective way to reduce the risk of data theft. Educating employees on the importance of password protection can help as well. The Trustwave report shared that it takes one day to break an eight-character password compared to 591 days it takes to crack a 10-digit code. More complex firewalls must be investigated and adopted as recommended by experts, driven by the nature of work that HR is called upon to guard.

HR may also research and form a business case to management to purchase cyber liability insurance, which covers employee and customer information should theft occur.

Taking action when a breach is discovered is an urgent task for HR. Practices begin by notifying those who may have been affected by the breach. Some employers take the additional precaution of offering credit monitoring protection for 12 to 24 months to help protect victims of data theft from experiencing a tangible loss.

Additionally, most employers have a very low tolerance for system emergencies. Reliance on computers, voice over Internet Protocol (VOIP) lines, and network connectivity disruptions can shut down operations for any length of time. HR may participate in the effort to develop software, hardware, and behavioral strategies for data maintenance and recovery in the event of an emergency.

Employee Communication and Safety Training

In the absence of employee compliance behaviors, a company's plans, procedures, and programs are mere paper tigers. Employees must know what is expected of them, and HR must take steps to test, audit, and measure the efficacy of the programs. In general, human resources should conduct:

- *New hire on-boarding and orientation presentations.* Too often new hires are handed the handbook and asked to sign an acknowledgment form without any interpretation and support. This is not an effective way to communicate safety plans and procedures.
- *Formal training sessions when a plan is changed* or to remind workers of the expectations. These sessions don't have to be classroom based. Asking employees to conduct safety walks with you while you point out what you are looking for trains them to be on the lookout for the same or similar issues. Training techniques is discussed more in the Human Resource Development chapter.
- *Compliance training as required by law.* Communication and training are so important that many safety standards have built these activities into employer efforts to comply with the law. HR must know what these requirements are and take steps to complete them.

Risk Management Techniques

There are four techniques an employer may use to manage the risks to the company.

1. **Abate/eliminate the risk.** Changing a work process to be safer is the ideal response to an identified hazard. Repositioning a computer server so the cords are shorter to eliminate a trip hazard is one example of hazard elimination. Another method is to substitute a less hazardous material or piece of equipment. For example, employers may switch to a water-based paint rather than a solvent-based paint to reduce employee exposure to hazardous chemicals. Physical changes are the most effective way to reduce injuries, particularly when you eliminate the choice. An employee who has access to company bank passwords must be relied upon to choose not to use them for nefarious purposes. Simply limiting who has access to this information reduces the risk of a financial loss.

2. **Mitigate/reduce the exposure.** Adding safety equipment such as machine guards, lockout/tag-out tools, or personal protective equipment is another way to respond to an identified hazard. So also is conducting employee training on proper use of equipment or tools. Checking for travel warnings prior to international business trips can also help employers make decisions that reduce or eliminate exposure.

3. **Transfer the risk.** Transferring risk may include outsourcing the work to a subcontractor or vendor. Some employers opt to purchase insurance so that if an incident occurs, they have some protection from liability. Not all risk can be transferred, but it is one technique that can be effective in shrinking the target. Examples include corporate governance insurance, professional liability insurance, and directors and officers liability insurance.

4. **Accept the risk.** The final risk management technique is for employers to accept a risk as a cost of doing business, and not engage in effort above and beyond normal business practices. For example, business bad debt seems to be unavoidable for many companies. Rather than employing a full-time collections agent or pursuing debtors through costly legal proceedings, an employer may identify a percentage of loss that is acceptable. The employer may then use the total as a tax write-off at the end of the year.

Metrics

Just as with any other HR function, employers must take steps to measure the success or failure of their workplace safety efforts. Conducting trend analysis using injury data from the past is one way to predict future hazards and identify whether current controls are effective. Workers' compensation costs are a tangible cash asset that can be controlled through careful monitoring and intervention. Department incident data can point HR to areas of threat, targeting resources to minimize exposure. By emphasizing and measuring the efforts of safety and health programs, employers and employees will be better off. Positive outcomes include safer workplaces, lower insurance costs, and increased productivity.

Suggested Study or Organizational Audit Activities

- Conduct an audit of your company's injury and illness prevention plan. Use the resources available at www.osha.gov by searching for the term "injury and illness prevention programs." Read through the various white papers, highlighting critical information, particularly those that are part of an overall compliance effort. In what areas does your employer's plan exceed the federal recommendations? How can your plan be improved?
- Call your workers' compensation provider and see if it offers any classes. If not, prepare interview questions ahead of time related to the administration of workers' compensation insurance. Ask questions related to nondiscriminatory treatment, the criteria for delaying or denying claims, the incidents of fraud, and the areas where it most often occurs.

- Conduct a risk assessment to identify the potential *financial* risks to your employer. Discuss/discover the executive strategy for dealing with these known risks. Does the C-suite prefer to eliminate, mitigate, transfer, or accept these risks? What internal financial controls have been established to reduce loss?
- Find your employer's OSHA Form 300 log for the past five years, and calculate the organization's incidence rate. Now calculate the incident rate for each department. Are there any action steps you can take based on the findings of this information?
- Complete a job hazard analysis for the three jobs within your organization that have the highest incidents of injury. Work with supervisors to identify and review them, and take note of their concerns and challenges in incorporating hazard elimination strategies. Are they most concerned with the time required to implement strategies? The cost? The employee buy-in and ownership? Resolve to work with management to find ways to reduce hazards to your workers.
- Log on to WorkersCompensation.com, and find its list of "Best Blogs." Research the links and discover information related to the risk management objectives found in this chapter. Search the blogs for related terms, such as "injury and illness prevention programs," "return to work programs," or types of "security risk assessments." Make note of questions or thoughts; create mind maps to show relationships.

Appendix A

Alphabetical Listing of Legal Issues

Affirmative Action Plans (AAPs)

All federal contractors and subcontractors who have at least 50 employees and designated monetary levels of government contracts or subcontracts must prepare and update annually two or three affirmative action plans (AAPs). Each AAP has specific requirements dictated by regulations. The three potential AAPs are:

Executive Order 11246 AAP Covers women and minorities and is required for each establishment, if a supply or services contractor (or subcontractor) has 50 or more employees and a government contract (or subcontract) of at least $50,000. Federally assisted construction contractors, however, do not prepare traditional EO 11246, but have 16 equal employment opportunity (EEO) and *affirmative action (AA)* specifications that they must meet and document.

Vietnam Era Veterans' Readjustment Assistance Action (VEVRAA) of 1974, as amended, 38 U.S.C. 4212 AAP Covers protected veterans and is required for each establishment, if a government contractor (or subcontractor) has 50 or more employees and has a government contract (or subcontract) of at least $150,000. Federally assisted construction contractors must also prepare the same type of AAP. The categories of protected veterans are: disabled veteran, recently separated veteran (three-year period), active duty wartime or campaign badge veteran, or an armed forces service medal veteran.

Section 503 of the Rehabilitation Act of 1973, as amended, 29 U.S.C. 793 AAP
Covers individuals with disabilities and is required for each establishment, if a government contractor (or subcontractor) has 50 or more employees and a government contract (or subcontract) of at least $50,000. Federally assisted construction contractors must also prepare the same type of AAP. The government allows the VEVRAA AAP and the Section 503 AAP to be combined into one if both are required.

> Even if an organization does not need to prepare written AAPs, there still are federal affirmative action requirements for government contracts or subcontracts that are greater than $10,000, if aggregated or for a contract or subcontract greater than $15,000.

The Office of Federal Contract Compliance Programs (OFCCP) in the U.S. Department of Labor constructs and enforces the affirmative action regulations. The OFCCP periodically will audit federal contractors and subcontractors on the contents of their AAPs and other regulatory requirements. The OFCCP's mission statement is:

Mission Statement
At the Office of Federal Contract Compliance Programs (OFCCP), we protect workers, promote diversity and enforce the law. OFCCP holds those who do business with the federal government—contractors and subcontractors—responsible for complying with the legal requirement to take affirmative action and not discriminate on the basis of race, color, sex, sexual orientation, gender identity, religion, national origin, disability, or status as a protected veteran. In addition, contractors and subcontractors are prohibited from discharging or otherwise discriminating against applicants or employees who inquire about, discuss or disclose their compensation or that of others, subject to certain limitations.

The required components of an Executive Order 11246 AAP appear in Table A.1.

VEVRAA AAP

The required components of the VEVRAA AAP include:

Policy statement The contractor's (note: when the term *contractor* is used, it also applies to subcontractors) equal opportunity policy statement should be included in the AAP, and be posted on the organization's bulletin board.

Table A.1   Required Components of Executive Order 11246 AAP

AAP Component	Description
Organizational profile	Employers choose the format that works best: organizational display (traditional organization chart) or workforce analysis (listing of job titles from lowest to highest paid).
Job group analysis	Places job titles with similar content, wages, and opportunities into job groups for analysis.
Placement of incumbents in job groups	Lists percentages of minorities and women employed in each job group.
Determining availability	Estimates the number of qualified minorities or women available for employment in a given job group, often within a specific geographic area.
Comparison of incumbency to availability	Compares the percentage of minorities and women in each job group with the availability for those job groups within a specific geographic area.
Placement goals	When the percentage of minorities or women employed in a particular job group is less than would reasonably be expected given their availability percentage in that particular job group, the contractor must establish a placement goal. Placement goals serve as objectives or targets reasonably attainable by means of applying every good-faith effort. Placement goals are not quotas or preferences.
Designation of responsibility	Assigns responsibility and accountability for the implementation of EEO and the affirmative action program to an official of the organization.
Identification of problem areas	Requires analysis of the total employment processes to determine whether and where impediments to equal opportunity exist.
Action-oriented programs	The contractor must develop and execute action-oriented programs designed to correct any problems identified and to attain established goals and objectives.
Internal audit and reporting system	The contractor must develop and implement an auditing system that periodically measures the effectiveness of its total affirmative action program.

Review of personnel processes The contractor shall periodically review such processes and make any necessary modifications to ensure that its obligations are carried out. A description of the review and any modifications should be documented.

Physical and mental qualifications Provides for a schedule for the periodic review of all physical and mental job qualification standards to ensure that to the extent that qualification standards tend to screen out qualified disabled veterans, they are job-related for the position in question and are consistent with business necessity.

Reasonable accommodation to physical and mental limitations Includes a statement that the contractor will make reasonable accommodation to the known physical or mental limitations of an otherwise qualified disabled veteran unless it can demonstrate that the accommodation would impose an undue hardship on the operation of the business.

Harassment Include a statement about what the contractor has done to develop and implement procedures to ensure that its employees are not harassed because of their status as protected veterans.

External dissemination of policy, outreach, and positive recruitment Includes listing the organization's outreach efforts, including sending written notification of the organization's EEO/AA policy to all subcontractors, vendors, and suppliers. Also requires the contractor to review, on an annual basis, the outreach and recruitment efforts it has taken over the previous 12 months to evaluate their effectiveness in identifying and recruiting qualified protected veterans. If not effective, the contractor shall identify and implement alternative efforts. These assessments are to be retained for a three-year period.

Internal dissemination of policy The contractor outlines its efforts to implement and disseminate its EEO/AA policy internally.

Audit and reporting system The contractor describes and documents the audit and reporting system that it designed and implemented to measure the effectiveness of its affirmative action program, among other things.

Responsibility for implementation The contractor documents which official of the organization has been assigned responsibility for implementation of the contractor's affirmative action program. His or her identity should appear on all internal and external communications regarding the contractor's affirmative action program.

Training Describe the efforts made to train all personnel involved in the recruitment, screening, selection, promotion, disciplinary actions, and related processes on the contractor's commitments in the affirmative action program.

Other VEVRAA requirements not included in the AAP, but required by the regulations, include:

Data collection analysis Annual documentation, maintained for a three-year period, of the number of applicants who self-identified as protected veterans, the total number of job openings and the total number of jobs filled, the total number of applicants for all jobs, the number of applicants hired, and the number of protected veterans hired.

Hiring benchmark The contractor shall either establish and document a hiring benchmark for protected veterans, based on specific criteria, or use the OFCCP-dictated hiring benchmark, which is 6.9 percent as of the time of publication. These records shall be retained for a period of three years.

- Contractors must now invite protected veterans to self-identify as such at both the pre- and postoffer stages. However, the protected veteran is not *required* to self-identify at any stage.
- Inclusion of the Equal Opportunity Clause in covered purchase orders and subcontracts.
- Annual notice to the State Employment Service Delivery System where the organization's jobs are located.
- Listing all external job openings with the State Employment Service Delivery System, except for temporary positions (for three days or less) or executive positions.

VEVRAA and Other Posters
- Allowing access to the protected veterans AAP for both applicants and employees.
- Annual union notification letter/e-mail.
- Annual filing of protected veterans VETS-4212 report (used to be VETS-100A).
- Required job listing, posting, or ad tagline.

Section 503, Individuals with Disabilities AAP

The required components of Section 503, Individuals with Disabilities AAP, include:

Policy statement The contractor's (always includes subcontractors) equal opportunity policy statement should be included in the AAP, and be posted on the organization's bulletin board.

Review of personnel processes The contractor shall periodically review such processes and make any necessary modifications to ensure its obligations are carried out. A description of the review and any modifications should be documented.

Physical and mental qualifications Provides for a schedule for the periodic review of all physical and mental job qualification standards to ensure that to the extent that qualification standards tend to screen out qualified individuals with disabilities, they are job-related for the position in question and are consistent with business necessity.

Reasonable accommodation to physical and mental limitations Includes a statement that the contractor will make reasonable accommodation to the known physical or mental limitations of an otherwise qualified individual with a disability unless it can demonstrate that the accommodation would impose an undue hardship on the operation of the business.

Harassment Includes a statement about what the contractor has done to develop and implement procedures to ensure that its employees are not harassed on the basis of disability.

External dissemination of policy, outreach, and positive recruitment Includes listing the organization's outreach efforts, including sending written notification of the organization's EEO/AA policy to all subcontractors, vendors, and suppliers. Also requires the contractor to review, on an annual basis, the outreach and recruitment efforts it has taken over the previous 12 months to evaluate their effectiveness in identifying and recruiting qualified protected veterans. If not effective, the contractor shall identify and implement alternative efforts. These assessments are to be retained for a three-year period.

Internal dissemination of policy The contractor outlines its efforts to implement and disseminate its EEO/AA policy internally.

Audit and reporting system The contractor describes and documents the audit and reporting system that it designed and implemented to measure the effectiveness of its affirmative action program, among other things.

Responsibility for implementation The contractor documents which official of the organization has been assigned responsibility for implementation of the contractor's affirmative action program. His or her identity should appear on all internal and external communications regarding the contractor's affirmative action program.

Training Describes the efforts made to train all personnel involved in the recruitment, screening, selection, promotion, disciplinary actions, and related processes on the contractor's commitments in the affirmative action program.

Other Section 503, Individuals with Disabilities, requirements not included in the AAP, but required by the regulations, include:

Data collection analysis Annual documentation, maintained for a three-year period, of the number of applicants who self-identified as individuals with disabilities, the total number of job openings and the total number of jobs filled, the total number of applicants for all jobs, the number of applicants hired, and the number of individuals with disabilities hired.

- Contractors must now invite individuals with disabilities to self-identify as such, at both the pre- and postoffer stages, using the OFCCP's designed form. However, the individual with disability is not *required* to self-identify at any stage.
- Inclusion of the Equal Opportunity Clause in covered purchase orders and subcontracts.
- Website accessibility language.
- Section 503 and Other Posters allowing access to the individuals with disabilities AAP for both applicants and employees.
- Annual union notification letter/e-mail.

- Annual utilization analysis with an OFCCP-determined goal of 7 percent individuals with disabilities per job group.
- Required job listing, posting, or ad tagline.
- Requirement to track any reasonable accommodation requests by applicants and employees and any resulting action taken.
- The contractor shall invite each of its employees to voluntarily inform the contractor whether the employee believes that he or she is an individual with a disability. This invitation shall be extended to employees the first year the contractor becomes subject to these regulations and at five-year intervals thereafter. At least once during the intervening years between these invitations, the contractor must remind its employees that they may voluntarily update their disability status at any time.

Affirmative Action (AA)

A process designed to treat all applicants and employees equally

An activity designed to correct previous inequality that may have existed for certain groups or classes of people

Age Discrimination in Employment Act of 1967 (ADEA)

The purpose of the Age Discrimination in Employment Act (ADEA) is to "promote employment of older persons based on their ability rather than age; to prohibit arbitrary age discrimination in employment; to help employers and workers find ways of meeting problems arising from the impact of age on employment."

The ADEA prohibits discrimination against persons 40 years of age or older in employment activities, including hiring, job assignments, training, promotion, compensation, benefits, terminating, or any other privileges, terms, or conditions of employment. The ADEA applies to private businesses, unions, employment agencies, and state and local governments with more than 20 employees. As with Title VII, the ADEA provides for the following exceptions:

- Bona fide occupational qualifications (BFOQs) that are reasonably necessary to business operations
- The hiring of firefighters or police officers by state or local governments
- Retirement of employees age 65 or older who have been in executive positions for at least two years and are eligible for retirement benefits of at least $44,000 per year
- Retirement of tenured employees of institutions of higher education at age 70
- Discharge or discipline for just cause

Individuals who think they have been subjected to an unlawful employment practice must file charges with the Equal Employment Opportunity Commission (EEOC), which has federal enforcement responsibility for the ADEA, or with the state equal employment agency (if one exists for the location in which the incident occurred). Timely filing of charges is essential for complainants, since the EEOC will not investigate charges that are not made according to the guidelines.

Amendment to the ADEA

Older Worker Benefit Protection Act

The Older Worker Benefit Protection Act (OWBPA) amended the ADEA in 1990 to include a prohibition on discrimination against older workers in all employee benefit plans unless any age-based reductions are justified by significant cost considerations. This amendment allows seniority systems as long as they do not require involuntary terminations of employees based on their age and extends ADEA protections to all employee benefits, as well as guidelines for legal severance agreements.

The OWBPA defines the conditions under which employees may waive their rights to make claims under the act. To be acceptable, waivers must include the following components:

- Waiver agreements must be written in a way that can be understood by the average employee.
- Waivers must refer specifically to the rights or claims available under the ADEA.
- Employees may not waive rights or claims for actions that occur subsequent to signing the waiver.
- Employees must receive consideration in exchange for the waiver in addition to anything to which they are already entitled.
- The waiver must advise employees of their right to consult an attorney prior to signing the document.
- In individual cases, employees must be given 21 days to consider the agreement before they are required to sign; when a group of employees is involved, employees age 40 and older must be given 45 days to consider their decision.
- Once the waiver is signed, employees may revoke the agreement within seven days.
- In cases of group terminations (such as a reduction in force or early retirement program), employees must be advised of the eligibility requirements for any exit incentive programs, any time limits for the programs, and a list of the job titles and ages of employees who have been selected or who are eligible for the program.

The federal agency responsible for enforcement of the OWBPA is the EEOC.

Americans with Disabilities Act of 1990 (ADA)

The *Americans with Disabilities Act (ADA)* of 1990 was based in large part on the Rehabilitation Act of 1973 (discussed later in this appendix), and it extended protected class status to qualified persons with disabilities. Employment discrimination is covered by Title I of the Act and identifies covered entities as employment agencies, labor unions, joint labor-management committees, and employers with 15 or more employees (including those who work on a part-time or temporary basis) for each working day in each of 20 weeks in the current or previous calendar year. Excluded from coverage are the federal government and 501(c) private membership clubs. The ADA prohibits discrimination in job application procedures; the hiring, advancement, or discharge of employees; employee compensation; job training; and other terms, conditions, and privileges of employment.

The ADA requires covered entities to make *reasonable accommodation* to develop employment opportunities for qualified persons with disabilities in two areas:

1. Facilities should be accessible to persons with disabilities.
2. Position requirements may be adjusted to accommodate qualified persons with disabilities.

The ADA allows that accommodations constituting an undue hardship to the business are not required and defines undue hardship as an accommodation that places an excessive burden on the employer. The Act identifies the factors to be considered in determining whether an accommodation is an undue hardship by looking at the cost, the financial resources of the organization, the size of the organization, and other similar factors.

In 2008, Congress enacted the ADA Amendments Act of 2008, which took effect on January 1, 2009. According to language in the amendment, Congress took the action to clarify the intention of the original legislation, which was to make the definition of "disability" consistent with the way the courts had defined the term under the Rehabilitation Act of 1973. In fact, court interpretations under the ADA had "narrowed the broad scope of protection" originally intended. The amendment more clearly describes the intent of Congress in the following areas:

Broadly defines "disability" A disability is a physical or mental impairment that causes substantial limitation to one or more major life activities for an individual, a record of impairment for an individual, or an individual who is regarded as being impaired.

Defines "major life activity" The amendment defines major life activities in two areas: general activities and major bodily functions. Table A.2 lists activities Congress cites in the law as examples but is not meant to be a complete list.

Table A.2   Major Life Activities

General Activities	Major Bodily Functions
Caring for oneself, performing manual tasks, seeing, hearing, eating, sleeping, breathing, learning, reading, concentrating, thinking, communicating, working	Functions of the immune system, normal cell growth, and functions of the digestive, bowel, bladder, neurological, brain, respiratory, circulatory, endocrine, and reproductive systems

Ignores mitigating measures Congress directs that, except for "ordinary glasses or contact lenses," mitigating measures such as medication, prosthetics, hearing aids, mobility devices, and others may not be used to limit the definition of disability for an individual.

Clarifies the definition of "regarded as" This amendment requires that individuals who are able to demonstrate that they have been the subject of prohibited activities under the ADA, whether or not they actually have some type of impairment, are protected by its requirements.

Explicitly authorizes the EEOC to regulate compliance The amendment mandates the EEOC to develop and implement regulations and guidance for employers to follow, specifying the inclusion of a definition for "substantially limits" that is consistent with the intent of Congress in the legislation.

Prohibits "reverse discrimination" claims The amendment clearly states that individuals without disability may not use the ADA to file claims of discrimination when disabled individuals receive favorable employment actions.

A key element of ADA compliance is the requirement to engage in an interactive process with disabled individuals requesting a reasonable accommodation that will enable them to perform essential job functions.

ADA

Americans with Disabilities Act

A U.S. law that prevents an organization or person from discriminating against an employee because of physical or mental disabilities

Reasonable Accommodation

Work adjustment for a disabled employee

Changing the process of applying for a job or the work environment for a qualified person with a disability

Australian Federal Privacy Act of 1988

The Australian Federal Privacy Act of 1988 regulates the use and storage of personably identifiable information such as an individual's name, signature, address, telephone number, date of birth, medical records, bank account details, and commentary or opinion about a person. It also regulates the privacy components of the credit reporting system, tax file numbers, and records related to health.

Schedule 1 of the Australian Privacy Principles (APP) includes:

- The open and transparent management of personal information, including having a privacy policy
- An individual having the option of transacting anonymously or using a pseudonym where practicable
- The collection of solicited personal information and receipt of unsolicited personal information, including giving notice about collection
- How personal information can be used and disclosed (including overseas)
- Maintaining the quality of personal information
- Keeping personal information secure
- The right of individuals to access and correct their personal information

The Act applies to most Australian and Norfolk Island government agencies, and all private-sector and nonprofit organizations with over $3 million in annual turnover, all health service providers, and some small businesses.

APP 8 outlines the steps entities must take when disclosing sensitive information across borders. These steps include ensuring that none of the privacy principles are violated and that the overseas receiver of personal information is capable of protecting the confidentiality of the data.

Civil Rights Act of 1964 (Title VII)

Title VII of the Civil Rights Act of 1964 introduced the concepts of protected classes and unlawful employment practices to American businesses. Unlawful employment practices are those that have an adverse impact on members of a protected class, which is a group of people who share common characteristics and are protected from discriminatory practices. Title VII established the basis for two types of unlawful practices: disparate treatment and disparate impact. Disparate treatment happens when employers treat some candidates or employees differently, such as requiring women to take a driving test when they apply for a job but not requiring men to take the test when they apply for the same job. Practices that have a disparate impact on members of protected classes seem fair on their face but result in adverse impact on members of protected classes, such as requiring all candidates for firefighter positions to be a certain height. Although the requirement applies to all candidates equally, some Asian and female candidates who might otherwise qualify for the position might be eliminated because they are generally shorter than male candidates of other races.

The Act identified five protected classes: race, color, religion, national origin, and sex. It also defined the following unlawful employment practices:

- Discriminatory recruiting, selection, or hiring actions
- Discriminatory compensation or benefit practices
- Discriminatory access to training or apprenticeship programs
- Discriminatory practices in any other terms or conditions of employment

Legitimate seniority, merit, and piece-rate payment systems are allowable under Title VII as long as they do not intentionally discriminate against protected classes.

Title VII allowed for limited exceptions to its requirements, some of which are listed here:

- Bona fide occupational qualifications (BFOQs) occur when religion, sex, or national origin is "reasonably necessary to the normal operation" of the business.
- Educational institutions were not originally subject to Title VII.
- Religious organizations may give preference to members of that religion.
- A potential employee who is unable to obtain, or loses, a national security clearance required for the position is not protected.
- Indian reservations may give preference to Indian applicants and employees living on or near the reservation.

Title VII created the Equal Employment Opportunity Commission (EEOC) with a mandate to promote equal employment opportunity, educate employers, provide technical assistance, and study and report on its activities to Congress and the American people. The EEOC is the enforcement agency for Title VII and other discrimination legislation.

Amendments to Title VII

Title VII was amended in 1972, 1978, and 1991 to clarify and expand its coverage.

Equal Employment Opportunity Act of 1972

Created in 1972, the Equal Employment Opportunity Act (EEOA) provides litigation authority to the EEOC in the event that an acceptable conciliation agreement cannot be reached. In those cases, the EEOC is empowered to sue non-governmental entities, including employers, unions, and employment agencies.

The EEOA extended coverage of Title VII to entities that had been excluded in 1964:

- Educational institutions
- State and local governments
- The federal government

In addition, the EEOA reduced the number of employees needed to subject an employer to coverage by Title VII from 25 to 15 and required employers to keep records of the discovery of any unlawful employment practices and provide those records to the EEOC upon request.

The EEOA also provided administrative guidance for the processing of complaints by providing that employers be notified within 10 days of receipt of a charge by the EEOC and that findings be issued within 120 days of the charge being filed. The EEOC was empowered to sue employers, unions, and employment agencies in the event that an acceptable conciliation agreement could not be reached within 30 days of notice to the employer. The EEOA also provided protection from retaliatory employment actions against whistle-blowers.

Pregnancy Discrimination Act of 1978

Congress amended Title VII with the Pregnancy Discrimination Act of 1978 to clarify that discrimination against women on the basis of pregnancy, childbirth, or any related medical condition is an unlawful employment practice. The Act specified that pregnant employees should receive the same treatment and benefits as employees with any other short-term disability.

Civil Rights Act of 1991

The Civil Rights Act (CRA) of 1991 contained amendments that affected Title VII, the Age Discrimination in Employment Act (ADEA), and the Americans with Disabilities Act (ADA) in response to issues raised by the courts in several cases that were brought by employees based on Title VII.

The purpose of the Civil Rights Act (CRA) of 1991, as described in the Act itself, is fourfold:

1. To provide appropriate remedies for intentional discrimination and unlawful harassment in the workplace

2. To codify the concepts of "business necessity" and "job relatedness" articulated by the Supreme Court in *Griggs v. Duke Power Co.* and in other Supreme Court decisions
3. To confirm statutory authority and provide statutory guidelines for the adjudication of disparate impact suits under Title VII of the Civil Rights Act of 1964
4. To respond to recent decisions of the Supreme Court by expanding the scope of relevant civil rights statutes in order to provide adequate protection to victims of discrimination

Amendments contained in the CRA affected Title VII, the ADEA, and the ADA. One of the issues addressed is that of disparate impact, first introduced by the *Griggs v. Duke Power Co.* case in 1971. Disparate impact occurs when an employment practice, which appears on its face to be fair, unintentionally discriminates against members of a protected class. The CRA places the burden of proof for discrimination complaints on the complainant when there is a job-related business necessity for employment actions. When an individual alleges multiple discriminatory acts, each practice in itself must be discriminatory unless the employer's decision-making process cannot be separated, in which case the individual may challenge the decision-making process itself. The CRA also provides additional relief for victims of intentional discrimination and harassment, codifies the concept of disparate impact, and addresses Supreme Court rulings over the previous few years that had weakened equal employment opportunity laws.

The CRA made the following changes to Title VII:

- Provided punitive damages when employers engage in discriminatory practices "with malice or with reckless indifference."
- Excluded back pay awards from compensatory damages.
- Established a sliding scale for compensatory and punitive damages based on company size.
- Provided that any party to a civil suit in which punitive or compensatory damages are sought may demand a jury trial.
- Expanded Title VII to include congressional employees and some senior political appointees.
- Required that the individual alleging that an unlawful employment practice is in use prove that it results in disparate impact to members of a protected class.
- Provided that job relatedness and reasonable business necessity are defenses to disparate impact and that if a business can show that the practice does not result in disparate impact, it need not show the practice to be a business necessity.
- Provided that business necessity is not a defense against an intentional discriminatory employment practice.
- Established that if discrimination was a motivating factor in an employment practice it was unlawful even if other factors contributed to the practice.

- Allowed that if the same employment decision would have been made whether or not an impermissible motivating factor was present, there would be no damages awarded.
- Expanded coverage to include foreign operations of American businesses unless compliance would constitute violation of the laws of the host country.

Common Law Doctrines

Common law doctrines are the result of legal decisions made by judges in cases adjudicated over a period of centuries. A number of doctrines have implications for employment relationships, the most common of which is the concept of *employment at will*. Other common law issues that affect employment relationships are respondeat superior, constructive discharge, and defamation.

Employment at Will

In *Payne v. The Western & Atlantic Railroad Company* in 1884, Justice Ingersoll of the Tennessee Supreme Court defined employment at will in this way: ". . . either party may terminate the service, for any cause, good or bad, or without cause, and the other cannot complain in law." This definition allowed employers to change employment conditions, whether it was to hire, transfer, promote, or terminate an employee, at their sole discretion. It also allowed employees to leave a job at any time, with or without notice. In the absence of a legally enforceable employment contract, this definition was unaltered for more than 70 years.

Although there have always been exceptions to at-will employment based on employment contracts, beginning in 1959 the doctrine began to be eroded by both court decisions and statutes. This erosion resulted in several exceptions to the at-will concept, including public policy exceptions, the application of the doctrine of good faith and fair dealing to employment relationships, and the concepts of promissory estoppel and fraudulent misrepresentation.

Contract Exceptions

Employment at will intentions may be abrogated by contracts, either express or implied. An express contract can be a verbal or written agreement in which the parties state exactly what they agree to do. Employers have been known to express their gratitude for a job well done with promises of continued employment, such as "Keep doing that kind of work and you have a job for life" or "You'll have a job as long as we're in business." Statements such as these can invalidate the at-will doctrine.

An implied contract can be created by an employer's conduct and need not be specifically stated. For example, an employer's consistent application of a progressive discipline policy can create an implied contract that an employee will not be terminated without first going through the steps set forth by the policy. A disclaimer can offset the effects of an implied contract; however, there is little agreement in the courts as to what and how the disclaimer must be presented in order to maintain at-will status.

Statutory Exceptions

The at-will doctrine has been further eroded by legislation. At-will employment may not be used as a pretext for terminating employees for discriminatory reasons as set forth in equal opportunity legislation or other legislation designed to protect employee rights.

Public Policy Exceptions

Erosion of the doctrine of at-will employment began in 1959 when the California Court of Appeals heard *Petermann v. International Brotherhood of Teamsters*, in which Mr. Petermann, a business agent for the union, alleged that he was terminated for refusing to commit perjury on behalf of the union at a legislative hearing. The court held that it is ". . . obnoxious to the interest of state and contrary to public policy and sound morality to allow an employer to discharge any employee, whether the employment be for a designated or unspecified duration, on the ground that the employee declined to commit perjury, an act specifically enjoined by statute."

The public policy exception to employment at will was initially applied conservatively by the courts, but over time, its application has been expanded. In general, the public policy exception has been applied in four areas. The first is exemplified by the *Petermann* case—an employee who refuses to break the law on behalf of the employer can claim a public policy exception. The second application covers employees who report illegal acts of their employers (whistle-blowers); the third covers employees who participate in activities supported by public policy, such as cooperating in a government investigation of wrongdoing by the employer. Finally, the public policy exception covers employees who are acting in accordance with legal statute, such as attending jury duty or filing a workers' compensation claim.

While the public policy exception to at-will employment originated in California, it has been adopted by many, although not all, states.

Employment at Will

A U.S. legal principle that defines a working relationship

An employment agreement in which an employee can quit, or can be fired, at any time and for any reason

---

Duty of Good Faith and Fair Dealing

This tenet of common law provides that parties to a contract have an obligation to act in a fair and honest manner with each other to ensure that benefits of the contract may be realized. The application of this doctrine to at-will employment issues varies widely from state to state. The Texas Supreme Court, for example, has determined that there is no duty for good faith and fair dealing in employment contracts. On the other hand, the Alaska Supreme Court has determined that the duty is implied in at-will employment situations.

Promissory Estoppel

Promissory estoppel occurs when an employer entices an employee (or prospective employee) to take an action by promising a reward. The employee takes the action, but the employer does not follow through on the reward. For example, an employer promises a job to a candidate who resigns another position to accept the new one and then finds the offered position has been withdrawn. If a promise is clear, specific, and reasonable, and an employee acts on the promise, the employer may be required to follow through on the promised reward or pay equivalent damages.

Fraudulent Misrepresentation

Similar to promissory estoppel, fraudulent misrepresentation relates to promises or claims made by employers to entice candidates to join the company. An example of this might be a company that decides to close one of its locations in six months but, in the meantime, needs to hire a general manager to run the operation. If, when asked about the future of the company during the recruiting process, the company tells candidates that the plant will be expanded in the future and withholds its intention to close the plant, the company would be fraudulently misrepresenting the facts about the position.

Respondeat Superior

The Latin meaning of *respondeat superior* is "let the master answer." What this means is that an employer can be held liable for actions of its employees that occur within the scope and course of assigned duties or responsibilities in the course of their employment, regardless of whether the act is negligent or reckless. This concept has implications for many employment situations; one is sexual harassment, which will be discussed later in this appendix. Another could be an auto accident where a third party is injured when an employee hits another vehicle while driving an employer's delivery truck. Respondeat superior could also come into play if a manager promised additional vacation time to a candidate and the candidate accepted the position based on the promise. Even if the promise was not in writing and was outside the employer's normal vacation policy, and the manager made the promise without prior approval, the employer could be required to provide the benefit based on this doctrine.

Constructive Discharge

Constructive discharge occurs when an employer makes the workplace so hostile and inhospitable that an employee resigns. In many states, this gives the employee a cause of action against the employer. The legal standard that must be met varies widely between the states, with some requiring the employee to show that the employer intended to force the resignation, and others requiring the employee to show only that the conditions were sufficiently intolerable that a reasonable person would feel compelled to resign.

Defamation

Accusations of defamation in employment relationships most often occur during or after termination. Defamation is a communication that damages an individual's reputation in the community, preventing the person from obtaining employment or other benefits. When an employer, out of spite or with a vengeful intent, sets out to deliberately damage a former employee, the result is malicious defamation.

Concerns about defamation have caused many employers to stop giving meaningful references for former employees, in many cases responding to reference requests only with dates of employment and the individual's last title. Employers are generally protected by the concept of "qualified privilege" if the information provided is job-related, truthful, clear, and unequivocal. Obtaining written authorization prior to providing references and limiting responses to the information being requested without volunteering additional information can reduce the risks of being accused of defamation.

Copyright Act of 1976

The use of musical, literary, and other original works without permission of the owner of the copyright is prohibited under most circumstances. The copyright owner is the author of the work with two exceptions. The first is that an employer who hires employees to create original works as part of their normal job duties is the owner of the copyright because the employer paid for the work to be done. The second exception is that the copyright for work created by a freelance author, artist, or musician who has been commissioned to create the work by someone else is owned by the person who commissioned the work. These exceptions are known as work-for-hire exceptions.

For trainers who want to use the work of others during training sessions, there are two circumstances that do not require permission. The first is related to works that are in the public domain. Copyrights protect original works for the life of the author plus 70 years; after that, the works may be used without permission. Works-for-hire are protected for the shorter of 95 years from the first year of publication or 120 years from the year of creation.

Other works in the public domain include those produced as part of the job duties of federal officials and those for which copyright protection has expired. Some works published without notice of copyright before January 1, 1978, or those published between then and March 1, 1989, are also considered to be in the public domain.

The second circumstance for use of published works without permission is known as the fair use doctrine. The Act specifies that use of a work for the purposes of criticism, commentary, news reporting, or teaching (including multiple copies for classroom use, scholarship, or research) is not an infringement, depending upon four factors:

1. *The purpose and character of the use.* Is it to be used for a profit or for a nonprofit educational purpose?
2. *The nature of the work itself.* Is it a work of fiction? Or is it based on facts? How much creativity did it require?
3. *The amount of work.* How much of the work (one copy or 50?) or what portion (a paragraph or an entire chapter?) will be used?
4. *The effect.* What effect will the use of the material have on the potential market value of the copyrighted work?

Permission for the use of copyright-protected material that is outside the fair use exceptions can generally be obtained by contacting the author or publisher of the work.

Davis-Bacon Act of 1931

The Davis-Bacon Act was the first federal legislation to regulate minimum wages. It requires that construction contractors and their subcontractors pay at least the prevailing wage for the local area in which they are operating if they receive federal funds. Employers with federal construction contracts of $2,000 or more must adhere to the Davis-Bacon Act.

Drug-Free Workplace Act of 1988

The Drug-Free Workplace Act of 1988 applies to businesses with federal contracts of $100,000 or more each year. Contractors subject to the Act must take the following steps to be in compliance:

Develop and publish a written policy Contractors must develop a written policy clearly stating that they provide a drug-free workplace and that illegal substance abuse isn't an acceptable practice in the workplace. The policy must clearly state what substances are covered and the consequences for violating the policy.

Establish an awareness program The employer must develop a program to educate employees about the policy, communicate the dangers of drug abuse in the workplace, discuss the employer's policy, inform employees of the availability of counseling or other programs to reduce drug use, and notify employees of the penalties for violating the policy. The program can be delivered through a variety of media—seminars, brochures, videos, web-based training—whatever methods will most effectively communicate the information in the specific environment.

Notify employees about contract conditions Employees must be made aware that a condition of their employment on a federal contract project is that they abide by the policy and inform the employer within five days if they're convicted of a criminal drug offense in the workplace.

Notify the contracting agency of violations If an employee is convicted of a criminal drug offense in the workplace, the employer must notify the contracting agency within 10 days of being informed of the conviction by the employee.

Establish penalties for illegal drug convictions The employer must have an established penalty for any employees convicted of relevant drug offenses. Within 30 days of notice by an employee of a conviction, the employer must take appropriate disciplinary action against the employee or require participation in an appropriate drug-rehabilitation program. Any penalties must be in accordance with requirements of the Rehabilitation Act of 1973.

Maintain a drug-free workplace Contractors must make a good-faith effort to maintain a drug-free workplace in accordance with the Act, or they're subject to penalties, including suspension of payments under the contract, suspension or termination of the contract, or exclusion from consideration from future contracts for a period of up to five years.

EEO Survey

Working together, the Equal Employment Opportunity Commission (EEOC) and the Office of Federal Contract Compliance Programs developed a reporting format designed to meet statistical reporting requirements for both agencies. This form, known as the EEO-1 survey or report, must be filed on or before September 30 of each year using employment data from one pay period in July, August, or September of the current survey year. All employers who meet the following criteria must complete the report:

- All federal contractors who are private employers and (a) are not exempt as provided by 41 CFR Section 60-1.5; (b) have 50 or more employees; *and* (i) are prime contractors or first-tier subcontractors, and have a contract, subcontract, or purchase order amounting to $50,000 or more, or (ii) serve as a depository of government funds in any amount, or (iii) are a financial institution that is an issuing and paying agent for U.S. Savings Bonds. Only those establishments located in the District of Columbia and the 50 states are required to submit. No reports should be filed for establishments in Puerto Rico, the Virgin Islands, or other American protectorates.
- All private employers who are subject to Title VII of the Civil Rights Act of 1964, as amended, with 100 or more employees.

Exceptions to the EEO-1 reporting requirements include:

- State and local governments
- Primary and secondary school systems
- Institutions of higher education
- Indian tribes
- Tax-exempt private membership clubs (other than labor organizations)

The preferred method for filing the EEO-1 survey is through the online filing application. Refer to the EEOC website at https://www.eeoc.gov for information on how to file the EEO-1 survey.

- Starting with the EEO-1 report of 2017 data, the "workforce snapshot period" will be October 1 to December 31, 2017. In other words, each employer may choose any pay period during this three-month "workforce snapshot period" to count its full-time and part-time employees for the EEO-1 report. To give employers more time to make the transition and to allow for alignment with the W-2 reporting cycle, the EEO-1 deadline for the 2017 report will be March 31, 2018. Employers will have a total of 18 months from October 1, 2016, to March 31, 2018 (2017 report deadline) to make the change.

Report Types

Employers with operations at a single location or establishment complete a single form, whereas those who operate at more than one location or establishment must file employment data on multiple forms.

All multiple-establishment employers must file a Headquarters Report, which is a report covering the principal or headquarters office.

Locations with 50 or more employees file a separate Establishment Report for each location employing 50 or more persons.

Locations with fewer than 50 employees may be reported on an Establishment Report or on an Establishment List. The Establishment List provides the name, address, and total number of employees for each location with fewer than 50 employees along with an employment data grid combining this data by race, sex, and job category.

Consolidated Report

Data from all the individual location reports and the headquarters report are combined on the Consolidated Report. The total number of employees on this report must be equal to data submitted on all the individual reports.

Parent corporations that own a majority interest in another corporation report data for employees at all locations, including those of the subsidiary establishments.

Race and Ethnicity Categories

Employers are required to report on seven categories of employees:

1. Hispanic or Latino
2. White
3. Black or African American
4. Native Hawaiian or Other Pacific Islander
5. Asian
6. American Indian or Alaska Native
7. Two or More Races (not Hispanic or Latino)

Job Categories

The EEO-1 report requires employers to group jobs into job categories based on the average skill level, knowledge, and responsibility of positions within their organizations.

- Executive/senior-level officials and managers
- Midlevel officials and managers
- Professionals
- Technicians
- Sales workers
- Administrative support workers
- Craft workers
- Operatives
- Laborers and helpers
- Service workers

Data Reporting

Beginning with the 2017 reporting period (October 1, 2017, to March 31, 2018), for private employers and federal contractors with 100 or more employees, the EEO-1 report will require additional reporting components of employment data. These reports include:

Employee Report Total employees in the workforce snapshot for each job category and pay band.

Pay Report W-2 Box 1 earnings for all employees identified in the workforce snapshot.

Hours Worked Report Hours worked for all employees in the snapshot in their job category and pay band.

The 12 pay bands are:

1. $19,239 and under
2. $19,240–$24,439
3. $24,440–$30,679
4. $30,680–$38,999
5. $39,000–$49,919
6. $49,920–$62,919
7. $62,920–$80,079
8. $80,080–$101,919

9. $101,920–$128,959
10. $128,960–$163,799
11. $163,800–$207,999
12. $208,000 and over

Employee Retirement Income Security Act of 1974 (ERISA)

The Employee Retirement Income Security Act (ERISA) was created by Congress to set standards for private pensions and some group welfare programs such as medical and life insurance. In July 2016, the Department of Labor, Internal Revenue Service, and Pension Benefit Guaranty Corporation proposed changes that, if accepted, will require plan sponsors and providers to comply with updated reporting requirements in 2019. While not accepted as of this publication, it will be important to watch for changes.

ERISA requires organizations to file three types of reports: a summary plan description, an annual report, and reports to individual participants of their benefit rights.

Summary Plan Description (SPD)

A summary plan description (SPD) provides plan participants with information about the provisions, policies, and rules established by the plan and advises them on actions they can take in utilizing the plan. ERISA requires that the SPD include the name and other identifying information about plan sponsors, administrators, and trustees, along with any information related to collective bargaining agreements for the plan participants. The SPD must describe what eligibility requirements must be met for participating in the plan and for receiving benefits, as well as the circum-stances under which participants would be disqualified or ineligible for participation or be denied benefits.

The SPD must also describe the financing source for the plan and the name of the organization providing benefits. Information on the end of the plan year and whether records are maintained on a calendar, plan, or fiscal year basis must be included in the description.

For health and welfare plans, the SPD must describe claim procedures, along with the name of the U.S. Department of Labor (DOL) office that will assist participants and beneficiaries with Health Insurance Portability and Accountability Act (HIPAA) claims. The SPD must also describe what remedies are available when claims are denied.

A new SPD reflecting all changes made must be prepared and distributed every five years unless no changes have occurred. Every 10 years, a new SPD must be distributed to participants whether or not changes have occurred.

Annual Reports

ERISA requires annual reports to be filed for all employee benefit plans. The reports must include financial statements, the number of employees in the plan, and the names and addresses of the plan fiduciaries. ERISA mandates that any persons compensated by the plan (such as an accountant) during the preceding year be disclosed, along with the amount of compensation paid to each, the nature of the services rendered, and any relationship that exists between these parties and any party in interest to the plan. Information that is provided with regard to plan assets must be certified by the organization that holds the assets, whether it is the plan sponsor, an insurance company, or a bank.

The annual reports must be audited by a CPA or other qualified public accountant, and any actuarial reports must be prepared by an enrolled actuary who has been licensed jointly by the Department of the Treasury and the Department of Labor to provide actuarial services for U.S. pension plans.

The DOL is given authority to simplify filing and reporting requirements for plans with less than 100 participants.

Once submitted, annual reports and other documents become public record and are made available in the DOL public document room. The DOL may also use this information to conduct research and analyze data.

Participant Benefit Rights Reports

Participants may request a report of the total benefits accrued on their behalf along with the amount of the benefit that is nonforfeitable. If there are no nonforfeitable amounts accrued at the time the report is requested, the earliest date that benefits will become nonforfeitable must be provided. Participants are entitled to receive the report no more than once per year.

ERISA records must be maintained for six years from the date they were due to be filed with the DOL. In addition to requiring the preparation of these reports, ERISA regulations stipulate that annual reports are to be filed with the DOL within 210 days of the end of the plan year. The DOL may reject reports that are incomplete or that contain qualified opinions from the CPA or actuary. Rejected plans must be resubmitted within 45 days, or the DOL can retain a CPA to audit the report on behalf of the participants. ERISA authorizes the DOL to bring civil actions on behalf of plan participants if necessary to resolve any issues.

In addition to the reporting requirements, ERISA sets minimum standards for employee participation or eligibility requirements, as well as vesting requirements for qualified pension plans.

Employee Participation

A participant is an employee who has met the eligibility requirements for the plan. The law sets minimum participation requirements as follows:

- When one year of service has been completed or the employee has reached the age of 21, whichever is later, unless the plan provides for 100 percent vesting after two years of service. In that case, the requirement changes to completion of two years of service or reaching age 21, whichever is later.
- Employees may not be excluded from the plan on the basis of age; that is, they may not be excluded because they have reached a specified age.
- When employees have met the minimum service and age requirements, they must become participants no later than the first day of the plan year after they meet the requirement, or six months after the requirements are met, whichever is earlier.

Vesting

Qualified plans must also meet minimum vesting standards. Vesting refers to the point at which employees own the contributions their employer has made to the pension plan whether or not they remain employed with the company. The vesting requirements established by ERISA refer only to funds that are contributed by the employer; any funds contributed by plan participants are owned by the employee. Employees are always 100 percent vested in their own money but must earn the right to be vested in the employer's contribution.

Vesting may be immediate or delayed. Immediate vesting occurs when employees are 100 percent, or fully, vested as soon as they meet the eligibility requirements of the plan. Delayed vesting occurs when participants must wait for a defined period of time prior to becoming fully vested. There are two types of delayed vesting—cliff vesting and graded vesting:

- With cliff vesting, participants become 100 percent vested after a specified period of time. ERISA sets the maximum period at five years for qualified plans, which means that participants are zero percent vested until they have completed the five years of service, after which they are fully vested.
- Graded vesting, which is also referred to as graduated or gradual vesting, establishes a vesting schedule that provides for partial vesting each year for a specified number of years. A graded vesting schedule in a qualified plan must allow for at least 20 percent vesting after three years and 20 percent per year after that, with participants achieving full vesting after seven years of service. See Table A.3 for a graded vesting schedule that complies with ERISA requirements.

Table A.3   ERISA Graded Vesting Schedule

Years of Service	Percent Vested
3	20 percent
4	40 percent
5	60 percent
6	80 percent
7	100 percent

Benefit Accrual Requirements

ERISA sets specific requirements for determining how much of an accrued benefit participants are entitled to receive if they leave the company prior to retirement. Plans must account for employee contributions to the plan separately from the funds contributed by the employer since the employees are entitled to all the funds contributed by them to the plan when they leave the company.

Form and Payment of Benefits

ERISA sets forth specific requirements for the payment of funds when participants either reach retirement age or leave the company. The act also provides guidance for employers to deal with qualified domestic relations orders (QDROs), which are legal orders issued by state courts or other state agencies to require pension payments to alternate payees. An alternate payee must be a spouse, former spouse, child, or other dependent of a plan participant.

ERISA also defines funding requirements for pension plans and sets standards for those who are responsible for safeguarding the funds until they are paid to employees. Finally, ERISA provides civil and criminal penalties for organizations that violate its provisions.

Funding

An enrolled actuary determines how much money is required to fund the accrued obligations of the plan, and ERISA requires that these funds be maintained in trust accounts separate from business's operating funds. These amounts must be deposited on a quarterly basis; the final contribution must be made no later than eight and a half months after the end of the plan year.

Fiduciary Responsibility

For purposes of ERISA, a fiduciary is a person, corporation, or other legal entity that holds property or assets on behalf of, or in trust for, the pension fund. ERISA requires fiduciaries to operate pension funds in the best interests of the participants and their beneficiaries and at the lowest possible expense to them. All actions taken with regard to the plan assets must be in accord with the prudent person standard of care, a common law concept that requires all actions be undertaken with "the care, skill, prudence, and diligence . . . that a prudent man acting in like capacity" would use, as defined in ERISA itself.

Fiduciaries may be held personally liable for losses to the plan resulting from any breach of fiduciary responsibility that they commit, and may be required to make restitution for the losses and be subject to legal action. They are not held liable for breaches of fiduciary responsibility that occur prior to the time they became fiduciaries.

ERISA specifically prohibits transactions between pension plans and parties in interest.

Administration and Enforcement

Criminal penalties for willful violations of ERISA include fines of between $5,000 and $100,000 and imprisonment for up to one year. Civil actions may be brought by plan participants or their beneficiaries, by fiduciaries, or by the DOL to recover benefits or damages or to force compliance with the law.

Amendments to ERISA

Consolidated Omnibus Budget Reconciliation Act of 1986 (COBRA)

Prior to 1986, employees who were laid off or resigned from their jobs lost any health care benefits that were provided as part of those jobs. ERISA was amended in 1986 by the Consolidated Omnibus Budget Reconciliation Act (COBRA), which requires businesses with 20 or more employees to provide health plan continuation coverage under certain circumstances. Employers who meet this requirement must continue benefits for those who leave the company or for their dependents when certain qualifying events occur.

Employers must notify employees of the availability of COBRA coverage when they enter the plan and again within 30 days of the occurrence of a qualifying event. Table A.4 shows the qualifying events that trigger COBRA, as well as the length of time coverage must be continued for each event.

Table A.4   COBRA Qualifying Events and Coverage Requirements

Qualifying Event	Length of Coverage
Employee death	36 months
Divorce or legal separation	36 months
Dependent child no longer covered	36 months
Reduction in hours	18 months
Reduction in hours when disabled*	29 months
Employee termination	18 months
Employee termination when disabled*	29 months
Eligibility for SSA benefits	18 months
Termination for gross misconduct	0 months

*An employee who is disabled within 60 days of a reduction in hours or a termination becomes eligible for an additional 11 months of COBRA coverage.

Employers may charge COBRA participants a maximum of 102 percent of the group premium for coverage and must include them in any open enrollment periods or other changes to the plans. Employers may discontinue COBRA coverage if payments are not received within 30 days of the time they are due.

Employees must notify the employer within 60 days of a divorce, a separation, or the loss of a child's dependent status. Employees who fail to provide this notice risk the loss of continued coverage.

Health Insurance Portability and Accountability Act of 1996 (HIPAA)

The Health Insurance Portability and Accountability Act (HIPAA) was another amendment to ERISA and prohibits discrimination on the basis of health status as evidenced by an individual's medical condition or history, claims experience, utilization of health care services, disability, or evidence of insurability. It also places limits on health insurance restrictions for preexisting conditions, which are defined as conditions for which treatment was given within six months of enrollment in the plan. Insurers may exclude those conditions from coverage for 12 months or, in the case of a late enrollment, for 18 months.

Insurers may discontinue an employer's group coverage only if the employer neglects to pay the premiums, obtained the policy through fraudulent or intentional misrepresentation, or does not comply with material provisions of the plan. Group coverage may also be discontinued if the insurer is no longer offering coverage in the employer's geographic area, if none of the plan participants reside in the plan's network area, or if the employer fails to renew a collective bargaining agreement or to comply with its provisions.

In April 2001, the Department of Health and Human Services (HHS) issued privacy regulations that were required by HIPAA. The regulations defined protected health information (PHI), patient information that must be kept private, including physical or mental conditions, information about health care given, and payments that have been made. Although these regulations were directed at covered entities that conduct business electronically, such as health plans, health care providers, and clearinghouses, they have had a significant impact on the way employers handle information related to employee health benefits. Many employers had to redesign forms for open enrollment periods and new hires, and update plan documents and company benefit policies to reflect the changes. The regulations have an impact on employers in other ways as well.

Although flexible spending accounts (FSAs) are exempt from other HIPAA requirements, they are considered group health plans for privacy reasons, so employers who sponsor FSAs must comply with the privacy requirements for them.

Employers who are self-insured or who have fully insured group health plans and receive protected health information are required to develop privacy policies that comply with the regulations, appoint a privacy official, and train employees to handle information appropriately.

Although the HIPAA regulations do not prevent employees from seeking assistance from HR for claim problems or other issues with the group health plan, they do require employees to provide the insurance provider or third-party administrator (TPA) with an authorization to release information about the claim to the HR department.

The new regulations include stiff civil and criminal sanctions for violations; civil penalties of $100 per violation and up to $25,000 per person each year can be assessed. There are three levels of criminal penalties:

1. A conviction for obtaining or disclosing PHI can result in a fine of up to $50,000 and one year in prison.
2. Obtaining PHI under false pretenses can result in fines of up to $100,000 and five years in prison.
3. Obtaining or disclosing PHI with the intent of selling, transferring, or using it to obtain commercial advantage or personal gain can be punished with a fine of up to $250,000 and 10 years in prison.

Health Insurance Portability and Accountability Act (HIPAA)

A U.S. law that protects workers' health benefits and medical privacy

The Health Insurance Portability and Accountability Act (HIPAA) protects American workers in assuring the continuation of health insurance coverage and protects their medical privacy.

Executive Orders

Executive orders (EOs) are presidential proclamations that, when published in the Federal Register, become law after 30 days. EOs have been used to ensure that equal employment opportunities are afforded by federal agencies and private businesses that contract or subcontract with those agencies. Certain executive orders relating to equal employment issues are enforced by the OFCCP.

Executive Order 11246, amended by 11375, 13279, and 13672

Executive Order 11246, established in 1965, prohibits employment discrimination on the basis of race, color, religion, sex, sexual orientation, gender identity, or national origin and requires affirmative steps be taken in advertising jobs, recruiting, employing, training, promotion, compensating, and terminating employees. Executive Order 13279 limits the impact of this executive order on religious corporations, associations, educational institutions, or societies in certain situations. Executive Order 11246 applies to federal contractors and federally assisted construction contractors and subcontractors who meet certain thresholds. See the section on affirmative action plans (AAPs) for additional information on the requirements for this executive order.

Executive Order 11478, amended by 13087, 13152, and 13672 This order, written in 1969, prohibits discrimination against federal government employees on the basis of race, color, religion, sex, sexual orientation, gender identity, status as a parent, national origin, handicap, or age.

Executive Order 12138 In 1979, with the implementation of EO 12138, the National Women's Business Enterprise policy was created. This EO also required federal contractors and subcontractors to take affirmative steps to promote and support women's business enterprises.

Executive Order 12989, amended by 13286 and 13465 This order requires contractors with qualifying federal contracts to electronically verify employment authorization of: (1) all employees hired during the contract term and (2) all employees performing work in the United States on contracts with a Federal Acquisition Regulation (FAR) E-Verify clause. A federal contractor may be exempt from these clauses if any of the following apply:

- The contract is for fewer than 120 days.
- It is valued at less than $150,000, the simplified acquisition threshold.
- All work is performed outside the United States.
- It includes only commercially available off-the-shelf (COTS) items and related services.

The E-Verify rule does not extend beyond the United States, applying only to employees working in the United States, which includes the 50 states, the District of Columbia, Guam, Puerto Rico, the U.S. Virgin Islands, and the Commonwealth of the Northern Mariana Islands (CNMI).

Fair Credit Reporting Act of 1970 (FCRA)

The FCRA was first enacted in 1970 and has been amended several times since then, most recently with the Fair and Accurate Credit Transactions (FACT) Act in 2003. Enforced by the Federal Trade Commission (FTC), the FCRA requires employers to take certain actions prior to the use of a consumer report or an investigative consumer report obtained through a consumer reporting agency (CRA) for use in making employment decisions.

Familiarity with three terms is valuable for understanding why these consumer protection laws are important for HR practitioners:

A consumer reporting agency (CRA) is an individual, business, or nonprofit association that gathers information about individuals with the intent of supplying that information to a third party.

A consumer report is a written document produced by a CRA containing information about an individual's character, reputation, lifestyle, or credit history for use by an employer in determining that person's suitability for employment.

An investigative consumer report is a written document produced by a CRA for the same purpose as a consumer report but is based on information gathered through personal interviews with friends, coworkers, employers, and others who are acquainted with the individual.

The FCRA established the following four-step process for employers to follow when using CRAs to perform background investigations:

1. A clear and conspicuous disclosure that a consumer report may be obtained for employment purposes must be made in writing to the candidate before the report is acquired.
2. The candidate must provide written authorization for the employer to obtain the report.
3. Before taking an adverse action based in whole or in part on the credit report, either the employer must provide the candidate with a copy of the report and a copy of the FTC notice, "A Summary of Your Rights Under the Fair Credit Reporting Act," or, if the application was made by mail, telephone, computer, or similar means, the employer must notify the candidate within three business days that adverse action is being taken based in whole or in part on the credit report. This notice must provide the name, address, and telephone number of the CRA and indicate that the CRA did not take the adverse action and cannot provide the reasons for the action to the candidate. If a candidate requests a copy of the

report, the employer must provide it within three days, along with a copy of the FTC notice just described.

4. Candidates must be advised of their right to dispute the accuracy of information contained in the report.

When employers request investigative consumer reports on candidates, they must comply with these additional steps:

- Provide written disclosure of its intent to the candidate within three days of requesting the report from a CRA.
- Include a summary of the candidate's FCRA rights with the written notice.
- Advise the candidate that he or she has a right to request information about the type and extent of the investigation.
- If requested, provide complete disclosure of the type and extent of the report within the later of five days of the request or receipt of the report.

The FCRA was amended in 2003 by the Fair and Accurate Credit Transactions (FACT) Act of 2003. Designed to improve the accuracy of consumer credit information, it gives consumers one free credit report per year. The Act also requires disclosure to consumers who are subject to risk-based pricing (less favorable credit offers) or who are denied credit altogether because of a credit-related record.

FACT describes "reasonable measures" for destroying credit reports, depending on the medium:

- Paper documents must be shredded, pulverized, or burned in a way that prevents them from being reassembled.
- Electronic files or media must be erased in a way that prevents them from being reconstructed.
- Either type may be destroyed by an outside vendor once the employer has conducted due diligence research to ensure the vendor's methods are reliable.

Fair Labor Standards Act of 1938 (FLSA)

Enacted in 1938, the Fair Labor Standards Act (FLSA) today remains a major influence on basic compensation issues for businesses in the United States. FLSA regulations apply to workers who are not already covered by another law. For example, railroad and airline employers are subject to wage and hour requirements of the Railway Labor Act, so the FLSA does not apply to their employees.

There are two categories of employers subject to the requirements of the FLSA: enterprise and individual. Enterprise coverage applies to businesses employing at least two employees with at least $500,000 in annual sales and to hospitals, schools, and government agencies. Individual coverage applies to organizations whose daily work involves interstate commerce. The FLSA defines interstate commerce so broadly that it includes those who have regular contact by telephone with out-of-state customers, vendors, or suppliers; on that basis, it covers virtually all employers in the United States.

The FLSA established requirements in five areas key areas to HRM:

1. It introduced a minimum wage for all covered employees.
2. It identified the circumstances in which overtime payments are required and set the overtime rate at one and one half times the regular hourly wage.
3. It identified the criteria for determining what jobs are exempt from FLSA requirements.
4. It placed limitations on working conditions for children to protect them from exploitation.
5. It identified the information employers must keep about employees and related payroll transactions.

Minimum Wage

The FLSA regulates the federal minimum wage, which is set at $7.25 per hour as of the most recent 2009 update. Some states, such as Alaska, California, and New York, have set the minimum wage at a higher rate than the federal government; when this is the case, the state requirement supersedes the federal minimum wage. In other states the minimum is lower than the federal rate. In those states, the federal minimum wage supersedes state requirements. The DOL provides a useful map showing current minimum wage requirements by state at https://www.dol.gov/whd/minwage/america.htm.

Nonexempt employees must be paid at least the minimum wage for all compensable time. The FLSA defines compensable time as the time an employee works that is "suffered or permitted" by the employer. For example, a nonexempt employee who continues to work on an assignment after the end of the business day to finish a project or make corrections must be paid for that time.

Maximum Hours and Overtime

The FLSA defined the maximum workweek for nonexempt employees as 40 hours per week and required overtime to be paid for any compensable time that exceeds that maximum. The FLSA defined overtime for nonexempt workers as one and one half times the regular hourly wage rate for all compensable time worked that exceeds 40 hours in a workweek (also commonly known as time and a half).

Although double-time, or two times regular pay, is not required by the FLSA, it may be required by some states or may be part of a labor agreement.

While the FLSA does not require payment of overtime for exempt employees, it also does not prohibit overtime payments for them. Employers who choose to compensate exempt employees for hours worked exceeding the regular workweek are free to do so without risking the loss of exemption status. As long as overtime payments are in addition to the regular salary, exemption status is not affected. Exempt overtime can be paid at straight time, at time and a half, or as a bonus.

State or local government agencies may compensate employees with what is known as compensatory time off, or comp time, instead of cash payment for overtime worked. For example, a road maintenance worker employed by a city government may work 20 hours of overtime during a snowstorm. Instead of being paid time and a half for the overtime hours, the employee may receive 30 hours of additional paid time off (1.5 times 20 hours) to be used just as paid vacation or sick leave. From time to time, initiatives to expand comp time to private employers are presented in Congress, but at this time, the FLSA does not permit private employers to use comp time.

Overtime calculations are based on time actually worked during the week. For example, in a week with a paid holiday, full-time nonexempt employees will actually work 32 hours even though they are paid for 40 hours. If some employees then work 6 hours on Saturday, for a total of 38 actual hours worked during the week, those hours are paid at straight time, not time and a half (unless, of course, a state law or union contract requires otherwise). This requirement also applies when employees use paid vacation or sick leave or some other form of paid time off (PTO).

To accurately calculate overtime payments, it is necessary to understand the difference between compensable time—hours that must be paid to nonexempt employees—and noncompensable time. The FLSA defines several situations for which nonexempt employees must be paid, such as the time spent in preparing for or cleaning up after a shift by dressing in or removing protective clothing. Other types of compensable time include the following.

Waiting Time

Time spent by nonexempt employees waiting for work is compensable if it meets the FLSA definition of engaged to wait, which means that employees have been asked to wait for an assignment. For example, a marketing director may ask an assistant to wait for the conclusion of a meeting in order to prepare a Microsoft PowerPoint presentation needed for a client meeting early the next morning. If the assistant reads a book while waiting for the meeting to end, that time is still compensable.

Time that is spent by an employee who is waiting to be engaged is not compensable. For example, time spent by an employee who arrives at work 15 minutes early and reads the newspaper until the beginning of a shift is not considered to be compensable.

On-Call Time

The FLSA does not require employees who are on call away from the work site and are able to effectively use the time for their own purposes to be paid for time they spend waiting to be called. These employees may be required to provide the employer with contact information. If, however, the employer places other constraints on the employee's activities, the time could be considered compensable.

Employees who are required to remain at or close to the work site while waiting for an assignment are entitled to on-call pay. For example, medical interns required to remain at the hospital are entitled to payment for all hours spent at the hospital waiting for patients to arrive.

Rest and Meal Periods

Although rest and meal periods are not required by the FLSA, if they are provided, that time is subject to its requirements. Commonly referred to as breaks, short periods of rest lasting less than 20 minutes are considered compensable time. Meal periods lasting 30 minutes or longer are not compensable time unless the employee is required to continue working while eating. For example, a receptionist who is required to remain at the desk during lunch to answer the telephone must be paid for that time.

Lectures, Meetings, and Training Programs

Nonexempt employees are not required to be paid to attend training events when all four of the following conditions are met:

1. The event takes place outside normal work hours.
2. It is voluntary.
3. It is not job related.
4. No other work is performed during the event.

Travel Time

Regular commute time (the time normally spent commuting from home to the regular work site) is not compensable. There are, however, some situations in which the FLSA requires that nonexempt employees receive payment for travel time.

Emergency Travel from Home to Work

Any time an employee is required to return to work for an emergency after working a full day, the employee must be compensated for travel time.

One-Day Offsite Assignments

When nonexempt employees are given a one-day assignment at a different location than their regular work site, the travel time may be considered compensable in certain circumstances. For example, if an employee drives to the off-site assignment, the travel time is compensable, but if he or she is a passenger in the car, the travel time is not compensable.

Travel between Job Sites

Nonexempt employees (such as plumbers or electricians) who are required to drive to different work sites to perform their regular duties must also be paid for the driving time between work sites.

Travel Away from Home

Travel away from home is defined as travel that keeps employees away from their homes overnight. When nonexempt employees must travel overnight, the FLSA considers the travel time during regular work hours as compensable time. This includes time traveled on nonworkdays (weekends, for example) when it occurs during the employee's regular work hours. The DOL excludes the time spent outside of working hours as a passenger on an airplane, train, boat, bus, or automobile from compensable time calculations. If the employee is driving or working while traveling, the time is compensable.

Exemption Status

The FLSA covers all employees except those identified in the law as exempt from the regulations. All other employees are considered nonexempt and must be paid in accordance with FLSA requirements.

Certain positions may be exempt from one or all of the FLSA requirements (minimum wage, overtime, or child labor). For example, police officers and firefighters employed by small departments of less than five employees are exempt from overtime requirements, but not exempt from the minimum wage requirement.

On the other hand, newspaper delivery jobs are exempt from the minimum wage, overtime, and child labor requirements.

The determination of exemption status is often misunderstood by both employers and employees. Employers often think that they will save money by designating jobs as exempt and paying incumbent employees a salary. Employees often see the designation of a job as exempt as a measure of status within the company. Neither of these perceptions is accurate, and jobs that do not meet the legal exemption requirements can have costly consequences for employers.

To assist employers in properly classifying positions, the DOL regulations include exemption tests to determine whether a job meets those requirements and is therefore exempt from FLSA regulations.

Salary Basis Requirement

The DOL defines a salary as a regular, predetermined rate of pay for a weekly or less frequent basis (for example, biweekly, semimonthly, monthly, and so on). Employees must be paid a minimum salary of $455 per week, or $23,660 per year, as well as meet certain tests outlined next regarding their job duties in order to qualify as exempt. Job titles alone do not determine an employee's exempt status.

Executive Exemption

Employees who meet the salary basis requirement may be exempt as executives if they meet all of the following requirements:

- They have as their primary duty managing the enterprise, or managing a customarily recognized department or subdivision of the enterprise.
- They customarily and regularly direct the work of at least two other full-time employees.
- They have the authority to hire, fire, promote, and evaluate employees or to provide input regarding those actions that carries particular weight.
- Employees who own at least a 20 percent equity interest in the organization and who are actively engaged in management duties are also considered bona fide exempt executives.

Administrative Exemption

Employees who meet the salary basis requirement may qualify for the administrative exemption if they meet all of the following requirements:

- The primary duty is to perform office or nonmanual work directly related to management or general business operations.

- The primary duty requires discretion and independent judgment on significant matters.

Professional Exemption

The DOL identifies two types of professionals who may qualify for exemption:

1. *Learned professional exemption.* Employees who meet the salary basis requirement may qualify for exemption as learned professionals if they also meet both of the following criteria:
   - The primary duty requires the use of this advanced knowledge for work that requires the consistent use of discretion and judgment.
   - They have advanced knowledge in a field of science or learning acquired through a prolonged course of intellectual instruction.
2. *Creative professional exemption.* Employees who meet the salary basis requirement may qualify for exemption as creative professionals if they also meet this criterion:
   - The primary duty requires invention, imagination, originality, or talent in a recognized field of artistic or creative endeavor.

Highly Compensated Employee Exemption

Highly compensated employees (HCEs, paid $100,000 or more) may also be considered exempt. To meet this exemption requirement, employees must perform office or nonmanual work and, on a customary and regular basis, at least one of the duties listed earlier for the executive, administrative, or professional exemptions.

Computer Employee Exemption

Employees who meet the weekly salary requirement or who are paid at least $27.63 per hour may qualify for the computer employee exemption if they perform one of the following jobs:

- Computer systems analyst
- Computer programmer
- Software engineer
- Other similarly skilled jobs in the computer field

and if they perform one or more of the following primary duties as part of the job:

- Apply systems analysis techniques and procedures, including consulting with users, to determine hardware, software, or system functional specifications.

- Design, develop, document, analyze, create, test, or modify computer systems or programs, including prototypes, based on and related to user or system design specifications.
- Design, document, test, create, or modify computer programs related to machine operating systems.
- A combination of the previously described duties, at a level requiring the same skill.

Specifically excluded from this exemption are employees engaged in manufacturing or repairing computer hardware or related equipment and those such as engineers, drafters, or computer-aided designers who rely on computers and software programs to perform their work.

Outside Sales Exemption

Unlike the other exemptions, there is no salary requirement for outside sales personnel. To qualify for this exemption, employees must meet both of the following requirements:

- The primary duty of the position must be making sales or obtaining orders or contracts for services or for the use of facilities for which a consideration will be paid by the client or customer.
- The employee must be customarily and regularly engaged away from the employer's place of business.

Salary Deductions

There are certain circumstances where an employer may make deductions from the pay of an exempt employee. The DOL defines permissible salary deductions as the following:

- Absence for one or more full days for personal reasons other than sickness or disability
- Absence for one or more full days because of sickness or disability if the deduction is made in accordance with a bona fide plan, policy, or practice of providing compensation for salary lost due to illness
- To offset amounts employees receive for jury or witness fees or military pay
- For good-faith penalties imposed for safety rule infractions of major significance
- Good-faith, unpaid disciplinary suspensions of one or more full days for infractions of workplace conduct rules
- During the initial or terminal weeks of employment when employees work less than a full week
- Unpaid leave under the Family and Medical Leave Act

Employers who have an "actual practice" of improper deductions risk the loss of exemption status for all employees in the same job classification, not just for the affected employee. The loss of exemption status will be effective for the time during which the improper deductions were made.

Actual Practice

The DOL looks at a variety of factors to determine whether employers have an actual practice of improper deductions from exempt pay. These factors include the following:

- The number of improper deductions compared to the number of employee infractions warranting deductions
- The time period during which the improper deductions were made
- The number of employees affected
- The geographic location of the affected employees and managers responsible for the deductions

Safe Harbor

The DOL provides a safe harbor provision for payroll errors that could affect exemption status. The safe harbor applies if all of the following are met:

- There is a clearly communicated policy prohibiting improper deductions that includes a complaint mechanism for employees to use.
- The employer reimburses employees for improper deductions.
- The employer makes a good-faith commitment to comply in the future.

Employers who meet these criteria will not lose exemption status for the affected employees unless they willfully violate the policy by continuing to make improper deductions after receiving employee complaints.

2016 Overtime Final Rule

In 2016, then President Obama updated the salary basis for executive, administrative, and professional workers. However, on November 22, 2016, a U.S. District Court judge in Texas granted an injunction that prevents the Department of Justice from implementing and enforcing the updated Final Rule. The injunction is currently on appeal as of December 1, 2016. If the injunction is lifted, then the following changes will be made to the FLSA.

Employees must be paid a minimum salary of $913 per week, or $47,476 per year, to be classified as exempt. Highly compensated employees (HCEs) are subject to a minimal duties test and must have an annual salary of at least $134,000. Employers are able to use nondiscretionary bonuses and incentive payments (including commissions) to satisfy up to 10 percent of the standard salary level. Such payments may include, for example, nondiscretionary incentive bonuses tied to productivity and profitability. The 2016 ruling also establishes an automatic update to salary thresholds every three years beginning in January 2020.

Child Labor

The FLSA regulates the employment of workers under the age of 18. Children 16 years of age and up may work for an unlimited amount of hours. Children of any age may work for businesses owned entirely by their parents, unless they would be employed in mining, manufacturing, or other hazardous occupations. There are no restrictions on a youth 18 years of age or older.

Children 14 and 15 years of age can work in nonmanufacturing, nonmining, and nonhazardous jobs outside of school hours if they work the following hours:

- No more than 3 hours a day or 18 hours in a workweek
- No more than 8 hours on a nonschool day or 40 hours in a nonschool workweek

During the school year, youths between the ages of 14 and 15 can work between 7 a.m. and 7 p.m. During the summer months, June 1 through Labor Day, the workday can be extended to 9 p.m.

Record Keeping

There are two common methods for reporting time worked: positive time reporting, in which employees record the actual hours they are at work along with vacation, sick, or other time off, and exception reporting, in which only changes to the regular work schedule are recorded, such as vacation, sick, or personal time. Although the DOL regulations accept either method, in general the positive time method is best for nonexempt employees because it leaves no doubt as to actual hours worked by the employee and protects both the employee and the employer if there is ever a question about overtime payments due. Exception reporting is more appropriate for exempt employees because their pay is not based on hours worked.

The FLSA does not prevent employers from tracking the work time of exempt employees. These records may be used for billing customers, for reviewing performance, or for other administrative purposes, but they may not be used to reduce pay based on the quality or quantity of work produced. Reducing the salary invalidates the exemption status and subjects the employee to all requirements of the FLSA.

The FLSA requires the maintenance of accurate records by all employers. The information that must be maintained includes the following:

- Personal information, including full name, SSN, home address, occupation, sex, and date of birth if younger than 19 years old
- The hour and day when the workweek begins
- The total hours worked each workday and each workweek
- The basis on which employee's wages are paid (e.g., "$9 per hour" or "$440 per week")
- The total daily or weekly straight-time earnings
- The regular hourly pay rate for any week, including overtime
- Total overtime pay for the workweek
- Deductions and additions to wages
- Total wages paid each pay period
- The pay period dates and payment date

These FLSA records are usually maintained by the payroll department. Records must be preserved for at least three years. They must include payroll records, collective bargaining agreements, and sales and purchase records.

Penalties and Recovery of Back Wages

It is not uncommon for an employer to make an inadvertent error in calculating employee pay. In most cases when that happens, the employer corrects the error as soon as the employee points it out or the employer catches the error in some other way. Although distressing for employees, employers who make a good-faith effort to rectify the error in a timely manner remain within FLSA requirements.

In other cases, employers intentionally violate FLSA regulations by either paying employees less than the minimum wage, not paying overtime, or misclassifying employees as exempt to avoid overtime costs. These and other employee complaints about wage payments are investigated by state or federal agencies. If the complaints are justified, the employers are required to pay retroactive overtime pay and penalties to the affected employees. The investigation of a complaint by a single employee at an organization can trigger a government audit of the employer's general pay practices and exemption classification of its other employees and may result in additional overtime payments or penalties to other employees if they are found to be misclassified.

Employees whose complaints are verified can recover back wages using one of the following four methods the FLSA provides. The least expensive cost to the employer requires payment of the back wages.

1. The Wage and Hour Division of the DOL can supervise the payment of back wages.
2. The DOL can file a lawsuit for the amount of back wages and liquidated damages equal to the back wages.
3. Employees can file private lawsuits to recover the wages plus an equal amount of liquidated damages, attorney fees, and court costs.
4. The DOL can file an injunction preventing an employer from unlawfully withholding minimum wage and overtime payments.

There is a two-year statute of limitations for back pay recovery unless the employer willfully violated the FLSA. In those cases, the statute extends to three years. Employers may not terminate or retaliate against employees who file FLSA complaints. Willful violators of the FLSA may face criminal prosecution and be fined up to $10,000; if convicted a second time, the violator may face imprisonment. A civil penalty of up to $1,100 per violation may be assessed against willful or repeat violators.

FLSA Amendments

The FLSA has been amended numerous times since 1938, most often to raise the minimum wage to a level consistent with changes in economic conditions.

Two significant federal amendments have been added to the FLSA since 1938, the Portal to Portal Act and the Equal Pay Act. Additionally, the Patient Protection and Affordable Care Act, commonly referred to as Obamacare, affected the FLSA requirements.

Portal to Portal Act (1947)

The Portal to Portal Act clarified what was considered to be compensable work time and established that employers are not required to pay for employee commute time. This Act requires employers to pay nonexempt employees who perform regular work duties before or after their regular hours or for working during their lunch period.

Equal Pay Act (EPA) (1963)

The Equal Pay Act, the first antidiscrimination act to protect women, prohibits discrimination on the basis of sex. Equal pay for equal work applies to jobs with similar working conditions, skill, effort, and responsibilities. The Equal Pay Act applies to employers and employees covered by FLSA and is administered and enforced by the Equal Employment Opportunity Commission (EEOC). The EPA allows differences in pay when they are based on a bona fide seniority system, a merit system, a system that measures quantity or quality of production, or any other system that fairly measures factors other than sex. Prior to the EPA, the comparable worth standard was used by the U.S. government to make compensation decisions. When Congress passed the EPA, it deliberately rejected the comparable worth standard in favor of the equal pay standard.

Patient Protection and Affordable Care Act (PPACA) (2010)

In March 2010, President Barack Obama signed into law the Patient Protection and Affordable Care Act (PPACA). Largely intended as substantial health care reform, it included provisions for lactation accommodation in the workplace. The amendment requires that employers provide a reasonable break time for an employee to express breast milk for her nursing child for one year after the child's birth each time such employee has need to express the milk, and an appropriate place (other than a bathroom) that provides privacy. There is some dispute as to whether this time must be paid, however. While the amendment states that the time need not be compensated, current FLSA language reads otherwise: "Rest periods of short duration, generally running from 5 minutes to about 20 minutes, are common in industry. They promote the efficiency of the employee and are customarily paid for as work time. It is immaterial with respect to compensability of such breaks whether the employee drinks coffee, smokes, goes to the rest room, etc." This is an excellent example of when existing employment practices must be considered when applying the law. For example, if an employer allows additional paid break time for employees who smoke (unprotected activity), it may be prudent for said employer to count lactation accommodation (protected activity) as paid time as well.

Family and Medical Leave Act of 1993 (FMLA)

In 1993, President Bill Clinton signed the Family and Medical Leave Act (FMLA), which was created to assist employees in balancing the needs of their families with the demands of their jobs. In creating the FMLA, Congress intended that employees not have to choose between keeping their jobs and attending to seriously ill family members.

In addition to protecting employees from adverse employment actions and retaliation when they request leave under the FMLA, the Act provides three benefits for eligible employees in covered organizations:

1. Twelve weeks of unpaid leave within a 12-month period (26 months for military caregiver leave)
2. Continuation of health benefits
3. Reinstatement to the same position or an equivalent position at the end of the leave

Designation of FMLA Leave

Employers are responsible to designate leave requests as FMLA-qualified based on information received from employees or someone designated by employees to speak on their behalf. When the employee does not provide enough information for the employer to determine if the leave is for a reason protected by the FMLA, it is up to the employer to request additional information. The FMLA regulations do not require employees to specifically request FMLA leave, but they must provide enough information to allow the employer to determine if the request is protected by the FMLA. If leave is denied based on a lack of information, it is up to the employee to provide enough additional information for the employer to ascertain that the leave is protected by the FMLA.

The regulations allow employers to retroactively designate leave as FMLA-qualified, as long as sufficient notice is given to the employee and the retroactive designation does not cause harm or injury to the employee. The retroactive designation can be made by mutual agreement between the employee and employer. When an employer fails to appropriately designate that a leave is FMLA-qualified at the time of the employee's request, the employee may be entitled to any loss of compensation and benefits caused by the employer's failure. This can include monetary damages, reinstatement, promotion, or other suitable relief.

Failure to Designate in a Timely Manner

In 2008, the FMLA was amended by the National Defense Authorization Act (NDAA). One of the changes incorporated the Supreme Court ruling in *Ragsdale v. Wolverine Worldwide, Inc.*, a case that addressed what happens when an employer fails to designate a leave as FMLA-qualified in a timely manner. Prior to the *Ragsdale* case, some employees interpreted the regulations in a way that required employers to provide more than the 12 weeks of unpaid leave required by the FMLA. The regulations now state that, if an employer neglects to designate leave as FMLA, employees who are harmed may be entitled to restitution for their losses.

Waiver of Rights

Prior to the 2008 changes, the DOL required any settlement of past claims, even those mutually agreeable to both parties, to be approved by either the DOL or a court. The 2008 final rules amend this, allowing employers and employees who mutually agree on a resolution to settle past claims between them, avoiding costly and unnecessary litigation. However, the regulations do not permit employees to waive their future FMLA rights.

Substitution of Paid Leave

DOL regulations permit employees to request, or employers to require, the use of all accrued paid vacation, personal, family, medical, or sick leave concurrently with the FMLA leave. Eligible employees who do not qualify to take paid leave according to policies established by their employers are still entitled to the unpaid FMLA leave.

Perfect Attendance Awards

Employers may now deny perfect attendance awards to employees whose FMLA leave disqualifies them as long as employees who take non-FMLA leave are treated the same way.

Light Duty Assignments

Some courts interpreted light duty assignments following an FMLA leave as a continuation of the leave. The 2008 final rules stipulate that light duty work assignments are not counted against an employee's FMLA entitlement. In addition, the employee's job restoration rights continue until the employee is released to full duty or until the end of the 12-month FMLA leave year.

Record-Keeping Requirements

FMLA leave records must be kept in accordance with record-keeping standards established by of the Fair Labor Standards Act (FLSA) and may be maintained in employee personnel files. The FMLA does not require submission of FMLA leave records unless requested by the DOL, but they must be maintained and available for inspection, copying, or transcription by DOL representatives for no less than three years. The DOL may not require submission more than once during any 12-month period without a reasonable belief that a violation has occurred.

Employers Covered

The FMLA applies to all public agencies and schools, regardless of their size, and to private employers with 50 or more employees working within a 75-mile radius. The law provides detailed descriptions on how employers determine whether these requirements apply to them.

Fifty or More Employees

Employers must comply with the FMLA when they employ 50 or more employees for each working day during each of 20 or more calendar workweeks in the current or preceding year. The statute does not require the workweeks to be consecutive. Guidelines in the FMLA count the number of employees at a work site as being determined by the number of employees on the payroll for that site.

Employers remain subject to FMLA rules until the number of employees on the payroll is less than 50 for 20 nonconsecutive weeks in the current and preceding calendar year. This means that if employers with 50 employees on the payroll for the first 20 weeks in 2016 reduce the number of employees for the rest of 2016 and remain at the reduced level throughout 2017, they must continue to comply with FMLA through the end of 2017.

Work Sites within a 75-Mile Radius

The number of employees at each work site is based on the employees who report to work at that site or, in the case of outside sales representatives or employees who telecommute, the location from which their work is assigned.

This can be either a single place of business or a group of adjacent locations, such as a business park or campus.

A work site may also consist of facilities that are not directly connected if they are in reasonable geographic proximity, are used for the same purpose, and share the same staff and equipment.

Employees such as construction workers or truck drivers who regularly work at sites away from the main business office are counted as employees in one of the three following ways:

1. At the business site to which they report
2. At the work site that is their home base
3. At the site from which their work is assigned

However, these employees may not be counted at a work site where they may be temporarily deployed for the duration of a project.

Notice Obligations

Employers have two notice obligations for the FMLA: the first obligation is to inform employees of their FMLA rights and the second requires specific information to be provided in response to an FMLA leave request.

Informational Notice

Upon hire, employers must provide employees with a general informational notice in two formats. The DOL provides a poster (WH Publication 1420) explaining FMLA rights and responsibilities. Employers must post this information in an area frequented by employees.

Employers must also provide information about employee rights and responsibilities in the employee handbook, collective bargaining agreement (CBA), or other written documents. When an employer does not have a handbook or CBA, DOL provides Fact Sheet #28, a four-page summary of the FMLA that the employer may distribute to employees.

Notice in Response to Leave Request

Once an employee requests an FMLA leave, the final rules require employers to respond within five business days. At this time, employers must inform employees of their eligibility, rights, and responsibilities for an FMLA leave, and designate the leave as FMLA. The DOL provides two forms for this purpose: WH-381 and WH-382.

The eligibility, rights, and responsibilities notice (Form WH-381) informs employees of the following:

- The date of leave request, and beginning and ending dates of the leave
- The reason for the leave (birth or adoption of a child or serious health condition of employee or family member)
- Employee rights and responsibilities under the FMLA
- That employee contributions toward health insurance premiums continue and whether or not the employee will be required to reimburse the employer for premiums paid if the employee does not return to work after the leave
- Whether or not the employer will continue other benefits
- Whether or not the employee is eligible for an FMLA leave
- Whether or not the employee is designated as a key employee and therefore may not be restored to employment upon the end of the leave
- Whether or not the employer requires periodic reports on the employee's status and intention to return to work

The designation notice (Form WH-382) informs employees of the following:

- Whether or not the requested leave will be counted against their FMLA leave entitlement
- Whether or not a medical certification is required
- Whether or not the employer requires them to use their accrued paid leave for the unpaid FMLA leave; if not required, whether or not the employee chooses to substitute accrued paid leave for all or part of the FMLA leave
- Whether or not the employer requires a fitness-for-duty certificate prior to the employee's return to work

Employers are not required to use the DOL forms, but if a substitute form is used, it must include all information required by the regulations.

Employers may not revoke an employee's eligibility, once confirmed. Similarly, if an employer neglects to inform an employee that he or she is ineligible for FMLA leave prior to the date the leave begins, the employee is considered eligible to take the leave, and the employer may not deny it at that point.

Employees Eligible for FMLA

The FMLA also provides guidelines for determining which employees are eligible for leave. This includes employees who:

- Work for an employer that is subject to FMLA as described previously.
- Have been employed by the employer for at least 12 months, which need not be consecutive, but time worked prior to a break in service of seven or more years does not need to be counted unless the service break was to fulfill a military service obligation. Employees who received benefits or other compensation during any part of a week are counted as having been employed for that week.
- Worked at least 1,250 hours during the 12 months immediately preceding the leave, based on the FLSA standards for determining compensable hours of work. If accurate time records are not maintained, it is up to the employer to prove that the employee did not meet the requirement; if this is not possible, the law provides that the employee will be presumed to have met the requirement. The determination of whether an employee meets the requirement for 1,250 hours of work within the past 12 months is counted from the date the leave begins.

Key Employee Exception

An FMLA leave is available to all employees of covered organizations who meet the FMLA eligibility requirements. FMLA includes a provision that key employees may be denied reinstatement to the position they held or an equivalent position if the employer demonstrates that the reinstatement would cause "substantial and grievous economic injury" to its operations. A key employee is defined by FMLA as a salaried employee among the highest-paid 10 percent of employees at the work site as defined previously. The law requires that the determination of which employees are the highest paid is calculated by taking the employee's year-to-date earnings (base salary, premium pay, incentive pay, and bonuses) and dividing the total earnings by the number of weeks worked. Whether an employee meets the definition of a key employee is to be determined at the time leave is requested. The employee must be advised of this status, either in person or by certified mail, as soon as possible. The employer must also explain why restoring the employee's job will cause substantial and grievous economic injury.

If the employee decides to take the leave after being informed of the implications of key employee status, the employee may still request reinstatement upon return to work. The employer must review the circumstances again and, if substantial and grievous economic injury would still occur under the circumstances at that time, notify the employee in writing, in person, or by certified mail that restoration is denied.

Key employees continue to be protected by the FMLA unless they notify their employer that they will not return to work, or until the employer denies reinstatement at the end of the leave.

Employee Notice Requirement

One FMLA requirement that caused difficulty for employers was an interpretation of previous rules that employees had up to two full days after an FMLA-qualifying event occurred to notify their employers of the need for FMLA leave. This made it difficult for employers to meet production schedules and ensure necessary coverage of critical work needs.

The 2008 final rules eliminated this language and clarified the timing of employee notices for two situations: foreseeable and unforeseeable leaves. In either case, employees must provide verbal notice so that the employer is aware of the need for FMLA-qualified leave, the expected timing and length of the leave, and information about the medical condition described in the upcoming section, "Reasons for FMLA Leave." Employees are not required to specifically request FMLA leave or mention FMLA for the first occurrence of a qualified event, but they are required to answer reasonable questions about the need for leave so that employers can determine whether the leave is qualified under the FMLA.

Foreseeable Leave

When the need for leave is foreseeable, FMLA rules require employees to notify their employers at least 30 days prior to the anticipated start date of leaves such as for the birth of a child, adoption, placement of a foster child, or planned medical treatment for a serious health condition. If the circumstances surrounding the planned leave change (such as a child is born earlier than expected), notice must be given as soon as practicable. This means as soon as both practical and possible, on the same day or the next business day. In these circumstances, a family member or someone else representing the employee may provide notice.

If the leave is foreseeable more than 30 days in advance and an employee fails to provide notice at least 30 days in advance without a reasonable excuse for delaying, the employer may delay FMLA coverage until 30 days after the date the employee provided notice.

If the need for FMLA leave is foreseeable less than 30 days in advance and the employee fails to notify the employer as soon as practicable, the employer may delay FMLA coverage of the leave. The amount of delay depends upon the circumstances of each leave request, and is evaluated on a case-by-case basis. Generally, the employer may delay the start of FMLA leave by the amount of delay in notice by the employee.

Unforeseeable Leave

At times, employees may be unable to notify their employers of the need for FMLA leave in advance. In these circumstances, the 2008 change to FMLA rules requires employees to provide notice in accordance with the usual and customary practice for calling in an absence unless unusual circumstances prevent the employee from doing so. An employee's representative, such as a spouse or another responsible person, may provide the notice if the employee is unable to do so. In emergencies when employees are unable to contact employers, they are permitted to supply the notice when they are able to use a telephone.

In order for employees to provide notice in accordance with the regulations, they must be aware of their responsibility to do so. The FMLA provides that proper posting of FMLA notice requirements by employers satisfies this requirement. Employers may waive FMLA notice requirements or their own rules on notice for employee leaves of absence at their discretion. In the absence of unusual circumstances, employers may choose not to waive their internal notice rules for employees who fail to follow those rules when requesting FMLA leaves, as long as those actions are consistent with practices regarding other leave requests. This is acceptable under the regulations as long as the actions do not discriminate against employees taking FMLA leave or violate the FMLA requirements described earlier.

Reasons for FMLA Leave

FMLA presents covered employers with a list of circumstances under which FMLA leave must be provided if requested by an eligible employee. Passage of the 2008

NDAA added care for military personnel and their families in some circumstances to existing circumstances that qualify for leave:

- *The birth of a child and caring for the infant.* FMLA leave is available to both fathers and mothers; however, if both parents work for the same employer, the combined total of the leave may not exceed the 12-week total. In addition, the leave must be completed within 12 months of the child's birth.
- *Placement of an adopted or foster child with the employee.* The same conditions that apply to the birth of a child apply here as well; in this case, the leave must be completed within 12 months of the child's placement.
- *To provide care for the employee's spouse, son, daughter, or parent with a serious health condition.* For purposes of FMLA leave, a spouse must be recognized as such by the state in which the employee resides.

A parent can be the biological parent of the employee or one who has legal standing in loco parentis, a Latin term that means "in place of the parent" and applies to those who care for a child on a daily basis. In loco parentis does not require either a biological or a legal relationship.

A son or daughter may be a biological child, adopted or foster child, stepchild, legal ward, or the child of someone acting in loco parentis. A child must also be younger than 18 years of age or, if older than 18, unable to care for him- or herself because of a physical or mental disability. Under the FMLA, persons who are in loco parentis include those with day-to-day responsibilities to care for or financially support a child. Courts have indicated some factors to be considered in determining in loco parentis status:

- The age of the child
- The degree to which the child is dependent on the person
- The amount of financial support, if any, provided
- The extent to which duties commonly associated with parenthood are exercised

In a 2015 amendment to the definition of spouse, eligible employees in legal same-sex marriages are able to take FMLA leave to care for their spouse or family member, regardless of where they live. The 2015 change means that eligible employees, regardless of where they live, will be able to take:

- FMLA leave to care for their lawfully married same-sex spouse with a serious health condition.
- Qualifying exigency leave due to their lawfully married same-sex spouse's covered military service, or
- Military caregiver leave for their lawfully married same-sex spouse.
- FMLA leave to care for their stepchild (child of employee's same-sex spouse) regardless of whether the in loco parentis requirement of providing day-to-day care or financial support for the child is met.

- FMLA leave to care for a stepparent who is a same-sex spouse of the employee's parent, regardless of whether the stepparent ever stood in loco parentis to the employee.

Employers may require those employees requesting FMLA leave to provide reasonable documentation to support the family relationship with the person for whom they will be providing care.

Employees may qualify for FMLA leave for their own serious health condition, defined as an illness, injury, impairment, or a physical or mental condition that requires the following:

- Inpatient care or subsequent treatment related to inpatient care.
- Continuing treatment by a health care provider because of a period of incapacity of more than three consecutive calendar days. *Incapacity* refers to an inability to work, attend school, or perform other daily activities as a result of the condition.
- Incapacity because of pregnancy or prenatal care.
- Treatment for a serious, chronic health condition.

FMLA time is available to employees who need to provide care for a covered service member with a serious injury or illness sustained while on active duty. In this situation, family members are eligible to take up to 26 weeks of leave in a 12-month period.

Additionally, FMLA-protected time is available to eligible employees for qualifying exigencies for families of members of the National Guard and Reserves. Qualifying exigencies include the following:

- Short-notice deployments
- Military events and related activities
- Child care and school activities
- Financial and legal arrangements
- Counseling
- Rest and recuperation
- Postdeployment activities
- Leave for other related purposes when agreed to by the employee and employer

Medical Certification Process

FMLA regulations allow employers to require medical certifications to verify requests for any qualified leave as long as the employee is notified of the requirements. The DOL provides the following forms for this purpose:

- WH-380-E (for employee's serious health condition)
- WH-380-F (for family member's serious health condition)

- WH-384 (for exigency leave for military families)
- WH-385 (for serious injury or illness to covered service member)

Employers should request initial certification within five business days of the employee's leave request. Additional certifications may be required at a later date to verify that the leave continues to be appropriate. Employers must provide at least 15 calendar days for the employee to submit the certification, but may allow more time.

FMLA regulations require employees to provide "complete and sufficient" certification for the employer. If the certification does not meet the complete and sufficient standard, employers may request, in writing, the additional information needed to comply. A certification is not considered complete and sufficient if one or more of the entries on the form are not completed or if the information is vague, ambiguous, or nonresponsive. Employees must be allowed a minimum of seven days to return the form with the additional information. When employers request the certification or additional information, they must advise employees of the consequences for failing to provide adequate certification of the serious illness or injury. If employees do not return the certification or they fail to provide a complete and sufficient certification upon notice of deficiencies in what was submitted, FMLA regulations allow employers to deny the FMLA leave.

Employers are not required to use the DOL forms, but may only request information that is directly related to the serious health condition necessitating the leave, including the following:

- Contact information for the health care provider.
- Approximate date the serious health condition began and an estimate of how long it will last.
- A description of the medical facts about the health condition, such as symptoms, diagnosis, hospitalization, doctor visits, prescribed medication, treatment referrals, or continuing treatments.
- For employees with serious health conditions, the certification must establish the inability to perform essential job functions, describe work restrictions, and indicate the length of the inability to perform job functions.
- For family members with serious health conditions, the certification must establish that the patient requires care, how often, and how long care will be necessary.
- Information that confirms the medical necessity for reduced or intermittent leave with estimated dates and length of treatment.

FMLA leave certifications may be complicated when workers' compensation, ADA, or employer-provided paid leave programs are used concurrently. FMLA regulations address certifications under these circumstances as follows:

- When FMLA runs concurrently with a workers' compensation leave, employers are prohibited from collecting information for workers' compensation purposes that exceeds what is allowed for FMLA purposes.

- Employers may require additional information in accordance with a paid leave or disability program, but must advise employees that the additional information is required in conjunction with the paid-leave plan, not with the FMLA leave. Whatever information is collected may be used to evaluate continuation of the FMLA leave. Failure to provide the additional information does not affect continuation of the FMLA leave.
- When FMLA leave runs concurrently with ADA, employers may follow ADA procedures for collecting information. This information may be used to evaluate the claim for FMLA-protected leave.

Employees are responsible for providing their own medical certifications. If they choose to do so, they may provide employers with an authorization or release to obtain information directly from their health care providers, but employers may not require them to do so.

Types of FMLA Leave

FMLA provides for three types of leave: continuous, reduced leave, and intermittent. A continuous FMLA leave is one in which the employee is absent from work for an extended period of time. A reduced FMLA leave schedule is one in which the employee's regular work schedule is reduced for a period of time. This can mean a reduction in the hours worked each day or in the number of days worked during the week. An intermittent FMLA leave is one in which the employee is absent from work for multiple periods of time because of a single illness or injury. When utilizing intermittent leave, employees must make an effort to schedule the leave to avoid disruption of regular business operations. In addition, the employer may assign an employee requesting intermittent leave to a different position with equivalent pay and benefits in order to meet the employee's needs.

Calculating the FMLA Year

FMLA provides four possible methods for employers to use in calculating the FMLA year, the 12-month period during which employees may use the 12 weeks of leave. An FMLA year can be calculated as any of the following:

- The calendar year
- Any fixed 12-month period (such as the fiscal year or anniversary date)
- The 12-month period beginning when an FMLA leave begins
- A rolling 12-month period that is measured back from the date FMLA is used by an employee

Although the most difficult to administer, for many employers the rolling 12-month period is best. Other methods are more open to abuse of FMLA by some employees, resulting in the use of 24 weeks of leave by bridging two 12-month periods, allowing an employee to be on continuous FMLA leave for 24 weeks.

If an employer does not have a stated policy, the FMLA year must be calculated in the way that provides the most benefit to employees. Whichever method is selected, it must be used to calculate FMLA for all employees. Employers that decide to change the way they calculate the FMLA year must provide written notice to employees 60 days in advance of the change and obtain written acknowledgment of the change.

Tracking Reduced and Intermittent FMLA Leave

Although keeping track of the amount of FMLA used for a continuous leave is fairly straightforward, ensuring that accurate records of reduced and intermittent FMLA records are maintained can be a bit more difficult. In either case, only the amount of leave used may be deducted from the 12 weeks available to the employee. For example, an employee whose regular work schedule of 40 hours per week is reduced to 20 hours per week would be charged one-half week FMLA leave for each week that the employee works the reduced schedule.

For intermittent leave, employers may charge for leave in increments of not less than one hour. Employees should provide at least two days' notice of the need to utilize the intermittent leave whenever possible.

Ending FMLA Leave

FMLA leave ends when the employee has used the full 12 weeks of leave, the serious illness of the employee or family member ends, or, in some cases, when the family member or the employee dies. When one of these three circumstances occurs (other than the employee's own death), the employee may return to the same or an equivalent position with no loss of benefits. If the employee wants to continue the leave at that point, the company is under no obligation to grant it, unless there is a company policy in place to provide a longer leave.

Employers may require employees returning from FMLA leaves to provide a fitness-for-duty certification from their health care providers, attesting to their ability to return to work. If they choose to do so, employers may require the fitness-for-duty report to specify the employee's ability to perform the essential functions of the job. Employers that choose this type of certification must provide a job description or list of the employee's essential job functions with the designation notice provided to the employee. Similarly to medical certifications, employers may contact health care providers to clarify and authenticate information contained in the fitness-for-duty certificate, but may not request information unrelated to the serious health condition that is the reason for the FMLA leave. Employees may be required to provide the fitness-for-duty certification prior to returning to work. Employees who neither provide the certificate nor request an extension of the leave are no longer entitled to reinstatement.

FMLA Implications for Employers

HR professionals need to ensure that supervisors and managers throughout their organizations are aware of the requirements for FMLA leaves and the consequences for noncompliance. FMLA requirements are complex and confusing, particularly when used in conjunction with workers' compensation or the ADA, and managers of other functional areas may not be aware of their obligations for FMLA requests.

There are some things employers can do to ensure that they comply with FMLA requirements. To start, review current leave practices to ensure that they comply with FMLA requirements and any state laws with more stringent requirements. FMLA leave policies should be included in the employee handbook; new hires must be advised of their rights to take leave under the Act. It is important for HR professionals to work with supervisors and managers throughout the organization to ensure that they understand the implications for situations that may be subject to FMLA regulations and encourage them to talk to HR about potential FMLA leave situations. HR needs to take an active role in educating the management team about the interaction of FMLA, ADA, and workers' compensation requirements. Before an FMLA situation occurs, a documentation procedure and policy should be developed, and HR should take an active role in ensuring that all leaves comply with established procedures to avoid possible claims of discriminatory practices. When workers' compensation and FMLA leaves occur simultaneously, make sure to advise the employee that the leaves run concurrently.

Foreign Corrupt Practices Act of 1977

The Foreign Corrupt Practices Act (FCPA) of 1977 made it unlawful for certain classes of people and entities to make payments to foreign government officials to assist in obtaining or retaining business. Made up of antibribery provisions, the FCPA prohibits people and entities from making any:

> offer, payment, promise to pay, or authorization of the payment of money or anything of value to any person, while knowing that all or a portion of such money or thing of value will be offered, given or promised, directly or indirectly, to a foreign official to influence the foreign official in his or her official capacity, induce the foreign official to do or omit to do an act in violation of his or her lawful duty, or

to secure any improper advantage in order to assist in obtaining or retaining business for or with, or directing business to, any person.

In 1988, amendments applied the antibribery provisions to foreign persons, prohibiting them from engaging in any of these activities within the United States.

The FCPA requires companies whose securities are listed in the United States to keep accurate records and maintain accounting controls to ensure that the records accurately and fairly represent corporate financial transactions.

Genetic Information Nondiscrimination Act of 2008 (GINA)

When research into the use of human genomic information made it possible to identify genetic predisposition to particular diseases, many people became uncomfortable with the idea of information so personal being made available to insurance companies or employers that could use it for discriminatory purposes. For more than 10 years, Congress worked on legislation that would prevent that from happening. President George W. Bush signed the resulting legislation, the Genetic Information Nondiscrimination Act (GINA), into law in May 2008.

GINA prohibits employers from unlawfully discriminating against employees or their family members in any of the terms or conditions of employment included in Title VII. The Act defines genetic information as the results of genetic tests for employees and their family members or as information about genetic diseases or disorders revealed through genetic testing.

The Act makes it unlawful for employers to request, require, or purchase genetic information but does not penalize them for inadvertently obtaining the information. GINA allows employers to obtain the information for wellness or health programs they offer when the employee authorizes access to the information in writing. In those cases, the information obtained through genetic testing may be provided only to health care professionals or board-certified genetic counselors providing services to employees. This information may be provided to employers only in aggregate form that does not identify specific employees.

Employers may request the information as required by the Family and Medical Leave Act (FMLA) or similar state laws but may use it only as required by those laws. Employers can also use genetic information if federal or state laws require genetic monitoring of biological effects from toxic substances in the workplace, but only if the employee receives written notice and provides informed, written consent to the monitoring and the monitoring complies with federal and state laws. Any test results may be provided to employers only in aggregate form without identifying individual information.

The Department of Labor (DOL) issued a request for comments on the implementation of GINA prior to beginning the rule-making process. The submission period ended in December 2008, and the DOL began evaluating regulatory needs with the Department of Health and Human Services and the Treasury Department since aspects of the law impact agencies in those departments as well.

Glass Ceiling Act of 1991

In 1991, Senator Robert Dole introduced legislation known as the Glass Ceiling Act, which was eventually signed into law as an amendment to Title II of the Civil Rights Act of 1991. An article in the *Wall Street Journal* in 1986 had coined the term *glass ceiling* to describe the limitations faced by women and minorities when it came to advancing into the senior ranks of corporate management. The Act established a commission whose purpose was to determine whether a glass ceiling existed and, if it did, to identify the barriers to placing more women and minorities in senior management positions. The commission found that although CEOs understood the need to include women and minorities in the ranks of senior management, this belief was not shared at all levels in the organization. The study went on to identify three barriers that prevented women and minorities from advancing to senior levels: societal, internal structural, and government barriers.

Societal Barriers

Societal barriers result from limited access to educational opportunities and biases related to gender, race, and ethnicity.

Internal Structural Barriers

Internal structural barriers encompass a wide range of corporate practices and shortcomings over which management has some control, including outreach and recruiting programs that do not try to find qualified women and minorities, as well as organizational cultures that exclude women and minorities from participation in activities that will lead to advancement, such as mentoring, management training, or career development assignments.

Governmental Barriers

Governmental barriers are related to inconsistent enforcement of equal opportunity legislation and poor collection and dissemination of statistics that illustrate the problem.

The commission also studied organizations that have successfully integrated glass ceiling initiatives into their operations and found some common traits that can be adopted by other organizations. Successful initiatives begin with full support of the CEO, who ensures that the initiative becomes part of strategic planning in the organization and holds management accountable for achieving goals by tracking and reporting on progress. These comprehensive programs do not exclude white men but do include a diverse workforce population. Organizations implementing programs to increase diversity benefit from improved productivity and bottom-line results for shareholders.

As a result of the study, the EEOC conducts glass ceiling audits to monitor the progress that organizations make toward including women and minorities at all levels.

Illegal Immigration Reform and Immigrant Responsibility Act of 1996 (IIRIRA)

The Illegal Immigration Reform and Immigrant Responsibility Act of 1996 reduced the number and types of documents allowable to prove identity, employment eligibility, or both in the hiring process, and established pilot programs for verification of employment eligibility. It also allowed for sanctions against employers who failed to comply with the hiring requirements.

Immigration Reform and Control Act of 1986 (IRCA)

The Immigration Reform and Control Act (IRCA) was enacted in 1986 to address illegal immigration into the United States. The law applied to businesses with four or more employees and made it illegal to knowingly hire or continue to employ individuals who were not legally authorized to work in the United States. Unfair immigration-related employment practices were defined as discrimination on the basis of national origin or citizenship status.

Employers were required to complete Form I-9 for all new hires within the first three days of employment and to review documents provided by the employee that establish identity or employment authorization or both from lists of acceptable documents on the Form I-9. IRCA requires employers to maintain I-9 files for three years from the date of hire or one year after the date of termination, whichever is later, and allows, but does not require, employers to copy documents presented for employment eligibility for purposes of complying with these requirements. The Act also provides that employers complying in good faith with these requirements have an affirmative defense to inadvertently hiring an unauthorized alien. Substantial fines for violations of both the hiring and record-

Table A.5   IRCA Fines

Violation	Amount of Fine
First	Not less than $375 or more than $3,200 for each unauthorized employee
Second	Not less than $3,200 or more than $6,500 for each unauthorized employee
Third	Not less than $4,300 or more than $16,000 for each unauthorized employee

keeping requirements were provided in the law. Failure to maintain acceptable Form I-9 records is subject to fines of not less than $110 (per United States Citizen and Immigration Services [USCIS]) or more than $1,100 for each employee without a completed form available upon request to an authorized agent of the USCIS. In addition for penalties assessed for missing or incomplete I-9 forms, IRCA established fines for unauthorized employees. Table A.5 outlines the fines for hiring violations under IRCA.

In addition to the fines listed, employers that knowingly hire unauthorized workers are subject to fines of $3,200 per employee and/or six months' imprisonment.

Employers are required to store I-9 forms on paper, on microfilm or microfiche, or on PDF files or other electronic formats, provided they meet the obligations for security and access upon demand.

E-Verify

E-Verify is a free service offered through the United States Citizen and Immigration Services (USCIS). It is a tool that helps employers comply with IRCA's requirement that employers must verify the identity and employment eligibility of new employees. Accessed through the Internet, the employer inputs basic information gleaned from the Form I-9 and receives a nearly instant "employment authorized" or "tentative nonconfirmation" (TNC) reply from the website. The employer then prints the results. A TNC result will give the employee more information about the mismatch and a statement of his or her rights and responsibilities under the law. It is important to note that an employer may not terminate an employee for the initial TNC; it is only when a final nonconfirmation is received that an employer may terminate under E-Verify.

To get started in the program, an employer must first enroll the company, distribute a memorandum of understanding (MOU), and commit to using E-Verify for every new employee at the affected hiring site. Under federal law, the use of E-Verify may be designated to certain locations, although this may be restricted under some state laws.

Table A.6 Employment Visas

Visa	Classification
	Visas for Temporary Workers
H-1B	Specialty occupations, DOD workers, fashion models
H-1C	Nurses going to work for up to three years in health professional shortage areas
H-2A	Temporary agricultural workers
H-2B	Temporary workers: skilled and unskilled, nonagricultural
H-3	Trainees
J-1	Visas for exchange visitors
	Visas for Intracompany Transfers
L-1A	Executive, managerial
L-1B	Specialized knowledge
L-2	Spouse or child of L-1
	Visas for Workers with Extraordinary Abilities
O-1	Extraordinary ability in sciences, arts, education, business, or athletics
	Visas for Athletes and Entertainers
P-1	Individual or team athletes
P-1	Entertainment groups
P-2	Artists and entertainers in reciprocal exchange programs
P-3	Artists and entertainers in culturally unique programs
	Visas for Religious Workers
R-1	Religious workers
	Visas for NAFTA Workers
TN	Trade visas for Canadians and Mexicans

Amendments to IRCA: Immigration Act of 1990

The Immigration Act of 1990 made several changes to IRCA, including adding the requirement that a prevailing wage be paid to H-1B immigrants to ensure that U.S. citizens did not lose jobs to lower-paid immigrant workers. The Act also restricted to 65,000 annually the number of immigrants allowed under the H-1B category and created additional categories for employment visas, as shown in Table A.6.

In 2016, several changes related to employees on work visas were made. Effective January 2017, they allowed certain high-skilled individuals in the United States with E-3, H-1B, H-1B1, L-1, or O-1 nonimmigrant status, including any applicable grace period, to apply for employment authorization for a limited period if:

- They are the principal beneficiaries of an approved Form I-140 petition,
- An immigrant visa is not authorized for issuance for their priority date, and
- They can demonstrate that compelling circumstances exist that justify DHS issuing an employment authorization document in its discretion. Such

employment authorization may be renewed in only limited circumstances and only in one-year increments.

- Clarified various policies and procedures related to the adjudication of H-1B petitions, including, among other things, providing H-1B status beyond the six-year authorized period of admission, determining cap exemptions and counting workers under the H-1B cap, H-1B portability, licensure requirements, and protections for whistle-blowers.
- Established two grace periods of up to 10 days for individuals in the E-1, E-2, E-3, L-1, and TN nonimmigrant classifications to provide a reasonable amount of time for these individuals to prepare to begin employment in the country, to depart the United States, or to take other actions to extend, change, or otherwise maintain lawful status.
- Established a grace period of up to 60 consecutive days during each authorized validity period for certain highly skilled nonimmigrant workers when their employment ends before the end of their authorized validity period, so they may more readily pursue new employment and an extension of their nonimmigrant status.
- Automatically extend the employment authorization and validity of Employment Authorization Documents (EADs or Form I-766s) for certain individuals who apply on time to renew their EADs.

For more information, visit the Working in the United States page found at: https://www.uscis.gov/working-united-states/working-us.

International Labour Organization (ILO)

The International Labour Organization (*ILO*) was established in 1919 to address working conditions and living standards in all countries. It has a tripartite structure comprised of member states' government, employers, and workers. The ILO currently has 185 member countries that agree to the labor standard development outcomes of *ILO conventions* and recommendations. Conventions are legally binding directives, whereas recommendations are nonbinding guidelines.

In 2000, the ILO adopted the Declaration of Fundamental Principles and Rights at Work, which includes the commitment by businesses to support, respect, and protect international human rights; the recognition of worker rights to organize and collectively bargain; to abolish child labor; and to eliminate unlawful discrimination.

ILO

International Labour Organization

A department of the United Nations that deals with human and labor rights

ILO Conventions

Standards of the International Labour Organization

International standards for employers and employees that become international law when a certain number of governments have adopted them

International Trade Organizations

For many reasons, some countries have found it to be mutually beneficial to enter into trade agreements. These agreements clarify expectations and establish rules that impact tariffs, employment visas, and employee rights between blocs of trading countries. Though not without controversy, the most prominent of these agreements are reviewed next.

European Union (EU)

The European Union is the world's largest international trading bloc, formed of a common market around which tariffs are reduced and free trade is established. It is designed to clarify the rules of trade, people movement (immigration), and social rights between member countries. Examples include standardized taxes and the rights of most service providers to practice in all member countries. Nineteen of the member countries use the euro as their form of currency.

The EU has both social and political influence over HR practices. The Social Charter of the EU was first adopted in 1989, establishing the 12 fundamental rights of workers. Since their passage, the EU has been working to translate the rights into specific directives to be observed by member countries. Various treaties have been adopted to reinforce the fundamental rights, including employee rights to data protection, the rights of asylum, equality under the law, nondiscriminatory treatment, protection against unfair dismissal, and access to social security. These directives in some form or another apply to all organizations, both local and foreign owned.

The EU currently has 28 (soon to be 27) member states: Austria, Belgium, Bulgaria, Croatia, Cyprus, Czech Republic, Denmark, Estonia, Finland, France, Germany, Greece, Hungary, Ireland, Italy, Latvia, Lithuania, Luxembourg, Malta, Netherlands, Poland, Portugal, Romania, Slovakia, Slovenia, Spain, Sweden, and the United Kingdom.

The Schengen area is the geographic locations where legal residents may move freely between member countries without special visas. Ireland and the United Kingdom have declined to participate.

In 2016, the United Kingdom voted to leave the European Union. Commonly referred to as Brexit, it is scheduled (as of this publication) to be completed sometime in 2019. Depending on the final terms of the separation, there may be an impact on work visas and permits for employees on assignment in neighboring countries.

Mercosur

Mercosur is a Southern trading bloc made up of four countries: Argentina, Brazil, Paraguay, and Uruguay. Venezuela was suspended in 2016 for failing to incorporate trade and human rights elements into its laws; also in 2016, Bolivia was in the final stages of becoming a member. Chile, Colombia, Ecuador, Guyana, Peru, and Suriname are considered associate members. Founded in 1991, Mercosur aims to form a common market, allowing for a common external tariff and free movement of goods, services, and people across member nations. A Common Market Council makes decisions, and a Trade Commission deals with tariffs and foreign affairs. The Economic and Social Consultative Forum was established in 1994 to serve in an advisory role to the Trade Commission about labor and social issues. One major goal of Mercosur is to establish a trade agreement with the European Union.

North American Free Trade Agreement (NAFTA)

Formed in 1994 as a trade agreement between the United States, Canada, and Mexico, the North American Free Trade Agreement (NAFTA) is aimed at promoting free trade and closer economic ties between the three participating members. In response to worries from labor unions, the North American Agreement on Labor Cooperation (NAALC) was included to provide problem-solving mechanisms to address the living and working conditions of workers. The NAALC agreement established national administrative offices (NAOs) in each of the countries to implement the Agreement and to serve as points of contact between national governments focused on improved working conditions and standards of living in each member country.

More recently, the Free Trade Area of the Americas is an agreement that has been in the process of negotiation for more than 10 years. If completed, it would expand NAFTA to include countries in South America, the Caribbean, and Central America, binding them together into a trading bloc similar to that of the European Union.

Mine Safety and Health Act of 1977 (MSHA)

The Mine Safety and Health Act of 1977 established the *Mine Safety and Health Administration* (MSHA) to ensure the safety of workers in coal and other mines. The act establishes mandatory safety and health standards for mine operators and monitors operations throughout the United States. MSHA has developed a comprehensive website (www.msha.gov/) that is a resource for miners and mine operators, providing access to information on preventing accidents, information on year-to-date fatalities, and guidance on specific mine hazards. The site also contains a link to the complete text of the Act.

Occupational Safety and Health Act of 1970 (OSHA)

For more than 100 years beginning in 1867, sporadic legislation was enacted by different states and the federal government to address specific safety concerns, usually in regard to mine safety or factory conditions, but there was no comprehensive legislation requiring employers to protect workers from injury or illness. That changed with the Occupational Safety and Health Act of 1970 (the OSH Act), a comprehensive piece of federal legislation that continues to have an impact on employers in virtually every company in America.

Although normally this law is referred to as OSHA, this Appendix talks at length about both the Act and the agency that is known by the same initials. For the sake of clarity, the law is referred to as the OSH Act throughout the discussion.

In the years prior to passage of the OSH Act, there was a growing recognition that employers were largely unwilling to take preventive steps to reduce the occurrence of injuries, illnesses, and fatalities in the workplace. On December 6, 1907, 362 miners died in an explosion at the Monongah coal mine in West Virginia—the worst mining disaster in American history. In that year alone, a total of 3,242 coal miners lost their lives. As a result, in 1910 Congress established the Bureau of Mines to investigate mining accidents.

There was a long period of time in the United States when it was cheaper for employers to fight lawsuits filed on behalf of workers killed or injured on the job than it was to implement safety programs. Because the courts rarely held employers accountable for worker injuries, many chose this approach. Employer attitudes in this regard didn't change until the shortage of skilled workers during World War II gave employees plentiful options for places to work—and they opted to work for employers that provided safe environments over those that didn't.

The tragic nature of large accidents in the railroad and mining industries captured public attention and created pressure on the federal government to take action. This led Congress to enact legislation requiring safety improvements in the coal mining and railroad industries, but these measures were specifically targeted to those industries. Little attention was paid to equally dangerous workplace safety and illness issues that didn't produce the spectacular accidents prevalent in mines or on railroads. In the late 1960s, 14,000 American workers lost their lives each year due to injuries or illnesses suffered while on the job. The federal government had been working on solutions but was mired in bureaucratic turf battles over which agency should have control of the process. The Department of Health, Education, and Welfare wanted legislation that applied only to federal contractors, and the Department of Labor (DOL), spurred by Secretary Willard Wirtz's personal interest in the subject, wanted to protect *all* American workers. After several years of this infighting, the proposal by the DOL was sent to the Congress and enacted as the Occupational Safety and Health Act of 1970. A key component of this legislation was the creation of the *Occupational Safety and Health Administration* (OSHA), which now sets safety standards for all industries. OSHA enforces those standards with the use of fines and, in the case of criminal actions, can call on the Department of Justice to file charges against offenders.

The intent of Congress, as stated in the preamble to the OSH Act, is to ensure safe and healthful working conditions for American workers. To accomplish this purpose, the Act establishes three simple duties:

1. Employers must provide every employee a place to work that is "free from recognized hazards that are causing or are likely to cause death or serious physical harm."
2. Employers must comply with all safety and health standards disseminated in accordance with the OSH Act.
3. Employees are required to comply with occupational safety and health standards, rules, and regulations that have an impact on their individual actions and behavior.

As mentioned previously, the OSH Act created OSHA and gave it the authority to develop and enforce mandatory standards applicable to all businesses engaged in interstate commerce. The definition of interstate commerce is sufficiently broad to cover most businesses, excepting only those sole proprietors without employees, family farms employing only family members, and mining operations, which are covered by the Mine Safety and Health Act (to be discussed later in this Appendix). The act encouraged OSHA to work with industry associations and safety committees to build upon standards already developed by specific industries, and it authorized enforcement action to ensure that employers comply with the standards. OSHA was charged with developing reporting procedures to track trends in workplace safety and health so that the development of preventive measures would be an ongoing process that changed with the development of new processes and technologies.

The OSH Act also created the *National Institute of Occupational Safety and Health* (NIOSH) as part of the Department of Health and Human Services. NIOSH is charged with researching and evaluating workplace hazards and recommending ways to reduce the effect of those hazards on workers. NIOSH also supports education and training in the field of occupational safety and health by developing and providing educational materials and training aids and sponsoring conferences on workplace safety and health issues.

In 2011, OSHA celebrated 40 years in the business of protecting American workers. Its focus in the coming years includes increasing enforcement of the standards through additional hiring, and making sure vulnerable workers, such as those who speak English as a second language, are heard. How this translates into the workforce remains to be seen, but we can infer from the statements several key points, discussed next.

More Inspections

With OSHA pushing for an increased budget, it stands to reason that the hiring of additional enforcement officers means more inspections and fines.

Emphasis on Safety Communication

The 2010 National Action Summit for Latino Worker Health and Safety helped to launch OSHA's Diverse Workforce Limited Proficiency Outreach program, designed to "enhance (vulnerable) workers' knowledge of their workplace rights and improve their ability to exercise those rights." Conducting training and providing material in a language all workers can understand is a logical outcome from this focus.

Reporting of Injuries

In 2016, OSHA issued a new rule prohibiting employers from discouraging workers from reporting an injury or illness, including through safety-incentive programs rewarding employees for no injuries being reported. This rule requires employers to inform employees of their right to report work-related injuries and illnesses free from retaliation, which can be satisfied by posting the already-required OSHA workplace poster. The rule also clarifies the existing implicit requirement that an employer's procedure for reporting work-related injuries and illnesses must be reasonable and not deter or discourage employees from reporting, and incorporates the existing statutory prohibition on retaliating against employees for reporting work-related injuries or illnesses. These provisions became effective.

Finally, the OSH Act encourages the states to take the lead in developing and enforcing safety and health programs for businesses within their jurisdictions, by providing grants to help states identify specific issues and develop programs for enforcement and prevention.

Employer Responsibilities

The OSH Act has three requirements, two of which pertain to employers. Not only must employers provide a workplace that is safe and healthful for employees, but they must also comply with established standards. OSHA has established other requirements for employers as required by the law:

- Employers are expected to take steps to minimize or reduce hazards, and ensure that employees have and use safe tools, equipment, and personal protective equipment (PPE) that are properly maintained.
- Employers are responsible for informing all employees about OSHA, posting the OSHA poster in a prominent location, and making employees aware of the standards that apply in the work site. If employees request a copy of a standard, the employer must provide it to them.
- Appropriate warning signs that conform to the OSHA standards for color coding, posting, or labels must be posted where needed to make employees aware of potential hazards.
- Compliance with OSHA standards also means employers must educate employees about safe operating procedures and train them to follow the procedures.
- Businesses with 11 or more employees must maintain records of all workplace injuries and illnesses and post them on Form 300A from February 1 through April 30 each year.
- Within eight hours of a fatal accident or one resulting in hospitalization for three or more employees, a report must be filed with the nearest OSHA office.
- An accident report log must be made available to employees, former employees, or employee representatives when reasonably requested.
- When employees report unsafe conditions to OSHA, the employer may not retaliate or discriminate against them.

Under a new OSHA rule effective January 1, 2017, certain employers must electronically submit injury and illness data that they are already required to record on their onsite OSHA Injury and Illness forms. Analysis of this data will be a factor used by OSHA to determine how to allocate its enforcement and compliance resources. Some of the data will also be posted to the OSHA website.

The new reporting requirements will be phased in over two years:

Establishments with 250 or more employees in industries covered by the record-keeping regulation must submit information from their 2016 Form 300A by July 1, 2017. These same employers will be required to submit information from all 2017 forms (300, 300A, and 301) by July 1, 2018. Beginning in 2019 and every year thereafter, the information must be submitted by March 2. These employers are required to submit OSHA Form 301, where prior to this new rule, they could submit either an OSHA Form 301 or other equivalent documentation such as workers' compensation records.

Establishments with 20 to 249 employees in certain high-risk industries must submit information from their 2016 Form 300A by July 1, 2017, and their 2017 Form 300A by

July 1, 2018. Beginning in 2019 and every year thereafter, the information must be submitted by March 2. A list of industries covered by this provision can be found at https://www.osha.gov/recordkeeping/NAICScodesforelectronicsubmission.html.

OSHA State Plan states must adopt requirements that are substantially identical to the requirements in this final rule within six months after publication of this final rule.

Employer Rights

Employers have some rights as well, including the right to seek advice and consultation from OSHA and to be active in industry activities involved in health and safety issues. Employers may also participate in the OSHA Standard Advisory Committee process in writing or by giving testimony at hearings. Finally, employers may contact NIOSH for information about substances used in work processes to determine whether they are toxic.

At times, employers may be unable to comply with OSHA standards because of the nature of specific operations. When this happens, they may apply to OSHA for temporary or permanent waivers to the standards along with proof that the protections developed by the organization meet or exceed those of the OSHA standards.

Employee Rights and Responsibilities

When the OSH Act was passed in 1970, employees were granted the basic right to a workplace with safe and healthful working conditions. The act intended to encourage employers and employees to collaborate in reducing workplace hazards. Employees have the responsibility to comply with all OSHA standards and with the safety and health procedures implemented by their employers. The Act gave employees the specific rights to do the following:

- Seek safety and health on the job without fear of punishment
- Know what hazards exist on the job by reviewing the OSHA standards, rules, and regulations that the employer has available at the workplace
- Be provided with the hazard-communication plan containing information about hazards in the workplace and preventive measures employees should take to avoid illness or injury, and to be trained in those measures
- Access the exposure and medical records employers are required to keep relative to safety and health issues
- Request an OSHA inspection, speak privately with the inspector, accompany the inspector during the inspection, and respond to the inspector's questions during the inspection

- Observe steps taken by the employer to monitor and measure hazardous materials in the workplace, and access records resulting from those steps
- Request information from NIOSH regarding the potential toxic effects of substances used in the workplace
- File a complaint about workplace safety or health hazards with OSHA and remain anonymous to the employer

OSHA Enforcement

OSHA's success is the result of strong enforcement of the standards it has developed. As demonstrated in the nineteenth and twentieth centuries, without the threat of financial penalty, some business owners would choose to ignore injury- and illness-prevention requirements. Construction and general industry continue to be the sources of the most frequently cited OSHA standards violations through 2011. That being the case, OSHA established fines and penalties that can be assessed against businesses when violations occur. Table A.7 describes the violation levels and associated penalties for noncompliance.

OSHA Record-Keeping Requirements

OSHA requires employers to record health and safety incidents that occur each year and to document steps they take to comply with regulations. Records of specific

Table A.7   Categories of Penalties for OSHA Violations

Violation	Description	Fine
Willful	Evidence exists of an intentional violation of the OSH Act or "plain indifference" to its requirements.	$5,000 to $70,000 per violation
Serious	Hazards with substantial probability of death or serious physical harm exist.	Up to $7,000
Other than serious	An existing hazard could have a direct and immediate effect on the safety and health of employees.	Up to $7,000
Repeat	OSHA previously issued citations for substantially similar conditions.	Up to $70,000 per violation
Failure to abate	The employer failed to abate a prior violation.	Up to $7,000 per day past the abatement date
De minimis	Violations exist but have no direct or immediate relationship to safety or health.	$0

Source: www.osha.gov/doc/outreachtraining/htmlfiles/introsha.html.

injuries and illnesses are compiled, allowing OSHA and NIOSH to identify emerging hazards for research and, if warranted, create new standards designed to reduce the possibility of similar injury or illness in the future. These records include up-to-date files for exposures to hazardous substances and related medical records, records of safety training meetings, and OSHA logs that record work-related injuries and illnesses.

As of January 1, 2002, OSHA revised the requirements for maintaining records of workplace injuries and illnesses in order to collect better information for use in prevention activities, simplify the information collection process, and make use of advances in technology. Three new forms were developed:

1. OSHA Form 300, Log of Work-Related Injuries and Illnesses
2. OSHA Form 300A, Summary of Work-Related Injuries and Illnesses
3. OSHA Form 301, Injury and Illness Incident Report

Completion of the forms doesn't constitute proof of fault on the part of either the employer or the employee and doesn't indicate that any OSHA violations have occurred. Recording an injury or illness on the OSHA forms also doesn't mean that an employee is eligible for workers' compensation benefits.

The following paragraphs cover the basic requirements for OSHA record keeping, including who should file OSHA reports, which employers are exempt from filing, and what injuries are considered work related.

Who Must Complete and File OSHA Forms?

All employers with 11 or more employees are required to complete and file the OSHA forms just discussed.

Are There Any Exemptions?

Employers with 10 or fewer employees aren't required to file the forms. In addition, OSHA has identified industries with low injury and illness rates and exempted them from filing reports. These include the retail, service, finance, insurance, and real estate industries. Unless OSHA has notified a business in writing that reports must be filed, the business is exempt from the requirement.

What Must Be Recorded?

OSHA regulations specify which employees are covered for reporting purposes. Injury or illness to any employee on the employer's payroll must be recorded, regardless of how the employee is classified: full-time or part-time, regular or temporary, hourly or salary, seasonal, and so on. Injuries to employees of temp agencies, if under the employer's direct supervision on a daily basis, must also be recorded. The owners and partners in sole proprietorships and partnerships aren't considered employees for OSHA reporting purposes.

Privacy concern cases are new protections developed by OSHA to protect employee privacy by substituting a case number for the employee name on the OSHA Form 300 log. Cases where this is appropriate include injury or illness that involved an intimate body part or resulted from a sexual assault; HIV infection, hepatitis, or tuberculosis; needle-stick injuries involving contaminated needles; and other illnesses when employees request that their names not be included on the log.

An injury or illness is generally considered to be work related if it occurred in the workplace or while performing work-related duties off-site. The basic OSHA requirement records any work-related injury or illness that causes death, days away from work, restricted or limited duty, medical treatment beyond first aid, or loss of consciousness. Diagnosis of an injury or illness by a physician or other health care professional, even if it doesn't result in one of the circumstances listed, must also be reported.

Once the employer has determined that the injury or illness is work related, the employer must determine whether this is a new case or a continuation of a previously recorded case. To a certain extent, this decision is left to the employer's common sense and best judgment. OSHA considers a new case to have occurred when an employee hasn't had a previous injury or illness that is the same as the current occurrence or when the employee has recovered completely from a previous injury or illness of the same type.

Annual Summary

At the end of each year, employers must review the OSHA Form 300 log and summarize the entries on Form 300A, which must then be certified by a company executive as correct and complete and posted, as previously mentioned, in February of the following year.

Retention

The OSHA Form 300 log and annual summary, privacy case list, and Form 301 Incident Report forms must be retained for five years following the end of the calendar year they cover.

Employee Involvement

Employers are required to provide employees and employee representatives, former employees, or a personal representative of an employee with information on how to properly report an injury or illness, and they're also required to allow employees or their representatives limited access to the records of injury and illness.

The OSHA Form 300 log must be provided to these requestors by the end of the following business day.

The OSHA Form 301 Incident Report must be provided by the end of the next business day when the employee who is the subject of the report requests a copy. When an employee representative requests copies, they must be provided within seven calendar days, and all information except that contained in the "Tell Us about the Case" section must be removed.

OSHA Assistance

OSHA provides many sources for employers and employees to obtain information about workplace health and safety issues. Chief among these is an extensive website (www.osha.gov) that provides access to the laws, regulations, and standards enforced by OSHA as well as general information on prevention. In addition to the website, OSHA publishes a number of pamphlets, brochures, and training materials that are available to employers. While OSHA exists to protect workers' safety rights, there are services such as consultation and voluntary participation programs that exist specifically to aid employers in complying with the standards.

OSHA Consultants

Educating employers and employees about workplace health and safety issues is key to preventing injuries and illnesses in the workplace. OSHA provides training programs for consultants who work with business owners in establishing effective health and safety programs. These free consultation services give employers an opportunity to learn which of the standards apply in their work site, involve employees in the safety process, and correct possible violations without a citation and penalty. Once the consultant becomes involved, the employer must abate any violations, or the consultant will refer the violation to an OSHA inspector.

The *Safety and Health Achievement Recognition Program* (SHARP) recognizes small, high-hazard employers that have requested a comprehensive OSHA consultation, corrected any violations, and developed an ongoing safety management program. To participate in the program, the business must agree to ask for additional consultations if work processes change.

Partnerships and Voluntary Programs

The Strategic Partnership Program is a means for businesses and employees to participate in solving health and safety problems with OSHA. Partnerships currently exist in 15 industries, including construction, food processing, logging, and health care, to develop solutions specific to their businesses.

The OSHA Alliance Program provides a vehicle for collaboration with employer organizations interested in promoting workplace health and safety issues. The program is open to trade and professional organizations, businesses, labor organizations, educational institutions, and government agencies, among others.

The Voluntary Protection Program (VPP) is open to employers with tough, well-established safety programs. VPP participants must meet OSHA criteria for the program and, having done so, are removed from routine scheduled inspection lists. The program serves to motivate employees to work more safely, reducing workers' compensation costs, and to encourage employers to make further improvements to safety programs. Acceptance into the VPP is an official recognition of exemplary occupational safety and health practices.

Health and Safety Inspections

The OSH Act authorizes both OSHA and NIOSH to investigate health or safety hazards in the workplace. The majority of OSHA inspections are focused on industries with higher hazard risks based on injury and illness rates. Some inspections occur at the request of an employer or employee in a specific organization. Less than 1 percent of OSHA inspections occur as part of the agency's Enhanced Enforcement Program that monitors employers with a history of repeat or willful violations.

NIOSH inspections, known as *health hazard evaluations*, always occur in response to the request of an employer, an employee, or a government agency.

No matter which agency conducts an investigation, employees who request or participate in them are protected by the OSH Act from retaliation or adverse employment actions.

OSHA Inspections

Most OSHA inspections are conducted without notice by a compliance safety and health officer (CSHO) who has been trained on OSHA standards and how to recognize safety and health hazards in the workplace. OSHA has established a hierarchy of situations to give priority to inspection of the most dangerous workplace environments.

During an inspection, OSHA follows a distinct procedure. In advance of the inspection, the CSHO prepares by reviewing records related to any previous incidents, inspections, or employee complaints. The inspector also determines what, if any, special testing equipment will be necessary for the inspection. Upon the inspector's arrival at the work site, the inspection commences with an opening conference, proceeds to a workplace tour, and ends with a closing conference:

1. The CSHO arrives at the work site and presents credentials. If the credentials aren't presented, the employer should insist on seeing them before the inspection begins. It's critical that any employee who may be the first person approached at the work site be instructed as to who should be contacted when a CSHO arrives. Employers have the right to require the inspector to have a security clearance before entering secure areas. Any observation of trade secrets during the inspection remains confidential; CSHOs who breach this confidentiality are subject to fines and imprisonment.

2. The CSHO holds an opening conference during which the inspector explains why the site was selected, the purpose of the visit, and the scope of the inspection, and discusses the standards that apply to the work site. The CSHO requests an employee representative to accompany the CSHO on the inspection along with the management representative. If no employee accompanies the inspector on the tour, the CSHO will talk to as many employees as necessary to understand the safety and health issues in the workplace.

3. The next step is a tour of the facilities. During the tour, the inspector determines what route to take, where to look, and which employees to talk to. During this part of the inspection, the CSHO may talk privately to employees, taking care to minimize disruptions to work processes. Activities that can occur during an inspection include the following:
   - Reviewing the safety and health program
   - Examining records, including OSHA logs, records of employee exposure to toxic substances, and medical records
   - Ensuring that the OSHA workplace poster is prominently displayed
   - Evaluating compliance with OSHA standards specific to the work site
   - Pointing out unsafe working conditions to the employer and suggesting possible remedial actions

4. The inspector holds a *closing conference* where the inspector, the employer, and, if requested, the employee representative discuss the observations made and corrective actions that must be taken. At this time the employer may produce records to assist in resolving any corrective actions to be taken. The CSHO discusses any possible citations or penalties that may be issued, and the OSHA area director makes the final determination based on the inspector's report.

Should the OSHA area director determine that citations are necessary to ensure employer compliance with OSHA, the director will issue the citations and determine the penalties to be assessed according to established guidelines that consider various factors, including the size of the company. The OSHA area director also determines the seriousness of the danger(s), how many employees would be impacted, and good-faith efforts on the part of the employer to comply with the standards, among others.

During the course of an OSHA inspection, an employer may raise an affirmative defense to any violations observed by the inspector. Possible affirmative defenses include the following:

- It is an isolated case caused by unpreventable employee misconduct. This defense may apply when the employer has established, communicated, and enforced adequate work rules that were ignored by the employee.
- Compliance is impossible based on the nature of the employer's work, and there are no viable alternative means of protection.
- Compliance with the standard would cause a greater hazard to employees, and there are no alternative means of protection.

The employer has the burden to prove that an affirmative defense exists. If it is successfully proven, the OSHA area director may decide that a citation and penalty aren't warranted.

Employers have specific responsibilities and rights during and after the inspection:

- Employers are required to cooperate with the CSHO by providing records and documents requested during the inspection and by allowing employees or their representatives to accompany the inspector on the work site tour.
- Should a citation be issued during the inspection, the employer must post it at or near the work site involved, where it must remain for three working days or until the violation has been abated, whichever is longer. It goes without saying, of course, that the employer is required to abate the violation within the time frame indicated by the citation.
- Employers may file a Notice of Contest within 15 days of a citation and proposed penalty. If there will be an unavoidable delay in abating a violation because the materials, equipment, or personnel won't be available, the employer may request a temporary variance until the violation can be corrected.

Within 15 days of receipt of a citation by an employer, employees have the right to object in writing to the abatement period set by OSHA for correcting violations. Employees who have requested an inspection also have the right to be advised by OSHA of the results of the inspection.

NIOSH Evaluations

The NIOSH mandate contained in the OSH Act is to identify and evaluate potential workplace hazards and recommend actions to reduce or eliminate the effects of chemicals, biological agents, work stress, excessive noise, radiation, poor ergonomics, and other risks found in the workplace. NIOSH established the *Health Hazard Evaluation* (HHE) program to respond to concerns about these and other risks expressed by employers, employees, unions, and government agencies.

NIOSH has an established process for responding to requests for assistance:

- A written response acknowledging the request is provided within a few weeks.
- NIOSH reviews the request and, depending on the nature and severity of the hazard being described, responds in one of three ways:
  1. NIOSH may have written materials that address the concern or may refer the request to another government agency better equipped to respond. If written materials aren't available, a project officer is assigned to assess the need for further assistance.
  2. The project officer telephones the requestor to discuss the request. In some cases, the request is resolved during the call.
  3. The project office may determine that the appropriate response is a site visit.

If an on-site visit is required, NIOSH will conduct an investigation, gathering information by touring the site, meeting with management and employees, and reviewing relevant records maintained by the employer. The project office may also use other investigative procedures such as sampling devices or medical tests to gather information. During an on-site visit, employees, employee representatives, and NIOSH project officers have seven legal rights considered nonnegotiable by NIOSH:

1. NIOSH has the right to enter the workplace to conduct an HHE.
2. NIOSH has the right to access relevant information and records maintained by the employer.
3. NIOSH has the right to meet privately with management and employees for confidential interviews.
4. An employee requestor or other employee representative has the right to accompany NIOSH during the evaluation inspection. NIOSH may also request participation from other employees if necessary to complete the evaluation.
5. Employee representatives have the right to attend opening and closing conferences.
6. Employees and managers have the right to participate in the investigation by wearing sampling devices and to take part in medical tests or in the use of sampling devices.
7. The interim and final HHE reports must be made available to employees; the employer must either post the final report in the workplace for 30 days or provide NIOSH with employee names and addresses so the report can be mailed to them.

Once the information-gathering phase is complete, NIOSH analyzes the data collected during the HHE and compiles a written report that is provided to the employer, employee, and union representatives.

Many activities that occur during either an OSHA consultation or NIOSH HHE seem similar and may cause confusion about which type of assistance is appropriate

Table A.8   OSHA Consultation versus NIOSH HHE

An OSHA Consultation Is Needed to . . .	A NIOSH HHE Is Needed to . . .
Identify workplace hazards	Identify the cause of employee illness
Suggest ways to correct hazards	Evaluate the potential for hazard from exposure to unregulated chemicals or working conditions
Assist in creating an effective safety and health program	Investigate adverse health effects from permissible exposures to regulated chemicals or working conditions
Assist in reducing workers' compensation costs	Conduct medical or epidemiologic hazard investigations
Assist in improving employee morale	Investigate higher-than-expected occurrences of injury or illness
	Evaluate newly identified hazards
	Investigate the possible hazard of exposure to a combination of agents
	Evaluate the potential for hazard from exposure to unregulated chemicals or working conditions

for any given situation. Table A.8 provides guidelines for determining which agency should be involved.

Organisation for Economic Co-operation and Development (OECD): Guidelines for Multinational Enterprises (MNEs)

The mission of the Organisation for Economic Co-operation and Development (OECD) is to promote policies that will improve the economic and social well-being of people around the world. This group works with government agencies and makes recommendations to address social, economic, and corruption/fairness issues in business dealings across boundaries (geographic, social, and political), all with a focus on the well-being of global citizens. The Guidelines for Multinational Enterprises lists responsible business conduct. They provide voluntary principles and standards in the areas of employment and industrial relations, human rights, environment, information disclosure, combating bribery, consumer interests, science and technology, competition, and taxation. First adopted in 1976, the guidelines have been reviewed and updated five times since then to reflect changing conditions. The most recent update in 2011 included a human rights addition, adapted from the United Nations' Guiding Principles on Business and Human Rights. Additionally, issues such as due diligence, sustainable supply chain management practices, and provisions on Internet freedom were reinforced.

The governments committed to adhering to the principles are responsible for establishing a National Contact Point (NCP). The NCPs establish relationships with other participants, the business community, labor unions, and any other group needing implementation support of the Guidelines. Governments must commit to the following through their NCP: visibility, accessibility, transparency, and accountability. The NCPs facilitate grievances, called "specific instances," although they are not judicial bodies. The NCPs facilitate problem solving through methods of conciliation and mediation.

Additionally, OECD Watch supports nongovernmental organizations (NGOs), helping them identify and hold businesses accountable for sustainable development and the eradication of poverty through policy development, education, and interactions with businesses and unions.

Patient Protection and Affordable Care Act of 2010 (PPACA, ACA, Obamacare)

On March 23, 2010, President Barack Obama signed into law a health care reform bill that had several employer implications. In addition to requiring provision for employees of accommodation for breast-feeding, it established criteria to ensure that Americans had access to affordable health care.

It is important to note that the PPACA does not require that employers provide health care insurance. It does, however, impose penalties upon large employers who fail to provide access to affordable "minimal essential coverage" beginning in the year 2014. A large employer is defined as those who employed an average of at least 50 full-time equivalent employees during the preceding calendar year, with an employee working 30 hours a week counted as one full-time worker, and the others prorated. In 2011, the following elements became active:

- Prohibition of lifetime limits for essential health services such as ambulatory care, emergency care, and maternity/newborn care.
- Prohibition of denial of preexisting conditions for dependents under the age of 19.
- The provision of health care for otherwise qualified under the age of 26.
- Reimbursement under Flexible Spending Accounts, Health Savings Accounts, Medical Savings Accounts, and Health Reimbursement Arrangements for over-the-counter drugs is no longer allowed; reimbursement is now limited to prescription drugs or insulin.
- The value of employee health benefits must be communicated on the employee's W-2.

In 2014, the state exchanges went live and individual responsibilities, employer obligations, and Medicaid expansions took effect. It is unclear how the results of the

2016 American election may impact all or part of the PPACA, so HR will need to stay updated to ensure ongoing compliance.

On his 2017 inauguration day, newly elected President Trump signed an executive order designed to "minimize the economic burden" of key provisions of the PPACA. While still unclear on how the order will affect the status and requirements of the current law, HR practitioners will need to keep a close eye on any changes as they occur as the result of the transition of power.

Pension Protection Act of 2006 (PPA)

The main focus of the Pension Protection Act of 2006 was to require employers to fully fund their pension plans to avoid future cash shortfalls in the plans as employees retire. Beginning in 2008, companies had seven years to bring their plans into compliance; for those that didn't comply, the Act provided a penalty in the form of a 10 percent excise tax. The Act also specified funding notices that must be provided by defined benefit plans.

One of the biggest changes to pension rules made by the PPA was to allow employers to automatically enroll employees in 401(k) plans. Employees who do not want to participate must now opt out of the plan. Another change was that plan advisers may now provide investment advice to plan participants and their beneficiaries under certain conditions.

Largely as a result of the Enron scandal, the PPA included a requirement for defined contribution plans that include employer stock to provide at least three alternative investment options and allow employees to divest themselves of the employer's stock.

When the Economic Growth and Tax Relief Reconciliation Act of 2001 (EGTRRA) was enacted, Congress increased contribution limits for 401(k) plans and individual retirement accounts (IRAs) and allowed catch-up contributions for taxpayers older than 50 years of age. These changes were set to expire in 2010, but the PPA made them permanent. Employees older than age 50 will be able to make 401(k) catch-up contributions to retirement funds. For 2009, the maximum contribution is $5,500; this amount may be adjusted for inflation in multiples of $500 each year.

Privacy Act of 1974

The Privacy Act of 1974 was an attempt by Congress to regulate the amount and type of information collected by federal agencies and the methods by which it was stored in an effort to protect the personal privacy of individuals about whom the information had been collected. The Act requires written authorization from an individual prior to releasing information to another person. The Act does not currently apply to private employers.

First, the Act provides individuals with the right to know what kind of information is being collected about them, how it is used and maintained, and whether it is disseminated. The Act prevents this information from being used for purposes other than that for which it was collected, and it allows individuals to obtain copies of the information, review it, and request amendments to inaccurate information. The Act requires the government to ensure that information collected is not misused. Except under specific circumstances covered by the Privacy Act, such as law enforcement or national security needs, the information collected by one agency must not be shared with another. Damages for violation of these requirements may be sought in federal district court and, if found by the judge to be warranted, are subject to reimbursement of attorney's fees and litigation costs, as well as a fine for actual damages incurred by the individual of up to $1,000 paid by the federal government.

Privacy Shield and Safe Harbor Frameworks

In 1998, the European Union prohibited the transfer of sensitive data to countries that do not meet the standard of "adequacy" for privacy protection. Because the United States and the European Union had different approaches to protecting individual privacy, a framework was adopted for evaluation and guidance. Organizations would need to become a member in the U.S.-EU Safe Harbor Program. In July 2016, the U.S.-EU Safe Harbor Program was replaced with the EU-U.S. Privacy Shield Framework. Key requirements include a privacy policy, individual rights to access their personal information, and which enforcement agency has jurisdiction. Free and accessible dispute resolution resources must also be made available. Companies in compliance with the framework must have steps in place to ensure that the integrity of the data is maintained, and must disclose or limit third-party access. Individuals must be notified of when and what type of data is being collected, and have the choice to opt out.

A similar but separate safe harbor program exists for information exchange between organizations in the United States and Switzerland, specifically providing a streamlined approach for the United States to comply with Switzerland's data protection requirements and join the U.S.-Swiss Safe Harbor Program.

While entirely voluntary, organizations self-certify to the U.S. Department of Commerce that they agree to the framework requirements in the following categories:

Notice Organizations must notify individuals what data will be collected and for what purpose, and who will use it.

Choice Individuals must be able to opt out or opt in, depending on the sensitivity and disclosure of the data.

Transfer to third parties The third party must subscribe to the safe harbor principles.

Access Individuals must have access and be able to correct or delete information about themselves.

Security Companies must take steps to protect information from loss, disclosure, and destruction.

Data integrity Organizations must take steps to ensure that information that is collected is used for its intended purpose.

Enforcement Individual complaints must be heard and investigated, with remedial procedures outlined and enforced.

Rehabilitation Act of 1973, Sections 501, 503, and 505

The Rehabilitation Act of 1973 was enacted to expand the opportunities available for persons with physical or mental disabilities. The employment clauses of the Act apply to agencies of the federal government and federal contractors with contracts of $10,000 or more during a 12-month period. Section 501 addresses employment discrimination, while Section 505 details the remedies available for those who have been subjected to unlawful employment practices. The EEOC has enforcement responsibility for Section 501. Under Section 503, individuals with disabilities who think a federal contractor has violated the requirements of the Rehabilitation Act may also file complaints with the Department of Labor through the Office of Federal Contract Compliance Programs (OFCCP).

Sarbanes-Oxley Act of 2002 (SOX)

Although the main focus of Sarbanes-Oxley Act (SOX) compliance is the reporting of financial transactions and activities, HR professionals may be called on to participate in SOX reporting requirements. SOX requires information that materially affects an organization's financial status to be reported to the Securities and Exchange Commission (SEC), in some cases immediately, when the organization becomes aware of the information. Some instances where this would apply to HR management are the following:

- Ensuring that material liabilities from pending lawsuits or settlements of employment practices claims are reported in the financial statements.

- Participating in the review and testing of internal controls for hiring, compensation, and termination practices.
- Reporting immediately any material changes to the organization's financial condition. Although in most cases this wouldn't be an HR responsibility, the settlement of a large class action lawsuit could potentially reach the threshold of a material change.

Failure to provide this information within the time frames required by SOX can result in criminal penalties, including incarceration, for employees who obstruct legal investigations into financial reporting issues. SOX also prohibits employers from retaliating against whistle-blowers who report financial conduct that they reasonably believe violates federal laws designed to protect shareholders from fraudulent activity.

Service Contract Act of 1965 (SCA)

The McNamara-O'Hara Service Contract Act of 1965 requires any federal service contractor with a contract exceeding $2,500 to pay its employees the prevailing wage and fringe benefits for the geographic area in which it operates, provide safe and sanitary working conditions, and notify employees of the minimum allowable wage for each job classification, as well as the equivalent federal employee classification and wage rate for similar jobs.

The SCA expands the requirements of the Davis-Bacon and Walsh-Healey Acts to contractors providing services to the federal government, such as garbage removal, custodial services, food and lodging, and the maintenance and operation of electronic equipment. Federal contractors already subject to the requirements of Davis-Bacon, Walsh-Healey, or laws covering other federal contracts, such as public utility services or transportation of people or freight, are exempt from the SCA.

Sexual Harassment

Title VII of the Civil Rights Act of 1964 and its subsequent amendments require employers to furnish a workplace that is free from *sexual harassment*. There are two forms of sexual harassment that must be prevented: quid pro quo and hostile work environment.

Quid pro quo is a legal term that means, in Latin, "this for that." Quid pro quo harassment, therefore, occurs when a supervisor or manager asks for sexual favors in return for some type of favorable employment action. "Sexual favors" is a broad term that covers actions ranging from unwanted touching to more explicit requests.

A *hostile work environment* has been defined by the EEOC as one in which an individual or individuals are subjected to unwelcome verbal or physical conduct "when submission to or rejection of this conduct explicitly or implicitly affects an individual's employment, unreasonably interferes with an individual's work performance, or creates an intimidating, hostile, or offensive work environment." When investigating these charges, the EEOC looks at many factors. In most cases, a single incident of inappropriate and unwelcome behavior does not rise to the level of a hostile work environment, but in some cases when the actions or behaviors are particularly offensive or intimidating, the EEOC may find that harassment has occurred. A hostile work environment can also be found to exist for victims who have been affected by unwelcome offensive conduct toward someone other than themselves.

Sexual Harassment

Inappropriate sexual advances

Unwelcome verbal, visual, or physical conduct of a sexual nature that is offensive or inappropriate

Hostile Work Environment Harassment

Harassment from coworkers rather than supervisors

A situation in which an employee's coworkers create an uncomfortable work environment, often through inappropriate sexual behavior or discrimination

---

Courts have held employers responsible for the harassing actions of their employees, whether or not the employer was aware of the harassment. Beginning in 1986, the Supreme Court issued a number of rulings to clarify employer responsibilities in the prevention of sexual harassment. The most commonly cited of these for HR purposes are *Meritor Savings Bank v. Vinson* (1986), *Harris v. Forklift Systems* (1993), and two cases decided at the same time in 1998, *Faragher v. City of Boca Raton* and *Burlington Industries v. Ellerth*.

Meritor Savings Bank v. Vinson (1986)

Mechelle Vinson applied for a job at a branch of Meritor Savings Bank in 1974 when Sidney Taylor was a vice president and manager of the branch. Taylor hired Vinson, who worked at the branch for four years, starting as a teller trainee and working her way up to assistant branch manager, based on her performance in the jobs she held. Once she passed her probationary period as a trainee, Vinson claims that Taylor began to harass her, requesting that they go to a motel to have sexual relations. Although Vinson refused Taylor's advances initially, she gave in eventually because she believed she would lose her job if she did not. Vinson claims that Taylor's harassment escalated to the point that she was fondled in front of other employees and expected to engage in sexual relations at the branch both during and after work. In September 1978, Vinson took an indefinite medical leave, and the bank terminated her in November 1978.

The Supreme Court issued its opinion in June 1986, finding that a claim of "hostile environment" sex discrimination is actionable under Title VII. The Court rejected the idea that the "mere existence of a grievance procedure and a policy against discrimination" is enough to protect an employer from the acts of its supervisors. The opinion indicated that a policy designed to encourage victims of harassment to come forward would provide greater protection.

Harris v. Forklift Systems (1993)

In April 1985, Teresa Harris was employed by Forklift Systems, Inc., as a manager, reporting to the company president, Charles Hardy. Hardy insulted Harris frequently in front of customers and other employees and made sexually suggestive remarks. When Harris complained in August 1987, Hardy apologized and said he would stop the conduct. But in September of that year, Hardy once again began the verbal harassment, and Harris quit on October 1.

Harris then filed a lawsuit against Forklift, claiming that Hardy had created a hostile work environment on the basis of her gender. The District Court found that although Hardy's conduct was offensive, it did not meet the required standard of severity to seriously affect her psychological well-being.

The Supreme Court agreed to hear the case in order to resolve conflicts in the lower courts on what conduct was actionable for a hostile work environment. The Court found that the appropriate standard is one that falls between that which is merely offensive and that which results in tangible psychological injury. Although this is not a precise guideline, it does allow courts to take into consideration a number of factors about the work environment, the frequency and severity of the conduct, the level of threat or humiliation that the victim is subjected to, and whether the conduct interferes unreasonably with performance of the employee's job.

Faragher v. City of Boca Raton (1998)

Beth Faragher and Nancy Ewanchew were two of about six females out of more than 40 lifeguards for the City of Boca Raton in Florida from 1985 to 1989. During their tenure, they were verbally and physically harassed by two supervisors, Bill Terry and David Silverman. They both complained to a third supervisor, Robert Gordon, about the harassment but did not file a formal complaint, and no corrective action was taken. Ewanchew resigned in 1989 and wrote to the city manager in 1990 to complain about the harassment. The city investigated and (when it found that both Terry and Silverman had acted inappropriately) reprimanded and disciplined both supervisors.

The Supreme Court found that employers are responsible for actions of those they employ and have a responsibility to control them. Going further, the Court determined that a supervisor need not make an explicit threat of an adverse tangible employment action (TEA), which the Court defined as "a significant change in employment status, such as hiring, firing, failing to promote, reassignment with significantly different responsibilities, or a decision causing a significant change in benefits" in order for harassment to be actionable. The Court determined that subordinates know that the possibility of adverse supervisory actions exists whenever requests are made, even if the adverse actions are not stated.

Burlington Industries v. Ellerth (1998)

Kimberly Ellerth worked for Burlington Industries in Chicago as a salesperson from March 1993 to May 1994. During that time, Ellerth claims that she was subjected to ongoing sexual harassment by Ted Slowick, who was not her direct supervisor but did have the power to approve or deny a TEA with regard to her employment. Although Ellerth was aware of Burlington's policy prohibiting sexual harassment during her employment, she did not complain about the harassment until after she resigned. After resigning, she filed a complaint with the EEOC and, when she received a right-to-sue letter in October 1994, filed suit against Burlington.

A key issue in this case was that of *vicarious liability* (an element of the legal concept of respondeat superior) that, in this context, means an employer may be held accountable for the harmful actions of its employees, whether or not the employer is aware of those actions. The Supreme Court decided in part that "An employer is subject to vicarious liability to a victimized employee for an actionable hostile environment created by a supervisor with immediate (or successively higher) authority over the employee."

Vicarious Liability

Responsibility for someone else's acts

A legal doctrine that makes a person liable for the negligence or crimes of another person

In 1997, the first case of same-sex harassment reached the U.S. Supreme Court. In the majority opinion issued for *Oncale v. Sundowner Offshore Services, Inc.,* Justice Antonin Scalia observed that ". . . male on male sexual harassment was assuredly not the principal evil Congress was concerned with when it enacted Title VII. But statutory prohibitions often go beyond the principal evil to cover reasonably comparable evils . . . ." A number of cases following *Oncale* resulted in substantial awards or settlements in cases of same-sex harassment. In 1998, President Bill Clinton amended an executive order to include sexual orientation as a protected class.

EEOC Guidelines for the Prevention of Sexual Harassment

The EEOC has developed detailed guidelines entitled "Enforcement Guidance: Vicarious Employer Liability for Unlawful Harassment by Supervisors" to assist employers in developing policies that clearly express the employer's prohibition against harassment and conducting investigations that meet EEOC standards.

To summarize the guidelines, employers are encouraged to develop antiharassment policies, along with complaint procedures for those who believe they have been harassed. The policy should clearly explain unacceptable conduct and reassure employees who complain that they will be protected against retaliation. The complaint process should describe multiple avenues for reporting harassment and provide assurances of confidentiality to the extent it is possible. Investigations of allegations should be prompt and impartial, and if the investigation finds that harassment did indeed occur, the policy should provide for immediate corrective action.

Uniformed Services Employment and Reemployment Rights Act of 1994 (USERRA)

Congress enacted the Uniformed Services Employment and Reemployment Rights Act (USERRA) in 1994 to protect the rights of reservists called to active duty in the armed forces. The Act provides reemployment and benefits rights and is administered through the Veterans Employment and Training Service (VETS) of the Department of Labor. USERRA applies to all public and private employers in the United States, including the federal government. The DOL issued revised rules for employers that became effective on January 18, 2006. These revisions clarified some of the requirements previously issued. Some of its stipulations are the following:

Coverage

- All employers, regardless of size, are required to comply with USERRA regulations.
- Members of all uniformed services are protected by USERRA.
- USERRA prohibits discrimination due to past, current, or future military obligations.
- In addition to service during times of war or national emergency, USERRA protects any voluntary or involuntary service such as active duty, training, boot camp, reserve weekend duty, National Guard mobilizations, and absence due to required fitness for duty examinations.

Notice Requirements

- In most circumstances, employees must give verbal or written notice to the employer that they have been called to active service. If an employee is unable to give notice, a military representative may provide the notice.
- If military necessity prevents advance notice, or if giving notice is impossible or unreasonable, employees are still protected by USERRA.
- To be eligible for reemployment rights, service members must report back to work within time frames that vary according to the length of service. Table A.9 shows the reporting time requirements established by USERRA for returning to work based on varying lengths of service.

Duration

- The employer must grant a leave of absence for up to five years, although there are several exceptions that extend coverage beyond five years.
- Types of leave protected without limits include the following:
  - Boot camp
  - Initial service period
  - Waiting for orders
  - Annual two-week mandatory training

Table A.9   USERRA Reemployment Reporting Times

Length of Service	Reporting Time
1 to 30 days *or* absence for "fitness for service" exam	The first regularly scheduled full workday that begins eight hours after the end of the service completion.
31 to 180 days	Submit application for reemployment no later than 14 days after the end of service, or on the next business day after that.
181 or more days	Submit application for reemployment no later than 90 days after the end of service or on the next business day after that.
Disability incurred or aggravated	Reporting or application deadline is extended for up to two years.

- Employees are permitted to moonlight during off-duty hours without losing reinstatement rights.
- Employees do not lose reinstatement rights if they leave their jobs to prepare for mobilization but the mobilization is canceled.

Compensation
- USERRA does not require employers to pay employees during military absences, unless the employer has an established policy of doing so.
- Employers may not require employees to apply accrued vacation pay to their military leaves, but employees may choose to do so.

Benefit Protection
- Employees on military leave are entitled to the same benefits employers provide for others on a leave of absence.
- Employees continue to accrue seniority and other benefits as though they were continuously employed.
- For leave greater than 30 days but less than 240 days in duration, the employer must offer COBRA-like health coverage upon request of the employee; for service less than 31 days, and at the employee's request, the employer must continue health coverage at the regular employee cost.
- Returning service members are entitled to participate in any rights and benefits provided to employees returning from nonmilitary leaves of absence.

Pension Protection
- Employee pension rights are protected by USERRA.
- Vesting and accrual for returning service members are treated as though there were no break in employment.
- Employer pension contributions must be the same as though the military leave did not occur.
- For defined contribution plans, service members must be given three times the period of the military leave absence (not to exceed five years) to make up contributions that were missed during the leave. Plans with an employer matching component are required to match the makeup funds.

Reinstatement
- The employer must "promptly" reinstate regular employees to positions that the employees would have earned had they remained on the job, referred to as an escalator position. The Act does not specify a definition of "promptly," since the timing will depend on the length of the leave. For example, an employee on leave for annual two-week training would be expected to be reemployed on the first workday following the end of leave. On the other hand, someone who has been serving on active duty for five years may be promptly reemployed after notice to vacate the position is given to the incumbent.
- Temporary employees do not have reinstatement rights.
- Seasonal or fixed-term contract employees are not entitled to reinstatement.

- Reemployment rights are forfeited if the employee has been discharged dishonorably or other than honorably from the service, has been expelled as a result of a court martial, or has been absent without leave (AWOL) for 90 days.

Continued Employment
- Employees returning to work from leaves of more than 30 but less than 181 days may not be discharged without cause for six months after the date of reemployment.
- Employees returning to work from leaves of 181 days or more may not be discharged without cause for one year from the date of reemployment.

Disabled Veterans

The employer must make reasonable accommodation to provide training or retraining to reemploy a returning service member disabled as a result of service; if reasonable accommodation creates an undue hardship, reemployment can be made to a position "nearest approximate" in terms of status and pay and with full seniority to which the person is entitled.

United Kingdom Bribery Act of 2010

The Bribery Act of 2010 was created to update and address bribery—both domestic and foreign—in business affairs. Offenses under the Bribery Act include offering, promising, or giving of an advantage, and requesting, agreeing to receive, or accepting of an advantage; a discrete offense of bribery of a foreign public official; and a new offense of failure by a commercial organization to prevent a bribe being paid to obtain or retain business or a business advantage. Companies must take steps to ensure that both policies and practices are in alignment with the requirements of this Act.

United States Patent Act of 1790

A patent allows inventors exclusive rights to the benefits of an invention for a defined period of time. Generally, the term of a new patent is 20 years from the date on which the application for the patent was filed in the United States or, in special cases, from the date an earlier related application was filed, subject to the payment of maintenance fees. U.S. patent grants are effective only within the United States, U.S. territories, and U.S. possessions. Patents protect an inventor's "right to exclude others from making, using, offering for sale, or selling" the invention in the United

States or "importing" the invention into the United States. Patent laws in the United States define three types of patents:

1. Design patents protect new, original, and ornamental designs of manufactured items. Design patents are limited to 14 years.
2. Utility patents protect the invention of new and useful processes, machines, manufacture or composition of matter, and new and useful improvements to the same. Utility patents are limited to 20 years.
3. Plant patents protect the invention or discovery of asexually reproduced varieties of plants for 20 years.

Wage Garnishment Law, Federal

The Federal Wage Garnishment Law is found in Title III of the Consumer Credit Protection Act (CCPA) of 1968 and applies to all employers and employees. Employers are required to withhold funds from an employee's paycheck and send the money to an entity designated in the court order or levy document.

Title III of the CCPA protects employees in three ways:

1. Prohibits employers from terminating employees whose wages are garnished for any one debt, even if the employer receives multiple garnishment orders for the same debt.
2. Sets limits on the amount that can be garnished in any single week. Currently, the weekly amount may not exceed the lesser of two figures: 25 percent of the employee's disposable earnings, or the amount by which an employee's disposable earnings are greater than 30 times the federal minimum wage (currently $7.25 an hour).
3. Defines how disposable earnings are to be calculated for garnishment withholdings.

Earnings that may be garnished include wages, salaries, bonuses, and commissions. Other income from pension plans or employer-paid disability may be subject to garnishment as well. The law does not protect employees from termination if the employer receives garnishments for more than one debt.

Walsh-Healey Public Contracts Act of 1936

The Walsh-Healey Public Contracts Act requires government contractors with contracts exceeding $10,000 (for other than construction work) to pay their employees the prevailing wage for their local area as established by the Secretary of Labor.

Worker Adjustment Retraining and Notification Act of 1988 (WARN)

The WARN Act was passed by Congress in 1988 to provide some protection for workers in the event of mass layoffs or plant closings. The Act requires that 60 days' advance notice be given to either the individual workers or their union representatives. The intent of Congress was to provide time for workers to obtain new employment or training before the loss of their jobs occurred. The WARN Act is administered by the Department of Labor and enforced through the federal courts.

Employers with 100 or more full-time employees or those with 100 or more full- and part-time employees who work in the aggregate 4,000 hours or more per week are subject to the provisions of the WARN Act. The employee count includes those who are on temporary leave or layoff with a reasonable expectation of recall.

The WARN Act established that a mass layoff occurs when either 500 employees are laid off or at least 50 employees making up 33 percent of the workforce and are laid off. A plant closing occurs when 50 or more full-time employees lose their jobs because a single facility shuts down, either permanently or temporarily. In cases where the employer staggers the workforce reduction over a period of time, care must be taken that appropriate notice is given if the total reductions within a 90-day period trigger the notice requirement.

The WARN Act also established rules on notice. For instance, notice is required to be given to all affected employees or their representatives, the chief elected official of the local government, and the state dislocated worker unit. Notice requirements vary according to which group the notices are being sent to, but they must contain specific information about the reasons for the closure, whether the action is permanent or temporary, the address of the affected business unit, the name of a company official to contact for further information, the expected date of closure or layoff, and whether bumping rights exist.

The WARN Act provides for three situations in which the 60-day notice is not required, but the burden is on the employer to show that the reasons are legitimate and not an attempt to thwart the intent of the Act:

1. The faltering company exception applies only to plant closures in situations where the company is actively seeking additional funding and has a reasonable expectation that it will be forthcoming in an amount sufficient to preclude the layoff or closure and that giving the notice would negatively affect the ability of the company to obtain the funding.
2. The unforeseeable business circumstance exception applies to plant closings and mass layoffs and occurs when circumstances take a sudden and unexpected negative turn that could not have reasonably been predicted, such as the cancellation of a major contract without previous warning.

3. The natural disaster exception applies to both plant closings and mass layoffs occurring as the result of a natural disaster, such as a flood, earthquake, or fire.

Workers' Compensation

Workers' compensation laws require employers to assume responsibility for all employee injuries, illnesses, and deaths related to employment. These laws are enacted and enforced by the individual states, and provide benefits for employees that cover medical and rehabilitation expenses, provide income replacement during periods of disability when employees are unable to work, and pay benefits to their survivors in the event of an employee's death.

The amount of compensation paid is based on actuarial tables that take into account the seriousness of the injury, whether the disability is permanent or temporary, whether it is a full or partial disability (such as the loss of an eye or hand), and the amount of income lost because of the injury. In most cases, employers fund workers' compensation obligations by purchasing coverage through private insurance companies or state-sponsored insurance funds. The premiums for workers' compensation coverage are based on a percentage of the employer's payroll in various job categories. The percentages are different and depend on previous claim activity in each category. The rate charged for a roofer, for example, is much higher than that for an office worker because of the inherent danger of the job and the number and severity of claims that result.

In some states, companies may self-fund workers' compensation programs, meaning that they pay the total costs of any injuries or illnesses when they occur instead of paying insurance premiums. These are known as nonsubscriber plans and are rare; generally, self-funded insurance plans make economic sense only for very large organizations with the financial base to support the payment of large claims when they occur.

Although increased emphasis on safety programs and training has led to a reduction in the number of nationwide workers' compensation claims filed each year, the insurance rates are increasing largely because of increased medical costs. This is most evident in California, where employers saw costs double between 2000 and 2003, but it has also led to state reform of workers' compensation programs in Florida, West Virginia, Washington, and Texas.

Implementing programs aimed at reducing the cost of workers' compensation coverage for their organizations is one way HR professionals can show a positive impact on the bottom line. Implementing safety training and injury prevention programs as discussed in Chapter 7, "Risk Management," is one way to reduce job-related injury and illness and to prevent claims. The costs of individual claims can be reduced by ensuring the availability of jobs that meet "light duty" medical requirements so that employees are able to return to work earlier, shortening the length of their leave.

Quick Reference Guide: Agencies, Court Cases, Terms, and Laws; General Record-Keeping Guidelines

Table A.10 presents information on agencies, court cases, terms, and laws, and Table A.11 provides general record-keeping guidelines.

Table A.10   Agencies, Court Cases, Terms, and Laws

Name	Description
Adverse impact	According to the Uniform Guidelines on Employee Selection Procedures, adverse impact is a substantially different rate of selection in hiring, promotion, or other employment decision, which works to the disadvantage of members of a race, sex, or ethnic group. Occurs when the selection rate (hiring, training, promotion, etc.) for protected class groups is less than four-fifths, or 80 percent, of the selection rate for the group with the highest selection rate.
Albemarle Paper v. Moody	Required that employment tests be validated; subjective supervisor rankings aren't sufficient validation; criteria must be tied to job requirements.
Automobile Workers v. Johnson Controls, Inc.	In response to a sex-based discrimination suit filed by women "capable of bearing children," the United States Supreme Court found that "decisions about the welfare of the next generation must be left to the parents who conceive, bear, support and raise them, rather than to the employers who hire those parents."
Bates v. United Parcel	Established that when employers apply an unlawful standard that bars employees protected by the ADA from an application process, the employees don't need to prove they were otherwise qualified to perform essential job functions. The employer must prove the standard is necessary to business operations.
Black Lung Benefits Act (BLBA)	Provided benefits for coal miners suffering from pneumoconiosis due to mine work.
Bureau of Labor Statistics (BLS)	An agency within the DOL that was established to study and publish statistical economic and industrial accidents data.
Burlington Northern Santa Fe Railway Co. v. White	Established that all retaliation against employees who file discrimination claims is unlawful under Title VII, even if no economic damage results.

Table A.10   Agencies, Court Cases, Terms, and Laws (*continued*)

Name	Description
Circuit City Stores v. Adams	Arbitration clauses in employment agreements are enforceable for employers engaged in interstate commerce except for transportation workers.
Citizen and Immigration Services, United States (USCIS)	A component of the Department of Homeland Security charged with overseeing lawful immigration to the United States. Individuals wishing to live or work in the United States must submit applications through the USCIS; employers must comply with Form I-9 and/or E-Verify for new hires.
Civil law	Regulations set by countries or legislative groups about the rights of people (different from common laws, which are set by judges).
Clause	A part of a document, agreement, proposal, or contract that gives more detail.
Clayton Act	Limited the use of injunctions to break strikes; exempted unions from the Sherman Antitrust Act.
Commercial diplomacy	The effort by multinational corporations to influence foreign government policy on issues such as tariffs, banking, and other financial regulations; antitrust/competition laws; workplace standards such as safety; data privacy; and corporate conduct in areas such as corruption, governance, and social responsibility.
Congressional Accountability Act (CAA)	Required all federal employment legislation passed by Congress to apply to congressional employees.
Davis v. O'Melveny & Myers	Established that arbitration clauses in employment agreements won't be enforced if they're significantly favorable to the employer and the employee doesn't have a meaningful opportunity to reject the agreement.
Department of Labor (DOL)	Charged with the administration and enforcement of U.S. labor laws.
Disability	A physical or mental condition that limits, but does not prevent, the performance of certain tasks.
Disparate impact	Occurs when protected class groups are treated differently than other groups in employment-related decisions; includes practices that are neutral on the surface but have a negative effect on protected groups (such as requiring a high school diploma in areas where minority groups have a lower graduation rate than nonminority groups).

(*continued*)

Table A.10   Agencies, Court Cases, Terms, and Laws (*continued*)

Name	Description
Due process	The way a government enforces laws; in the United States, the way a government enforces its laws to protect its citizens (e.g., guaranteeing a person a fair trial).
Energy Employees Occupational Illness Compensation Program Act (EEOICPA)	Provided compensation for employees and contractors subjected to excessive radiation during production and testing of nuclear weapons.
Energy Policy Act of 1992	Allowed employers to provide a nontaxable fringe benefit to employees engaged in qualified commuter activities such as bicycling and mass transit.
Equal employment opportunity (EEO)	U.S. laws that guarantee equal treatment and respect for all employees.
Equal Employment Opportunity Act (EEOA)	Established that complainants have the burden of proof for disparate impact; provided litigation authority for the EEOC; extended the time to file complaints.
Equal Employment Opportunity Commission (EEOC)	U.S. agency charged with investigating complaints of job discrimination based on race, color, religion, sex (including pregnancy, gender identity, and sexual orientation), national origin, disability, age (40 or older), or genetic information, and with taking action to stop the discriminatory behavior when found.
Extraterritorial laws	Laws from a multinational enterprise's home country that have application in other countries. U.S. laws with extraterritorial application include Sarbanes-Oxley, Foreign Corrupt Practices Act, Americans with Disabilities Act, Age Discrimination in Employment Act, and Title VII of the Civil Rights Act of 1964. These laws give American workers the right to sue in the United States for unlawful acts that occurred outside of the country.
Federal Employees Compensation Act (FECA)	Provided benefits similar to workers' compensation for federal employees injured on the job.
Federal Insurance Contributions Act (FICA)/ Social Security Act	Required employers and employees to pay Social Security taxes.
Federal regulations	In the United States, laws that apply in every state (as opposed to laws unique to every state).
Federal Unemployment Tax Act (FUTA)	Required employers to contribute a percentage of payroll to an unemployment insurance fund.

Table A.10   Agencies, Court Cases, Terms, and Laws (*continued*)

Name	Description
Forum shopping	Looking for a legal venue most likely to result in a favorable outcome; the practice of trying to get a trial held in a location that is most likely to produce a favorable result.
Griggs v. Duke Power	Required employers to show that job requirements are related to the job; established that lack of intention to discriminate isn't a defense against claims of discrimination.
Immigration and Nationality Act (INA)	Eliminated national origin, race, and ancestry as bars to immigration; set immigration goals for reunifying families and preference for specialized skills.
Intellectual property	Creations or inventions protected by law; an original invention or something created by the mind, which is usually protected by patents, trademarks, or copyrights.
Internal Revenue Service (IRS)	The U.S. government agency responsible for collecting taxes and enforcing tax laws.
Jespersen v. Harrah's Operating Co.	Established that a dress code requiring women to wear makeup doesn't constitute unlawful sex discrimination under Title VII.
Jurisdiction	The right and power to interpret and apply the law, often within a certain geographical region.
Labor-Management Relations Act (LMRA; Taft-Hartley)	Prohibited closed shops; restricted union shops; allowed states to pass "right to work" laws; prohibited jurisdictional strikes and secondary boycotts; allowed employers to permanently replace economic strikers; established the Federal Mediation and Conciliation Service; allowed an 80-day cooling-off period for national emergency strikes.
Labor-Management Reporting and Disclosure Act (LMRDA; Landrum-Griffin)	Controlled internal union operations; provided a bill of rights for union members; required a majority vote of members to increase dues; allowed members to sue the union; set term limits for union leaders.
Licensing	Giving permission to use, produce, or sell; a written contract in which the owner of a trademark or intellectual property gives rights to a licensee to use, produce, or sell a product or service.
Lobbying	The act of monitoring and seeking to influence new labor laws and regulations by contacting local, state, and national representatives of the U.S. government.

(*continued*)

Table A.10   Agencies, Court Cases, Terms, and Laws (*continued*)

Name	Description
Longshore and Harbor Workers' Compensation Act	Provided workers' compensation benefits for maritime workers injured on navigable waters of the United States or on piers, docks, and terminals.
Mental Health Parity Act (MHPA)	Required insurers to provide the same limits for mental health benefits that are provided for other types of health benefits.
National Labor Relations Act (NLRA; Wagner Act)	Protected the right of workers to organize and bargain collectively; identified unfair labor practices; established the National Labor Relations Board (NLRB).
Needlestick Safety and Prevention Act	Mandated record keeping for all needle-stick and sharps injuries; required employee involvement in developing safer devices.
NLRB, *Epilepsy Foundation of Northeast Ohio v.*	Extended *Weingarten* rights to nonunion employees by allowing employees to request a coworker be present during an investigatory interview that could result in disciplinary action.
NLRB: *IBM Corp.*	NLRB reversed its 2000 decision in *Epilepsy*, withdrawing *Weingarten* rights from nonunion employees.
NLRB: *M.B. Sturgis, Inc.*	Established that temporary employees may be included in the client company's bargaining unit and that consent of the employer and temp agency aren't required to bargain jointly.
NLRB v. J. Weingarten, Inc.	U.S. Supreme Court: Established that union employees have the right to request union representation during any investigatory interview that could result in disciplinary action.
Norris–La Guardia Act	Protected the right to organize; outlawed yellow-dog contracts.
Omnibus Budget Reconciliation Act (OBRA)	Revised rules for employee benefits; set the maximum deduction for executive pay at $1,000,000; mandated some benefits for medical plans.
Payne v. The Western & Atlantic Railroad Company	Defined employment at will.
Personal Responsibility and Work Opportunity Reconciliation Act	Required employers to provide information about all new or rehired employees to state agencies to enforce child support orders.
Pharakhone v. Nissan North America, Inc.	Established that employees who violate company rules while on FMLA leave may be terminated.
Phason v. Meridian Rail Corp.	Established that when an employer is close to closing a deal to sell a company, WARN Act notice

Table A.10   Agencies, Court Cases, Terms, and Laws (*continued*)

Name	Description
	requirements are triggered by the number of employees actually employed and the number laid off on the date of the layoff, even if the purchasing company hires some of the employees shortly after the layoff.
Proprietary	Relating to an owner or ownership; rights of property ownership relating to key information, materials, or methods developed by an organization.
Public Contracts Act (PCA; Walsh-Healey Act)	Required contractors to pay prevailing wage rates.
Railway Labor Act	Protected unionization rights; allowed for a 90-day cooling-off period to prevent strikes in national emergencies. Covers railroads and unions.
Repa v. Roadway Express, Inc.	Established that when an employee on FMLA leave is receiving employer-provided disability payments, the employee may not be required to use accrued sick or vacation leave during the FMLA absence.
Retirement Equity Act	Lowered the age limits on participation and vesting in pension benefits; required written spousal consent to not provide survivor benefits; restricted conditions placed on survivor benefits.
Rule of law	A political system in which the law is supreme; all citizens are subject to the laws of their country, no individual is above the law, and everyone must obey it.
Service Contract Act	Required government contractors to pay prevailing wages and benefits.
Sharia	Islamic religious law; the code of law from the Koran that regulates both civil and criminal justice as well as individual behaviors and morals.
Sherman Antitrust Act	Controlled business monopolies; allowed court injunctions to prevent restraint of trade. Used to restrict unionization efforts.
Sista v. CDC Ixis North America, Inc.	Established that employees on FMLA may be legally terminated for legitimate, nondiscriminatory reasons, including violations of company policy if the reason is unrelated to the exercise of FMLA rights.
Small Business Job Protection Act	Redefined highly compensated individuals; detailed minimum participation requirements; simplified 401(k) tests; corrected qualified plan and disclosure requirements.

(*continued*)

Table A.10   Agencies, Court Cases, Terms, and Laws (*continued*)

Name	Description
Small Business Regulatory Enforcement Fairness Act (SBREFA)	Provided that a Small Business Administration (SBA) ombudsman act as an advocate for small business owners in the regulatory process.
Smith v. City of Jackson, Mississippi	Established that ADEA permits disparate impact claims for age discrimination comparable to those permitted for discrimination based on sex and race.
Supranational laws	Agreements, standards, and laws that transcend national boundaries or governments. Examples include directives and regulations from the EU to its member countries.
Taxman v. Board of Education of Piscataway	Found that in the absence of past discrimination or underrepresentation of protected classes, preference may not be given to protected classes in making layoff decisions.
Taylor v. Progress Energy, Inc.	Established that the waiver of FMLA rights in a severance agreement is invalid. FMLA clearly states that "employees cannot waive, nor may employers induce employees to waive, any rights under the FMLA."
Uniform Guidelines on Employee Selection Procedures (UGESP)	Established guidelines to ensure that selection procedures are both job related and valid predictors of job success.
Velazquez-Garcia v. Horizon Lines of Puerto Rico, Inc.	Established that the burden of proof that a termination wasn't related to military service is on an employer when an employee protected by USERRA is laid off.
Visas and work permits	Documents used by various countries to control immigration and job placement of foreign workers. Most countries require a work permit whenever a foreign individual is transferred or takes a job in the country for a period of six months or more.
Washington v. Davis	Established that employment selection tools that adversely impact protected classes are lawful if they have been validated to show future success on the job.
World Trade Organization (WTO)	An international body in which members negotiate tariffs and trade barriers, and trade disputes are reviewed and adjudicated.
Works council	Group that represents employees; organization that functions like a trade union and represents the rights of workers. Works councils are most common in Europe and the United Kingdom.

Table A.11 General Record-Keeping Guidelines

Record Type	Length of Retention	Requirements
Affirmative action plan/data	Two years	Applications and other personnel records that support employment decisions (e.g., hires, promotions, terminations) are considered "support data" and must be maintained for the present AAP and the prior AAP. Records required by 41CFR60-300.44(f)(4), 60-300.44(k), and 60-300.45(c) must be kept for a period of three years from the date of making the record. This also applies to records required by 41CFR60-741.44(f)(4) and (k).
Applications for employment	One year from making the record or making the hiring decision, whichever is later; two years if a federal contractor or subcontractor has 150 or more employees and a government contract of at least $150,000	If a charge or lawsuit is filed, the records must be kept until the charge is disposed.
Drug test records	One year for non-DOT employers	Department of Transportation records for commercial drivers: 1 year: Negative drug test results. Alcohol test results less than 0.02. 2 years: Records related to the alcohol and drug collection process. 3 years: Previous employer records. 5 years: Annual MIS reports. Employee evaluation and referrals to SAPs. Follow-up tests and follow-up schedules. Refusals to test. Alcohol test results 0.02 or greater. Verified positive drug test results. EBT calibration documentation.

(continued)

Table A.11 General Record-Keeping Guidelines (*continued*)

Record Type	Length of Retention	Requirements
Employment benefits	Until no longer relevant to determine benefits due to employees	Except for specific exemptions, ERISA's reporting and disclosure requirements apply to all pension and welfare plans, including summary plan descriptions, annual reports, and plan termination. Pension and insurance plans for the full period the plan is in place.
EEO-1	Annually, unless a federal contractor or subcontractor	The current EEO-1 report must be kept on file. Federal contractors and subcontractors must produce three years' worth of EEO-1 reports, if audited by the OFCCP.
Family Medical Leave records	Three years	Basic employee data, including name, address, occupation, rate of pay, terms of compensation, daily and weekly hours worked per pay period, additions to/deductions from wages, and total compensation. Dates of leave taken by eligible employees. Leave must be designated as the FMLA leave. For intermittent leave taken, the hours of leave. Copies of employee notices and documents describing employee benefits or policies and practices regarding paid and unpaid leave. Records of premium payments of employee benefits. Records of any dispute regarding the designation of leave.
Form I-9	Three years after date of hire or one year after date of termination, whichever is later	See retention formula in Workforce Planning & Employment

Table A.11   General Record-Keeping Guidelines (*continued*)

Record Type	Length of Retention	Requirements
Merit and seniority pay systems	Two years	Includes wage rates, job evaluations, seniority and merit systems, and collective bargaining agreements or any other document that explains the basis for paying different wages to employees of opposite sexes in the same establishment.
Payroll records, etc.	Three years (EEOC, FLSA, ADEA): Payroll records, collective bargaining agreements, sales and purchase records Two years: Time cards and piecework tickets, wage rate tables, work and time schedules, and records of additions to or deductions from wages	If a charge is filed, all related records must be kept until the charge is settled. Basic payroll records that must be kept according to the FLSA are: 1. Employee's full name and Social Security number 2. Address, including zip code 3. Birth date, if younger than 19 4. Sex and occupation 5. Time and day of week when employee's workweek begins 6. Hours worked each day 7. Total hours worked each workweek 8. Basis on which employee's wages are paid (e.g., "$9 per hour," "$440 a week," "piecework") 9. Regular hourly pay rate 10. Total daily or weekly straight-time earnings 11. Total overtime earnings for the workweek 12. All additions to or deductions from the employee's wages 13. Total wages paid each pay period 14. Date of payment and the pay period covered by the payment

(*continued*)

Table A.11 General Record-Keeping Guidelines (*continued*)

Record Type	Length of Retention	Requirements
Personnel records	One year from making the record or taking the action, whichever is greater (EEOC) Three years if applicable under the Davis-Bacon Act Two years if a federal contractor or subcontractor with 150 or more employees, or government contract of $150,000 or more	Records related to promotions, demotions, transfers, performance appraisals, terminations, requests for reasonable accommodations.
Polygraph test records	Three years	Polygraph test result(s) and the reason for administering.
Selection and hiring records	One year after creation of the document or the action is taken, whichever is later Two years if a federal contractor or subcontractor with 150 or more employees, or government contract of $150,000 or more	Job ads, assessment tools, credit reports, interview records, and other documents related to hiring decisions.
Tax records	Four years from date tax is due or paid	Amounts of wages subject to withholding. Agreements with employee to withhold additional tax. Actual taxes withheld and dates withheld. Reason for any difference between total tax payments and actual tax payments. Withholding forms.
Work permits	No retention requirements	Employers must keep current work permits for minors.

Appendix B

Four Steps to Domestic Certification

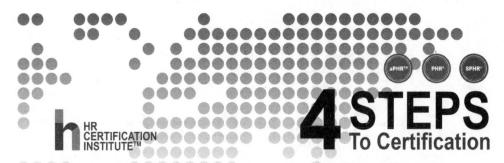

4 STEPS To Certification

① Choose the Right Certification for you

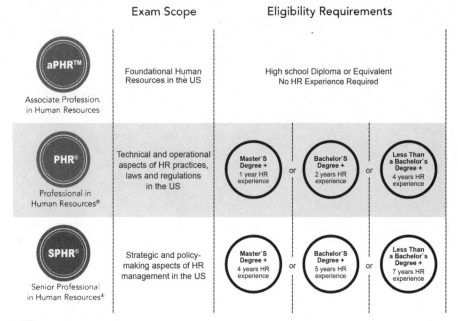

	Exam Scope	Eligibility Requirements		
aPHR™ Associate Profession. in Human Resources	Foundational Human Resources in the US	High school Diploma or Equivalent No HR Experience Required		
PHR® Professional in Human Resources®	Technical and operational aspects of HR practices, laws and regulations in the US	Master's Degree + 1 year HR experience *or*	Bachelor's Degree + 2 years HR experience *or*	Less Than a Bachelor's Degree + 4 years HR experience
SPHR® Senior Professional in Human Resources.	Strategic and policy-making aspects of HR management in the US	Master's Degree + 4 years HR experience *or*	Bachelor's Degree + 5 years HR experience *or*	Less Than a Bachelor's Degree + 7 years HR experience

② Apply for the Exam

Exam registration for the aPHR, PHR and SPHR is available throughout the year.

- Go to hrci.org/login
- Create an account
- Complete the online application
- Schedule your exam at **prometric.com/hrci** once you receive eligibility confirmation

For more information, go to: **www.hrci.org/application-steps**

Note: Used with permission by Human Resource Certification Institute, Inc.

③ Prepare for Your Exam

Each exam assesses your knowledge and competencies based on HR functional areas:

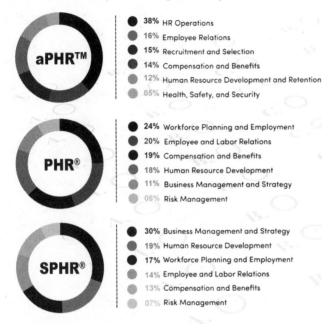

aPHR™
- 38% HR Operations
- 16% Employee Relations
- 15% Recruitment and Selection
- 14% Compensation and Benefits
- 12% Human Resource Development and Retention
- 05% Health, Safety, and Security

PHR®
- 24% Workforce Planning and Employment
- 20% Employee and Labor Relations
- 19% Compensation and Benefits
- 18% Human Resource Development
- 11% Business Management and Strategy
- 06% Risk Management

SPHR®
- 30% Business Management and Strategy
- 19% Human Resource Development
- 17% Workforce Planning and Employment
- 14% Employee and Labor Relations
- 13% Compensation and Benefits
- 07% Risk Management

There are hundreds of exam prep options to choose from. To find out which options suit your needs and learning style, go to hrci.org/exam-preparation.

④ Take the Exam

Earning a credential from HR Certification Institute® (HRCI®) speaks volumes—about you as an HR professional, about the organization you serve and about the employees who put their trust in you. HRCI wants you to succeed, and we are here to guide you through your certification journey.

Check out our test-taking tips at: hrci.org/exam-day-tips.

Please contact us should you have questions

HR CERTIFICATION INSTITUTE™

info@hrci.org
+1 866 898 4724 (US)
+1 571 551 6700
hrci.org

🅕 hrcertificationinstitute
🅧 @hrcertinstitute

🅛 HRCI Voices
▶ HRCertInstitute

Appendix C

Four Steps to Global Certification

1 Choose the Right Certification for You

	Exam Scope	Eligibility Requirements		
PHRi™ Professional in Human Resources-international™	Technical and operational HR principles in a geographic region outside the U.S.	Master's Degree + 1 year HR experience	Bachelor's Degree + 2 years HR experience	Less Than a Bachelor's Degree + 4 years HR experience
SPHRi® Senior professional in Human Resources-Inernational™	HR strategy, policy development and service delivery, and employment laws in geographic regions outside the U.S.	Master's Degree + 4 years HR experience	Bachelor's Degree + 5 years HR experience	Less Than a Bachelor's Degree + 7 years HR experience
GPHR® Global Professional in Human Resources®	Multinational HR responsibilities, policies and initiatives.	Master's Degree + 2 years HR Exp (2 years global)	Bachelor's Degree + 3 years HR Exp (2 years global)	Less Than a Bachelor's Degree + 4 years HR Exp (2 years global)

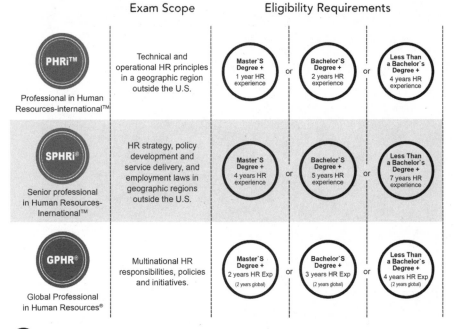

2 Apply for the Exam

Exam registration for the PHRi™, SPHRi™ and GPHR® is available throughout the year.

- Go to hrci.org/login
- Create an account
- Complete the online application
- Schedule your exam at **prometric.com/hrci** once you receive eligibility confirmation

For more information, go to: **www.hrci.org/application-steps**

③ Prepare for Your Exam

Each exam assesses your knowledge and competencies based on HR functional areas:

PHRi™
- 22% HR Administration
- 22% Recruitment and Selection
- 20% Employee Relations and Communications
- 15% Training and Development
- 14% Compensation and Benefits
- 07% Health, Safety, and Security

SPHRi®
- 32% HR as a Business Leader
- 29% People Development and Talent Management
- 23% HR Service Delivery
- 16% Measurement

GPHR®
- 25% Strategic HR Management
- 22% Talent and Organizational Development
- 21% Global Talent Acquisition and Mobility
- 17% Global Compensation and Benefits
- 15% Workforce Relations and Risk Management

There are hundreds of exam prep options to choose from. To find out which options suit your needs and learning style, go to hrci.org/exam-preparation.

④ Take the Exam

Earning a credential from HR Certification Institute® (HRCI®) speaks volumes—about you as an HR professional, about the organization you serve and about the employees who put their trust in you. HRCI wants you to succeed, and we are here to guide you through your certification journey.

Check out our test-taking tips at: hrci.org/exam-day-tips.

Please contact us should you have questions

HR CERTIFICATION INSTITUTE™

info@hrci.org
+1 866 898 4724 (US)
+1 571 551 6700
hrci.org

 hrcertificationinstitute
 @hrcertinstitute

 HRCI Voices
 HRCertInstitute

6533/J38385

Appendix D

Some Questions You May Have About Form I-9

Part Seven
Some Questions You May Have About Form I-9

Employers should read these questions and answers carefully. They contain valuable information that, in some cases, is not found elsewhere in this handbook.

For more information on Form I-9, employers and employees can also visit I-9 Central at uscis.gov/i-9-central.

Questions about the Verification Process

1. **Q. Do citizens and noncitizen nationals of the United States need to complete Form I-9?**

    A. Yes. While citizens and noncitizen nationals of the United States are automatically eligible for employment, they too must present the required documents and complete a Form I-9. U.S. citizens include persons born in the United States, Puerto Rico, Guam, the U.S. Virgin Islands, and the Commonwealth of the Northern Mariana Islands. U.S. noncitizen nationals are persons who owe permanent allegiance to the United States, which include those born in American Samoa, including Swains Island.

    NOTE: Citizens of the Federated States of Micronesia (FSM) and the Republic of the Marshall Islands (RMI) are not noncitizen nationals, however they are eligible to work in the U.S.

2. **Q. Do I need to complete Form I-9 for employees working in the CNMI?**

    A. Yes. You need to complete Form I-9 for employees hired for employment in the CNMI on or after Nov. 27, 2011. Employers in CNMI should have used Form I-9 CNMI between Nov. 28, 2009 and Nov. 27, 2011. If the employer did not complete Form I-9 CNMI as required during this period the employer should complete a new Form I-9 as soon as the employer discovers the omission. You should not complete Form I-9 for any employees already working for you on Nov. 27, 2009, even if you assign them new job responsibilities within your company. For more information

on federal immigration law in the CNMI, go to uscis.gov/CNMI.

3. **Q. Do I need to complete Form I-9 for independent contractors or their employees?**

    A. No. For example, if you contract with a construction company to perform renovations on your building, you do not have to complete Form I-9 for that company's employees. The construction company is responsible for completing Form I-9 for its own employees. However, you may not use a contract, subcontract or exchange to obtain the labor or services of an employee knowing that the employee is unauthorized to work.

4. **Q. May I fire an employee who fails to produce the required documents within three business days of their start date?**

    A. Yes. You may terminate an employee who fails to produce the required document or documents, or an acceptable receipt for a document, within three business days of the date employment begins.

5. **Q. What happens if I properly complete and retain a Form I-9 and DHS discovers that my employee is not actually authorized to work?**

    A. You cannot be charged with a verification violation. You will also have a good faith defense against the imposition of employer sanctions penalties for knowingly hiring an unauthorized individual, unless the government can show you had knowledge of the unauthorized status of the employee.

Questions about Documents

6. **Q. May I specify which documents I will accept for verification?**

    A. No. The employee may choose which document(s) they want to present from the Lists of Acceptable Documents. You must accept

Note: Excerpted from U.S. Citizenship and Immigration Services, *Handbook for Employers: Guidance for Completing Form I-9 (Employment Eligibiilty Verification Form)* (2017, p. 42-51). Available at https://www.uscis.gov/sites/default/files/files/form/m-274.pdf .

any document (from List A) or combination of documents (one from List B and one from List C) listed on Form I-9 and found in Part Eight of this handbook that reasonably appear on their face to be genuine and to relate to the person presenting them. To do otherwise could be an unfair immigration-related employment practice in violation of the anti-discrimination provision in the INA. Individuals who look and/or sound foreign must not be treated differently in the recruiting, hiring, or verification process. Please see Part Eight of this handbook for more information on acceptable documents.

For more information relating to discrimination during the Form I-9 process, contact IER at 1-800-255-8155 (employers) or 1-800-237-2515 (TDD) or visit IER's website at justice.gov/ier.

NOTE: An employer participating in E-Verify can only accept a List B document with a photograph.

7. **Q.** **What is my responsibility concerning the authenticity of document(s) presented to me?**

A. You must physically examine the document(s), and if they reasonably appear on their face to be genuine and to relate to the person presenting them, you must accept them. To do otherwise could be an unfair immigration-related employment practice. If the document(s) do not reasonably appear on their face to be genuine or to relate to the person presenting them, you must not accept them.

However, you must provide the employee with an opportunity to present other documents from the Lists of Acceptable Documents.

8. **Q.** **My employee has presented a U.S. passport card. Is this an acceptable document?**

A. Yes. The passport card is a wallet-size document issued by the U.S. Department of State. While its permissible uses for international travel are more limited than the U.S. passport book, the passport card is a fully valid passport that attests to the U.S. citizenship and identity of the bearer. As such, the passport card is considered a "passport" for purposes of Form I-9 and has been included on List A of the Lists of Acceptable Documents on Form I-9.

9. **Q.** **Why was documentation for citizens of the Federated States of Micronesia (FSM) and the Republic of the Marshall Islands (RMI) added to the Lists of Acceptable Documents on Form I-9?**

A. Under the Compacts of Free Association between the United States and FSM and RMI, most citizens of FSM and RMI are eligible to reside and work in the United States as nonimmigrants. An amendment to the Compacts eliminated the need for citizens of these two countries to obtain Employment Authorization Documents (Forms I-766) to work in the United States. However, FSM and RMI citizens may also apply for Employment Authorization Documents (Forms I-766) if they wish, or present a combination of List B and List C documents. The List A document specific to FSM and RMI citizens is a valid FSM or RMI passport with a Form I-94/Form I-94A indicating nonimmigrant admission under one of the Compacts.

10. Q. How do I know whether a Native American tribal document issued by a U.S. tribe presented by my employee is acceptable for Form I-9 purposes?

A. In order to be acceptable, a Native American tribal document should be issued by a tribe recognized by the U.S. federal government. Because federal recognition of tribes can change over time, to determine if the tribe is federally recognized, please check the Bureau of Indian Affairs website at bia.gov.

11. Q. Can the Certificate of Indian Status, commonly referred to as the status card or INAC card, be used as a Native American tribal document for Form I-9 purposes?

A. No. This card is not a Native American tribal document. It is issued by Indian and Northern Affairs Canada (INAC), which is a part of the Canadian government.

12. Q. May I accept an expired document?

A. No. Expired documents are no longer acceptable for Form I-9. However, you may accept Employment Authorization Documents (Forms I-766) and Permanent Resident Cards (Forms I-551) that appear to be expired on their face, but have been extended by USCIS.

For example, Temporary Protected Status (TPS) beneficiaries whose Employment Authorization Documents (Forms I-766) appear to be expired may be automatically extended in a Federal Register notice or, if the employee timely filed for a new Employment Authorization Document (Form I-766) the corresponding I-797C from USCIS indicating timely filing may be presented with the expired EAD to the employer as a List A document. These individuals may continue to work based on their expired Employment Authorization Documents (Forms I-766) during the automatic extension period. When the automatic extension of the Employment Authorization Document (Form I-766)

expires, you must reverify the employee's employment authorization.

Please see *Automatic Extensions of Employment Authorization Document in Certain Circumstances* for more information.

NOTE: Some documents, such as birth certificates and Social Security cards, do not contain an expiration date and should be treated as unexpired.

13. Q. How can I tell if a DHS-issued document has expired? If it has expired, should I reverify the employee?

A. Some INS-issued documents, such as older versions of the Alien Registration Receipt Card (Form I-551), do not have expiration dates, and are still acceptable for Form I-9 purposes. However, all subsequent DHS-issued Permanent Resident Cards (Forms I-551) contain two-year or 10-year expiration dates. You should not reverify an expired Alien Registration Receipt Card/Permanent Resident Card (Form I-551). Other DHS-issued documents, such as the Employment Authorization Document (Form I-766) also have expiration dates. These dates can be found on the face of the document. Generally, Employment Authorization Documents (Forms I-766) must be reverified upon expiration.

14. Q. May I accept a photocopy of a document presented by an employee?

A. No. Employees must present original documents. The only exception is that an employee may present a certified copy of a birth certificate.

15. Q. I noticed on Form I-9 that under List A there are three spaces for document numbers and expiration dates. Does this mean I have to see three List A documents.

A. No. Form I-9 (Rev. 11/14/16 N) includes an expanded document entry area in Section 2. The additional spaces are provided in case an employee presents a List A document that is really a combination of more than one document. For example, an F-1 student in curricular practical training may present, under List A, a foreign passport, Form I-94/Form I-94A and Form I-20 that specifies that you are their approved employer. Form I-9 provides space for you to enter the document number and expiration date for all three documents. Another instance where an employer may need to enter document information for three documents is for J-1 exchange visitors. If an employee provides you with one document from List A (such as a U.S. passport), or a combination of two documents (such as a foreign passport and Form I-94/94A), you do not need to fill out any unused space(s) under List A.

16. Q. When I review an employee's identity and employment authorization documents, should I make copies of them?

A. If you participate in E-Verify and the employee presents a document used as part of Photo Matching, currently the U.S. passport and passport card, Permanent Resident Card (Form I-551) and the Employment Authorization Document (Form I-766), you must retain a photocopy of the document they present. Other documents may be added to Photo Matching in the future. If you do not participate in E-Verify you are not required to make photocopies of documents. However, if you wish to make photocopies of documents other than those used in E-Verify, you must do so for all employees. Photocopies must not be used for any other purpose. Photocopying documents does not relieve you of your obligation to fully complete Section 2 of Form I-9, nor is it an acceptable substitute for proper completion of Form I-9 in general.

17. Q. When can employees present receipts for documents in lieu of actual documents from the Lists of Acceptable Documents?

A. The "receipt rule" is designed to cover situations in which an employee is authorized to work at the time of initial hire or reverification, but they are not in possession of a document listed on the Lists of Acceptable Documents accompanying Form I-9. Receipts showing that a person has applied for an initial grant of employment authorization are not acceptable.

An individual may present a receipt in lieu of a document listed on Form I-9 to complete

Section 2 or Section 3 of Form I-9. The receipt is valid for a temporary period. There are three different documents that qualify as receipts under the rule:

1. A receipt for a replacement document when the document has been lost, stolen, or damaged. The receipt is valid for 90 days, after which the individual must present the replacement document to complete Form I-9.

2. Form I-94/I-94A containing a temporary I-551 stamp and a photograph. The individual must present the actual Form I-551 by the expiration date of the temporary I-551 stamp or within one year from the date of issuance of Form I-94/Form I-94A if the I-551 stamp does not contain an expiration date.

3. A Form I-94/Form I-94A containing an unexpired refugee admission stamp. This is considered a receipt for either an Employment Authorization Document (Form I-766) or a combination of an unrestricted Social Security card and List B document. The employee must present an Employment Authorization Document (Form I-766) or an unrestricted Social Security card in combination with a List B document to complete Form I-9 within 90 days after the date of hire or, in the case of reverification, the date employment authorization expires. For more information on receipts, see Table 1 in Part Two.

18. Q. My nonimmigrant employee has presented a foreign passport with a Form I-94/Form I-94A (List A, Item 5). How do I know if this employee is authorized to work?

A. You, as the employer, likely have submitted a petition to USCIS on the nonimmigrant employee's behalf. However, there are some exceptions to this rule:

1. You made an offer of employment to a Canadian passport holder who entered the United States under the North American Free Trade Agreement (NAFTA) with an offer letter from your company. This nonimmigrant worker will have a Form I-94/Form I-94A indicating a TN immigration status, and may choose to

present it with their passport under List A. The employee may also present Form I-94/Form I-94A indicating a TN immigration status as a List C document, in which case your employee will need to present a List B document (such as a Canadian driver's license) to satisfy Section 2 of Form I-9.

2. A student working in on-campus employment or participating in curricular practical training (See Part Two.)

3. A J-1 exchange visitor. (See Part Two.)

Most employees who present a foreign passport in combination with a Form I-94 or I-94A (List A, Item 5) are restricted to work only for the employer who petitioned on their behalf. If you did not submit a petition for an employee who presents such documentation, then that non- immigrant worker is not usually authorized to work for you. See Part Two for more information on nonimmigrant employees.

19. Q. My new employee presented two documents to complete Form I-9, each containing a different last name. One document matches the name she entered in Section 1. The employee explained that she had just gotten married and changed her last name, but had not yet changed the name on the other document. Can I accept the document with the different name?

A. You may accept a document with a different name than the name entered in Section 1 provided that you resolve the question of whether the document reasonably relates to the employee. You also may wish to attach a brief memo to Form I-9 stating the reason for the name discrepancy, along with any supporting documentation the employee provides. An employee may provide documentation to support their name change, but is not required to do so. If, however, you determine that the document with a different name does not reasonably appear to be genuine and to relate to her, you may ask her to

provide other documents from the Lists of Acceptable Documents on Form I-9.

20. Q. My employee entered a compound last name in Section 1 of Form I-9. The documents she presented contain only one of these names. Can I accept this document?

A. DHS does not require employees to use any specific naming standard for Form I-9. If a new employee enters more than one last name in Section 1, but presents a document that contains only one of those last names, the document they present for Section 2 is acceptable as long as you are satisfied that the document reasonably appears to be genuine and to relate to the employee. It is helpful for individuals attesting to lawful permanent resident status who have more than one name to enter their name on Form I-9 as it appears on their Permanent Resident Card (Form I-551).

21. Q. The name on the document my employee presented to me is spelled slightly differently than the name they entered in Section 1 of Form I-9. Can I accept this document?

A. If the document contains a slight spelling variation, and the employee has a reasonable explanation for the variation, the document is acceptable as long as you are satisfied that the document otherwise reasonably appears to be genuine and to relate to the employee.

22. Q. My employee's Employment Authorization Document (Form I-766) expired and the employee now wants to show me a Social Security card. Do I need to see a current DHS document?

A. No. During reverification, an employee must be allowed to choose what documentation to present from either List A or List C. If an employee presents an unrestricted Social Security card upon reverification, the employee does not also need to present a current DHS document. However, if an employee presents a restricted Social Security card upon reverification, you must reject the restricted Social Security card, since it is not an acceptable Form I-9 document, and ask the employee to choose different documentation from List A or List C of Form I-9.

23. Q. My employee presented me with a document issued by INS rather than DHS. Can I accept it?

   A. Yes, you can accept a document issued by INS if the document is unexpired and reasonably appears to be genuine and to relate to the individual presenting it. Effective March 1, 2003, the functions of the former INS were transferred to three agencies within the new DHS: USCIS, CBP, and ICE. Most immigration documents acceptable for Form I-9 use are issued by USCIS. Some documents issued by the former INS before March 1, 2003, such as Permanent Resident Cards or Forms I-94 noting asylee status, may still be within their period of validity. If otherwise acceptable, a document should not be rejected because it was issued by INS rather than DHS. It should also be noted that INS documents may bear dates of issuance after March 1, 2003, as it took some time in 2003 to modify document forms to reflect the new USCIS identity.

Questions about Completing and Retaining Form I-9

24. Q. Can an employee leave any part of Section 1 on Form I-9 blank?

   A. Employees must complete every applicable field in Section 1 of Form I-9 with the exception of the Social Security number field. However, employees must enter their Social Security number in this field if you participate in E-Verify. The e-mail address and telephone number fields are optional but if an employee chooses not to provide this information, they must enter "N/A." Do not leave these fields blank.

   NOTE: Not all employees who attest to being an Alien Authorized to Work will have an expiration date for their employment authorization. However, refugees and asylees who present an Employment Authorization Document (Form I-766) have employment authorization that does not expire. These

individuals should put "N/A" where Section 1 asks for an expiration date.

25. Q. How do I correct a mistake on an employee's Form I-9?

   A. If you find a mistake on an employee's Form I-9, you must have the employee correct errors in Section 1. Employers must make corrections in Section 2. The best way to correct Form I-9 is to line through the portions of the form that contain incorrect information and then enter the correct information. Initial and date your correction. If you have previously made changes on Form I-9 using correction fluid, USCIS recommends that you attach a note to the corrected Form I-9 explaining what happened. Be sure to sign and date the note.

26. Q. What should I do if I need to reverify an employee who filled out an earlier version of Form I-9?

   A. If you used a version of Form I-9 when you originally verified the employee that is no longer valid, and you are now reverifying the employment authorization of that employee, the employee must provide any document(s) they choose from the current Lists of Acceptable Documents. Enter this new document(s) in Section 3 of the current version of Form I-9 and retain it with the previously completed Form I-9. To see if your form is an acceptable version of Form I-9, go to uscis.gov/i-9.

   For more information on reverification, please see Part Two.

27. Q. Do I need to complete a new Form I-9 when one of my employees is promoted within my company or transfers to another company office at a different location?

   A. No. You do not need to complete a new Form I-9 for employees who have been promoted or transferred.

28. Q. What do I do when an employee's employment authorization expires?

   A. To continue to employ an individual whose employment authorization has expired, you will need to reverify the employee in Section 3 of Form I-9. Reverification must occur no later than the date that employment authorization expires. The employee must present a document from either List A or List C that shows either an extension of their initial employment authorization or new employment authorization. You must review this document and, if it reasonably appears on its face to be genuine and to relate to the person presenting it, enter the document title, number, and expiration date (if any), in the Reverification and Rehires section (Section 3), and sign in the appropriate space.

If the version of Form I-9 that you used for the employee's original verification is no longer valid, you must complete Section 3 of the current Form I-9 upon reverification and attach it to the original Form I-9.

You may want to establish a calendar notification system for employees whose employment authorization will expire and provide the employee with at least 90 days' notice prior to the expiration date of the employment authorization.

You may not reverify an expired U.S. passport or passport card, an Alien Registration Receipt Card/Permanent Resident Card (Form I-551), or a List B document that has expired.

Some workers are eligible for an automatic extension of their Employment Authorization Document for 180 days, in certain circumstances. If your employee presents an expired Employment Authorization Document (Form I-766) in combination with an I-797C Notice of Action from USCIS indicating both timely filing for a renewal of their Employment Authorization document and eligibility for a 180-day automatic extension of their Employment Authorization Document (Form I-766), you should not reverify the employee based on the expiration date on the face of the Employment Authorization Document (Form I-766); instead, update Section 2 of Form I-9 at that time. When the automatic extension of the Employment Authorization Document (Form I-766) expires (180 days after the expiration date on the face of the Employment Authorization Document (Form I-766)), you must reverify the employee's employment authorization. Please see *Automatic Extensions*

of Employment Authorization Document in Certain Circumstances for eligible categories and additional information.

NOTE: You cannot refuse to accept a document because it has a future expiration date. You must accept any document (from List A or List C) listed on Form I-9 that on its face reasonably appears to be genuine and to relate to the person presenting it. To do otherwise could be an unfair immigration-related employment practice in violation of the anti-discrimination provision of the INA.

29. Q. **Can I avoid reverifying an employee on Form I-9 by not hiring persons whose employment authorization has an expiration date?**

A. No. You cannot refuse to hire persons solely because their employment authorization is temporary. The existence of a future expiration date does not preclude continuous employment authorization for an employee and does not mean that subsequent employment authorization will not be granted. In addition, consideration of a future employment authorization expiration date in determining whether an individual is qualified for a particular job may be an unfair immigration-related employment practice in violation of the anti-discrimination provision of the INA.

30. Q. **Can I contract with someone to complete Form I-9 for my business?**

A. Yes. You can contract with another person or business to verify employees' identities and employment authorization and to complete Form I-9 for you. However, you are still responsible for the contractor's actions and are liable for any violations of the employer sanctions laws.

31. Q. **How does the Immigrant and Employee Rights Section in the Department of Justice's Civil Rights Division (IER) obtain the necessary information to determine whether an employer has committed an unfair immigration-related employment practice**

under the anti-discrimination provision of the INA?

A. IER will notify you in writing to initiate an investigation, request information and documents, and interview your employees. If you refuse to cooperate, IER can obtain a subpoena to compel you to produce the information requested or to appear for an investigative interview.

32. Q. Do I have to complete Form I-9 for Canadians or Mexicans who entered the United States under the North American Free Trade Agreement (NAFTA)?

A. Yes. You must complete Form I-9 for all employees. NAFTA entrants must show identity and employment authorization documents just like all other employees.

33. Q. If I am a recruiter or referrer for a fee, do I have to fill out Form I-9 on individuals that I recruit or refer?

A. No, with three exceptions: Agricultural associations, agricultural employers, and farm labor contractors must complete Form I-9 on all individuals who are recruited or referred for a fee. However, all recruiters and referrers for a fee must complete Form I-9 for their own employees hired after Nov. 6, 1986. Also, all recruiters and referrers for a fee are liable for knowingly recruiting or referring for a fee individuals not authorized to work in the United States and must comply with federal anti-discrimination laws.

34. Q. If I am self-employed, do I have to fill out a Form I-9 on myself?

A. A self-employed person does not need to complete a Form I-9 on their own behalf unless the person is an employee of a separate business entity, such as a corporation or partnership. If the person is an employee of a separate business entity, he or she, and any other employees, will have to complete Form I-9.

35. Q. I have heard that some state employment agencies, commonly known as state workforce

agencies, can certify that people they refer are authorized to work. Is that true?

A. Yes. A state employment agency may choose to verify the employment authorization and identity of an individual it refers for employment on Form I-9. In such a case, the agency must issue a certification to you so that you receive it within 21 business days from the date the referred individual is hired. If an agency refers a potential employee to you with a job order, other appropriate referral form, or telephonically authorized referral, and the agency sends you a certification within 21 business days of the referral, you do not have to check documents or complete a Form I-9 if you hire that person. Before receiving the certification, you must retain the job order, referral form, or annotation reflecting the telephonically authorized referral as you would Form I-9. When you receive the certification, you must review the certification to ensure that it relates to the person hired and observe the person sign the certification. You must also retain the certification as you would a Form I-9 and make it available for inspection, if requested. You should check with your state employment agency to see if it provides this service and become familiar with its certification document.

Questions about Avoiding Discrimination

36. Q. What is the INA's Anti-Discrimination Provision?

A. The Immigration and Nationality Act's (INA) anti-discrimination provision, codified at 8 U.S.C. § 1324b, is a law that prohibits four types of discriminatory unfair employment practices:

- Citizenship or immigration status discrimination with respect to hiring, firing, and recruitment or referral for a fee, by employers with four or more workers, subject to certain exceptions. Employers may not treat individuals differently because they are or are not U.S. citizens or because of their work-authorized immigration status. U.S. citizens, U.S. nationals, recent lawful permanent residents, asylees, and refugees are protected from citizenship status discrimination. An employer may restrict hiring to U.S. citizens only when required to do so by law, regulation, executive order, or government contract.

- National origin discrimination with respect to hiring, firing, and recruitment or referral for a fee, by employers with four to 14 workers. Employers may not treat individuals differently because of their place of birth, country of origin, ancestry, native language, accent or because they are perceived as looking or sounding "foreign." All work-authorized individuals are protected from national origin discrimination. The Equal Employment Opportunity Commission has jurisdiction over national origin discrimination claims against employers with 15 or more workers, regardless of the work authorization status of the discrimination victims.

- Unfair documentary practices related to verifying the employment eligibility of employees during the I-9 or E-Verify processes. Employers may not, on the basis of citizenship, immigration status, or national origin, request more or different documents than are required to verify employment eligibility and identity, reject reasonably genuine-looking documents, or specify certain documents over others. All work-authorized individuals are protected from unfair documentary practices.

- Intimidation or Retaliation. Employers may not intimidate, threaten, coerce, or retaliate against individuals who file charges with IER, who cooperate with an IER investigation, who contest an action that may constitute unfair documentary practices or discrimination based upon citizenship, immigration status, or national origin, or who otherwise assert their rights under the INA's anti-discrimination provision.

37. Q. Can I limit hiring only to U.S. citizens?

A. Employers cannot limit positions to U.S. citizens only unless they are required to do so by a law, executive order, regulation, or government contract that requires specific positions to be filled only by U.S. citizens. If a job applicant is discouraged or rejected from employment based on citizenship status, the employer may be committing citizenship status discrimination in violation of the anti-discrimination provision of the INA.

38. Q. Can I refuse to hire someone based on national origin?

A. Failure to hire an individual based on the person's national origin may violate the anti-discrimination provision of the INA if the employer employs between four and 14 employees, or may violate Title VII of the Civil Rights Act (enforced by the Equal Employment Opportunity Commission (EEOC)) if the employer has 15 or more employees. If a small employer has rejected your employment application based on your national origin, contact IER to determine whether IER or the EEOC has jurisdiction to assist you.

39. Q. Can I ask an employee to show a specific document for the Form I-9?

A. No. For employment eligibility verification, an employee must be allowed to choose which documents to show from the Form I-9 Lists of Acceptable Documents. If the documentation reasonably appears to be genuine and to relate to the employee, the employer must accept it. An employer may be violating the anti-discrimination provision of the INA if the employer requires an employee to show specific documents or more documents than required based on the employee's citizenship, immigration status or national origin.

40. Q. Can I refuse to accept an employee's documentation if I would prefer to see another type of documentation?

A. No. For employment eligibility verification, an employee must be allowed to choose which documents to show from the Form I-9 Lists of Acceptable Documents. If the documentation reasonably appears to be genuine and to relate to the employee, the employer must accept it. An employer may be violating the anti-discrimination provision of the INA if the employer rejects the valid documentation an employee presents based on the employee's citizenship, immigration status or national origin.

41. Q. Can I ask my employee to show the same type of document for reverification as the employee showed to complete Section 2?

A. No. For reverification, an employee may choose which unexpired List A or List C document to present. An employer may be violating the anti-discrimination provision of the INA if the employer requires an employee to show specific documents for reverification based on the employee's citizenship, immigration status or national origin.

For more information on these or any other discrimination-related questions, call IER's employer hotline at 1-800-255-8155 or 1-800-237-2515 (TTY). You can also visit IER's website at justice.gov/ ier.

For more information on avoiding discrimination in the Form I-9 and E-Verify processes, visit justice.gov/ ier.

Questions about Different Versions of Form I-9

42. Q. Is Form I-9 available in different languages?

A. Form I-9 is available in English and Spanish. However, only employers in Puerto Rico may use the Spanish version to meet the verification and retention requirements of the law. Employers in the United States and other U.S. territories may use the Spanish version as a translation guide for Spanish-speaking employees, but the English version must be completed and retained in the employer's records. Employees may also use or ask for a preparer and/or translator to assist them in completing the form.

43. Q. Are employers in Puerto Rico required to use the Spanish version of Form I-9?

A. No. Employers in Puerto Rico may use either the Spanish or the English version of Form I-9 to verify new employees.

44. Q. May I continue to use earlier versions of Form I-9?

A. No, employers must use the current version of Form I-9. A revision date with an "N" next to it indicates that all previous versions with earlier revision dates, in English or Spanish, are no longer valid. You may also use subsequent versions that have a "Y" next to the revision date. If in doubt, go to uscis.gov/i-9 to view or download the most current form.

45. Q. Where do I get the Spanish version of Form I-9?

A. You may download the Spanish version of this form from the USCIS website at uscis.gov/i-9. For employers without internet access, you may call the USCIS Forms Request Line toll-free at 800-870-3676.

For more questions and answers on Form I-9 topics, go to uscis.gov/i-9-central and select I-9 Central Questions & Answers.

Appendix E

Sample Affirmative Action Plan

SAMPLE AFFIRMATIVE ACTION PROGRAM (AAP)

The following sample AAP is for illustrative purposes only and does not represent the only styles and formats that meet regulatory requirements. While this sample has been constructed around a company with less than 150 employees, thereby allowing the AAP job groups to be formulated according to OFCCP occupational categories as authorized by 41 CFR 60-2.12(e)[1], it may be used as a guide for larger employers.

When preparing an AAP, it should be customized to reflect an employer's organizational structure, policies, practices, programs, and data. Usually a separate AAP is required for each establishment. In appropriate circumstances, an establishment may include several facilities located at two or more sites if the facilities are in the same labor market or recruiting area.

In addition to the records an employer is required to compile and maintain to support the AAP *[41 CFR 60-1.12 and 60-2.17(d)]*, the employer should also keep materials evidencing its affirmative action efforts. This may include items such as copies of collective bargaining agreements and other documents that indicate employment policies and practices; copies of letters sent to suppliers and vendors stating the EEO/affirmative action policy; copies of letters sent to recruitment sources and community organizations; and copies of contract language incorporating the regulatory EEO clause [*41 CFR 60-1.4*].

---

[1] Employers may use the EEO-1 categories for this purpose. See footnote 2 for further discussion.

Note: Reprinted from The Department of Labor, Office of Federal Contract Compliance.
Available at https://www.dol.gov/ofccp/regs/compliance/AAPs/Sample_AAP_final_JRF_QA_508c.pdf.

FEDERAL CONTRACTOR, INC. (FCI)
EXECUTIVE ORDER 11246
SAMPLE AFFIRMATIVE ACTION PROGRAM

	Title 41 CFR Section
Organizational Profile	60-2.11
Job Group Analysis	60-2.12
Utilization Analysis	
Placement of Incumbents in Job Groups	60-2.13
Determining Availability	60-2.14
Comparing Incumbency to Availability	60-2.15
Placement Goals	60-2.16
Additional Required Elements	60-2.17
Designation of Responsibility for Implementation	60-2.17(a)
Identification of Problem Areas	60-2.17(b)
Action-Oriented Programs	60-2.17(c)
Internal Audit and Reporting System	60-2.17(d)
Support Data	60-2.17(b) and 60-3
General Requirement (optional inclusion in AAP)	
Guidelines on Discrimination because of Religion or National Origin	60-50

Organizational Display

The **Organizational Display** is a detailed chart of the contractor's organizational structure. For each organizational unit, the display must indicate the following:

- The name of the unit and the job title, race and gender of the unit supervisor
- The total number of male and female incumbents and the total number of male and female incumbents in each of the following groups: Blacks, American Indians, Asians, Hispanics, and whites other than Hispanics[2].

Federal Contractor, Inc. (FCI)

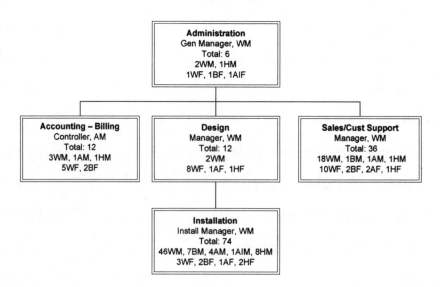

Note that the organizational display shows each department, the race/sex of the supervisor(s) and employees within each department, and how all of the departments relate to each other.

---

[2] OFCCP's regulations regarding the race, ethnicity, and job categories to be used by contractors have not changed to reflect the new categories required for the EEO-1 Report. However, OFCCP will accept AAPs and supporting records that reflect the categories outlined in either 41 CFR Part 60-2 or the new EEO-1 Report. For more information, see OFCCP's Directive at
http://www.dol.gov/ofccp/regs/compliance/directives/dirindex.htm

Workforce Analysis

DEPARTMENT/WORK UNIT: Administration

Job Title	Wage Rate	EEO-1 Category	Job Group	Total Employees	MALES						FEMALES					
					Total	White	Black/AA	Asian/PI	American Indian/AN	Hispanic	Total	White	Black/AA	Asian/PI	American Indian/AN	Hispanic
General Manager	S-A	1	1	1	1	1										
Personnel Manager	S-D	1	1	1	1	1										
Executive Assistant	S-J	5	5	1							1	1				
Administrative Assistant	H-8	5	5	1							1		1			
File Clerk	H-11	5	5	2	1					1	1				1	
DEPARTMENT TOTAL				6	3	2				1	3	1	1		1	

Workforce Analysis

DEPARTMENT/WORK UNIT: Accounting – Billing

Job Title	Wage Rate	EEO-1 Category	Job Group	Total Employees	MALES						FEMALES					
					Total	White	Black/AA	Asian/PI	American Indian/AN	Hispanic	Total	White	Black/AA	Asian/PI	American Indian/AN	Hispanic
Controller	S-C	1	1	1	1			1								
Pricing-Billing Manager	S-E	1	1	1	1	1										
General Ledger Accountant	S-F	2	2	1							1	1				
Payroll Administrator	S-H	2	2	1	1	1										
Billing Clerk	H-5	5	5	3	1					1	2	2				
Material Pricing Clerk	H-5	5	5	3	1	1					2	1	1			
Administrative Assistant	H-8	5	5	2							2	1	1			
DEPARTMENT TOTAL				12	5	3		1		1	7	5	2			

Workforce Analysis

DEPARTMENT/WORK UNIT: Accounting – Design

Job Title	Wage Rate	EEO-1 Category	Job Group	Total Employees	MALES Total	MALES White	MALES Black/AA	MALES Asian/PI	MALES American Indian/AN	MALES Hispanic	FEMALES Total	FEMALES White	FEMALES Black/AA	FEMALES Asian/PI	FEMALES American Indian/AN	FEMALES Hispanic
Interior Design Manager	S-E	1	1	1	1	1										
Interior Designer	S-M	2	2	2							2	1				1
Office Space Planner	S-M	2	2	5	1	1					4	4				
Administrative Assistant	H-8	5	5	2							2	2				
File Clerk	H-11	5	5								2	1		1		
Material Pricing Clerk	H-5	5	5	3							2	1	1			
Administrative Assistant	H-8	5	5	2							2	1	1			
DEPARTMENT TOTAL				12	2	2					10	8		1		1

Workforce Analysis

DEPARTMENT/WORK UNIT: Sales - Customer

Job Title	Wage Rate	EEO-1 Category	Job Group	Total Employees	MALES						FEMALES					
					Total	White	Black/AA	Asian/PI	American Indian/AN	Hispanic	Total	White	Black/AA	Asian/PI	American Indian/AN	Hispanic
Customer Support Manager	S-G	1	1	1	1	1										
Pricing Specialist	S-J	2	2	6	5	3	1	1			1					
Purchasing Agent	S-J	2	2	7	5	5					2	2				
Office Equipment Sales Representative	S-K	4	4	10	8	8					2	2				
Customer Information Sales Representative	H-7	5	5	6							6	4		1		
Call Center Agent	H-7	5	5	3	1	1					2	1	1			
Customer Service Complaints Clerk	H-8	5	5	3	1					1	2	1		1		
DEPARTMENT TOTAL				36	21	18	1	1		1	15	10	2	2		1

Workforce Analysis

DEPARTMENT/WORK UNIT: Installation

Job Title	Wage Rate	EEO-1 Category	Job Group	Total Employees	MALES Total	White	Black/AA	Asian/PI	American Indian/AN	Hispanic	FEMALES Total	White	Black/AA	Asian/PI	American Indian/AN	Hispanic
Installation Manager	S-F	1	1	1	1	1										
Installation Supervisor	S-G	1	1	1	1	1										
Furniture Repair Supervisor	S-G	1	1	1	1	1										
Inventory Control Clerk	H-9	5	5	2							2	1				1
Systems Specialist	H-9	6	6	12	10	8				2	2	1	1			
Installer	H-10	6	6	18	17	12	2	1		2	1					1
Furniture Repair	H-10	6	6	13	12	7		3		2	1		1			
Truck Driver	H-11	7	7	8	7	5	1		1		1	1				
Forklift Operator	H-12	7	7	2	2	1	1									
Installer Helper	H-13	8	8	13	12	8	2			2	1			1		
Receiving	H-13	8	8	3	3	2	1									
DEPARTMENT TOTAL				74	66	46	7	4	1	8	8	3	2	1		2

Job Group Analysis:
Listing of Job Titles

Job Titles	Job Group Name	EEO-1 Category
General Manager Controller Pricing – Billing Manager Sales – Customer Support Manager Interior Design Manager Personnel Manager Installation Manager Installation Supervisor Furniture Repair Supervisor	1	Officials & Managers
Interior Designer Office Space Planner General Ledger Accountant Payroll Administrator Purchasing Agent Pricing Specialist	2	Professionals
Office Sales Representative	4	Sales Workers
Executive Assistant Administrative Assistant File Clerk Billing Clerk Inventory Control Clerk Material Pricing Clerk Customer Information Sales Representative Call Center Agent Customer Service Complaints Clerk	5	Office & Clericals
Systems – Specialist Installer Furniture Repair	6	Craftworkers
Truck Driver Forklift Operator	7	Operatives
Installer Helper Receiving	8	Laborers

Utilization Analysis:
Placement of Incumbents in Job Groups

Job Group	Total # of Incumbents	# of Females	Female Incumbency %	# of Minorities	Minority Incumbency %
1	9	0	0.0	1	11.1
2	22	10	45.5	4	18.2
4	10	2	20.0	0	0.0
5	30	25	83.3	13	43.3
6	43	4	9.3	15	34.9
7	10	1	10.0	3	30.0
8	16	1	6.3	6	37.5

Utilization Analysis:
Determining Availability[3]

Job Group: 6	Raw Statistics		Value Weight	Weighted Statistics		Source of Statistics	Reason for Weighting
	Minority	Female		Minority	Female		
1. Percentage of minorities or women with requisite skills in the reasonable recruitment area	18.4%	40.2%	10%	1.84%	4.02%	2000 Census Data	
2. Percentage of minorities or women among those promotable, transferable, and trainable within the contractor's organization.	20.1%	44.6%	90%	18.09%	40.14%		
Totals:			100%	19.93%	44.16%	‹ Final Factor	

[3] The example is of one job group only. Contractors must conduct an analysis of each of the job groups and determine availability for each [41 CFR 60-2.12 – 60-2.14]. Please note that the chart includes fictionalized numbers designed for illustrative purposes.

Utilization Analysis:
Comparing Incumbency to Availability
and
Establishing Placement Goals

Job Group	Female Incumbency %	Female Availability %	Establish Goal? Yes/No	If Yes, Goal for Females	Minority Incumbency %	Minority Availability %	Establish Goal? Yes/No	If Yes, Goal for Minorities
1	0.0	47.6%	Yes	**47.6%**	11.1%	18.1%	Yes	**18.1%**
2	45.5%	43.8%	No		18.2%	8.2%	No	
4	20.0%	34.5%	Yes	**34.5%**	0.0%	12.4%	Yes	**12.4%**
5	83.3%	87.7%	No	*	43.3%	27.6%	No	
6	9.3%	5.5%	No		34.9%	23.2%	No	
7	10.0%	6.3%	No		30.0%	37.5%	No	*
8	6.3%	19.1%	Yes	**19.1%**	37.5%	26.3%	No	

*The 80% rule of thumb was followed in declaring underutilization and establishment goals when the actual employment of minorities or females is less than 80% of their availability. If the female/minority incumbency percent (%) is less than the female/minority availability percent (%) <u>and</u> the ratio of incumbency to availability is less than 80%, a placement goal should be included in the appropriate "If Yes" column.

Designation of Responsibility for Implementation

Responsibilities of the Equal Employment Opportunity Manager:

The Personnel Manager has the responsibility for designing and ensuring the effective implementation of Federal Contractor, Inc's. (FCI's) Affirmative Action Program (AAP). These responsibilities include, but are not limited to, the following:

1. Developing Equal Employment Opportunity (EEO) policy statements, affirmative action programs and internal and external communication procedures;

2. Assisting in the identification of AAP/EEO problem areas;

3. Assisting management in arriving at effective solutions to AAP/EEO problems;

4. Designing and implementing an internal audit and reporting system that:

   a. Measures the effectiveness of FCI's program;
   b. Determines the degree to which AAP goals and objectives are met; and
   c. Identifies the need for remedial action;

5. Keeping FCI's General Manager informed of equal opportunity progress and reporting potential problem areas within the company through quarterly reports;

6. Reviewing the company's AAP for qualified minorities and women with all managers and supervisors at all levels to ensure that the policy is understood and is followed in all personnel activities;

7. Auditing the contents of the company's bulletin board to ensure compliance information is posted and up-to-date; and

8. Serving as liaison between FCI and enforcement agencies.

Responsibilities of Managers and Supervisors:

It is the responsibility of all managerial and supervisory staff to implement FCI's AAP. These responsibilities include, but are not limited to:

1. Assisting in the identification of problem areas, formulating solutions, and establishing departmental goals and objectives when necessary;

2. Reviewing the qualifications of all applicants and employees to ensure qualified individuals are treated in a nondiscriminatory manner when hiring, promotion, transfer, and termination actions occur; and

3. Reviewing the job performance of each employee to assess whether personnel actions are justified based on the employee's performance of his or her duties and responsibilities.

Identification of Problem Areas

Areas of Concern	Corrective Actions
• Underutilization of minorities and women in Job Groups 1 and 4 where external hiring opportunities occurred. Concern regarding low minority and female applicant flow rate resulting from inadequate recruitment for both job groups.	• No later than March 1, 2010, notify management and professional recruitment sources, in writing, of FCI's interest in attracting qualified minorities and women to apply for job openings. • No later than March 1, 2010, expand FCI's recruitment program to colleges and universities with a significant percentage of minority and female students.
• Underutilization of women in Job Group 8 entry-level blue-collar jobs. Concern regarding low female applicant flow rate resulting from inadequate recruitment.	• No later than January 1, 2010, contact the local YWCA, local vocational school, and training centers to inform them of FCI's interest in attracting qualified female applicants.
• High termination rate for females in Job Group 8.	• Immediately review exit interview survey of terminated females to confirm voluntary reason for leaving.

Action-Oriented Programs

FCI has instituted action programs to eliminate identified problem areas and to help achieve specific affirmative action goals. These programs include:

1. Conducting annual analyses of job descriptions to ensure they accurately reflect job functions;

2. Reviewing job descriptions by department and job title using job performance criteria;

3. Making job descriptions available to recruiting sources and available to all members of management involved in the recruiting, screening, selection and promotion processes;

4. Evaluating the total selection process to ensure freedom from bias through:

   a. Reviewing job applications and other pre-employment forms to ensure information requested is job-related;

   b. Evaluating selection methods that may have a disparate impact to ensure that they are job-related and consistent with business necessity;

   c. Training personnel and management staff on proper interview techniques; and

   d. Training in EEO for management and supervisory staff;

5. Using techniques to improve recruitment and increase the flow of minority and female applicants. FCI presently undertakes the following actions:

   a. Include the phrase "Equal Opportunity/Affirmative Action Employer" in all printed employment advertisements;

   b. Place help wanted advertisement, when appropriate, in local minority news media and women's interest media;

   c. Disseminate information on job opportunities to organizations representing minorities, women and employment development agencies when job opportunities occur;

   d. Encourage all employees to refer qualified applicants;

   e. Actively recruit at secondary schools, junior colleges, colleges and universities with predominantly minority or female enrollments; and

   f.   Request employment agencies to refer qualified minorities and women;

6. Hiring a statistical consultant to help FCI perform a self-audit of its compensation practices; and

7. Ensuring that all employees are given equal opportunity for promotion. This is achieved by:

   a.   Posting promotional opportunities;

   b.   Offering counseling to assist employees in identifying promotional opportunities, training and educational programs to enhance promotions and opportunities for job rotation or transfer; and

   c.   Evaluating job requirements for promotion.

Internal Audit and Reporting System

The Personnel Manager has the responsibility for developing and preparing the formal documents of the AAP. The Personnel Manager is responsible for the effective implementation of the AAP; however, responsibility is likewise vested with each department manager and supervisor. FCI's audit and reporting system is designed to:

- Measure the effectiveness of the AAP/EEO program;

- Document personnel activities;

- Identify problem areas where remedial action is needed; and

- Determine the degree to which FCI's AAP goals and objectives have been obtained.

The following personnel activities are reviewed to ensure nondiscrimination and equal employment opportunity for all individuals without regard to their race, color, sex, sexual orientation, gender identity, religion, or national origin:

- Recruitment, advertising, and job application procedures;
- Hiring, promotion, upgrading, award of tenure, layoff, recall from layoff;
- Rates of pay and any other forms of compensation including fringe benefits;
- Job assignments, job classifications, job descriptions, and seniority lists;
- Sick leave, leaves or absence, or any other leave;
- Training, apprenticeships, attendance at professional meetings and conferences; and
- Any other term, condition, or privilege of employment.

The following documents are maintained as a component of FCI's internal audit process:

1. An applicant flow log showing the name, race, sex, date of application, job title, interview status and the action taken for all individuals applying for job opportunities;

2. Summary data of external job offers and hires, promotions, resignations, terminations, and layoffs by job group and by sex and minority group identification;

3. Summary data of applicant flow by identifying, at least, total applicants, total minority applicants, and total female applicants for each position;

4. Maintenance of employment applications (not to exceed one year); and

5. Records pertaining to FCI's compensation system.

FCI's audit system includes a quarterly report documenting FCI's efforts to achieve its EEO/AAP responsibilities. Managers and supervisors are asked to report any current or foreseeable EEO problem areas and are asked to outline their suggestions/recommendations for solutions. If problem areas arise, the manager or supervisor is to report problem areas immediately to the Personnel Manager. During quarterly reporting, the following occurs:

1. The Personnel Manager will discuss any problems relating to significant rejection ratios, EEO charges, etc., with the General Manager; and

2. The Personnel Manager will report the status of the FCI's AAP goals and objectives to the General Manager. The Personnel Manager will recommend remedial actions for the effective implementation of the AAP.

Support Data:
Personnel Activity

OFCCP Category: Officials and Managers Job Group: 1	External Hires		External Applicants		Promotions – Into Job Group		Promotions - Within Job Group	
	MALES	FEMALES	MALES	FEMALES	MALES	FEMALES	MALES	FEMALES
White	1		8		1			
Black/African American				1				
Asian/Pacific Islander								
American Indian/Alaskan Native								
Hispanic								
Race Missing or Unknown								
TOTAL (count each person once only)	1		8	1	1			

Support Data:
Personnel Activity

OFCCP Category: Officials and Managers Job Group: 1	Voluntary Terminations & Retirements		Involuntary Terminations		Layoffs		Recalls	
	MALES	FEMALES	MALES	FEMALES	MALES	FEMALES	MALES	FEMALES
White								
Black/African American			1					
Asian/Pacific Islander								
American Indian/Alaskan Native								
Hispanic								
Race Missing or Unknown								
TOTAL (count each person once only)			1					

Support Data:
Personnel Activity

OFCCP Category: Professionals Job Group: 2	External Hires		External Applicants		Promotions – Into Job Group		Promotions - Within Job Group	
	MALES	FEMALES	MALES	FEMALES	MALES	FEMALES	MALES	FEMALES
White	2		6	9			1	
Black/African American			1	1				
Asian/Pacific Islander								
American Indian/Alaskan Native								
Hispanic			1			1		
Race Missing or Unknown								
TOTAL (count each person once only)	2		8	10		1	1	

Support Data:
Personnel Activity

OFCCP Category: Professionals **Job Group: 2**	Voluntary Terminations & Retirements		Involuntary Terminations		Layoffs		Recalls	
	MALES	FEMALES	MALES	FEMALES	MALES	FEMALES	MALES	FEMALES
White								
Black/African American								
Asian/Pacific Islander								
American Indian/Alaskan Native								
Hispanic								
Race Missing or Unknown								
TOTAL (count each person once only)								

Support Data:
Personnel Activity

OFCCP Category: Sales Workers Job Group: 4	External Hires		External Applicants		Promotions – Into Job Group		Promotions - Within Job Group	
	MALES	FEMALES	MALES	FEMALES	MALES	FEMALES	MALES	FEMALES
White								
Black/African American								
Asian/Pacific Islander								
American Indian/Alaskan Native								1
Hispanic								
Race Missing or Unknown								
TOTAL (count each person once only)								1

Support Data:
Personnel Activity

OFCCP Category: Sales Workers Job Group: 4	Voluntary Terminations & Retirements		Involuntary Terminations		Layoffs		Recalls	
	MALES	FEMALES	MALES	FEMALES	MALES	FEMALES	MALES	FEMALES
White			1					
Black/African American								
Asian/Pacific Islander								
American Indian/Alaskan Native								
Hispanic								
Race Missing or Unknown								
TOTAL (count each person once only)			1					

Support Data:
Personnel Activity

OFCCP Category: Office and Clerical Job Group: 5	External Hires		External Applicants		Promotions – Into Job Group		Promotions - Within Job Group	
	MALES	FEMALES	MALES	FEMALES	MALES	FEMALES	MALES	FEMALES
White	1		5	46				1
Black/African American		1	2	3				
Asian/Pacific Islander			2					
American Indian/Alaskan Native				1				
Hispanic			1	3				
Race Missing or Unknown								
TOTAL (count each person once only)	1	1	10	53				1

Support Data:
Personnel Activity

OFCCP Category: Office and Clerical Job Group: 5	Voluntary Terminations & Retirements		Involuntary Terminations		Layoffs		Recalls	
	MALES	FEMALES	MALES	FEMALES	MALES	FEMALES	MALES	FEMALES
White								
Black/African American								
Asian/Pacific Islander								
American Indian/Alaskan Native								
Hispanic			1					
Race Missing or Unknown								
TOTAL (count each person once only)			1					

Support Data:
Personnel Activity

OFCCP Category: Craftworkers Job Group: 6	External Hires		External Applicants		Promotions – Into Job Group		Promotions - Within Job Group	
	MALES	FEMALES	MALES	FEMALES	MALES	FEMALES	MALES	FEMALES
White	2		15	2	1		1	
Black/African American		1	1	1				
Asian/Pacific Islander			2	1	1			
American Indian/Alaskan Native								
Hispanic	1							
Race Missing or Unknown								
TOTAL (count each person once only)	3	1	18	4	2		1	

Support Data:
Personnel Activity

OFCCP Category: Craftworkers Job Group: 6	Voluntary Terminations & Retirements		Involuntary Terminations		Layoffs		Recalls	
	MALES	FEMALES	MALES	FEMALES	MALES	FEMALES	MALES	FEMALES
White	1			1				
Black/African American								
Asian/Pacific Islander								
American Indian/Alaskan Native								
Hispanic								
Race Missing or Unknown								
TOTAL (count each person once only)	1			1				

Support Data:
Personnel Activity

OFCCP Category: Operatives Job Group: 7	External Hires		External Applicants		Promotions – Into Job Group		Promotions – Within Job Group	
	MALES	FEMALES	MALES	FEMALES	MALES	FEMALES	MALES	FEMALES
White					1		1	
Black/African American								
Asian/Pacific Islander							1	
American Indian/Alaskan Native								
Hispanic								
Race Missing or Unknown								
TOTAL (count each person once only)					1		2	

Support Data:
Personnel Activity

OFCCP Category: Operatives Job Group: 7	Voluntary Terminations & Retirements		Involuntary Terminations		Layoffs		Recalls	
	MALES	FEMALES	MALES	FEMALES	MALES	FEMALES	MALES	FEMALES
White								
Black/African American								
Asian/Pacific Islander								
American Indian/Alaskan Native								
Hispanic								
Race Missing or Unknown								
TOTAL (count each person once only)								

Support Data:
Personnel Activity

OFCCP Category: Laborers Job Group:8	External Hires		External Applicants		Promotions – Into Job Group		Promotions - Within Job Group	
	MALES	FEMALES	MALES	FEMALES	MALES	FEMALES	MALES	FEMALES
White			19	1			1	
Black/African American	1		3					
Asian/Pacific Islander			1					
American Indian/Alaskan Native								
Hispanic			4					
Race Missing or Unknown								
TOTAL (count each person once only)	1		27	1			1	

Support Data:
Personnel Activity

OFCCP Category: Laborers Job Group: 8	Voluntary Terminations & Retirements		Involuntary Terminations		Layoffs		Recalls	
	MALES	FEMALES	MALES	FEMALES	MALES	FEMALES	MALES	FEMALES
White								
Black/African American			1					
Asian/Pacific Islander			1					
American Indian/Alaskan Native								
Hispanic								
Race Missing or Unknown								
TOTAL (count each person once only)			2					

Support Data:

Applicant Flow Log

NAME	RACE/ETHNICITY	SEX	DATE OF APPLICATION	JOB TITLE	INTERVIEW (Y/N)*	ACTION TAKEN (H/NH)) & DATE

*Legend: Y – Yes N-No H – Hired NH – Not Hired

Support Data

ANALYSIS OF AFFIRMATIVE ACTION PROGRAM PROGRESS: ☐ PRIOR YEAR AAP ☐ CURRENT YEAR AAP

JOB GROUP*		GOAL PLACEMENT RATE (%)**	ACTUAL PLACEMENT RATE (%)***	ANALYSIS OF GOOD FAITH EFFORTS
	MINORITY			
	FEMALE			
	MINORITY			
	FEMALE			
	MINORITY			
	FEMALE			
	MINORITY			
	FEMALE			

* JOB GROUPS WHERE GOALS ARE REQUIRED
** GOAL PLACEMENT RATE EQUALS AVAILABILITY PERCENTAGE RATE FOR MINORITIES OR FEMALES AS APPLICABLE
*** ACTUAL PLACEMENT RATE FOR MINORITIES OR FEMALES FOR A PARTICULAR JOB GROUP IS EQUAL TO THE NUMBER OF MINORITY OR FEMALE PLACEMENTS
DIVIDED BY THE TOTAL NUMBER OF PLACEMENTS. FOR EXAMPLE, IF JOB GROUP A EXPERIENCED 45 FEMALE PLACEMENTS OUT OF 90 TOTAL PLACEMENTS,
THE ACTUAL PLACEMENT RATE FOR FEMALES IS (45/90=.50) OR 50%.

Guidelines on Discrimination Because of Religion or National Origin

It is the policy of FCI, Inc. to take affirmative action to insure that applicants are employed, without regard to their religion or national origin. Such action includes, but is not limited to the following employment practices: hiring, promotion, demotion, transfer, recruitment or recruitment advertising, layoff, termination, rates of pay or other forms of compensation and selection for training.

Employment practices have been reviewed to determine whether members of the various religions and/or ethnic groups are receiving fair consideration for job opportunities. Attention has been directed toward executive and middle management levels.

1. The policy concerning FCI's obligation to provide equal employment opportunity without regard to religion or national origin is communicated to all employees via employee handbooks, policy statement and the Affirmative Action Program.

2. Internal procedures have been developed in this program to insure that FCI's obligation to provide equal employment opportunity without regard to religion or national origin is being fully implemented. **[LIST PROCEDURES]**

3. Employees are informed at least annually of FCI's commitment to equal employment opportunity for all persons, without regard to religion or national origin.

4. Recruiting sources have been informed of our commitment to provide equal employment opportunity without regard to religion or national origin.

5. Employment records of all employees are reviewed to determine the availability of promotable and transferable employees.

6. Contacts with religious and ethnic organizations will be made for purposes of advice, education, technical assistance and referral of potential employees as necessary to accomplish the purpose of this program.

7. FCI engages in recruitment activities at educational institutions with substantial enrollments of students from various ethnic and religious groups.

8. Ethnic and religious media may be used for employment advertising.

Reasonable accommodations to the religious observances and practices of employees or prospective employees will be made, unless doing so would result in undue hardship. In determining whether undue hardship exists, factors such as the cost to the company and the impact on the rights of other employees would be considered.

Appendix F

OSHA Form 300

OSHA
Forms for Recording
Work-Related Injuries and Illnesses

Dear Employer:

This booklet includes the forms needed for maintaining occupational injury and illness records for 2004. These new forms have changed in several important ways from the 2003 recordkeeping forms.

In the December 17, 2002 Federal Register (67 FR 77165-77170), OSHA announced its decision to add an occupational hearing loss column to OSHA's Form 300, Log of Work-Related Injuries and Illnesses. This forms package contains modified Forms 300 and 300A which incorporate the additional column M(5) Hearing Loss. Employers required to complete the injury and illness forms must begin to use these forms on January 1, 2004.

In response to public suggestions, OSHA also has made several changes to the forms package to make the recordkeeping materials clearer and easier to use:

- On Form 300, we've switched the positions of the day count columns. The days "away from work" column now comes before the days "on job transfer or restriction."
- We've clarified the formulas for calculating incidence rates.
- We've added new recording criteria for occupational hearing loss to the "Overview" section.
- On Form 300, we've made the column heading "Classify the Case" more prominent to make it clear that employers should mark only one selection among the four columns offered.

The Occupational Safety and Health Administration shares with you the goal of preventing injuries and illnesses in our nation's workplaces. Accurate injury and illness records will help us achieve that goal.

Occupational Safety and Health Administration
U.S. Department of Labor

What's Inside...

In this package, you'll find everything you need to complete OSHA's *Log* and the *Summary of Work-Related Injuries and Illnesses* for the next several years. On the following pages, you'll find:

► **An Overview: Recording Work-Related Injuries and Illnesses** — General instructions for filling out the forms in this package and definitions of terms you should use when you classify your cases as injuries or illnesses.

► **How to Fill Out the Log** — An example to guide you in filling out the *Log* properly.

► **Log of Work-Related Injuries and Illnesses** — Several pages of the *Log* (but you may make as many copies of the *Log* as you need.) Notice that the *Log* is separate from the *Summary*.

► **Summary of Work-Related Injuries and Illnesses** — Removable *Summary* pages for easy posting at the end of the year. Note that you post the *Summary* only, not the *Log*.

► **Worksheet to Help You Fill Out the Summary** — A worksheet for figuring the average number of employees who worked for your establishment and the total number of hours worked.

► **OSHA's 301: Injury and Illness Incident Report** — A copy of the OSHA 301 to provide details about the incident. You may make as many copies as you need or use an equivalent form.

Take a few minutes to review this package. If you have any questions, *visit us online at www.osha. gov* **OR** *call your local OSHA office.* We'll be happy to help you.

U.S. Department of Labor
Occupational Safety and Health Administration

Note: Reprinted from The Department of Labor, Occupational Safety and Health Administration.
Available at https://www.osha.gov/recordkeeping/new-osha300form1-1-04.pdf.

An Overview:
Recording Work-Related Injuries and Illnesses

The Occupational Safety and Health (OSH) Act of 1970 requires certain employers to prepare and maintain records of work-related injuries and illnesses. Use these definitions when you classify cases on the Log. OSHA's recordkeeping regulation (see 29 CFR Part 1904) provides more information about the definitions below.

The *Log of Work-Related Injuries and Illnesses* (Form 300) is used to classify work-related injuries and illnesses and to note the extent and severity of each case. When an incident occurs, use the *Log* to record specific details about what happened and how it happened. The *Summary* — a separate form (Form 300A) — shows the totals for the year in each category. At the end of the year, post the *Summary* in a visible location so that your employees are aware of the injuries and illnesses occurring in their workplace.

Employers must keep a *Log* for each establishment or site. If you have more than one establishment, you must keep a separate *Log and Summary* for each physical location that is expected to be in operation for one year or longer.

Note that your employees have the right to review your injury and illness records. For more information, see 29 *Code of Federal Regulations Part 1904.35, Employee Involvement.*

Cases listed on the *Log of Work-Related Injuries and Illnesses* are not necessarily eligible for workers' compensation or other insurance benefits. Listing a case on the *Log* does not mean that the employer or worker was at fault or that an OSHA standard was violated.

When is an injury or illness considered work-related?

An injury or illness is considered work-related if an event or exposure in the work environment caused or contributed to the condition or significantly aggravated a preexisting condition. Work-relatedness is presumed for injuries and illnesses resulting from events or exposures occurring in the workplace, unless an exception specifically applies. See 29 CFR Part 1904.5(b)(2) for the exceptions. The work environment includes the establishment and other locations where one or more employees are working or are present as a condition of their employment. See 29 CFR Part 1904.5(b)(1).

Which work-related injuries and illnesses should you record?

Record those work-related injuries and illnesses that result in:

▶ death,
▶ loss of consciousness,
▶ days away from work,
▶ restricted work activity or job transfer, or
▶ medical treatment beyond first aid.

You must also record work-related injuries and illnesses that are significant (as defined below) or meet any of the additional criteria listed below.

You must record any significant work-related injury or illness that is diagnosed by a physician or other licensed health care professional. You must record any work-related case involving cancer, chronic irreversible disease, a fractured or cracked bone, or a punctured eardrum. See 29 CFR 1904.7.

What are the additional criteria?

You must record the following conditions when they are work-related:

▶ any needlestick injury or cut from a sharp object that is contaminated with another person's blood or other potentially infectious material;
▶ any case requiring an employee to be medically removed under the requirements of an OSHA health standard;
▶ tuberculosis infection as evidenced by a positive skin test or diagnosis by a physician or other licensed health care professional after exposure to a known case of active tuberculosis.
▶ an employee's hearing test (audiogram) reveals 1) that the employee has experienced a Standard Threshold Shift (STS) in hearing in one or both ears (averaged at 2000, 3000, and 4000 Hz) and 2) the employee's total hearing level is 25 decibels (dB) or more above audiometric zero (also averaged at 2000, 3000, and 4000 Hz) in the same ear(s) as the STS.

What is medical treatment?

Medical treatment includes managing and caring for a patient for the purpose of combating disease or disorder. The following are not considered medical treatments and are NOT recordable:

▶ visits to a doctor or health care professional solely for observation or counseling;

1. Within 7 calendar days after you receive information about a case, decide if the case is recordable under the OSHA recordkeeping requirements.

2. Determine whether the incident is a new case or a recurrence of an existing one.

3. Establish whether the case was work-related.

4. If the case is recordable, decide which form you will fill out as the injury and illness incident report.

   You may use *OSHA's 301: Injury and Illness Incident Report* or an equivalent form. Some state workers compensation, insurance, or other reports may be acceptable substitutes, as long as they provide the same information as the OSHA 301.

How to work with the Log

1. Identify the employee involved unless it is a privacy concern case as described below.

2. Identify when and where the case occurred.

3. Describe the case, as specifically as you can.

4. Classify the seriousness of the case by recording the **most serious outcome** associated with the case, with column G (Death) being the most serious and column J (Other recordable cases) being the least serious.

5. Identify whether the case is an injury or illness. If the case is an injury, check the injury category. If the case is an illness, check the appropriate illness category.

U.S. Department of Labor
Occupational Safety and Health Administration

- diagnostic procedures, including administering prescription medications that are used solely for diagnostic purposes; and
- any procedure that can be labeled first aid. (See below for more information about first aid.)

What is first aid?

If the incident required only the following types of treatment, consider it first aid. Do NOT record the case if it involves only:

- using non-prescription medications at non-prescription strength;
- administering tetanus immunizations;
- cleaning, flushing, or soaking wounds on the skin surface;
- using wound coverings, such as bandages, Band-Aids™ gauze pads, etc., or using SteriStrips™ or butterfly bandages.
- using hot or cold therapy;
- using any totally non-rigid means of support, such as elastic bandages, wraps, non-rigid back belts, etc.;
- using temporary immobilization devices while transporting an accident victim (splints, slings, neck collars, or back boards).
- drilling a fingernail or toenail to relieve pressure, or draining fluids from blisters;
- using eye patches;
- using simple irrigation or a cotton swab to remove foreign bodies not embedded in or adhered to the eye;
- using irrigation, tweezers, cotton swab or other simple means to remove splinters or foreign material from areas other than the eye;
- using finger guards;
- using massages;
- drinking fluids to relieve heat stress

How do you decide if the case involved restricted work?

Restricted work activity occurs when, as the result of a work-related injury or illness, an employer or health care professional keeps, or recommends keeping, an employee from doing the routine functions of his or her job or from working the full workday that the employee would have been scheduled to work before the injury or illness occurred.

How do you count the number of days of restricted work activity or the number of days away from work?

Count the number of calendar days the employee was on restricted work activity or was away from work as a result of the recordable injury or illness. Do not count the day on which the injury or illness occurred in this number. Begin counting days from the day after the incident occurs. If a single injury or illness involved both days away from work and days of restricted work activity, enter the total number of days for each. You may stop counting days of restricted work activity or days away from work once the total of either or the combination of both reaches 180 days.

Under what circumstances should you NOT enter the employee's name on the OSHA Form 300?

You must consider the following types of injuries or illnesses to be privacy concern cases:

- an injury or illness to an intimate body part or to the reproductive system,
- an injury or illness resulting from a sexual assault,
- a mental illness,
- a case of HIV infection, hepatitis, or tuberculosis.
- a needlestick injury or cut from a sharp object that is contaminated with blood or other potentially infectious material (see 29 CFR Part 1904.8 for definition), and
- other illnesses, if the employee independently and voluntarily requests that his or her name not be entered on the log.

You must not enter the employee's name on the OSHA 300 *Log* for these cases. Instead, enter "privacy case" in the space normally used for the employee's name. You must keep a separate, confidential list of the case numbers and employee names for the establishment's privacy concern cases so that you can update the cases and provide information to the government if asked to do so.

If you have a reasonable basis to believe that information describing the privacy concern case may be personally identifiable even though the employee's name has been omitted, you may use discretion in describing the injury or illness on both the OSHA 300 and 301 forms. You must enter enough information to identify the cause of the incident and the general severity of the injury or illness, but you do not need to include details of an intimate or private nature.

What if the outcome changes after you record the case?

If the outcome or extent of an injury or illness changes after you have recorded the case, simply draw a line through the original entry or, if you wish, delete or white-out the original entry. Then write the new entry where it belongs. Remember, you need to record the most serious outcome for each case.

Classifying injuries

An injury is any wound or damage to the body resulting from an event in the work environment.

Examples: Cut, puncture, laceration, abrasion, fracture, bruise, contusion, chipped tooth, amputation, insect bite, electrocution, or a thermal, chemical, electrical, or radiation burn. Sprain and strain injuries to muscles, joints, and connective tissues are classified as injuries when they result from a slip, trip, fall or other similar accidents.

Classifying illnesses

Skin diseases or disorders

Skin diseases or disorders are illnesses involving the worker's skin that are caused by work exposure to chemicals, plants, or other substances.

Examples: Contact dermatitis, eczema, or rash caused by primary irritants and sensitizers or poisonous plants; oil acne; friction blisters, chrome ulcers; inflammation of the skin.

Respiratory conditions

Respiratory conditions are illnesses associated with breathing hazardous biological agents, chemicals, dust, gases, vapors, or fumes at work.

Examples: Silicosis, asbestosis, pneumonitis, pharyngitis, rhinitis or acute congestion; farmer's lung, beryllium disease, tuberculosis, occupational asthma, reactive airways dysfunction syndrome (RADS), chronic obstructive pulmonary disease (COPD), hypersensitivity pneumonitis, toxic inhalation injury, such as metal fume fever, chronic obstructive bronchitis, and other pneumoconioses.

Poisoning

Poisoning includes disorders evidenced by abnormal concentrations of toxic substances in blood, other tissues, other bodily fluids, or the breath that are caused by the ingestion or absorption of toxic substances into the body.

Examples: Poisoning by lead, mercury, cadmium, arsenic, or other metals; poisoning by carbon monoxide, hydrogen sulfide, or other gases; poisoning by benzene, benzol, carbon tetrachloride, or other organic solvents; poisoning by insecticide sprays, such as parathion or lead arsenate; poisoning by other chemicals, such as formaldehyde.

Hearing Loss

Noise-induced hearing loss is defined for recordkeeping purposes as a change in hearing threshold relative to the baseline audiogram of an average of 10 dB or more in either ear at 2000, 3000 and 4000 hertz, and the employee's total hearing level is 25 decibels (dB) or more above audiometric zero (also averaged at 2000, 3000, and 4000 hertz) in the same ear(s).

All other illnesses

All other occupational illnesses.

Examples: Heatstroke, sunstroke, heat exhaustion, heat stress and other effects of environmental heat; freezing, frostbite, and other effects of exposure to low temperatures; decompression sickness; effects of ionizing radiation (isotopes, x-rays, radium); effects of nonionizing radiation (welding flash, ultra-violet rays, lasers); anthrax; bloodborne pathogenic diseases, such as AIDS, HIV, hepatitis B or hepatitis C; brucellosis; malignant or benign tumors; histoplasmosis; coccidioidomycosis.

When must you post the Summary?

You must post the *Summary* only — not the *Log* — by February 1 of the year following the year covered by the form and keep it posted until April 30 of that year.

How long must you keep the Log and Summary on file?

You must keep the *Log* and *Summary* for 5 years following the year to which they pertain.

Do you have to send these forms to OSHA at the end of the year?

No. You do not have to send the completed forms to OSHA unless specifically asked to do so.

How can we help you?

If you have a question about how to fill out the *Log*,

☐ *visit us online at www.osha.gov* or
☐ *call your local OSHA office.*

U.S. Department of Labor
Occupational Safety and Health Administration

Optional

Calculating Injury and Illness Incidence Rates

What is an incidence rate?

An incidence rate is the number of recordable injuries and illnesses occurring among a given number of full-time workers (usually 100 full-time workers) over a given period of time (usually one year). To evaluate your firm's injury and illness experience over time or to compare your firm's experience with that of your industry as a whole, you need to compute your incidence rate. Because a specific number of workers and a specific period of time are involved, these rates can help you identify problems in your workplace and/or progress you may have made in preventing work-related injuries and illnesses.

How do you calculate an incidence rate?

You can compute an occupational injury and illness incidence rate for all recordable cases or for cases that involved days away from work for your firm quickly and easily. The formula requires that you follow instructions in paragraph (a) below for the total recordable cases or those in paragraph (b) for cases that involved days away from work, *and* for both rates the instructions in paragraph (c).

(a) *To find out the total number of recordable injuries and illnesses that occurred during the year,* count the number of line entries on your OSHA Form 300, or refer to the OSHA Form 300A and sum the entries for columns (G), (H), (I), and (J).

(b) *To find out the number of injuries and illnesses that involved days away from work,* count the number of line entries on your OSHA Form 300 that received a check mark in column (H), or refer to the entry for column

(H) on the OSHA Form 300A.

(c) *The number of hours all employees actually worked during the year.* Refer to OSHA Form 300A and optional worksheet to calculate this number.

You can compute the incidence rate for all recordable cases of injuries and illnesses using the following formula:

Total number of injuries and illnesses X 200,000 ÷ Number of hours worked by all employees = Total recordable case rate

(The 200,000 figure in the formula represents the number of hours 100 employees working 40 hours per week, 50 weeks per year would work, and provides the standard base for calculating incidence rates.)

You can compute the incidence rate for recordable cases involving days away from work, days of restricted work activity or job transfer (DART) using the following formula:

(Number of entries in column H + Number of entries in column I) X 200,000 ÷ Number of hours worked by all employees = DART incidence rate

You can use the same formula to calculate incidence rates for other variables such as cases involving restricted work activity (column (I) on Form 300A), cases involving skin disorders (column (M-2) on Form 300A), etc. Just substitute the appropriate total for these cases, from Form 300A, into the formula in place of the total number of injuries and illnesses.

What can I compare my incidence rate to?

The Bureau of Labor Statistics (BLS) conducts a survey of occupational injuries and illnesses each year and publishes incidence rate data by various classifications (e.g., by industry, by employer size, etc.). You can obtain these published data at www.bls.gov/iif or by calling a BLS Regional Office.

Worksheet

Total number of injuries and illnesses [ ] X 200,000 ÷ Number of hours worked by all employees [ ] = Total recordable case rate [ ]

Number of entries in Column H + Column I [ ] X 200,000 ÷ Number of hours worked by all employees [ ] = DART incidence rate [ ]

U.S. Department of Labor
Occupational Safety and Health Administration

How to Fill Out the Log

The *Log of Work-Related Injuries and Illnesses* is used to classify work-related injuries and illnesses and to note the extent and severity of each case. When an incident occurs, use the *Log* to record specific details about what happened and how it happened.

If your company has more than one establishment or site, you must keep separate records for each physical location that is expected to remain in operation for one year or longer.

We have given you several copies of the *Log* in this package. If you need more than we provided, you may photocopy and use as many as you need.

The *Summary* — a separate form — shows the work-related injury and illness totals for the year in each category. At the end of the year, count the number of incidents in each category and transfer the totals from the *Log* to the *Summary*. Then post the *Summary* in a visible location so that your employees are aware of injuries and illnesses occurring in their workplace.

You don't post the *Log*. You post only the *Summary* at the end of the year.

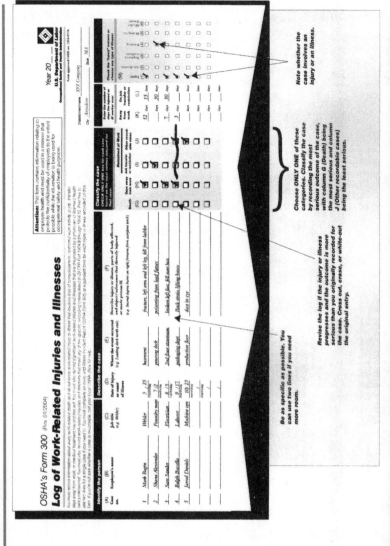

OSHA's Form 300 (Rev. 01/2004)

Log of Work-Related Injuries and Illnesses

Attention: This form contains information relating to employee health and must be used in a manner that protects the confidentiality of employees to the extent possible while the information is being used for occupational safety and health purposes.

U.S. Department of Labor
Occupational Safety and Health Administration

Form approved OMB no. 1218-0176

Year 20 ____

You must record information about every work-related death and about every work-related injury or illness that involves loss of consciousness, restricted work activity or job transfer, days away from work, or medical treatment beyond first aid. You must also record significant work-related injuries and illnesses that are diagnosed by a physician or licensed health care professional. You must also record work-related injuries and illnesses that meet any of the specific recording criteria listed in 29 CFR Part 1904.8 through 1904.12. Feel free to use two lines for a single case if you need to. You must complete an Injury and Illness Incident Report (OSHA Form 301) or equivalent form for each injury or illness recorded on this form. If you're not sure whether a case is recordable, call your local OSHA office for help.

Establishment name _____
City _____ State _____

Identify the person

(A) Case no.	(B) Employee's name	(C) Job title (e.g., Welder)

Describe the case

(D) Date of injury or onset of illness	(E) Where the event occurred (e.g., Loading dock north end)	(F) Describe injury or illness, parts of body affected, and object/substance that directly injured or made person ill (e.g., Second degree burns on right forearm from acetylene torch)

(D) month/day (repeated for each row)

Classify the case

CHECK ONLY ONE box for each case based on the most serious outcome for that case:

Death (G)	Days away from work (H)	Remained at Work — Job transfer or restriction (I)	Remained at Work — Other recordable cases (J)

Enter the number of days the injured or ill worker was:

Away from work (K)	On job transfer or restriction (L)
____ days	____ days

Check the "Injury" column or choose one type of illness:

(M)	Injury (1)	Skin disorder (2)	Respiratory condition (3)	Poisoning (4)	Hearing loss (5)	All other illnesses (6)

Page totals ▶

Be sure to transfer these totals to the Summary page (Form 300A) before you post it.

	Injury (1)	Skin disorder (2)	Respiratory condition (3)	Poisoning (4)	Hearing loss (5)	All other illnesses (6)

Page ____ of ____

Public reporting burden for this collection of information is estimated to average 14 minutes per response, including time to review the instructions, search and gather the data needed, and complete and review the collection of information. Persons are not required to respond to the collection of information unless it displays a currently valid OMB control number. If you have any comments about these estimates or any other aspects of this data collection, contact: US Department of Labor, OSHA Office of Statistical Analysis, Room N-3644, 200 Constitution Avenue, NW, Washington, DC 20210. Do not send the completed forms to this office.

OSHA's Form 300A (Rev. 01/2004)

Summary of Work-Related Injuries and Illnesses

Year 20____

U.S. Department of Labor
Occupational Safety and Health Administration

Form approved OMB no. 1218-0176

All establishments covered by Part 1904 must complete this Summary page, even if no work-related injuries or illnesses occurred during the year. Remember to review the Log to verify that the entries are complete and accurate before completing this summary.

Using the Log, count the individual entries you made for each category. Then write the totals below, making sure you've added the entries from every page of the Log. If you had no cases, write "0."

Employees, former employees, and their representatives have the right to review the OSHA Form 300 in its entirety. They also have limited access to the OSHA Form 301 or its equivalent. See 29 CFR Part 1904.35, in OSHA's recordkeeping rule, for further details on the access provisions for these forms.

Number of Cases

Total number of deaths

_____
(G)

Total number of cases with days away from work

_____
(H)

Total number of cases with job transfer or restriction

_____
(I)

Total number of other recordable cases

_____
(J)

Number of Days

Total number of days away from work

_____
(K)

Total number of days of job transfer or restriction

_____
(L)

Injury and Illness Types

Total number of . . .
(M)

(1) Injuries _____

(2) Skin disorders _____

(3) Respiratory conditions _____

(4) Poisonings _____

(5) Hearing loss _____

(6) All other illnesses _____

Establishment information

Your establishment name _____

Street _____

City _____ State _____ ZIP _____

Industry description (e.g., Manufacture of motor truck trailers)

_____

Standard Industrial Classification (SIC), if known (e.g., 3715)

_ _ _ _ — _ _ _ _

OR

North American Industrial Classification (NAICS), if known (e.g., 336212)

_____

Employment information (If you don't have these figures, see the Worksheet on the back of this page to estimate.)

Annual average number of employees _____

Total hours worked by all employees last year _____

Sign here

Knowingly falsifying this document may result in a fine.

I certify that I have examined this document and that to the best of my knowledge the entries are true, accurate, and complete.

_____
Company executive   Title

(_____) _____ — _____
Phone   Date

Post this Summary page from February 1 to April 30 of the year following the year covered by the form.

Public reporting burden for this collection of information is estimated to average 58 minutes per response, including time to review the instructions, search and gather the data needed, and complete and review the collection of information. Persons are not required to respond to the collection of information unless it displays a currently valid OMB control number. If you have any comments about these estimates or any other aspects of this data collection, contact: US Department of Labor, OSHA Office of Statistical Analysis, Room N-3644, 200 Constitution Avenue, NW, Washington, DC 20210. Do not send the completed forms to this office.

Optional

Worksheet to Help You Fill Out the Summary

At the end of the year. OSHA requires you to enter the average number of employees and the total hours worked by your employees on the summary. If you don't have these figures, you can use the information on this page to estimate the numbers you will need to enter on the Summary page at the end of the year.

How to figure the average number of employees who worked for your establishment during the year:

➊ Add the total number of employees your establishment paid in all pay periods during the year. Include all employees: full-time, part-time, temporary, seasonal, salaried, and hourly.

The number of employees paid in all pay periods = _____ ➊

➋ Count the number of pay periods your establishment had during the year. Be sure to include any pay periods when you had no employees.

The number of pay periods during the year = _____ ➋

➌ Divide the number of employees by the number of pay periods.

$$\frac{➊}{➋} = \text{_____} \quad ➌$$

➍ Round the answer to the next highest whole number. Write the rounded number in the blank marked *Annual average number of employees.*

The number rounded = _____ ➍

For example, Acme Construction figured its average employment this way:

For pay period...	Acme paid this number of employees...
1	10
2	0
3	15
4	30
5	40
▶	
24	20
25	15
26	+10
	830

Number of employees paid = 830   ➊

Number of pay periods = 26   ➋

$$\frac{830}{26} = 31.92 \quad ➌$$

31.92 rounds to 32   ➍

32 is the annual average number of employees

How to figure the total hours worked by all employees:

Include hours worked by salaried, hourly, part-time and seasonal workers, as well as hours worked by other workers subject to day to day supervision by your establishment (e.g., temporary help services workers).

Do not include vacation, sick leave, holidays, or any other non-work time, even if employees were paid for it. If your establishment keeps records of only the hours paid or if you have employees who are not paid by the hour, please estimate the hours that the employees actually worked.

If this number isn't available, you can use this optional worksheet to estimate it.

Optional Worksheet

Find the number of full-time employees in your establishment for the year.

_____

Multiply by the number of work hours for a full-time employee in a year.

X _____

This is the number of full-time hours worked.

_____

Add the number of any overtime hours as well as the hours worked by other employees (part-time, temporary, seasonal)

+ _____

Round the answer to the next highest whole number. Write the rounded number in the blank marked *Total hours worked by all employees last year.*

_____

U.S. Department of Labor
Occupational Safety and Health Administration

OSHA's Form 301
Injury and Illness Incident Report

U.S. Department of Labor
Occupational Safety and Health Administration

Form approved OMB no. 1218-0176

Attention: This form contains information relating to employee health and must be used in a manner that protects the confidentiality of employees to the extent possible while the information is being used for occupational safety and health purposes.

This *Injury and Illness Incident Report* is one of the first forms you must fill out when a recordable work-related injury or illness has occurred. Together with the *Log of Work-Related Injuries and Illnesses* and the accompanying *Summary*, these forms help the employer and OSHA develop a picture of the extent and severity of work-related incidents.

Within 7 calendar days after you receive information that a recordable work-related injury or illness has occurred, you must fill out this form or an equivalent. Some state workers' compensation, insurance, or other reports may be acceptable substitutes. To be considered an equivalent form, any substitute must contain all the information asked for on this form.

According to Public Law 91-596 and 29 CFR 1904, OSHA's recordkeeping rule, you must keep this form on file for 5 years following the year to which it pertains.

If you need additional copies of this form, you may photocopy and use as many as you need.

Completed by _____

Title _____

Phone (___) ___ - ___ Date ___ / ___ / ___

Information about the employee

1) Full name _____

2) Street _____
   City _____ State _____ ZIP _____

3) Date of birth ___ / ___ / ___

4) Date hired ___ / ___ / ___

5) ☐ Male ☐ Female

Information about the physician or other health care professional

6) Name of physician or other health care professional _____

7) If treatment was given away from the worksite, where was it given?
   Facility _____
   Street _____
   City _____ State _____ ZIP _____

8) Was employee treated in an emergency room?
   ☐ Yes ☐ No

9) Was employee hospitalized overnight as an in-patient?
   ☐ Yes ☐ No

Information about the case

10) Case number from the *Log* _____ *(Transfer the case number from the Log after you record the case.)*

11) Date of injury or illness ___ / ___ / ___

12) Time employee began work _____ AM / PM

13) Time of event _____ AM / PM ☐ Check if time cannot be determined

14) **What was the employee doing just before the incident occurred?** Describe the activity, as well as the tools, equipment, or material the employee was using. Be specific. *Examples:* "climbing a ladder while carrying roofing materials"; "spraying chlorine from hand sprayer"; "daily computer key-entry."

15) **What happened?** Tell us how the injury occurred. *Examples:* "When ladder slipped on wet floor, worker fell 20 feet"; "Worker was sprayed with chlorine when gasket broke during replacement"; "Worker developed soreness in wrist over time."

16) **What was the injury or illness?** Tell us the part of the body that was affected and how it was affected; be more specific than "hurt," "pain," or sore." *Examples:* "strained back"; "chemical burn, hand"; "carpal tunnel syndrome."

17) **What object or substance directly harmed the employee?** *Examples:* "concrete floor"; "chlorine"; "radial arm saw." *If this question does not apply to the incident, leave it blank.*

18) **If the employee died, when did death occur?** Date of death ___ / ___ / ___

If You Need Help...

If you need help deciding whether a case is recordable, or if you have questions about the information in this package, feel free to contact us. We'll gladly answer any questions you have.

▼ **Visit us online at www.osha.gov**

▼ **Call your OSHA Regional office and ask for the recordkeeping coordinator**

or

▼ **Call your State Plan office**

Federal Jurisdiction

Region 1 - 617 / 565-9860
Connecticut; Massachusetts; Maine; New Hampshire; Rhode Island

Region 2 - 212 / 337-2378
New York; New Jersey

Region 3 - 215 / 861-4900
DC; Delaware; Pennsylvania; West Virginia

Region 4 - 404 / 562-2300
Alabama; Florida; Georgia; Mississippi

Region 5 - 312 / 353-2220
Illinois; Ohio; Wisconsin

Region 6 - 214 / 767-4731
Arkansas; Louisiana; Oklahoma; Texas

Region 7 - 816 / 426-5861
Kansas; Missouri; Nebraska

Region 8 - 303 / 844-1600
Colorado; Montana; North Dakota; South Dakota

Region 9 - 415 / 975-4310

Region 10 - 206 / 553-5930
Idaho

State Plan States

Alaska - 907 / 269-4957

Arizona - 602 / 542-5795

California - 415 / 703-5100

*Connecticut - 860 / 566-4380

Hawaii - 808 / 586-9100

Indiana - 317 / 232-2688

Iowa - 515 / 281-3661

Kentucky - 502 / 564-3070

Maryland - 410 / 527-4465

Michigan - 517 / 322-1848

Minnesota - 651 / 284-5050

Nevada - 702 / 486-9020

*New Jersey - 609 / 984-1389

New Mexico - 505 / 827-4230

*New York - 518 / 457-2574

North Carolina - 919 / 807-2875

Oregon - 503 / 378-3272

Puerto Rico - 787 / 754-2172

South Carolina - 803 / 734-9669

Tennessee - 615 / 741-2793

Utah - 801 / 530-6901

Vermont - 802 / 828-2765

Virginia - 804 / 786-6613

Virgin Islands - 340 / 772-1315

Washington - 360 / 902-5554

Wyoming - 307 / 777-7786

*Public Sector only

U.S. Department of Labor
Occupational Safety and Health Administration

Have questions?

If you need help in filling out the *Log* or *Summary*, or if you have questions about whether a case is recordable, contact us. We'll be happy to help you. You can:

▶ Visit us online at: **www.osha.gov**

▶ Call your regional or state plan office. You'll find the phone number listed inside this cover.

U.S. Department of Labor
Occupational Safety and Health Administration

Appendix G

HRCI's Ethical Standards

HR Certification Institute® (HRCI®) determines who is certified and thus authorized to use the marks. Implicit in the acceptance of this authorization is an obligation not only to comply with the mandates and requirements of all applicable laws and regulations but also to take responsibility to act in an ethical and professionally responsible manner. Adherence to these standards is expected from all who hold an HR Certification Institute credential and serves to ensure public confidence in the integrity of these individuals.

Those holding an HR Certification Institute credential commit to the following:

Professional Responsibility

As an HR Certification Institute certificant, you are responsible for adding value to the organizations you serve and contributing to the ethical success of those organizations. You accept professional responsibility for your individual decisions and actions. You are also an advocate for the HR profession by engaging in activities that enhance its credibility and value. You will:

- Adhere to the highest standards of ethical and professional behavior.
- Measure the effectiveness of human resources in contributing to or achieving organizational goals.

Note: From HR Certification Institute, "HRCI Code of Ethical and Professional Responsibility." Available at https://www.hrci.org/docs/default-source/web-files/code-of-ethics-and-responsiblity .pdf?sfvrsn=10. Used with permission by Human Resource Certification Institute, Inc.

- Comply with the law.
- Work consistently within the values of the profession.
- Strive to achieve the highest levels of service, performance, and social responsibility.
- Advocate for the appropriate use and appreciation of human beings as employees.
- Advocate openly and within the established forums for debate in order to influence decision making and results.

Professional Development

As an HR Certification Institute certificant, you must strive to meet the highest standards of competence and commit to strengthen your competencies on a continuous basis. You will:

- Commit to continuous learning, skills development, and application of new knowledge related to both HR management and the organizations you serve.
- Contribute to the body of knowledge, the evolution of the profession, and the growth of individuals through teaching, research, and dissemination of knowledge.

Ethical Leadership

As an HR Certification Institute certificant, you are expected to exhibit individual leadership as a role model for maintaining the highest standards of ethical conduct. You will:

- Be ethical and act ethically in every professional interaction.
- Question pending individual and group actions when necessary to ensure that decisions are ethical and are implemented in an ethical manner.
- Seek expert guidance if ever in doubt about the ethical propriety of a situation.
- Through teaching and mentoring, champion the development of others as ethical leaders in the profession and in organizations.

Fairness and Justice

As an HR Certification Institute certificant, you are ethically responsible for promoting and fostering fairness and justice for all employees and their organizations. You will:

- Respect the uniqueness and intrinsic worth of every individual.
- Treat people with dignity, respect, and compassion to foster a trusting work environment free of harassment, intimidation, and unlawful discrimination.

- Ensure that everyone has the opportunity to develop their skills and new competencies.
- Assure an environment of inclusiveness and a commitment to diversity in the organizations you serve.
- Develop, administer, and advocate policies and procedures that foster fair, consistent, and equitable treatment for all.
- Regardless of personal interests, support decisions made by your organizations that are both ethical and legal.
- Act in a responsible manner and practice sound management in the country or countries in which the organizations you serve operate.

Conflicts of Interest

As an HR Certification Institute certificant, you must maintain a high level of trust with your stakeholders. You must protect the interests of those stakeholders as well as your professional integrity and should not engage in activities that create actual, apparent, or potential conflicts of interest. You will:

- Adhere to and advocate the use of published policies on conflicts of interest within your organization.
- Refrain from using your position for personal, material, or financial gain or the appearance of such.
- Refrain from giving or seeking preferential treatment in HR processes.
- Prioritize your obligations to identify conflicts of interest or the appearance thereof. When conflicts arise, you will disclose them to relevant stakeholders.

Use of Information

As an HR Certification Institute certificant, you must consider and protect the rights of individuals, especially in the acquisition and dissemination of information while ensuring truthful communications and facilitating informed decision making. You will:

- Acquire and disseminate information through ethical and responsible means.
- Ensure that only appropriate information is used in decisions affecting the employment relationship.
- Investigate the accuracy and source of information before allowing it to be used in employment-related decisions.
- Maintain current and accurate HR information.
- Safeguard restricted or confidential information.
- Take appropriate steps to ensure the accuracy and completeness of all communicated information about HR policies and practices.
- Take appropriate steps to ensure the accuracy and completeness of all communicated information used in HR-related training.

Appendix H
Glossary of Terms

absenteeism   Not coming to work
Not coming to work because of illness or personal problems. Many companies calculate the rate of absenteeism of their employees, which is the average number of days they do not come to work.

accountability   Responsibility
An obligation to accept responsibility for one's actions

accrual   A method of accounting
An accounting method that recognizes a company's financial performance by recording income and expenses at the time a transaction occurs, rather than when a payment is received or an invoice is paid

acquiring company   A company that buys another company
The business or organization that is buying another business

acquisition   An acquired company
A process in which one organization buys another organization

active listening   Checking for understanding
A communication method that a listener uses to interpret and evaluate information from a speaker

---

Note: Used with permission by Human Resource Certification Institute, Inc. Please see www .hrci.org/glossary for updates.

ADA Americans with Disabilities Act
A U.S. law that prevents an organization or person from discriminating against an employee because of physical or mental disabilities

ADDIE model A training design technique
A process for designing training programs that has five steps: analysis, design, development, implementation, and evaluation

ad hoc Not planned, for a specific case
A solution to a specific problem that is not planned, or cannot be used in other situations

ADR Alternative dispute resolution
A method for resolving a disagreement without going through formal legal procedures

advocacy Support, encouragement
Supporting an idea or cause, influencing outcomes

affirmative action A process designed to treat all applicants and employees equally
An activity designed to correct previous inequality that may have existed for certain groups or classes of people

align Line up, make parallel
To place in a line or arrange in a similar way

alliance Agreement, cooperation
A partnership between organizations that helps both sides

allowance Amount of money
Money for a specific purpose

Angoff method An exam scoring process
A way to set the standard score for passing a test

appeal A request to a higher authority
To challenge an official decision (for example, in court)

appraisals Evaluations
Assessments of the value or performance of something (for example, job appraisals)

apprentice A person learning a skill, trade, or profession
A person learning a trade or skill from a qualified person for a specific length of time

arbitration Resolving a dispute
The process of coming to an agreement about something without using a judge or court

assessment center A method of selecting personnel
A system of tests and interviews that evaluate employee performance and help companies select the right people for job positions

assignee   Expatriate, transferee
A person who is on (or will go on) an international work assignment

assignment   Job or position
A job, usually in a new location

assimilation   A process of integration
The process of becoming a member of a team, organization, or culture

asynchronous learning   An online teaching method
A teaching method where the students and teachers are online at different times

ATS   Applicant tracking system
Computer software that helps an organization recruit employees

attrition   Reduction, decrease in numbers of employees
The number of employees who leave the organization for any reason: resignation, termination, end of agreement, retirement, sickness, or death

authority   Expert or person in control
Someone with extensive knowledge of a specific subject; a person in a superior position

background check   Process of confirming a job candidate's personal and public information
Gathering data to determine the accuracy of a candidate's experience and records during employment screening (for example, verifying personal data, checking credentials, determining any criminal activity)

balanced scorecard   An analysis technique
A method or tool that organizations use to measure the success of their strategies by looking at both financial and nonfinancial areas

balance-sheet approach   A model for international compensation
A way to set the salary and living allowances for employees on international assignments

base salary   A fixed amount of money paid for work performed
Compensation that does not include benefits, bonuses, or commissions

behavioral interview   Job interview method based on past work behavior
Interview process to predict future performance based on how the candidate acted in past work situations

benchmarks   Measures or markers
A basis for judging or measuring something else

beneficiary   Receiver of benefits
A person who is eligible to gain benefits under a will, insurance policy, retirement plan, or other contract

benefit programs   Compensation in addition to wages
Workers' entitlements in addition to base salary (for example, health insurance, life insurance, disability pay, retirement pension, and so on)

benefits   Noncash compensation provided to employees
Compensation that the employee receives in addition to a base salary (for example, health insurance, company housing, company meals, clothing allowance, pension, and gym membership)

best practices   Techniques or activities that give the best results
The methods, processes, or activities that have proven to produce outstanding results for organizations' opportunities

biodata   Information about a person
A shortened term for "biographical data": information about a person's education, background, and work history

blackout period   Temporary denial of access
A brief period in which employees cannot access or change things about their retirement or investment plans

blended learning   A mix of different types of learning
A learning method that combines face-to-face teaching with online learning

brain drain   Loss of skilled workers
When smart and talented people leave their own country for better opportunities

brainstorming   A process for producing new ideas and solutions
A method in which individuals or groups spontaneously find solutions to a problem

breakdown analysis   Listing things according to categories
Analyzing and classifying, such as an analysis of revenue sources or a report on attrition numbers

briefings   Instructions or summary
Discussions that provide detailed information

brownfield operation   Previously used land
Reuse of land previously used for industry or manufacturing

buy-in   Obtaining support
Acquiring backing or sponsorship from a person or group

career development   Progress in a job or profession
An employee's progress through each stage in his or her career

career ladder promotion   A structured job advancement
Job advancement through a series of defined positions, from lower level to higher level

career management   Planning and controlling the professional development of an employee
Preparing, implementing, and monitoring the career path of an employee, with a focus on the goals and needs of the organization

career planning   Managing professional goals
Taking steps to improve professional skills and create new opportunities

career plateau   No possibility for advancing in a career
Inability of an employee to advance further in the company due to mediocre performance or lack of opportunities

cascading goals   Goals that flow from the top to the bottom of an organization
Goals that an organization sets at a high level, which flow down as goals for departments, and then become goals for specific people

cause-and-effect diagram   A tool used to examine quality factors
A visual tool to organize factors that contribute to certain outcomes; also called a fishbone diagram

Caux principles   Ethical guidelines for international organizations
A set of ethical principles developed for global organizations by the Caux Round Table, a group of global business leaders from around the world

center of excellence   An area where high standards produce the best results
A team or division that uses best practices within a specific area to achieve business goals

central tendency   Average value of a data set
A measure of the middle of a statistical distribution of data

certification   A procedure to grant an official designation
Confirmation of specific achievements or characteristics given by an authority, usually by issuing a certificate or diploma after a test

chain of command   Order of authority
The sequence of power in an organization, from the top to the next levels of authority

change agent   Something or someone that causes change
A person or department that deliberately causes change within an organization

cloud computing   A type of computing that uses groups of servers and resources, made available on the Internet
Using a network of remote servers hosted on the Internet to access, manage, and process data, rather than using a local server

coaching   Guiding, giving information, or training
A method of developing specific skills in which a coach gives information and objective feedback to a person or group

code of conduct   A set of principles and behavioral expectations
A written description of the principles, behaviors, and responsibilities that an organization expects of its employees

codetermination   A management structure involving employees
An organizational structure in which employees share responsibility for the operation of a company

cognitive ability   Intelligence
Thinking skills and mental abilities

commuter assignment   A type of expatriate position requiring frequent travel between two countries
An international job that requires an employee to live in one country and work in another country, and to travel regularly between them (for example, an expatriate who lives in Bahrain and works in Saudi Arabia)

company culture   The beliefs and behaviors of an organization
The values, language, rules, procedures, expectations, and processes that affect how employees of an organization think, act, and view the world

compa-ratio   Math formula for comparing salaries
A number comparing a person's salary to other salaries for the same job; the comparison ratio is calculated by taking a person's salary and comparing it to the midpoint of other salaries (if a person earns $45,000 per year in a job where the salary midpoint is $50,000 per year, the compa-ratio is $45,000/$50,000 = 90%).

compensation   Salary and benefits
Everything that an employee receives for working, including pay and nonmonetary benefits

competencies   The abilities needed to do well in a specific job
The skills, behaviors, and knowledge that are needed to succeed in a specific job

competency-based pay   Salary based on demonstrated skills and knowledge
Pay based on the skills and knowledge that make an employee valuable to an organization

competency model   A description of the skills needed for a specific job
A list of the behaviors, skills, and knowledge needed to do well in a specific job

compliance   Obedience, conforming
Following established laws, guidelines, or rules

conflict resolution   Process of negotiation, arbitration
A method of negotiating agreements or solving problems

consolidation   Process of combining, bringing together
Combining separate companies, functional areas, or product lines; in finance, combining the assets, equity, liabilities, and operating accounts of a company with those of its subsidiaries

contingent worker   Part-time or temporary employee
A person who is hired part-time to work under a contract or for a fixed period of time

contract manufacturing   Producing private-label goods
A production method in which one company hires another company to manufacture parts or goods under its label and according to its specifications

core competency   Specific expertise
The skills or knowledge that an organization or employee needs to do work

corporate citizenship   Responsibility to employees and to the community
A practice in which organizations take steps to improve their employees' lives and the communities in which they operate

corporate culture   The beliefs and behaviors of an organization
The values, language, rules, procedures, expectations, and processes that affect how employees of an organization think, act, and view the world

corporate social responsibility   An organization's commitment to improving the community and the environment
A business philosophy in which an organization helps to improve social and environmental problems

co-sourcing   Using both internal and external resources to perform a service
A business practice in which the employees of a company work with an outside organization to perform a service

cost-benefit analysis (CBA)   A process of measuring business decisions
A financial review of various options to determine if the benefits are greater than the costs

cost-of-living adjustment (COLA)   Pay change due to economic conditions
An increase or decrease in pay based on changes in economic conditions in a geographic location or country

cost per hire   Recruitment measuring tool
The amount of money needed to recruit a new employee, which includes advertising, recruiting fees, referral fees, travel expenses, and relocation costs

cost sharing   Expenses for a project being divided among those involved
Method of saving money by dividing the costs of a program, project, or business operation

credentials Certified documents, diplomas
Proof of a person's earned authority, status, or rights, usually in writing (for example, a university diploma, a digital certification badge, or other proof of passing a professional exam)

criterion A standard or rule
A test, standard, or rule on which something is judged or measured

cross-border Country to country
Taking place across the geographic boundaries of two or more countries (for example, cross-border trade)

cross-cultural Comparing or interacting with two or more groups of people
Involving two or more cultures (such as national, regional, or professional cultures)

cross-training Learning new skills beyond one's current job responsibilities
Teaching employees the skills and responsibilities of other positions in the company to increase their effectiveness and to provide greater staffing flexibility in the organization

cultural coaching Guidance to help a person interact to achieve greater success with other cultures
Giving support and suggestions to help employees achieve greater success with different cultures

cultural intelligence Measure of competence in culturally diverse situations
A person's ability to function in multicultural situations and to interact appropriately with people from different backgrounds

danger premium Additional pay for high-risk work
Extra pay that employees receive for working in dangerous jobs or places (for example, environments that are hazardous or politically unstable)

days to fill The time it takes to hire someone
The average number of days it takes to hire someone for an open job position

dedicated HR Person committed to human resources in an organization
A human resources position that works only on HR responsibilities within an organization

deductive Reasoning from the general to the specific
A method of reasoning that forms a conclusion from general information; the opposite of inductive reasoning, where a conclusion is formed from particular facts

deferred compensation plan An employee pension program
A pension program that allows an employee to contribute a portion of income over time to be paid as a lump sum at retirement when the employee's income tax rate will probably be lower

defined benefit plan   A retirement plan with predetermined payments
A retirement plan that tells participants exactly how much money (lump sum or regular payments) they will receive on a specific later date (usually the day they retire)

Delphi technique   A forecasting technique
A method of forecasting where a group of experts provides individual opinions, which are later shared in order to reach a more objective decision

demographics   Data, information about people
Statistics about groups of people that give information such as age, gender, income, and ethnic background

development   Event, happening, occurrence
Something that happens or has happened, or the act of making or improving something

didactic   Instructive, teaching
Intending to teach or demonstrate

distance learning   Remote teaching method
A method of education that uses TV, audiotapes or videotapes, computers, and the Internet, instead of traditional classroom teaching where students are physically present with their teacher

distributed training   A method of instruction over time and distance
A method of training that allows instructors, students, and content to be located in different places. This type of training can be used together with a traditional classroom, or it can be used to create virtual classrooms.

diversity   Composed of different elements
A combination of various types of people working together, often with differences in culture, race, generation, gender, or religion

divestiture   The sale of a company's asset(s)
Property that an organization sells or gives to another organization (for example, a company's sale of a business unit)

document retention   Maintaining important employee records
Managing employee data and records as required by the organization or rule or law

downsizing   Reduction in the number of employees
A decrease in a company's workforce to create efficiency and profitability

downward communication   Flow of information from superiors to subordinates
Information that is conveyed by upper management to lower-level employees in the organization

drive   Guide, steer
To push or move forward a plan or project

due diligence   An investigation
The gathering and analysis of important information related to a business acquisition or merger, such as assets and liabilities, contracts, and benefit plans

due process   The way a government enforces laws
In the United States, the way a government enforces its laws to protect its citizens (for example, guaranteeing a person a fair trial)

economic valuation   Value given to nonfinancial factors
Giving monetary value to environmental factors (for example, the quality of air and water, which are not normally part of a financial valuation)

e-learning   Online training or education
A method of education where students attend classes on a computer or on the Internet

eligible   Qualified
To be qualified to participate in a program or apply for a job

employee assistance program   Services and counseling that employees receive to help them solve problems that could affect their work productivity
Examples include counseling for drug or alcohol problems or family issues.

employee benefits   Compensation in addition to salary
Payments or allowances that organizations give to their employees (for example, medical insurance, Social Security taxes, pension contributions, education reimbursement, and car or clothing allowances)

employee engagement   Level of satisfaction with work
A measurement of employees' involvement, satisfaction, happiness, and loyalty with their employment (how hard they work and how long they stay with their organization)

employee handbook   A reference document for workers in an organization
A manual that contains information about an organization's policies, procedures, and benefits

employee relations   Interaction between employees and the organization
Interaction between employees and an organization (for example, communications, conflict resolution, compliance with legal regulations, career development, and performance measurement)

employee retention   Keeping employees
Methods of motivating employees to stay with the organization and making sure employees are satisfied and rewarded

employee self-service   A method allowing employees to access and update data
A trend in human resources management that allows employees to handle many job-related tasks (such as updates to their personnel data) using technology

employee turnover   The ratio of unfilled positions
The percentage of a company's employees that must be replaced at any time

employer branding   How a company presents itself to the public
The image an organization presents to its employees, stakeholders, and customers

employer of choice   An organization highly valued by employees
An organization that people want to work for because it attracts, motivates, and keeps good employees

employer-paid benefits   Something extra that employees receive in addition to salary
Benefits that an organization gives its employees in addition to salary (for example, medical insurance, payments to retirement funds, and allowances for cars or clothing)

employment at will   A U.S. legal principle that defines a working relationship
An employment agreement in which an employee can quit, or can be fired, at any time and for any reason

employment branding   Changing how others perceive an organization
Process of turning an organization into an employer of choice

empowerment   Authorized to make decisions
The ability for employees to manage their work, share information, and make decisions without close supervision

environmental responsibility   Concern and care for the environment
The management of products and processes that show concern for health, safety, and the environment

environmental scanning   Gathering internal and external information for strategic purposes
Acquiring and using information about the internal and external business environments that influence an organization's strategy (for example, determining how to respond to a talent shortage)

equal employment opportunity   EEO
U.S. laws that guarantee equal treatment and respect for all employees

equity compensation   A type of payment that gives employees an ownership interest in a company
Noncash payment that represents an ownership interest in a company (for example, stock options and restricted stock)

equity partnership   Business arrangement with financial investors
An agreement for a person or an organization to own part of a company by providing start-up funds to the new business

ergonomic   Safe and comfortable equipment
Designed to be comfortable and avoid injuries (for example, an ergonomic chair or keyboard)

ERP   Enterprise resource planning
Computer software that combines information from all areas of an organization (such as finance, human resources, operations, and materials), and also manages contact with people outside the organization (such as customers, suppliers, and stakeholders)

ESOP   Employee stock ownership plan
A tax-qualified benefit plan with defined contributions that allows employees to own shares in a company

essential functions   Required job duties
An employee's main responsibilities or tasks to succeed in a job

ethnocentric staffing orientation   Filling key positions with employees from the headquarters' country
Filling important positions in an international organization by choosing new hires from the country where the organization has its headquarters

ethnocentrism   Belief that one's own culture is superior
The belief that one's own culture is the center of everything and other cultures are less effective or less important

ethnorelativism   Understanding one culture in the context of other cultures
The ability to recognize different values and behaviors as cultural and not universal

exempt-level employee   Employee whose position is not bound to hourly job rules
A U.S. term that describes employees who work however many hours are necessary to perform the tasks of their position. They do not receive overtime pay, unlike hourly workers.

exit interview   Final interview before leaving an organization
An interview that HR has with an employee to get feedback about the job the employee held, the work environment, and the organization

expatriate   A citizen of one country who lives in another country
An employee who has been transferred from the person's country of citizenship (home country) to live and work in another country (host country)

expatriate assignment   A job outside the home country
A position in one country that is filled by a person from another country who moves there to live and work

external forces   Events an organization cannot control
Things that occur outside of an organization that might affect its financial health, employees, products, services, or customers (for example, political, economic, or environmental challenges)

extraterritorial laws   Provisions whereby foreigners are sometimes exempt from local laws
Laws from one country that apply to that country's citizens when they travel or live in countries where they might be exempt from some local laws. Similar exceptions can apply to companies operating abroad.

extraterritoriality   Being exempt from local law
Being exempt from the laws of the foreign country in which one is living (for example, foreign diplomats)

extrinsic rewards   Measurable recognition
Work or actions where the motivating factors are material and are measured through monetary benefits, grades, prizes, and praise

face-to-face   Being physically present with another person
Interacting while in the presence of another person, as opposed to on the telephone, in a webinar, or by e-mail

feasibility study   Investigation, analysis of what is possible
Research and analysis to determine if a project will succeed

financial viability   Ability to survive financially
The ability of an organization to achieve financial goals, growth, and stability, while also paying expenses and debt

forced distribution   A rating system for evaluating employees
A performance measurement system that ranks employees against each other on a bell curve and according to predetermined categories such as high, low, or average

forecasting   A planning tool that helps with future decisions
Analyzing the probability of future outcomes to help lessen uncertainty

foreign compulsion exception   Exemption from a home country's law
When a law of an organization's home country does not apply because it is in conflict with laws of the country where the organization is doing business

foreign direct investment (FDI)   Ownership of a business or property by a foreign entity
An overseas investment in structures, equipment, or property controlled by a foreign corporation

foreign service premium   Financial reward for moving to a foreign country
Extra pay that an employee receives for accepting an international work assignment

foreign subsidiary A legal term defining ownership of a foreign company
A company that is more than 50 percent owned or controlled by a parent organization in another country

formalization Structured work roles and rules
The degree to which processes and procedures define job functions and organizational structure

franchising A business model that involves licensing
Selling a license for the use of a trademark, product, or service in order to do business a certain way and receiving ongoing payment for the license

fringe benefits Payments other than, or in addition to, salary
Payments that the employee receives other than or in addition to a salary, such as for health insurance

front-back format An organizational design that separates customer service and production
An organization that has two parts: one part that focuses on the customers and the market (the front), and one part that develops products and services (the back)

full-time equivalent (FTE) A ratio of employee hours worked each week
A percentage comparing the number of hours that an organization's part-time employees work to the number of hours that full-time employees work

functional area Group of people performing similar tasks
A department in which people have similar specialties or skills (for example, the accounting or IT department in an organization)

functional HR Dedicated tasks of the human resources position in an organization
The human resources role within an organization that focuses on strategy, recruitment, management, and the direction of the people in the organization

functional structure Group of people performing similar tasks
A department or division where people have similar specialties or skills (for example, the accounting or IT department in an organization)

gap analysis A technique used to compare the current state with the future desired state
An analysis process that helps organizations or people compare their actual performance with their potential performance

generalization An objective conclusion
A perception based on observations (for example, "Americans are usually friendly"); different from a stereotype (for example, "All Americans are friendly")

geocentric staffing orientation   Management of global talent
The practice of choosing the best employees for a job, regardless of their nationality or where the job is located

geographic structure   Organizational model based on location
An organizational model in which divisions, functions, or departments are organized by location in a specific country or region

global ethics policy   Company behavioral guidelines
An outline of how a company expects employees to behave around the world, often intended to prevent bribery and corruption

global mind-set   A worldview that embraces cultural diversity
A perspective that helps people understand and function successfully in a range of cultures, markets, and organizations

global mobility   International relocation
The transfer of employees from one part of the world to another

global organization   An organization that views the world as one market
An organization that views the whole world as one market, and does not divide it into separate markets by country

global staffing   Worldwide employees
The process of identifying the number and type of employees an organization needs worldwide, and searching for the best candidates

Global Sullivan Principles   Rules for ethics and human rights
A voluntary set of rules to help an organization advance human rights and equality

global team   Group of employees from different countries who are working on a project together
A group of employees who are working on the same project but who are located in different countries or come from different cultures

glocalization   A strong local and global presence
Characteristic of a company that "thinks globally, but acts locally"; when a company has a strong presence both in its own country and around the world

governance   System of rules to regulate behavior
System of rules and processes an organization creates in order to comply with local and international laws, accounting rules, ethical norms, and environmental and social codes of conduct

graphic rating scale   Method of evaluating employees
A method of giving employees a numerical rating for having certain traits (for example, being reliable or honest)

greenfield operation   New business facility built in a new location
Start-up of a new business plant or operation, usually in a new location

grievance   Serious complaint
A cause of distress that can lead to an official complaint (for example, difficult work conditions)

grievance procedure   The method used by employees to address problems at work with their employer
The steps that employees must follow when they want to express their concerns about work-related issues to their employer

group consensus   Agreement between people
A decision process in which a group of people agree to a decision or come to the same conclusion

halo effect   Transfer of positive feelings
The transfer of the positive qualities of a person or thing to related people or things

hardship premium   Extra compensation for difficult living conditions
Extra payment or benefits that an expatriate receives on assignment in a country where the living and working conditions are challenging

hardships   Difficult living or working conditions for expatriates
Situations in a country that cause political or economic uncertainty that make it challenging for expatriates to live and work there. Often, expatriates receive extra hardship pay.

head count   Number of employees
The number of employees an organization has on its payroll

headhunter   An employment recruiter
An informal name for an employment recruiter, sometimes referred to as an executive search firm

headhunting   Recruiting employees
The practice of recruiting employees from one company to work at another company

health care benefits   Medical support plans provided to employees
Company-sponsored medical plans that help employees pay for the cost of doctor visits, hospitalization, surgery, and so on

Health Insurance Portability and Accountability Act (HIPAA)   A U.S. law that protects workers' health benefits and medical privacy
The Health Insurance Portability and Accountability Act (HIPAA) protects American workers in assuring the continuation of health insurance coverage and protects their medical privacy.

hidden costs   Expenses that occur in addition to the purchase price
Expenses such as maintenance, supplies, training, upgrades, and other costs in addition to the purchase price

high-context culture   Society that communicates indirectly
A culture that communicates indirectly, through the context of a situation more than through words, and that builds relationships slowly (for example, Japan)

high-potential (Hi-Po) employees   Employees identified for advancement due to their talents and skills
Employees who have the capacity to grow into higher levels of leadership in the organization

histogram   A bar graph showing frequency distribution
A bar graph that shows the upper and lower limits in a set of data

homogeneous   The same or similar
Description of a group whose members are all the same or similar (for example, people from the same background and heritage); opposite of heterogeneous

hostile work environment harassment   Harassment from coworkers rather than supervisors
A situation in which an employee's coworkers create an uncomfortable work environment, often through inappropriate sexual behavior or discrimination

HR   Human Resources
Function within an organization that focuses on implementing organizational strategy, as well as recruiting, managing performance, and providing direction for the people who work in the organization

HR audit   Assessment of an organization's human resources
An evaluation of the strengths, weaknesses, and development needs of human resources required for organizational performance

HR business partner   Strategic role for human resources
A role in which the human resources function works closely with an organization to develop strategies and achieve business results

HRD   Human resource development
The part of human resource management that deals with training employees and giving them the skills they need to do their jobs both now and in the future

HR partner   An ally in providing HR services
A manager or department that has a relationship with HR in order to provide services to the organization

human capital   Knowledge and talents of employees
Employees' knowledge, talents, and skills that add to the value of the organization

human capital strategies   Employment tactics, plan for managing employees
Methods and tools for recruiting, managing, and keeping important employees

hybrid structure   A vertical and horizontal organizational model
An organizational model that combines different operational, functional, product, and geographic structures

ILO   International Labour Organization
A department of the United Nations that deals with human and labor rights

ILO conventions   Standards of the International Labour Organization
International standards for employers and employees that become international law when a certain number of governments have adopted them

in-basket exercise   A method of evaluating candidates
A test used to hire or promote employees to management positions that measures the candidate's ability to prioritize and respond to daily tasks

incentive   Motivation, inducement
A monetary or nonmonetary reward to motivate an employee (for example, a bonus or extra time off)

independent contractors   People who provide goods or services under an agreement
Workers who contract to do specific work for other people or organizations and are not considered employees

individualism   Self-reliant, personal independence
Cultural belief that the individual is the most important part of society; one of Hofstede's cultural dimensions, the opposite of collectivism

inducement   Incentive
A benefit that management offers to employees as motivation for producing specific results

industrial relations   The relationship between an employer and its employees
The relationship between the management of an industrial enterprise and its employees, as guided by specific laws and regulations

informants   Suppliers of useful information
People who provide business, social, or cultural data to others

initiatives   Ideas, programs, projects
Actions related to new ideas or to starting new plans

inpatriate   An employee on assignment in the country of an organization's headquarters
A foreign employee who is on a work assignment in the country where an organization's headquarters are located

insourcing   Assigning a job or function within a company
Assigning a job to an internal department instead of to an outside organization; opposite of outsourcing

instant awards   Immediate employee recognition
Rewards for employees that are provided immediately after the desired behavior is produced

integrate   Combine, mix together
To combine or bring together different parts

intellectual property   Creations or inventions protected by law
An original invention or something created by the mind, which is usually protected by patents, trademarks, or copyrights

internal equity   Fairness in pay and benefits for similar jobs
Making sure that employees with jobs of similar value to the organization receive equal compensation

internal forces   Drivers of change inside an organization
Key people and influences inside an organization that shape its future (the opposite of external forces, such as the economy and competitors)

internal rate of return   A way of measuring profits
A calculation of the average return each year during the life of an investment

international assignee   Expatriate employee
A person who moves to a new country to work on an international assignment

international organization   A business that operates in more than one country
A company that has operations and services in different parts of the world

interpersonal skills   Traits for effective social interaction
Effective social qualities for communicating and building good relationships with different people

interpretation   Explanation of meaning
An explanation of the meaning of something; translating spoken language

intranet   A private computer network with limited access
A restricted computer network that allows only authorized people to access the site (for example, a company intranet that allows only its employees access to its data)

intrinsic rewards   Nonmaterial satisfaction
Nonmaterial motivation that comes from personal satisfaction (for example, job status, job satisfaction, or human interest)

investment   A commitment of money for expected return
Money and capital that is spent in order to make more money (for example, stocks, bonds, real estate)

job analysis   Review of job tasks and requirements
A study of the major tasks and responsibilities of jobs to determine their importance and relation to other jobs in a company

job competencies   Skills needed for a job
The skills and behaviors that will help an employee succeed in a specific job

job-content-based job evaluation   Method to decide an employee's salary
A way of estimating how much people should be paid based on what they do

job description   Description of work tasks and responsibilities
Written document describing an employee's work activities

job family   A set of related jobs performed within a work group or occupation
Groups of occupations based on the type of work performed, skills, education, training, and credentials

job matching   A process of placing employees in the right positions
The use of objective skill assessment data combined with common sense to determine the best fit for an employee to a specific job

job preview   A method that gives applicants an understanding of job duties before being hired
A strategy for introducing job candidates to the realities of the position, both good and bad, prior to making a hiring decision

job ranking   A way to compare all jobs based on their value
A job evaluation method that compares jobs to each other based on their importance to the organization

job requisition   Request to hire a person for an open position
A procedure used when a company wants to hire a new employee to fill a position

job rotation   Changing work assignments
A way to develop employees by giving them different jobs to perform

job shadowing   Observing another person's work practices
Learning a new job by watching another employee work

job specification   Requirements for an employment position
A description of employee qualifications required to perform a specific job

joint venture (JV)   Partnership between two or more organizations
When two or more organizations work together and share risks and rewards

key talent   Important and valued workers
Employees that perform extremely good work and are highly valued by the organization

kidnap and ransom insurance   Protection for employees in high-risk areas
Policies that reimburse employees' losses due to kidnapping or extortion in high-risk areas of the world

knowledge management Organizing information to improve business performance
The process of gathering, documenting, and sharing important information to improve the performance of employees and the organization

KPI   Key performance indicator
A measure an organization uses to see its progress and show what it needs to improve

labor union   A trade organization or works council
A group of employees with the same job who join together to ask their employers for things such as better wages, benefits, or working conditions

lagging economic indicators   Signs that confirm change in the economy
Signs that confirm the economy has already changed (for example, the unemployment rate)

layoff   Loss of employees' jobs owing to business reasons
Temporary suspension or termination of an employee or groups of employees because of business reasons

leadership   A management ability
The ability to influence other people or groups to achieve a goal

leadership development   Activities that enhance leadership performance
Investment in programs to help current leaders become more effective and to build future leaders

leadership pipeline   Source of future leaders
The people in a company who will be developed to move into higher levels of leadership over time

leading economic indicators   Signs that predict the future of the economy
Signs that show ahead of time that the economy will change (for example, a predicted rise or fall in interest rates)

learning curve   The rate at which a person acquires new skills and knowledge
The time it takes for a person to acquire new information and skills and to perform successfully

learning effectiveness model   Method of assessing results of development programs
Measuring the impact of employee training and development programs on business goals

learning management system (LMS)   Computer software for employee development
Computer software that administers, tracks, and reports on employee development opportunities such as classroom and online events, e-learning programs, and training content

learning pace   How fast a person learns
The time it takes for a person to understand and retain information

learning portal   Website for learning
Internet site where employees can use educational resources

learning style   The way a person learns
The way people process new information and learn most effectively (for example, some people learn best visually, through lectures, or by reading, whereas others learn best by action or doing)

lease   A contract to use a property
An agreement for a person or organization to rent a property (lessee) from its owner (lessor) for a specific period of time and amount of money

leniency error   Favoritism in performance evaluations
Rating employees higher than their actual performances deserve

leverage   The ability to multiply the return on an investment
The act of applying a small investment to bring a high level of return

liaison   Contact, connection, link
A communication link between people or groups

licensing   Giving permission to use, produce, or sell
A written contract in which the owner of a trademark or intellectual property gives rights to a licensee to use, produce, or sell a product or service

line management   People who create revenue for organizations
Work groups that conduct the major business of an organization, such as manufacturing or sales

loan   Lending of money or goods
Money or goods that a person or organization lends temporarily, usually charging interest

localization compensation strategy Expatriate salary based on the salary structure of the host country
Salary for an international assignee that is the same as the salary that a local employee receives for a similar job

long-term assignment An expatriate job that is more than six months
A job in a different culture that lasts longer than six months, usually three to five years

low-context culture Society that communicates directly
A culture that communicates directly, using words more than situations, and that builds relationships quickly (for example, the United States)

lump-sum compensation A single payment made at one time
An extra amount of money paid at one time rather than on a regular basis (for example, an expatriate may receive a lump-sum payment to cover the extra costs of the assignment related to housing, taxes, dependent education, and transportation)

management contract An agreement to oversee a project or operations
An arrangement in which a person or company operates a project or business in return for a fee

mandatory benefits Laws that require certain benefits to protect workers
Laws that outline benefits to provide economic security for employees and their dependents

manpower An organization's workforce
The total number of individuals who make up the workforce of an organization

market-based job evaluation Comparison of current salaries for a specific job
An evaluation that compares the salaries for particular jobs offered on the external job market

marketplace The geographic area in which business is conducted
A physical or virtual place in which business operates (for example, the global marketplace or the online marketplace)

market salary survey Research summary of fair wages
Review of median pay for specific positions in the same labor market

mastery Ability, expertise
Great ability and knowledge of some subject or activity

matrix structure A system of reporting where employees have both vertical and horizontal relationships
A system of managing staff where employees have more than one reporting relationship (for example, they could report to a direct supervisor as well as a team leader)

mean   A way to calculate the average of a series of numbers
An average determined by adding up a group of numbers, and then dividing that total by the number of numbers. For example, to calculate the mean of 10, 20, 30, 40, 50: first, add the numbers (10 + 20 + 30 + 40 + 50 = 150), then count the numbers (5), and then divide the total by the number of numbers (150/5 = 30).

median   The middle value in a series of numbers
The middle number in a series. For example, in the series 13, 13, 13, 13, 14, 14, 16, 18, 21, the median is 14, with four numbers to the left and four numbers to the right.

mediation   Helping others negotiate
An attempt to help other people or groups come to an agreement

mentoring   Helping a person learn
When an experienced person shares knowledge with someone who has less experience

merger   Two or more organizations coming together to form a new legal entity
Two or more organizations that come together through a purchase, acquisition, or sharing of resources. Usually the new organization intends to save money by eliminating duplicate jobs.

merit increase   Pay raise for meeting performance goals
An increase in wages for meeting or exceeding the performance goals of a job

minimum wage   Least amount paid for work
The lowest hourly, daily, or monthly salary that employers must legally pay to employees or workers

mission statement   A description of the purpose of an organization
A short description of the main purpose of an organization, which does not change (unlike strategy and business practices, which can change frequently)

mobility   The ability to move from one place to another
An HR term that refers to employees and their families who move from one location to another

mobility premium   Financial benefit for expatriates
Extra salary paid to expatriates to encourage them to move to a new country

mode   The value that occurs most often in a series of numbers.
In the following series of numbers, 8 is the mode: 6, 5, 8, 3, 7, 8, 9, 8, 4.

module   A unit or segment of an educational program
One section of a training program that is presented alone or as part of a series of other units

moonlighting   Working for more than one company at the same time
To have a second job in addition to full-time employment

moral absolutes   Beliefs that are right or wrong
The idea that there is a clear definition of what is right and wrong

motivation   Inspiration for action
Reasons or influences that lead to specific desired behavior such as commitment to a job or continuing efforts to achieve a goal

multicultural   Refers to a group of people from several cultures or ethnic groups
Employees of diverse cultures and backgrounds who are part of an organization's workforce

multinational organization   A company operating in many countries
A company that has its headquarters in one country and has offices and operations in other countries; also known as a multinational corporation (MNC)

needs analysis   Assessment to determine next steps
Assessing the present situation to determine the steps necessary to reach a desired future goal

nepotism   Favoritism shown to relatives and friends
A practice where people of influence appoint their relatives or friends to positions in a business, even though they may be less qualified than other candidates

network   People or things that are connected
A group of people who connect with one another; a computer system that allows people to access shared resources and data

NGO   Nongovernmental organization
Any nonprofit, voluntary, and independent organization that is not connected with any government, and that usually works to improve social or environmental conditions

norms   Standards, averages
A standard model or pattern that is considered typical

offshoring   Relocation of a business process to another country
Transferring service or manufacturing operations to a foreign country where there is a supply of skilled and less costly labor

on-boarding   Training and orientation of new employees
The process of helping new employees learn the organization's policies, procedures, and culture in addition to their job responsibilities

one-on-one meetings   Direct interaction between two people
Person-to-person communication, such as a conversation between an HR manager and an employee

on-the-job experience   Skills and knowledge gained through work
The skills and knowledge a person learns from day-to-day work experience

on-the-job training (OJT)   Receiving instruction while working
Acquiring knowledge, practical skills, and competencies while engaged in daily work

open sourcing   Freely sharing
Made available for others to use or modify

organizational chart (org chart)   Diagram showing reporting relationships
A graphic representation of how authority and responsibility are distributed within a company; it includes all work processes of the company.

organizational development (OD)   Planned process to improve an organization
Planned process that uses the principles of behavioral science to improve the way an organization functions

organizational structure   The grouping of employees and processes
The way that employees and processes are grouped into departments or functions in an organization, along with a description of reporting relationships

outsourcing   Contracting or subcontracting noncore business activities
Transferring certain business functions outside of the organization so that the organization can focus on core activities (examples of outsourced functions may be data processing, telemarketing, and manufacturing)

outstanding loan   An unpaid debt
Money that a person or organization has borrowed but not yet paid back

overhead   Business operating expenses
Direct costs associated with operating a business, such as rent, salaries, benefits, equipment, technology, and so on

overtime   Time worked in addition to regular paid work hours
Extra time worked beyond the normal hours of employment or the payment for extra time worked

ownership interest   Equity in a company
Owning part of a company or business

parent country nationals   Citizens of the headquarters country
People who live and work abroad but are citizens of the country where an organization's headquarters are located

Pareto chart   Chart that shows most frequently occurring items
A vertical bar graph in which values are plotted in decreasing order of frequency, from left to right; often used in quality control

parochialism   Narrow interest or view
A view of the world that does not consider other ways of living and working

pay for performance   Salary based on merit or on meeting goals
A payment strategy where management links an employee's pay to desired results, behaviors, or goals

peers   People equal to each other
People who are similar to one another in age, background, profession, or status

per diem   Daily expenses or reimbursements for an employee
The amount of money a person receives for working for one day, or the amount an organization allows an employee to spend on expenses each day (for example, meals and hotels on a business trip)

performance appraisals   Evaluations of employees
A method of measuring how effective employees are

performance-based pay   Earnings based on merit or how well the employee meets goals
Pay linked to how well the employee meets expectations; better performance results in more pay.

performance management   Supervising employees
The process of setting goals, measuring progress, and rewarding or correcting performance of employees

performance management system   Process of creating a productive work environment
The process of helping people perform to the best of their abilities, which begins by defining a job and ends when an employee leaves the organization

performance review   Formal evaluation of an employee's work activities
A documented discussion about an employee's development and performance that involves managers, HR, and the employee

performance standards   Expected behaviors and results from employees
The behaviors and results that management expects employees to achieve on the job

permanent assignment   Regular or usual position
An employee's regular or usual job or position in a company

perquisites (perks)   Benefits and special treatment
Special nonmonetary privileges (such as a car or club membership) that come with senior job positions; also called executive perks or fringe benefits

PEST analysis   Method of gathering external data for organizational analysis
Political, economic, sociopolitical, and technological (PEST) data that is gathered and reviewed by organizations for planning purposes

phantom stock arrangement   An employee incentive plan
A technique in which a company gives its employees the benefits that come with owning stock, including dividends, but does not actually give them stock in the company

piece rate   Payment determined by the amount produced
A wage system in which the employee is paid for each unit of production at a fixed rate

placement   Placing applicants in jobs
Finding suitable jobs for applicants

planned absence   Scheduled time away from work
Missing work after asking permission in advance, such as for a vacation or a medical appointment

political unrest   Disturbance or turmoil about government issues
Unrest, agitation, or turmoil about a government's actions or beliefs

polycentric staffing orientation   Hiring citizens of the local country
Recruiting host country nationals to manage subsidiaries in their own country, and recruiting parent country nationals to fill management positions at headquarters

power distance   The degree of hierarchy
A term Geert Hofstede uses in his cultural theory to describe hierarchical relationships between people in a culture. For example, high power distance means there are strong hierarchical relationships. Low power distance means greater equality and accessibility among members of the population.

predictive validity   Relationship between a test score and a work task
The extent to which a score on a scale or test predicts future behavior

premiums   Payments or incentives
Payments for insurance; also, payments employees receive for meeting goals by a certain time

prevailing wage   Usual wage paid to workers in an area
The hourly wage, usual benefits, and overtime that most workers receive in a certain location

primacy errors   Incorrect assumptions or judgments
Incorrect conclusions where the first impression of someone or something continues despite contradictory evidence

process-flow analysis   Method of assessing critical business functions
A diagram used to assess business processes; sometimes called "process mapping"

product structure   A way of organizing a company
A method of organizing a company in which the departments are grouped by product

progress review   Evaluation of an employee's performance
Formal or informal evaluation of an employee's progress toward goals and recommendations for improvements and development

project management   Planning and guiding processes
A methodical approach to planning and guiding project processes from start to finish

promotion   Job advancement
Advancement of an employee's rank, usually with greater responsibility and more money

proprietary   Relating to an owner or ownership
Rights of property ownership relating to key information, materials, or methods developed by an organization

psychological contract   Beliefs that influence the employee-employer relationship
An unwritten agreement of the mutual beliefs, perceptions, and informal obligations between an employer and an employee, which influence how they interact

purchase   Buy
Acquire something through payment or barter

quantification   Counting and measuring
Giving a number to a measurement of something

raise   Salary increase
An increase in salary that an employee receives, often for good performance

range   The difference between the most and least
The amount covered, or the amount of difference (for example, a salary range is the difference between the lowest and highest amount paid for a particular job)

range penetration   An employee's pay compared to the total pay range
An employee's pay compared to the total pay range for the same job function

ranked performance   A method of evaluating employees
Rating employees from best to worst against each other according to a standard measurement system

reasonable accommodation   Work adjustment for a disabled employee
Changing the process of applying for a job or the work environment for a qualified person with a disability

recency errors Inaccurate assessments based on recent behavior
Incorrect conclusions due to recent actions that are weighed more heavily than overall performance

record retention schedule A defined plan for keeping and disposing of documents
A listing of key documents and the length of time that each is required by law to be stored or disposed of by the organization

recruitment Process of identifying and hiring qualified people
Process of attracting, screening, and hiring qualified people for a job

redeployment Moving employees from one location or task to another
A change in an employee's location or task, often to reduce layoffs or to make the best use of employees

red flag A warning signal
An indicator of a problem, or something that calls for attention

reduce turnover Lower the number of unfilled positions
To retain employees and lower the number of vacancies in a company

reduction in force (RIF) Temporary or permanent layoffs
Loss of employment positions due to lack of funding or change in work requirements

redundancies Elimination of jobs
Elimination or reduction of jobs because of downsizing or outsourcing

reference check Verification of a job applicant's employment history
Contact with a job applicant's past employers, or other references, to verify the applicant's job history, performance, and educational qualifications

referral program Using employees to recruit applicants
Recruitment method that rewards employees for recommending candidates

regiocentric staffing orientation Staffing policy for a particular geographic area
Focus on recruitment and hiring of employees within a particular region with opportunities for interregional transfers

reimbursements Compensation paid for money already spent
Payments made for money already spent (for example, a company pays an employee for the cost of travel or supplies after the employee has spent his or her own money)

reliability Being dependable or consistent
Having the same results after many tests

relocation Changing residence, moving employees
Transferring employees to another location for work

relocation services   Support provided to transferring employees
Help given to relocating employees (for example, predeparture orientation, home-finding assistance, tax and legal advice, and in-country assistance)

remuneration   Pay or salary
Money paid for work, including wages, commissions, bonuses, overtime pay, and pay for holidays, vacations, and sickness

remuneration surveys   Gathering information on salary and benefits
Surveys that gather information on what other companies pay employees and what kinds of benefits they provide

repatriate   To return to the country of origin
To return home from an international work assignment

replacement planning   Identifying employees to fill future vacancies
Using past performance to identify employees who can fill future vacancies (unlike succession planning, which focuses on future potential)

reprimand   Formal warning or scolding
A warning given to an employee who violates an organization's rules and that may result in dismissal

responsibility   Duty
A task that is part of an employee's job description

restricted stock   Stock with rules about its transfer
Stock with rules about when it can be sold (restricted stock is usually issued as part of a salary package, and has a time limit on when it can be fully transferred)

return on investment (ROI)   A financial calculation to evaluate an investment
Performance measure used to evaluate the financial outcome of an investment

risk management   Assessing and preventing threats
The process of analyzing potential threats and deciding how to prevent them

sabbatical leave   Paid time off for a predetermined period
A benefit provided by some organizations that allows eligible employees paid time off during a specific time period for study, rest, or travel

salary midpoint   The center point of the middle range paid for a certain job
The amount of money halfway between the highest and lowest amount paid for a particular job

salary range   Wage band, pay scale, compensation rate
The lowest and highest wages paid to employees who work in the same or similar jobs

Sarbanes-Oxley Act   A U.S. law that sets specific standards for public companies
A broad range of legal regulations that strengthen corporate accounting controls in the United States

scaled score   An adjusted score
A conversion of a raw score to a common scale that can be used for comparison

scatter diagram   Chart that shows relationships between variables
A graph with a vertical axis and a horizontal axis with dots at each data point; also called a scatter plot or dot chart.

screening tool   An instrument used to assess an employee's suitability for a particular job
An instrument used in employee selection to help assess job suitability (for example, in-basket exercises, psychometric tests, and cultural adaptability inventories)

selection   Choosing employees
Method for choosing the best candidate for a job

self-assessment   Evaluating one's own performance
Evaluation of one's own performance, abilities, and developmental needs

separation rate   The percentage of employees who leave their jobs
The ratio of the number of employees who leave their jobs to the total number of employees in the organization

severance   Separation payment
An additional payment (other than salary) given to an employee when employment termination occurs

sexual harassment   Inappropriate sexual advances
Unwelcome verbal, visual, or physical conduct of a sexual nature that is offensive or inappropriate

shared services   Business strategy to centralize administrative functions
An operational approach where each country or unit uses administrative services from a central source rather than repeating these services in different locations (examples of services include finance, purchasing, inventory, payroll, hiring, and information technology)

short term   A brief period of time
Occurring over a brief time (for example, a short-term loan or a short-term assignment)

situational interview   Technique for assessing a job candidate's problem-solving skills
A method of assessing job candidates' skills by asking them how they would respond to specific work-related issues and problems

Six Sigma   Business management strategy
A strategy to improve current business processes by continuously reviewing and revising them

S.M.A.R.T. goal setting   Process used to help achieve business success
Applying specific, measurable, action-oriented, realistic, and time-based goals to help a company achieve business success

social media   Technology that helps people connect
Technology that lets people communicate over the Internet to share information and resources (for example, Twitter, Facebook, LinkedIn, and podcasts)

social network   Group of people with similar interests
A group of people who interact because they have a common interest. The group communicates either in person or by using technology (for example, Facebook or Twitter).

social responsibility   An ethical theory that guides organizations to consider the welfare of society
An organization's voluntary obligation toward the good of the environment in which it operates

sourcing   Finding qualified people for a job
Identifying candidates who are qualified to do a job by using proactive recruiting techniques

span of control   The number of employees a manager supervises
The number of employees who report to one manager in an organization. The more people that a manager supervises, the wider the span of control.

split payroll   A method of paying expatriates
A method of paying expatriates that gives part of their salary in the currency of the home country and part in the currency of the host country

staffing   Hiring and firing employees
The act of selecting, hiring, and training people for specific jobs, as well as reducing the workforce when needed

staff units   People who support line management
Work groups that support the major business of an organization with activities such as accounting, customer service, maintenance, and personnel

stakeholder   An interest holder in an organization
A person, group, or organization that has a direct or indirect interest in the organization (for example, owners, investors, employees, suppliers, unions, or the community)

start-up   A new business venture
A company or business that recently began operating and is in an early phase of development

statutory benefit   Employee benefits that are required by law
Employee benefits mandated by federal or local laws, such as Social Security and unemployment insurance

stay interview   A method of determining why employees remain with the organization
A retention strategy that helps organizations understand why their employees remain with the organization and how the organization can motivate them to continue their employment

stereotype   Fixed opinion or belief
An oversimplified opinion, image, or attitude that people from a particular group are all the same

stock option   An employee's right to buy or sell shares in the company
A benefit that gives employees the right to buy or sell stock in their company at a certain price for a specific period of time

strategic alliance   An agreement to cooperate between two organizations
An arrangement between two organizations to pursue common goals and share resources. Unlike a joint venture, the organizations do not form a new legal entity.

strategic partnership   An association based on common objectives
A mutually beneficial relationship based on the common goals of people or organizations

strategic planning   Process of defining the organization's future direction
The process of defining a company's direction for the future in four stages: analysis, development, implementation, and evaluation

strategy   Plan of action
A plan of action that starts with examining the current state of an organization and then deciding how to achieve the best state for the organization's future

stretch objectives   Goals that require maximum effort
Setting personal or business targets that require extra effort to achieve

subsidiary   A company that is controlled by another company
A company whose voting stock is more than 50 percent owned by another company. The company with the majority interest is called the "parent company."

substance abuse   Excessive use of drugs, alcohol, or other addictions
Use of habit-forming drugs or substances that impair behavior

succession planning   Determining and preparing for future talent needs
Identifying and developing high-potential employees for the organization's future success

supervisor A person in charge of other employees
Someone who oversees employees in a department or business unit to assign tasks and make sure work is completed, among other duties

supply chain management (SCM) The steps taken from initial planning through customer support
Process of planning, implementing, and controlling operations, which begins with acquiring raw materials and continues to customer delivery and support

sustainability The capacity to endure over time
The capacity to stay, hold, or maintain something, such as a concept, economy, geography, environment, and so on

SWOT audit or analysis Strategic planning method
A strategic planning technique used to assess the internal and external environment in which a company operates, its strengths and weaknesses (internal), and opportunities and threats (external)

synchronous learning An online teaching method
A type of e-learning in which participants interact without a time delay, which requires them to attend at specific times

talent management An approach to attract, develop, and keep skilled employees
The process of recruiting, integrating, and developing new workers, developing and keeping current workers, and attracting skilled workers

talent pool Group of available skilled workers
A group of available skilled workers, or database of resumes that a company can use to recruit in a particular location

targeted selection Evaluation of a candidate's abilities based on past behavior
An assessment of job-related behavior from the candidate's previous employment to predict future performance

tax bill Amount of money owed for taxes
A document that lists the tax money owed to a government or legal body

tax equalization policy A policy ensuring that the expatriate assignment is tax-neutral
A policy that makes sure that expatriates' combined home and host taxes are no more than they would have paid if they remained in their home country. The expatriate's company pays for any additional taxes.

telecommuting Working from home via computer
A flexible work arrangement that allows part-time or full-time employees to work at home via a computer

tenure   Permanent position
Holding a permanent job or position without the need for periodic contract renewals

territorial rule   A tax law
A rule that employees must follow the tax laws of the country where they are working

third-country national (TCN)   An expatriate who works for a company that is foreign in the host country
An expatriate who works for a foreign company that is located in the host country (for example, a French person working in China for a German company)

third party   A term describing those who are not directly involved in a transaction
A person or group in addition to those who are directly involved, such as a company that supplies outsourced services to an organization

360-degree feedback   Method of appraising job performance
Employee appraisal data gathered from internal and external sources (such as peers, subordinates, supervisors, customers, and suppliers); also known as multi-rater feedback

time-to-fill   Average time to hire people for job vacancies
The average number of days that a certain job position remains open

total compensation   Complete pay package
An employee's complete pay package, including cash, benefits, and services

totalization agreement   Arrangement to avoid double social taxes of expatriates
An agreement between countries that says an expatriate needs to pay social taxes to only the country in which he or she is working

total quality management (TQM)   Continuous improvement
A method for improving the organization by continuously changing its practices, structures, and systems

total rewards   All the tools available for attracting, motivating, and keeping employees
Financial and nonfinancial benefits that the employee sees as valuable

trainee   A person learning skills for a certain job
A person who is learning and practicing the necessary skills for a particular job

training method   A way of helping people learn
A way of communicating skills and knowledge (for example, classroom training, distance learning, online training, and on-the-job training)

transfer of learning Sharing knowledge and information from one person or place to another
The continuous exchange of information, knowledge, and skills from one context to another

translation Interpreting text from one language to another
Changing a message from one language to another while keeping the meaning

transnational corporation (TNC) Organization that operates globally, multi-national enterprise
An organization whose operations, production, or service processes take place in more than one country and are interconnected

trend analysis A review of historical data to predict future outcomes
Gathering information from the past to identify patterns that will help predict future outcomes

tuition reimbursement Payment for an employee's school fees
A benefit whereby the employer provides full or partial payment for educational courses completed by employees

turnkey operation A business that is ready to operate
A business that includes everything needed to start operating in a certain location

uncertainty avoidance The degree of tolerance for risk and preference for clarity
One of Geert Hofstede's cultural dimensions, uncertainty avoidance describes the degree to which cultures accept ambiguity and risk. For example, in cultures with high uncertainty avoidance, people prefer clear, formal rules. In cultures with low uncertainty avoidance, people are comfortable with flexible rules.

up-front costs Paid or due in advance
Paid in advance, or invested as beginning capital

upward communication Flow of information from subordinates to superiors
Information that is conveyed by employees to upper management

user interface Software that allows people and machines to share information
Software that allows a human and a computer to share information

validity Reliability, true evaluation
The extent to which something is accurate (for example, the extent to which an exam actually measures what it claims to measure)

value chain Model of how businesses create value
Model of how businesses receive raw materials, add value to the raw materials, and sell finished products to customers

value proposition   The benefits of a product or service
The unique benefits, costs, and value that a business delivers to its customers

values   Beliefs of a person or social group
The lasting beliefs of members of a culture about what is good or desirable and what is not

variable pay plan   Compensation that is less predictable than standard base pay
Profit sharing, incentives, bonuses, or commissions that align compensation with performance

vendor/supplier   Service provider, seller
A person or company that sells services and/or products, such as a recruiting firm, financial consultant, or relocation company

vicarious liability   Responsibility for someone else's acts
A legal doctrine that makes a person liable for the negligence or crimes of another person

virtual team   People who work together in different locations or time zones
A group of people who work in different times, locations, or organizations, who communicate using technology

vision statement   Declaration of what an organization wants to become
A written statement that clarifies what the organization wants to be in the future

voluntary benefits   Programs offered to and paid by employees
Extra benefits or discounted services offered to employees with little extra cost to the employer (for example, additional life insurance, gym memberships, and concierge services)

wage band   Salary range, pay scale, compensation rate
The lowest and highest wages paid to employees who work in the same or similar jobs

webinar   Meetings, training, or presentations on the Internet
An interactive seminar on the Internet (usually a live presentation)

workforce   Workers, employees
The people working for a single company, industry, or geographic region

workforce analytics   Metrics used in HR strategic planning
Metrics used to determine the effectiveness of HR functions, such as turnover rates, organizational culture, and succession planning

workforce planning   Analyzing the type and number of employees
Identifying and analyzing what an organization needs to achieve its goals, in terms of the size, type, and quality of its employees

workforce rotation   Moving employees when work requirements change
The regular movement of employees from one function, time, or place to another, as needed

work/life balance   The time allocated to the work and to the personal parts of one's life
The ability to effectively manage time at work with the time spent on life demands, leisure, or with family members

work/life balance programs   Support for the employee's job and personal well-being
Services to support the well-being of employees and to help them balance their jobs, families, and personal lives

workplace   A place where people work
A place, such as an office or factory, where people work

works councils   Groups that represent employees
Organizations that function like trade unions and represent the rights of workers, most commonly found in Europe and the United Kingdom

work unit   Smallest work group in a company
A business function that produces one product or focuses on a single area

zero-based budgeting   An approach to financial planning and decision making
A budgeting process that requires that every budget item is approved instead of only budget changes being approved. No reference is made to previous budget expenditures.

Index

cyber vulnerability and liability, 346
description, 322
employee communication and safety
training, 347
injury and illness prevention programs,
331–335
overview, 321–322
physical asset protection, 345–346
prevention, 336–347, 344
responsibilities and knowledge, 322
return to work programs, 319–322,
335–336
risk assessments, 323–331
techniques, 347–348
RM. *See* Risk management
ROI. *See* Return on investment
Rollerblade, 61–62
Romney, Mitt, 64
Roosevelt, President Theodore, 260, 307.
See also Social Security Act
Roth IRA, 276
R. Riveter, 137, 138
RTW. *See* Return to work programs
Rule of law, 45

Sabbaticals, 218, 220. *See also* Leaves of
absence
Safe Harbor, 391, 433–434
Safety, 343. *See also* Risk management
OSHA and, 419
personal protective equipment, 420
Salary basis requirement, 388
Salary deductions, 390–392
Salary midpoint, 264
Salary range, 264
Sales, 45
Sales force, 273
Salting, 308
SAM. *See* Successive Approximation Model
Same-sex marriage, 403–404
Samsung, 87
SAP, 132–133
Sarbanes-Oxley Act of 2002 (SOX), 101,
103, 434–435, 448
Saturn, 294
SBA. *See* Small Business Administration
SBREFA. *See* Small Business Regulatory
Enforcement Fairness Act
SCA. *See* Service Contract Act of 1965
Scalia, Justice Antonin, 439

Scatter diagram, 227, 228
Schein, Edgar, 77
SCM. *See* Supply chain management
S corporations, 36
Screening tools, 139
SEC. *See* Securities and Exchange
Commission
Section 505, Individuals with Disabilities
AAP, 355–357
Securities and Exchange Commission
(SEC), 42, 94, 270, 434
reporting, 285
Selection interviewing, 144
Self-assessment, 210, 211
Self-paced programs, 194
Senge, Peter, 86
Seniority pay system, record-keeping
guidelines, 455
Senior Professional in Human Resources
(SPHR), 26
Senior Professional in Human Resources,
International (SPHRi), 27–28
Separation process, 156–157
Separation rate, 159
Service Contract Act of 1965 (SCA), 435, 451
Severance, 280, 303
Sexual harassment, 435–436
EEOC guidelines for prevention, 439
Shared services, 93, 96–97
Sharia, 451
Shark Tank, 36
Sherman Antitrust Act, 255, 447, 451
Short term, 116
SHRM. *See* Society for Human Resource
Management
Simple Sugars, 36
SIOP. *See* Society for Industrial and
Organizational Psychology
Sista v. CDC Ixis North America, Inc., 451
Situational interview, 144, 145
Six Sigma, 227, 228
Skills
employee, 128
inventory, 129
variety, 186
Skinner, B.F., 109, 188–189, 300–301
Small Business Administration (SBA), 452
Small Business Job Protection Act, 451
Small Business Regulatory Enforcement
Fairness Act (SBREFA), 452